STAR TREK
AND
SACRED GROUND

STAR TREK
AND
SACRED GROUND

Explorations of
Star Trek, Religion,
and American Culture

edited by

Jennifer E. Porter
and
Darcee L. McLaren

STATE UNIVERSITY OF NEW YORK PRESS

Published by
State University of New York Press, Albany

© 1999 State University of New York

For information, address State University of New York Press,
State University Plaza, Albany, N.Y., 12246

Production by Marilyn P. Semerad
Marketing by Dana E. Yanulavich

Library of Congress Cataloging-in-Publication Data

Star trek and sacred ground : explorations of Star trek, religion, and
    American culture / edited by Jennifer E. Porter and Darcee L.
    McLaren.
        p.   cm.
    Includes bibliographical references and index.
    ISBN 0-7914-4333-7 (hc : alk. paper). — ISBN 0-7914-4334-5 (pb :
alk. paper)
    1. Star Trek films—Religious aspects. 2. Star Trek television
programs—Religious aspects. I. Porter, Jennifer E., 1964–   .
II. McLaren, Darcee L., 1965–   .
PN1995.9.S694S72 1999
791.43'75—dc21
                                                                98-52147
                                                                CIP

10 9 8 7 6 5 4 3 2 1

For John Porter, Andrew Porter,
and James Gavin Wilce, with love.

Contents

Acknowledgments

This volume was a group effort, from the two editors, to the talented and insightful contributors, to the many people who offered their time, effort, and encouragement. We would like to thank those who helped make this book possible. We are indebted to Praeger and the Greenwood Publishing Group for their assistance with regard to Jon Wagner's chapter, "Intimations of Immortality: Death/Life Mediations in *Star Trek.*" This article expands on material in pages 75–79 of the book *Deep Space and Sacred Time: Star Trek in the American Mythos* by Jon Wagner and Jan Lundeen (Westport, CT and London: Praeger Publishers, 1998). We are also indebted to David Nottage and the crew of the U.S.S. Golden Gate fan club, and to the other members of the United Federation of Planets Internationale fan organization who welcomed us and responded to our questions. Many other fans that attended the TorontoTrek and GrandSlam conventions also gave generously of their time, and their help and gracious goodwill is gratefully acknowledged. Special thanks are due to Kelli-Ann Maidment and Ron Barter for access to their collection of *Star Trek* episodes.

A volume of essays such as this ultimately depends upon the contributors. We had the great good fortune to work with a group of people who not only produced quality work, but produced it in a timely fashion and within the length requirements imposed upon them. It has been a pleasure to work with each of these contributors and we are sincerely grateful for all their hard work and their many insights.

On a personal note, we would like to thank Dr. Brad Eastman for helping to conceive the idea for this book during weekly *Star Trek* watching nights in graduate school. We would also like to thank Dr. Anne Pearson for organizing the session of *Star Trek* and Religion for the annual meeting of the Canadian Society for the Study of Religion in 1996 that convinced us to turn thought into deed. We are grateful to the faculty members in the Department of Religious Studies at Memorial University (St. John's) for their encouragement, and to Dr. Ellen Badone at McMaster University (Hamilton) for her encouragement, the training she gave us, and the fine example she sets for all her students. Finally, we would like to thank our family and friends—Ardella and Don McLaren; Patricia Sherry and Bill Walker; John, Andrew, Elizabeth, and Liam Porter; Joanne Scott, and Rick Wybou—for being there from the beginning, listening to our ideas, helping to refine them and encouraging us to put them into print.

1

Introduction

Star Trek, Religion, and American Culture

JENNIFER E. PORTER
AND DARCEE L. McLAREN

T elevision programs provide one of the most popular forms of entertainment today. From *The Simpsons* to *The X-Files*, television shows amuse, shock, sadden, and excite us by turns. Television does more, however, than simply entertain. Television shows are cultural products, and as such, they reflect, reinforce, and challenge cultural ideals. As a pre-eminent forum for the expression of popular culture, television acts as a mirror and a model for society. In examining and coming to an understanding of the cultural messages and popular appeal of certain television shows, we come to understand something about the society that has created and sustained them.

Arguably, *Star Trek* is the most popular television show ever produced. To date the *Star Trek* franchise includes four television series and nine motion pictures.[1] The *Star Trek* phenomenon includes countless unofficial fan-generated novels, short stories, songs, poems, drawings, paintings, models, costumes, and videos, as well as officially sponsored merchandise including hundreds of novels, guidebooks, technical manuals, encyclopedias, autobiographies, comic books, collector cards, action figures, and games. There are hundreds of fan clubs and millions of self-identified fans representing most of the countries of the world. The popularity, longevity, and creativity of *Star Trek* and its fandom is unparalleled in television history.

Nonetheless, as *Star Trek* fans everywhere acknowledge, *Star Trek* is "just a television show." Like other television shows, *Star Trek* has been subject to the vagaries of producers, writers, and Nielsen ratings. It is thus difficult to generalize about the "intent" of the "authors" of *Star Trek*, or the viewpoint of the "readers". Yet, it is also clear that *Star Trek*, like other television shows, has at various times been reflective, informative, and critical of American culture. Over the past thirty years, *Star Trek* has addressed a wide variety of issues, including war, capitalism, individualism, technology, race, gender, prejudice, and religion. As portrayed on television, such issues are representations of socio-cultural perspectives on broad human concerns. Television shows both shape and reflect the socio-cultural concerns of the times. Consequently, an examination of *Star Trek*'s treatment of these issues is an examination of the culture reflected, informed, and critiqued therein. This is particularly true of *Star Trek*'s portrayal and treatment of religion, within which these other issues are often contextualized. Although religion is the explicit focus of only a few episodes in each series and one of the motion pictures,[2] concern with religion and religious issues and themes represents a consistent subtext throughout the entire *Star Trek* franchise.

Analyses of the relationship between religion and television have previously focused almost exclusively on the issues of religious broadcasting and televangelism (e.g. Alexander 1994; Peck 1993; Schultze 1991). Such an approach is inappropriate to the study of *Star Trek*. With very few exceptions (Skill 1994), little attention has been given to the portrayal and treatment of fictional religion in television. With the notable exception of Kreuziger's work (1986), studies of science fiction rarely explore the issue of religion. Studies of *Star Trek* itself have focused primarily on the audience (Jenkins 1992; Bacon-Smith 1992; Tulloch and Jenkins 1995). Even in works exploring questions of meaning and metaphysics as portrayed in *Star Trek* (Richards 1997; Hanley 1997) the topic of religion is largely ignored.

The contributors to this volume suggest that the portrayal and treatment of religion in the *Star Trek* television series and films provides an important cultural commentary on the place of religion in society. Although no single coherent approach to religion appears in *Star Trek*, the series is nevertheless variously reflective of, informed by, and critical of societal attitudes toward religion. The portrayal and treatment of religion in much of the *Star Trek* franchise is negative: religion is often presented as superstitious, outdated, and irrational. An underlying and consistent theme of the *Star Trek* series is the presentation of rational scientific humanism as an alternative to religious faith. A newer theme, notably found in episodes from the *Deep Space Nine* and *Voyager* series, explores the potentially positive value of religion. Since the viability and popularity of *Star Trek* have spanned such a long period of time, it is inevitable that the series would begin to diverge from original assumptions in response to changing cultural attitudes. The recent potentially positive portrayal of religion within *Star Trek* both reflects and reinforces a particular cultural change.

Contributors to this volume further suggest that the *Star Trek* franchise reveals an ongoing exploration of powerful mythic and religious themes. Whether *Star Trek* is generally unsympathetic toward religion or not, the series and movies contain many religious and mythic themes, including themes of resurrection, sacrifice, immortality, faith, and the spiritual quest. *Star Trek* fandom itself also reveals many religious and ritual elements, from the adoption of *Star Trek*–inspired philosophies, ethical systems, and worldviews by fans to the ritual practice of pilgrimage in pursuit of *Star Trek*–inspired ideals.

This volume is organized into three sections. In the first section, contributors examine the explicit portrayal and treatment of religion in the various *Star Trek* series. What do *Star Trek* and *Star Trek*'s creator, Gene Roddenberry, have to say about religion, and what does this reveal about changing American perceptions about the role, value, and place of religion in everyday life? The papers in this section explore the ways in which religion has been understood in the *Star Trek* franchise in relation to science and technology, scientism, and secular humanism. The changing dynamics of this relationship provide the focus for the following analyses. In her chapter "From Thwarted Gods to Reclaimed Mystery? An Overview of the Depiction of Religion in *Star Trek*," Anne Pearson suggests that the dismissal of religion in Classic *Star Trek* is primarily the result of *Star Trek* creator Gene Roddenberry's own humanistic values and personal rejection of organized religion. Roddenberry's views on religion are explored in this chapter, and their impact on Classic *Star Trek* is analyzed. Pearson also argues that there has been an increasing and positive interest in personal religion as portrayed in later *Star Trek* series. She suggests that both the death of Gene Roddenberry and a sustained and perhaps increasingly popular interest among North Americans in alternative forms of spirituality lie at the root of this shift toward a more positive portrayal of religion in *Star Trek*. According to Pearson, religious mystery now has a place in the *Star Trek* universe.

Robert Asa's chapter—"Classic *Star Trek* and the Death of God: A Case Study of 'Who Mourns for Adonais?'"—addresses what he calls the "paradoxical treatment of theism" in the original *Star Trek* series. Asa suggests that the explicit message of the episode "Who Mourns for Adonais?" mirrors the death of God theology in the 1960s. Classic *Star Trek* is shown to be reflective of the theological concerns of its time. As a result, *Star Trek*'s cosmology is not only dismissive of religion, Asa argues, but haunted by it. Through a careful analysis of the Adonais episode, Asa argues that religious questions, themes, metaphors, and symbols abound in *Star Trek*, even when religion itself is explicitly rejected. This rejection is a result of a naive scientism that naturalizes religious issues and supplants traditional forms of religion in Classic *Star Trek*. However, as Asa argues, Classic Trek cannot escape the larger religious questions. As a result, he concludes, reports of the death of God in *Star Trek* may well have been exaggerated.

Gregory Peterson provides a detailed examination of *Star Trek: The Next Generation*'s portrayal of religion in "Religion and Science in *Star Trek: The Next Generation*: God, Q, and Evolutionary Eschatology on the Final Frontier." The "naive scientism" noted by Asa in Classic *Star Trek* is, according to Peterson, an explicit and competing "religious" paradigm in *The Next Generation*. Peterson argues that the portrayal and treatment of religion in this *Star Trek* series reflects the conviction that science and religion are diametrically opposed ways of understanding the universe. Within the series, religious phenomena are explained (or explained away) by science, and science itself serves as the basis for a new, non-traditional, religious worldview. This worldview encompasses an "evolutionary eschatology" in which divinity and salvation are naturalized. The religions of non-humans are treated with respect only insofar as they do not conflict with this evolutionary eschatology. Peterson argues that this portrayal and treatment of religion perpetuates a philosophy that is fundamentally hostile to traditional forms of religion.

In "Deeds of Power: Respect for Religion in *Star Trek: Deep Space Nine*," Peter Linford suggests that this series attempts a more thoughtful exploration of religion than the earlier *Star Trek* series and than science fiction generally. This more thoughtful portrayal of religion is coupled with an explicit questioning of the 'sterile' scientific and technological world of StarFleet (and hence *Star Trek*.) Focusing on the character of Captain Sisko, Linford examines the explicit and implicit messages communicated through the treatment of religion in *Deep Space Nine*. He suggests that while the series makes a conscious and laudatory attempt to treat religion with respect, this approach nonetheless marginalizes and dismisses the faith of believers. Linford argues that *Deep Space Nine*, in positing a model of "local" religion, reinforces rather than challenges the idea that religion is something that societies and cultures outgrow. As a result, Linford argues, *Deep Space Nine* ultimately entrenches the dismissive view of religion with which science fiction in general and *Star Trek* in particular initially began.

In "(Re)Covering Sacred Ground: New Age Spirituality in *Star Trek: Voyager*," Darcee L. McLaren and Jennifer Porter suggest that a shift toward a more positive portrayal of religion can be identified in the fourth *Star Trek* series. Addressing the apparent openness toward spirituality portrayed in *Star Trek: Voyager*, McLaren and Porter suggest that the issue of religious intolerance apparent in earlier *Star Trek* series is mediated in *Star Trek: Voyager* within the framework of the relationship between religion and science established previously within the *Star Trek* franchise. This mediation, they argue, occurs through the depiction of the spiritual experiences of two main characters: Commander Chakotay, the Native American First Officer, and Captain Kathryn Janeway, former science officer and head of the *Voyager* crew. Through the beliefs and experiences of these two characters, religion is introduced alongside science as normative, and as legitimately and appropriately "human." McLaren and Porter argue that the approach taken to religion in *Star Trek: Voyager* is particularly "New Age" and that this form of spirituality is compatible with the *Star Trek* worldview in ways that more institutional, doctrinal forms of religion apparently are not.

The second section of this volume examines the religious and mythic themes that run throughout *Star Trek*. How does *Star Trek* deal with the powerful issues of life and death, suffering and sacrifice, meaning and purpose? How does *Star Trek*'s exploration of these themes both reflect and potentially inform societal attempts to deal with these issues? Chapters in this section address the mythic power and appeal of *Star Trek* and highlight the mythic and symbolic parallels between *Star Trek* storylines and themes taken from both Western religious tradition and the scientific and technological emphasis of contemporary North American society. In "Intimations of Immortality: Death/Life Mediations in *Star Trek*," Jon Wagner explores the mythic mediations of life and death found within *Star Trek* episodes. Understanding myths as those narratives within which human beings encode issues of deepest ambivalence, Wagner argues that *Star Trek* provides new narrative mediations of an old and pervasive contradiction: our desire for immortality versus the need to come to terms with inexorable death. Although traditional religious myths deal with this dilemma, modernism invites a mythology that frames such mediation in naturalistic terms. Science fiction, Wagner suggests, can confront this need by setting its narratives in a hypothetical, usually futuristic frame. Immortal beings, resurrected characters, alternate universe doubles, disembodied intelligences, holographic personalities, androids, and a host of other alternate life-forms transmute contradictions of life/death and mortality/immortality in *Star Trek* into other hypothetical oppositions that subsequently lend themselves to ambiguous mediation. By problematizing the boundaries separating person and thing, mortal and immortal, Wagner argues, *Star Trek* provides a rich corpus of narrative that addresses the pervasive themes of traditional theology and mythology.

According to Larry Kreitzer, in "Suffering, Sacrifice and Redemption: Biblical Imagery in *Star Trek*," the Bible forms an important source for some of the most pervasive themes found within *Star Trek* episodes and films. According to Kreitzer, the characters of Kirk, Spock, and McCoy often play out between them the themes of suffering, sacrifice, and redemption as modeled on biblical imagery. Focusing first on the original *Star Trek* episode "The Empath," Kreitzer reveals the striking parallels between this episode and the crucifixion and resurrection imagery of the Christ story and the suffering and sacrifice imagery of the story of the Suffering Servant (Isaiah 53). Kreitzer then analyzes the parallels between Christ imagery and the figure of Spock within the films *Star Trek II: The Wrath of Khan* and *Star Trek III: The Search for Spock*. Here too, Kreitzer suggests, the biblical imagery of suffering, sacrifice, and redemption come to the fore. Kreitzer consequently suggests that the prevalence of this imagery reveals a significant theological core to *Star Trek*'s mythological world. This in turn, he suggests, reveals the ongoing fruitfulness of the Christian theological message. Theology and *Star Trek*, Kreitzer concludes, are perhaps much closer than we might have previously supposed.

Ian Maher addresses the human quest for meaning and purpose in his chapter "The Outward Voyage and the Inward Search: *Star Trek* Motion Pictures and the Spiritual Quest." Like Kreitzer, Maher suggests that there are recurring Christian religious themes to be found within the *Star Trek* franchise. Maher focuses his analysis on the eight *Star Trek* motion pictures to date. From the search of the V-ger probe for its creator in *Star Trek: The Motion Picture* to the mysterious encounter with the force of the Nexus in *Star Trek VII*, Maher suggests that the films frequently focus attention on the transcendent. According to Maher, fundamental questions of meaning remain significant within the scientific and technological world of *Star Trek*. What is the purpose of life? What does it mean to be human? Where does humanity fit into the broader scheme of the universe? Is there a 'God' behind it all? In positing and attempting to explore these questions, Maher concludes, the voyages of the starship *Enterprise* can be read as a metaphor for the human spiritual quest.

In Jeffrey Lamp's chapter, "Biblical Interpretation in the *Star Trek* Universe: Going Where Some Have Gone Before," the parallels between themes found in *Star Trek* and issues found in biblical interpretation are explored. Lamp examines selected episodes of *Star Trek: The Next Generation* and *Star Trek: Deep Space Nine* to uncover three issues in contemporary biblical interpretation that contribute to the storylines. The *Next Generation* episode "Rightful Heir" is examined in light of its reflection of the search for the historical Jesus; the *Next Generation* episode "Birthright" is examined in light of its portrayal of the role of narrative in the religious life of a community, and the *Deep Space Nine* episode "Destiny" is examined in light of its portrayal of issues relating to the fulfilment and interpretation of prophetic revelation. Lamp argues that these episodes reflect concerns at the forefront of scholarly interpretations of biblical literature, as well as attempts by religious individuals to maintain the essential core of religious belief in the midst of an intellectual and cultural framework generally unsympathetic toward a supernaturalist worldview. The struggles of the characters in these episodes to hold personal convictions of faith in a hostile intellectual environment can be seen, Lamp suggests, as models for those in American society who seek a similar integration.

Finally, in the third section of this volume, contributors discuss the religious, mythic, and ritual aspects of *Star Trek* fandom. No examination of the *Star Trek* phenomenon would be complete without addressing the subject of *Star Trek* fans. Fandom is not religious in and of itself, and *Star Trek* is not a religion. Nevertheless, *Star Trek* fandom both reveals and participates in classic religious and mythic themes. Chapters in this section explore the ways in which *Star Trek* fans have found meaning and value in *Star Trek*, and the ways in which they express that meaning in their actions and lives. Michael Jindra examines the folk philosophy of *Star Trek* fandom in "'*Star Trek* to Me Is a Way of Life': Fan Expressions of *Star Trek* Philosophy." Jindra argues that *Star Trek* fans integrate the philosophy portrayed in *Star Trek* into their own lives in numerous ways. His chapter explores how *Star Trek* has been used as folk philosophy by fans.

How are North American and other fans getting meaning from *Star Trek*? What does the *Star Trek* fan phenomenon tell us about our society? Jindra suggests that for many people, *Star Trek* takes the place of previous metanarratives and mythologies, such as nationalism or Christianity, that have allowed people to make sense of their identity and place in history. In supplanting these previous metanarratives, however, *Star Trek* has nonetheless capitalized on themes and symbols dominant in Western religious and cultural discourse. As a result, Jindra concludes, the folk philosophy of *Star Trek* is firmly embedded within the context of fundamental American cultural themes.

Darcee L. McLaren's "On the Edge of Forever: Understanding the *Star Trek* Phenomenon as Myth," also explores the question of how *Star Trek* fans find meaning in *Star Trek*. According to McLaren, scholars and fans alike frequently refer to *Star Trek* as modern myth. It is consequently within the study of myth that insight into the worldview, beliefs, and practices of fandom can be found. What, McLaren therefore asks, does it mean to say that *Star Trek* is myth? McLaren suggests that myth operates on two levels: first, on the level of meaning, in which exemplary models for human action are communicated symbolically, and second, on the level of action, in which the meaning of myth is lived by those to whom the stories have a mythic dimension. *Star Trek* operates on both of these levels, she suggests, but it is at the lived, participatory level that *Star Trek* truly emerges as modern myth. At this level, fans learn to see new possibilities for human action, as modeled on the relationships found within *Star Trek*. As a result, McLaren argues, *Star Trek* is an "origin myth" of the future, in which now and forever become actively linked for fans as they seek to actualize in their present-day lives the futuristic vision of humanity found within *Star Trek*. According to McLaren, IDIC ("Infinite Diversity in Infinite Combination") becomes the paradigm for this model of transformative action. Fans seek to live this paradigm and, in doing so, live the myth. *Star Trek*, McLaren therefore concludes, is more than "just a television show," it is a myth for modern times.

In "To Boldly Go: *Star Trek* Convention Attendance as Pilgrimage," Jennifer Porter explores the ritual aspects of *Star Trek* convention attendance. It is in the convention context that the paradigm of IDIC truly becomes lived or embodied. Cultural ideals are likewise embodied, negotiated, and expressed in the convention context. According to Porter, traveling to attend a convention in search of this embodied meaning places the convention setting on a par with traditional pilgrimage sites. Furthermore, she argues, the meaning that fans find in *Star Trek* is shared and reinforced at conventions, and convention attendees come to see themselves as living out *Star Trek*'s ideals. Drawing upon the concepts of liminality and communitas, Porter argues that fandom convention attendance consequently represents, for some fans, secular pilgrimage. Just as pilgrims in conventional pilgrimage contexts experience a sense of liberation from everyday statuses and roles, so too do fans in the convention context experience a "place and moment in and out of time," in which social boundaries diminish and egalitarian ideals become realized. In understanding convention attendance within the framework of pilgrimage, Porter concludes, new insights into *Star Trek* fandom and convention attendance are gained.

Star Trek continues to hold a place of importance within popular American culture. Since the series first premiered in the 1960s, *Star Trek* has reflected, informed, and often challenged prevailing social attitudes toward a wide variety of often controversial topics. Concern with religion and religious issues has constituted a consistent subtext within the *Star Trek* franchise. This engagement with religion is on-going: the more recent *Star Trek* series have made religion an explicit focus of concern. The reciprocal relationship between *Star Trek*'s portrayal and treatment of religion and changing societal attitudes toward religion provides the focus for the current work. This volume of articles represents the first comprehensive attempt to address the topic of religion and *Star Trek*. As such, it raises issues of interest to scholars and fans alike.

NOTES

1. These include the original *Star Trek* television series (TOS) and the three spin-off series, *Star Trek: The Next Generation* (*TNG*), *Star Trek: Deep Space Nine* (*DS9*), and *Star Trek: Voyager* (*VOY*). The movies include *Star Trek: The Motion Picture* (*1979*), *Star Trek II: The Wrath of Khan* (1982), *Star Trek III: The Search for Spock* (1984), *Star Trek IV: The Voyage Home* (1986), *Star Trek V: The Final Frontier* (1989), *Star Trek VI: The Undiscovered Country* (1991), *Star Trek: Generations* (1994), *Star Trek: First Contact* (1996), and *Star Trek: Insurrection* (1998).

2. The episodes and even the movies which deal explicitly with religion are generally regarded by *Star Trek* fans as marginal. They are not believed to be in any sense key narrations in the *Star Trek* corpus. Yet, religious themes and symbols are wound throughout the episodes and movies, and as at least one contributor to this volume will argue, a new eschatology is proposed over the course of the four series.

PART I

Religion in *Star Trek*

2

From Thwarted Gods to Reclaimed Mystery?

An Overview of the Depiction of Religion in Star Trek

ANNE MACKENZIE PEARSON

"**D**uring the darkest days of the sixties and seventies," writes David Gerrold (1984: 204) an avowed fan, *Star Trek* scriptwriter, and author of a book called *The World of Star Trek*, "it was easy to explain [the appeal of] *Star Trek*: '*Star Trek* says that there will be a future, and that we can and will solve our problems and learn how to live in peace.' It was such a clear opposite to what confronted us every morning on the front pages of the newspaper." But more than this, he argues, "Star Trek is about challenging ourselves. It is about finding our limits by being willing to go beyond them . . . it is about the ultimate nobility of the human spirit . . . it inspires. It leads individuals to pursue larger goals and discover possibilities in themselves that they might not otherwise have realized." This statement could describe an essential spiritual teaching articulated in many of the world's religions since a recurrent challenge offered to humanity by the world's religious founders and teachers has been for humans to recognize and then to develop the potential within themselves; to move beyond the limits imposed by their own egos in order to more fully express such divine attributes as love, mercy, and justice. Yet, despite what could be seen as a confluence of views about humanity's inherent nobility and unlimited potential for social and moral maturity expressed both by many of the world's religions and by *Star Trek*, the series has displayed an ambivalent view of religion and of the role that religion might play in humanity's future.

Gene Roddenberry (1921–1991) was *Star Trek's* creator and executive producer. While he was alive and continued to have a direct hand in the production of the show, religion as a theme was rarely treated. When it was, this chapter argues, the portrayal of religion reflected Roddenberry's own distrust of and antipathy toward organized religion. In *Star Trek*, organized religion tends to be portrayed as the product of a prerational age, antithetical to science and reason, and God is depicted as a category mistake—an advanced alien life-form mistaken for a god. However, after Roddenberry's death, and particularly evident in *Star Trek: Deep Space Nine* and *Star Trek: Voyager*, religion appears as a theme far more often and, while not uniformly the case, tends to be treated in a more sophisticated and sympathetic manner. Thus, while many Americans tend to share Roddenberry's distrust of organized religion in both its traditional and more recent incarnations (e.g., televised evangelism and new forms of fundamentalism), since Roddenberry's death the show has reflected more accurately the fact that the vast majority of Americans believe in God (around 95 percent) and a majority accept religious membership (Bellah 1985: 219, 324). The portrayal of religion in *Star Trek* has shifted from the point of view of secular individualists to the point of view of contemporary religious individualists—those who often speak of themselves today as "spiritual" rather than "religious," and for whom spirituality operates on a personal therapeutic model.[1] Present-day North Americans' interest in, if not acceptance of, diverse expressions of spirituality is reflected in *Star Trek* episodes of the 1990s and it seems that God/god no longer needs to be exposed and dethroned. There is a place for mystery.

GENE RODDENBERRY AND THE CONSTRUCTION OF THE *STAR TREK* VIEW OF RELIGION

Any examination of the portrayal of religion in *Star Trek* ought properly to begin with an inquiry into the views on religion and God held by Gene Roddenberry for Roddenberry was not only the series' creator and executive producer, he also wrote or rewrote many of the scripts and insisted on approving them all.[2] "Nowhere was one man's vision so personified on one show as on *Star Trek*," commented A&E's *Biography* feature on Gene Roddenberry. As Roddenberry himself remarked in 1991, "I am as near to an absolute monarch as is possible in this industry. I have complete control over what my show says and does" (Fern 1996: 62).

In another context Roddenberry explained, "I've been sure from the first that the job of 'Star Trek' was to use drama and adventure as a way of portraying humanity in its various guises and beliefs. The result was that 'Star Trek'—in the original series but even more powerfully in the second series—is an expression of my own beliefs using my characters to act out human problems and equations."[3] One of those human problems is humanity's relationship to God and to institutionalized religion. Roddenberry disliked the hypocrisy and inconsistency he saw manifested in religion. He admitted to ignoring religion and keeping quiet about his views of it until the making of *Star Trek*, when he could finally allow his views to be aired indirectly (Alexander 1991: 7). However, even then, he restrained himself in order to have general audience approval for the show: "Should I start venting my feelings on God, religion and so on," he remarked to the editor of *The Humanist* in 1991, "to the point it becomes hurtful of people and of their feelings, I would not be doing a good job" (Alexander 1991: 17).

Roddenberry was raised as a Baptist and taken to church every Sunday by his pious mother. But, when he began to really listen to sermons as a teenager, he reports that he became disenchanted. "I guess from that time it was clear to me that religion was largely nonsense—largely magical, superstitious things. . . . For me, religion was full of misstatements and reaches of logic that I just couldn't agree with."[4] He stopped going to church, rejected the traditional theist's notion of God, and rejected organized religion in general. He came to view conventional religious faith as a product and "a vestige of a pre-rational age" (Engel 1994: 7).

Roddenberry was an iconoclast, a man who fiercely cherished his right, indeed his responsibility as he would see it, to think for himself and to investigate truth through his own power of reasoning and imagination. He believed every person should be afforded the opportunity to express this right and responsibility (Engel 1994: 7). Roddenberry condemned organized religion for eclipsing this opportunity by offering its adherents ready-made answers and claims to exclusive truth bolstered by a religious hierarchy wrapped in symbols of its own authority. Further, religious hierarchy had shown itself powerfully capable of exploiting the faithful obedience of its adherents. According to Roddenberry, religious institutions and the closedmindedness they helped to sustain among their followers served to keep people in a passive or nonquestioning state of ignorance of themselves, of the world, and especially of other points of view.[5] Yet, Roddenberry was also an optimist, and he believed passionately in both the fundamental goodness and dignity of human beings and in their unlimited potential for development. He was thus a humanist, and in fact, he formalized that identity by becoming a member of the American Humanist Association in 1986 (Alexander 1991: 5).

While Roddenberry's views on the function of organized religion and on the nature of conventional faith were generally negative, toward the end of his life, at least, he evidently was not prepared to dismiss the concept of God. He was uncomfortable with the kind of personalized views of God he saw expressed by the mostly Judeo-Christian faiths he saw around him for he felt that such views limited God and subsequently limited humans.[6] He disliked the idea of humans denigrating themselves before a God largely conceived of by themselves or, rather, by the authoritative interpreters of religion. Yet, for Roddenberry the universe is a "marvellously complex thing" (Alexander 1991: 568), and he was prepared to accept a place for some notion of God in this universe, just not the "humanified" Judeo-Christian God, as he understood it. "God, to me," Roddenberry suggested to Yvonne Fern, "is intrinsic to humanity. To the whole cause of humanity. To the imaginative principle. To what we create, and think" (Fern 1996: 67–68). Roddenberry told another interviewer, Terrance Sweeney, that "God equals consciousness," and that humans, insofar as they participate in creativity, in "thought," are in some sense divine, are part of God. But, Roddenberry insisted, the concept of "being God" has nothing to do with religion.[7] Roddenberry's view, reflected in *Star Trek*, is that humanity has unlimited capacity to develop, even to become "god-like." Of course, the *Enterprise* crews often encounter in their journeys beings—organic and machine—with god-like powers (powers to manipulate the physical laws of the universe), but usually they are shown either to be devoid of an emotional and moral capacity or, from a human-centered perspective, to be morally and emotionally immature or irresponsible.[8] Thus, their powers are dangerous. The god-like qualities toward which humanity might evolve are suggested in *Next Generation* episodes such as those that feature "the traveller," and also perhaps the beings featured in the episode "Transfigurations" (1990).

In sum, philosophically, Roddenberry was an agnostic humanist. His view of organized religion was that it hampers humanity's progress toward self-actualization and overall advancement. Religion in general is a product of superstition and the human proclivity to rely on irrational but comfortingly unambiguous answers in the form of doctrines, myths, rules, and laws to make sense of, and order, life. Organized religion, in short, constrains freedom of thought. Roddenberry's view of God generally seems to be that God is simply the self, magnified, in contrast to the view that sees God as confronting humanity from the outside.[9]

As a result, in *Star Trek* the basic outlook of the *Enterprise* crew is humanistic and individual religious beliefs are generally presumed to be a private matter. None of the regular human characters, with the exception of Chakotay, the Native American commander on the fourth *Star Trek* series *Voyager*, are portrayed as having any kind of religious commitment. An assumption of *Star Trek* seems to be that organized religion had no direct role in helping to achieve humanity's peaceful and prosperous twenty-third and twenty-fourth century future. Rather, it is reason and humanist values, that is, religious values stripped of their dogma, institutional association, and reference to a transcendent being, reality, or source of Truth, that have helped to bring humanity together and continue to guide her course. According to Alexander (1991:8), "One of the underlying messages of [the original series (*TOS*) and *The Next Generation* (*TNG*)] is that human beings can, with critical thinking, solve the problems that are facing them without any outside or supernatural help." Roddenberry had great faith in the power of science and technology to solve humanity's problems. In *Star Trek*, science and religion, or reason and faith, are usually presented as incompatible (e.g. "For the World is Hollow and I Have Touched the Sky," 1968). Nevertheless, the show does suggest that science and technology are morally blind and offer no guarantee of the well-being of humankind. A core of agreed-upon ethical standards (related to safeguarding law and freedom, implementing justice, and exercising tolerance, compassion, and respect for life) are necessary to guide the use of science and technology. For example, in the episode "The Devil in the Dark" (1967), the use of technology to mine a planet results in the death of several miners. When it is discovered that the deaths were caused by a "rock creature" the first impulse of the humans is to kill it. When Spock then discovers that the creature is a mother trying to protect her offspring, Captain Kirk insists that respect for the right of this creature to exist must override the miners' desire to use their technology to promote their own material interests. A Vulcan mind-meld with the creature allows for the possibility of a mutually advantageous peaceful co-existence.

Despite Roddenberry's opinions about religious institutions, his second marriage in 1969 to Majel Barrett (Nurse Chapel in *TOS*, the voice of the computer in all series, and Lwaxana Troi in *TNG*) took place in a Japanese Buddhist ceremony, with both bride and groom dressed in traditional Japanese apparel. Roddenberry's apparent sympathy for Japanese Buddhism may help to explain the Zen-like atmosphere of Vulcan culture which, like Zen, is presented as very ordered, disciplined, and contemplative. Vulcan culture is, of course, also super-rational and, like Zen, has no beliefs in a personal god, yet it accepts a (benevolent) priestly hierarchy that oversees ritual rites of passage (e.g. the Vulcan "pon-farr" and "kohlinar"). The moral philosophy of Vulcan culture is based on nonviolence, an important ethical precept of Buddhism. And for all the emphasis on logic and the purging of emotion, there are definite mystical elements to Vulcan ways. The picture seems to reflect a rather typical Western understanding of Zen Buddhism: simple, even austere but mystical, and, above all, supporting a philosophy that locates the search for truth as beginning and ending with the self. Truth is thus directly available to any serious enquirer through a disciplined journey of self-discovery. Interestingly, just as Zen is one of the most popular of the transplanted Eastern religions in the United States, so Spock is by far the most popular character of *TOS*, and Gene Roddenberry's favorite as well.[10]

CLASSIC *TREK*: CHALLENGING THE MACHINE IN THE GOD

No specific human religious tradition is ever mentioned directly in *Star Trek*. However, "religion," generally presented in the series as a set of rituals and beliefs whose source, efficacy, and authority are attributed to some sort of superior being, is occasionally depicted among "primitive" alien cultures. A recurrent motif in *Star Trek* is that a highly advanced civilization or the products of its technology may be mistaken for gods by a "primitive," i.e. much less technologically advanced race (see Dubreuil 1994: 210). This motif has three related themes: a computer mistaken for a god, an advanced being or race mistaken for a god(s), and an advanced being or race that tries to present itself as god-like.

First, a favorite storyline, especially evident in the first series—and saying much about popular fears concerning the future direction of the emergent computer technology in the 1960s—features a group of people who have come under the control of a machine, or a super-computer, regarded as a god. Thus, in the first series episode, "For the World is Hollow and I Have Touched the Sky" (1968), a people living on a world which, unknown to them is actually a space ship, willingly submit to the directives of the Oracle—a sophisticated computer. In "The Apple" (1967), an ancient computer named Vaal controls every aspect of a child-like and stagnant race's "edenic" existence (including the weather and food production). The *Enterprise* doctor and others are appalled: "Jim," Dr. McCoy says, "you can't just blind yourself to what is happening. These are humanoids—intelligent! They've got to advance—progress! . . . This isn't life, it's stagnation!" Despite the supposedly overarching constraint on the Federation of the Prime Directive,[11] the moral imperative to interfere and rescue the humanoid race held captive to a machine is irresistible to Kirk and his crew, and they devise a plan leading to the destruction of the computer-god. After its demise, Kirk addresses the child-people (making a statement that could well have come from Roddenberry's own mouth): "Listen to me, all of you. From this day on, you will not depend on Vaal. You are your own masters. You will be able to think what you wish, say what you wish, do what you wish. You will learn many things that are strange, but they will be good."

Similarly, in "The Return of the Archons" (1967), whose teleplay was based on a story by Roddenberry, a computer once programmed by a technological wizard to help ensure peace among his formerly warring people, now controls the minds and bodies of their descendants in its own machine image. Though peaceful (except for an imposed annual twelve-hour period of violent chaos), the people lack individual initiative; their minds are submerged into the "common being of the Body" of the machine-god Landru, who thinks of himself as maintaining the "Absolute Good." The people have lost their own "humanity," until, that is, the *Enterprise* crew arrives and uses logic to persuade the "false god" to self-destruct.[12] In this episode, those who enforce the law for Landru—and are described as his limbs—are depicted wearing dark robes with hoods and cowls and carrying lethal staffs. They appear as caricatures of imagined medieval European stern and fearful servants of an all-powerful religious hierarchy. At the end of the episode, Spock remarks: "I was reflecting on the frequency with which mankind has wished for a world as peaceful and secure as the one Landru provides." "Quite so, Mr. Spock," Kirk replies. "And see what happens when we get it! It's our luck and our curse that we're forced to grow, whether we like it or not."

The "Paradise Syndrome" (1968) is an example of the highly technologically advanced race mistaken for gods by a low-technology race. In this episode, Captain Kirk resuscitates a child who has just drowned, and the "primitive" people on the planet (who are made to resemble a Hollywood version of Native Americans) view the resuscitation as the proof they are looking for that this strange man who emerged out of their temple is a god. In this case, the amnesiac Kirk almost believes it himself though with his failure to perform other god-like feats, the people begin to turn against the imposter. Faith is fickle when beliefs are irrational, this episode suggests to the viewers.

During a discussion about observing the Prime Directive in the episode "Bread and Circuses" (1968), McCoy exclaims: "Once, just once, I would like to land someplace and say, 'Behold! I am the Archangel Gabriel!'" In other words, he would like to set himself up as a messenger of God (or of the gods from the sky) in front of a technologically primitive, and therefore, we are expected to assume, gullible race and see what happens. Interestingly, while this show made it past the censors whom Roddenberry would wish to challenge boldly, especially in the 1960s, the teleplay written by Roddenberry and Gene Coon still retained a barely concealed reference to Christianity and the "cult of the Son." Of course, the audience along with the *Enterprise* crew are fooled into thinking, until the end of the show, that the characters are speaking about a cult of the Sun!

Finally, the third theme concerns a race technologically or physiologically advanced in comparison to humans who try to command the obedience or even worship of humans. This theme is the subject of the episodes "Who Mourns for Adonais?" (1967) and "Plato's Stepchildren" (1968). However, in the twenty-third century, most humans are unwilling to submit to postures of humiliation before other species. "Who Mourns for Adonais?" is a particularly striking example of an episode that suggests (along Roddenberrian lines) that humans "overcame" their need to worship a "higher" being.

THE NEXT GENERATION OF
FALSE GODS AND MISPLACED FAITH

Two decades later we once again meet with an advanced race assuming a godly mantle before its beguiled "child-race" followers. In "Justice" (1987), a first season episode of *Star Trek: The Next Generation* (*TNG*), Wesley, the young teenage son of the starship's doctor, is condemned to death for violating a seemingly trivial taboo on an edenic planet of, as descriptions would have it, "scantily clad" "blonde fitness fiends" called the Edo. The well-being of the Edo is guarded, and the laws governing their lives are determined and controlled by a large alien ship that exists "inter-dimensionally" and hovers, unseen, around the planet. To the Edo this being, who benevolently, if arbitrarily, looks after them, is God. The crew of the *Enterprise-D* has a run-in with this god when Wesley inadvertently breaks a law. The captain and other officers try to argue their way out of the only punishment for any crime—death. Yet, even when the *Enterprise* crew reveals the "god" to be nothing more than a technologically advanced race, the Edo quake in fear of it, and prefer to hold on to their known ways. The "god" also makes it amply clear that it will tolerate no interference with its "children." The main message of this episode is that an absolutist interpretation of law creates injustice. As Captain Jean-Luc Picard states: "There can be no justice so long as laws are absolute. Justice itself is an exercise in exceptions." However, the other message of the episode reflects Roddenberry's view of how readily people accept a false god when they have not been encouraged to question received truth and to think for themselves. "Why are they so certain it's a god?" Picard asks Data concerning the Edo. "Any sufficiently advanced life-form would appear to be that, sir," Data replies.

The third-season episode "Who Watches the Watchers" (1989) is a relevant case study for our purposes as it takes as its theme what the writers evidently view as the alarmingly easy backward slide from an emergent rationality and science to superstition and religion that can occur among a people grappling with an inexplicable and threatening event. This episode thus encapsulates a simplistic dichotomization of religion and science where the two realms are presented as mutually exclusive. Further, the characters in this episode explicitly articulate a view of the effects of organized religion on a culture with which Roddenberry would likely have been in agreement.[13]

In "Who Watches the Watchers" a three-member Federation anthropological field team is studying an extended family of "proto-Vulcan humanoids of the Bronze-age level" on a planet called Mintaka. The people are described as "quite peaceful and highly rational." When the anthropologists' reactor (which provides power for their holographic camouflage) begins to malfunction, a distress call is sent out. The *Enterprise* responds and arrives as the generator explodes, injuring the scientists and dissolving the camouflage. When a team beams down to assist the scientists on the planet they are observed by a native Mintakan (the "watchers are watched") who later identifies Picard as the "Overseer," the Mintakan term for god.

In an effort to explain the existence of the alien observers and the effects of their technology, the Mintakans resurrect the old beliefs of their forebears. Meanwhile, in an effort to exercise damage control, the head anthropologist suggests that Picard beam down to the planet and give the Mintakans a set of guidelines, to "let them know what the Overseer expects of them." He fears that "without guidance [the Mintakans'] religion would degenerate into inquisitions, holy wars, chaos." Picard refuses to "send [the Mintakans] back into the dark ages of superstition, ignorance, of fear." The Mintakans are finally convinced that the *Enterprise* crew are not gods when they see one of the anthropologists die from her injuries. Their forward path to rationality and progress is restored. "You have taught us that there is nothing beyond our reach," the female leader, Nuria,[14] says to Picard in the closing scene.

The old beliefs of the Mintakans are described essentially as a collection of superstitions revolving around the attempt to please the gods in order to ensure security and well-being. But pleasing the gods can never be confidently undertaken. Beliefs such as these, the anthropologist and Picard assume, have no rational coherence, no ethical framework or rules that could prevent the unleashing of chaos, intolerance, and violence. This horror is supposedly religion and only a codified set of guidelines, provided by the advanced representatives of the Federation, can prevent the re-emergent Mintakan beliefs from degenerating into such a religion with its unfortunate concomitant effects. Picard rejects this solution not because it violates respect for the Mintakans, but because it violates the "essence" of the Prime Directive: noninterference in the natural course of a race's evolution (or in this case, devolution).[15]

Finally, the episode "Rightful Heir" (1993) also deals with the issue of religion, although it departs from the previously mentioned episodes in several ways. First, "Rightful Heir" is a more thoughtful and serious treatment of the function of religion in people's lives than that found in earlier episodes. Perhaps significantly, Roddenberry had died more than a year before this show was aired. Second, the episode deals not with a race who is never to be seen in the series again, but with a race who have occupied a great deal of attention in three of the four series, namely, the Klingons. This episode focuses on the spiritual quest of one member of the *Enterprise* crew, the Klingon, Lieutenant Worf. If the Vulcans are modeled at least in part on a Western perception of Zen Buddhists, the Klingons are modeled on the Western perception of the Russians (a perception which, of course, changed between the first and second series), and the Russian Orthodox Church. The chanting, the semi-darkness, the smokiness, beards, long hair and heavy garments of the Klingon priests are all suggestive of a Russian Orthodox service. In *TNG* the Klingons are depicted with much greater depth and subtlety than the cardboard bad-guy figures who appear in the original series. They are still swarthy and aggressive, ready to engage in battle at the first hint of insult or glimmer of glory, but these characteristics are given a richer cultural background, particularly through the character of Worf, the only Klingon serving on a Federation ship. Just as Spock is the only Vulcan on the *Enterprise* in the first series, and his is the only regular character for whom some glimpses of a ritual and spiritual or mystical life are drawn, so Worf, an outsider, is the only regular character in *TNG* who is depicted as having a spiritual life.[16] Perhaps from the producers' and writers' point of view it is safer as well as creatively more expansive to experiment with depictions of a spiritual and ritual life for a non-human character than for a regular human character. Yet, the very fact that there is a mystical or religious dimension to these characters' lives, not evident in the lives of other regular characters, serves to further distinguish, if not alienate these aliens.

Seeking answers to a crisis of his faith in Klingon beliefs about Kahless, the heroic founder of the Klingon way of life, Worf in "Rightful Heir" makes a pilgrimage to Borath, a sacred planet predicted to be the site of the return of Kahless. After many days of chanting and meditation Kahless appears to Worf, not in a vision but in the flesh. The appearance of Kahless produces varied reactions among the Klingons. Some disbelieve it is him, others are not sure, and still others joyfully celebrate. Worf waffles. He wants to believe, but can't, at least not until a scan matches Kahless' DNA with a sample of the original Kahless' blood preserved on a knife. For Worf, science had to prove his faith, and he is exuberant when it does so. "Only with [Kahless'] help," Worf tells Gowron, the leader of the Klingon High Council who wants to kill the imposter, "can we revive the pure warriors within ourselves. Listen to him, open your heart, hear his words, let him restore your faith as he has mine, give him a chance to cleanse and restore your spirit." However, doubt creeps back in, and faith is lost again for Worf when the guardians are forced to reveal that Kahless is a clone of the original, a "false god," Worf calls him. Ultimately it is decided that the clone Kahless should return to the Klingon home world as a figurehead emperor, after Worf gives an impassioned speech: "They need something to believe in, just as I did, something larger than themselves, something that will give their lives meaning—they need Kahless. . . . Our people are becoming decadent and corrupt—they need moral leadership, Kahless can be that leader . . . he will lead by example, and will guide them in spiritual matters. . . . Real power comes from within the heart."

The last scene is between Worf and Kahless. As Kahless is about to transport off the ship he notices that Worf looks troubled, and he asks him why. Worf confesses: "I went to Borath to find my faith—for a while I thought I had—but my heart is empty again; I do not know what to believe." Kahless responds: "Kahless left us a powerful legacy—a way of thinking and acting that makes us Klingon. . . . If his words hold wisdom, and his philosophy is honorable, what does it matter if he returns. What is important is that we follow his teachings. Perhaps the words are more important than the man."

Among other things, this episode is a commentary on the Christian expectation of the return of Christ, an expectation increasingly fueled by the approach of the end of the second millennium. However, while, as in the previous episodes, the notion of a supernatural intervention in history is rejected (Kahless is just a product of modern cloning technology), the need for moral leadership, "spiritual guidance," and for belief in "something larger than ourselves" that can provide lives with meaning and coherence is acknowledged as legitimate. Further, the show acknowledges that there are special people—like Kahless or, by implication, Jesus or the Buddha—whose wisdom and exemplary lives are recorded in "holy texts" and who, through these texts, can continue to provide guidance and meaning to life. While this episode continues the premise that belief in God, an after-life, or a soul are not "necessary conditions of human worth and dignity" (Lalli 1994: 204), it does come close to saying that such beliefs may not, after all, obstruct progress toward a mature, rational, and peaceful world.

In sum, the view of religion generally portrayed in the first and second *Star Trek* series reflects the humanistic tradition rooted in the Enlightenment's characterization of religion as anti-rational superstition, a source of backwardness, and a relic of pre-industrial societies that modern culture has outgrown or will outgrow. *Star Trek's* attractive humanistic vision of the future is based on a faith in the ability of human rationality (and self-interest) alone to play the divine physician: to "take the pulse" of humankind, prescribe the best remedy, overcome all adversity and direct humanity, finally, to a peaceful, democratic, and united world.[17] Such a view would seem to support the argument made by two authors of a recent book on religion and film that, "during the same period in which film has risen to prominence, Europeans and Americans have shifted from a focus on the power of God toward one that emphasizes the power of humanity" (Martin and Ostwelt 1995: 65).

DEEP SPACE NINE AND VOYAGER: PRIVATE FAITH AND THE REDEMPTION OF RELIGION IN SPIRITUALITY

If it can be argued that *Star Trek* mirrors and expresses the beliefs and values of a substantial portion of North American culture, then this culture's confidence in the power of humanity on its own to provide guidance, cohesion, and meaning is much less assured now than it was in the 1960s, 1970s, and 1980s. The need for moral and spiritual guidance and for a belief in something larger than ourselves, articulated in the *Next Generation* episode described earlier, has become a recurring theme in *Star Trek: Deep Space Nine (DS9)* and *Star Trek: Voyager.*

The setting of *DS9* is a Federation space station situated next to the planet Bajor. The people of Bajor are united by their common religious faith guided by a religious oligarchy, itself directed by invisible spiritual guides called "the Prophets." This setting allows for the periodic examination of the nature of religious faith and leadership. The two-hour premiere episode of *DS9* ("Emissary," 1993) featured then-Commander Sisko's encounter with the Prophets, one that led both to his emotional healing and to his identification as the Bajoran's long-awaited spiritual Emissary. This introductory episode so explicitly involving a spiritual motif set a compelling tone for the exploration of religious themes in this series. On *DS9* religious faith is treated as more than simply the product of superstition and the suspension of rationality depicted in the earlier series. On the other hand, certain episodes that deal with the Bajoran oligarchy convey the idea that this religious leadership is also not immune to ambition and corruption (see, e.g. the episode "Shakaar," 1995).

Like two other central but not fully human characters, Spock and Worf, Major Kira Nerys, the Bajoran liaison officer serving on the space station, is the one regular character whose personal religious life is portrayed. She prays, performs rituals, and is seen both to ask vexing spiritual questions and to demonstrate the abiding and supportive role of her examined (though sometimes troubling) religious beliefs. "Your faith seems to have led you to something of a contradiction," says the Changeling security officer Odo after he asks Kira how there could have existed two emissaries, in the episode "Accession" (1996). "I don't see it as a contradiction," replies Kira. "I don't understand," Odo says. "That's the thing about faith," Kira responds, "If you don't have it you can't understand it. And if you do, no explanation is necessary." Kira's faith, even if not always explicable to others, is portrayed as providing her not just with guidance but with a moral and spiritual axis that helps to center and strengthen her.

A theme occurring regularly though infrequently in this series is the question of the Prophets' identity. In other words, the series asks, who is God?[18] In *DS9* the identity of the Prophets is alternately suggested to be a non-corporeal species existing outside of time with little interest in Bajor, and "real" spiritual powers or beings who do take interest in and guide the course of the Bajoran people. The Prophets of the Bajorans are thus allowed to retain their enigmatic divine quality and are somewhat sympathetically depicted.

Interestingly, Commander Sisko's identification by the Bajorans as their Emissary means that he is now the only regular human character on *Star Trek* who has a religious function. As the Emissary, he is thought to be able, and consequently expected at certain critical times, to convey the will of the Prophets. Though he resists this identity—or resists its spiritual implications—Sisko accepts the role and assumes its ceremonial functions for the sake of furthering Federation-Bajoran relations. He is uncomfortable with this identity, however, for he does not see himself as a believer, even while he has learned to respect the Bajorans' faith. The enigma of the Prophets' identity and Sisko's link to them would seem to encapsulate the ambivalent, uncertain, "maybe, maybe not" attitude toward religion and spirituality that has characterized the *Star Trek* point of view on religion since Roddenberry's death.

The appearance of a Native American character, Commander Chakotay, as the second-in-command on the most recent *Star Trek* incarnation, *Star Trek: Voyager* (*VOY*) has allowed writers to explore the inner space of Native American religiosity and in the process reflect a persistent, if not growing, interest among North Americans (and Europeans) in aboriginal spirituality. The glimpses we are offered of Chakotay's cultural heritage and spiritual practices, however, do not conform to any specific Native American tradition. We do learn that Chakotay's boyhood skepticism of his ancestors' spiritual heritage has been replaced by an experiential appreciation of its value, especially as a repository of practical wisdom.

This series has also brought back as a regular character a Vulcan, Lieutenant Tuvok, who brings with him the logical yet mystical legacy of the ever popular Spock. Like Spock, Tuvok regularly meditates and engages in particular rituals to aid him in controlling his emotions and developing the powers of his mind. In *Voyager*, Tuvok also assists one of his crew members to develop her innate mental capacities, always within a disciplined and somewhat ritualistic setting.

In one *Voyager* episode entitled "Sacred Ground" (1996), the captain of the starship *Voyager* undertakes a classic spiritual journey and in the process seriously grapples with the limits of science-based knowledge to solve or even potentially solve all problems. When a member of her crew is rendered comatose after encountering a "biogenic field" surrounding a holy sanctuary on an alien planet where the people's ancestral spirits are said to exist, Captain Janeway attempts to uncover clues for a treatment. She is led on a ritual journey during which she keeps seeing things in terms of tests and challenges and continually tries to use the categories of science and reason to understand what is happening. She insists that she is not interested in personal enlightenment but only in doing whatever is necessary to save her crew member. Toward the end of this ritual journey, Captain Janeway's guide tells her, not for the first time, that everything she has gone through is meaningless and that "You have what you need to save her yourself."

Meanwhile, the ship's doctor monitors the captain's biochemical state through an implant placed in her before the start of the ritual and concludes that he has received sufficient "biometric" information to treat Kes, the injured crew member. He tries but the treatment does not work. He cannot explain it. He reiterates to the captain who has returned to the ship: "It appears that everything you went through is meaningless." Science has failed to provide a solution. Janeway returns to the planet and confronts her guide, who tells her: "I haven't led you anywhere. . . . You've taken me along wherever you wanted to go. This was your ritual. You set these challenges for yourself." Janeway admits to having had certain expectations of what the ritual would entail and finally confesses that she does not know what she is seeking. In a state of new humility but still looking for rational answers, she is again made to confront her own unquestioning faith in the ultimate explanatory triumph of science. Not until Janeway is finally able to "let go" of her beliefs in the supremacy of science is she able to save Kes. She is told to take Kes back into the shrine and "trust the spirits to return her soul." Janeway realizes that this was the challenge all along, and she decides to accept it—to take this new and, for her, utterly alien and frightening kind of leap of faith. The voices of doubt and hesitation are represented by her colleagues who question her judgement and her state of mental competence. Quelling these voices, she takes Kes into the sanctuary/biogenic field and Kes revives. Back on the ship, the doctor—the epitome of science, and necessarily soulless because he is artificial—comes up with a complicated physiological explanation for Kes' "miraculous" recovery. Yet her brief response, the look on her face and her colleagues' reactions to it, make it clear that Janeway no longer finds such "perfectly sound scientific" explanations entirely satisfying.

It appears that Janeway's "ordeal" was not meaningless after all. It simply was not meaningful in the way that she had expected it to be, that is, to provide information, hard data that could be used to find a cure for her comatose crew member. The ordeal and its initial failure represented the necessary prelude to her confrontation with her own total faith in one form of knowledge—based on science—to explain away every "mystery." Though she was not seeking personal enlightenment, she did receive it in the form of a "revelation" of the extent to which her beliefs constituted their own form of unexamined faith. Other forms of knowledge, specifically what may be called spiritual knowledge, even while apparently not always rational, may "work."

Captain Janeway's confident statement uttered at the beginning of the episode "Sacred Ground" that, "if we scratch deep enough, we'll find a scientific basis for most religious doctrines" reflects, not an affirmation of the fundamental irrationality of religion typical of *TOS*, but a functionalist view of religion. Human beliefs and actions that have withstood the test of time must have some utilitarian purpose which, while not always immediately discernible, must nevertheless be there. But this view too is challenged in *Voyager*. It seems that religion and science may not be incompatible but rather are distinctive domains which offer different sorts of explanatory models for human experience. Both *DS9* and *Voyager*, then, have shifted the generally negative ambivalence toward religion and spirituality characteristic of the older series to a positive ambivalence that accepts the possible efficaciousness of spiritual knowledge. Religion is thus redeemable.

CONCLUSION

What have traditionally been construed as quintessentially religio-philosophical questions concerning morality and the meaning of human existence have appeared frequently in *Star Trek*, but these questions have usually been addressed independently of any religious context. Clearly, religion as an explicit subject has not figured prominently in the series, nor has it been ignored in any of the four *Star Trek* series. When religion is treated, five themes are prominent. The first theme notable in the original series, is that technological advancement may be equated to godhood by less developed (and therefore naive) people. The second theme is religion as a source of conflict and superstition. The third theme is religion in opposition to rationality and science. Each of these themes expresses aspects of Gene Roddenberry's personal view of religion, a view that fore-saw conventional organized religion and traditional images of God being left behind and saw humanity as the appropriate locus for faith. A fourth theme is that religion properly belongs to the Other (Spock, Worf, Kira, Chakotay). This device, in the case of the first three characters, has allowed the show to explore forms of spirituality without implicating any "real" human religions and without compromising Roddenberry's view of the nature and effects of organized religion in human history (both its past and projected future). Giving these characters a "mystical" or "spiritual" dimension to their lives has also helped to underscore their difference. Nonetheless, this sense of difference is sympathetically drawn and serves to render these characters more attractive and interesting. The fifth theme, evident particularly in the post-Roddenberry *TNG* as well as in *DS9* and *Voyager*, is that a religious worldview and beliefs can, after all, provide individuals with a legitimate source of guidance and strength which may not necessarily be incompatible with rationality and science. This theme suggests that there may be forms of "spiritual knowledge" which can illuminate facets of truth and reality unavailable to purely scientific forms of inquiry.

In sum, while dismissed if not ridiculed in the first series, religion has made a comeback in the later series, albeit in something of a New Age package, full of unanswered questions, speculation, and hints of "something more out there." *Star Trek* has come close to acknowledging the fundamentally spiritual nature of human beings, or of the human spirit, which inclines us toward transcendence. From most religions' point of view, our capacity for spiritual growth (or moral perfection, if you will) is what defines us as humans. For Roddenberry, this perfection was achievable by human will alone, without any assistance from conventional forms of religion. As he reflects in his interview with Terrance Sweeny: "As nearly as I can concentrate on the question today, I believe I am God; certainly you are, I think we intelligent beings on this planet are all a piece of God, are becoming God. In some sort of cyclical non-time thing we have to become God, so we can end up creating ourselves, so that we can be in the first place." The boy-genius Wesley of *TNG*, may well exemplify Roddenberry's view of humans, just described. In the episode, "Journey's End" (1994), Wesley successfully utilizes his potential, and by implication, all humans' potential, to tap into and manipulate the power of thought to travel through space and time—to explore other dimensions of reality.

The final word is left to the film *Star Trek: The Motion Picture* (1979). This film features V-ger, a machine that amassed so much information that it became sentient. V-ger wants to grow, it wants answers to questions unanswerable by its science-based machine intelligence, and it seeks these answers from its creator. V-ger's troubling question, "Is this all I am?" is getting a repeated hearing on *Star Trek* in recent years.

NOTES

1. For a discussion of "secular individualists" and "religious individualists" see Bellah et al. (1985: 247).

2. Roddenberry wrote the screenplay and/or the story for twelve out of the seventy-nine episodes of the first series, including the pilot. In addition, he "rewrote major portions of the first two seasons of the show" (Alexander 1994: 564). For the second series, he continued to be executive producer for the first five seasons. He also wrote the show's "Writer's Guide," and three of the episodes. With *Star Trek: The Next Generation* Roddenberry is said to have been able to "fix" things that he hadn't been happy with in the first series—like the portrayal of the Klingons.

3. Quoted in *The Humanist*, 1991: 10.

4. From an interview in *The Humanist*, March/April, 1991: 6–7.

5. See Roddenberry's statements quoted in Fern (1996: 66, 93,166). Roddenberry reports to his Jesuit interlocutor Terrance Sweeny (published in Sweeny's book *God &* [1985] reprinted in Alexander [1994: 571]) about a "major" experience in his life when, at the age of about seventeen, he attended a Baptist young people's Christian Association meeting where he heard a Scottish ex-minister ridiculing war and patriotism and who then lent Roddenberry a book called *Days of Our Years* by P. Van Passen. "It was the first revelation in my life that things are not as they are said to be." Roddenberry then describes a similar revelatory experience much later in his life when he was developing *Star Trek*. The "idea began to grow in me that Star Trek adventures could be about many different creatures and events, so that I could get many different ideas by the censors on religion, on sex, on unions, on management, or on Vietnam"

6. "My own feeling is that relation to God as a person is a petty, superstitious approach to the All, the Infinite." (Roddenberry quoted in the Sweeny interview in Alexander 1991: 570)

7. See the Sweeny interview with Roddenberry in Alexander (1991: 568, 571).

8. Episode examples of amoral or immature god-like beings would include *TOS*: "Where no Man has Gone Before" (1966); "The Changeling"

(1967); "The Squire of Gothos" (1967); *TNG*: "Where Silence Has Lease" (1988); and episodes featuring the character Q.

9. In this description of Roddenberry's view of God, I have used Bellah's words wherein he was comparing the beliefs of "radical individualistic" religion with "conservative" religion (Bellah et al. 1985: 235).

10. For Roddenberry's views on the character of Spock, see Fern (1996: 73–74, and *passim*).

11. The Prime Directive, as the name implies, is the central ethical principle governing the Federation's interaction with non-Federation species. Federation starships are not to involve themselves in the natural evolution of a pre-space faring people or planet's sentient population.

12. The *Enterprise* crew commits or is an accessory to deicide in a number of *TOS* episodes ("The Apple" [1968] , "The Return of the Archons" [1967], and "For the World is Hollow and I have Touched the Sky" [1968]) and in the fifth film, *Star Trek V: The Final Frontier* (1989).

13. Roddenberry says as much with respect to this episode in comments made in his interview with Sweeney (Alexander 1991:8).

14. *Nur* means "light" (as opposed to "dark") in Farsi (Persian).

15. Of course, abuse, violence, and intolerance perpetrated in the name of religion are very real features of humanity's past and present, but it is facile to suggest that these behaviors are a necessary attribute of religious people, or that they exist because of the presence or absence of a rule book. In the episode "Justice" (1987), the Edo describe their past as violent and chaotic until "God" came along and provided a set of laws. However, though these laws had provided them with peace and security, and the Edo were content with this, the rigidity of the laws was judged by Picard and crew as ultimately unjust because of their inflexibility. The suggestion here is that religious laws are always inflexible and therefore are not capable of consistently bringing justice to people.

16. Data is a special case, and his spiritual quest warrants a separate treatment, beyond the scope of the present chapter.

17. The unity of the human race is another premise of the series. However, while *Star Trek* assumes the attainment of this consciousness for the human family, it illustrates the novelty of the idea for us even today in the episode "The Chase" (1993), which develops the premise (first seen in the episode "The Paradise Syndrome") that the galaxy was genetically "seeded" by a single original race eons ago. Thus, the humans, the Cardassians, the Klingons, and the Romulans are all biologically related, much to their dismay.

18. As previously noted, the theme of the identity of God occupies the core of *Star Trek V: The Final Frontier* (1989). In this film, the question concerning

the identity of the would-be god beyond "the great barrier" is certainly not conclusively resolved. The "god" that is finally encountered turns out to be a powerful and capricious alien being (and not the supreme being that the Vulcan Sybok (Spock's brother), the Klingons, and a few of the humans on the *Enterprise* had hoped to discover). Yet a "Roddenberrian" answer to the god question is suggested for the audience at the end of the film. "Is God really out there?," McCoy asks Kirk at the end of this film. "Maybe he's not out there, Bones," Kirk replies, "he's really here, in the human heart."

3

Classic *Star Trek* and the Death of God

A Case Study of "Who Mourns For Adonais?"

ROBERT ASA

On September 22, 1967, at 8:30 P.M. (EST), NBC television aired a drama that was a parable of the state of religion in American society during the 1960s and beyond. *Star Trek* was indeed boldly going where no one had gone before, but only the insightful few knew it at the time. Mature viewers and television critics had accurately perceived that this innovative series was no vacuous space opera, nor some innocuous "wagon train to the stars," as Gene Roddenberry, its creator, described it (Whitfield and Roddenberry 1968:124).[1] It was a generally well-written, well-acted, serious attempt to comment on current social issues in the guise of science fiction. Previously, only *The Twilight Zone* had used the genre for so lofty a purpose, though not all of its episodes could be considered science fiction in content.

Star Trek certainly was "far out" for the times, both literally and figuratively. Not only did the events of the show take place in outer space, strange creatures appeared who taxed the credulity of the average television viewer. While Americans were anticipating a manned landing on the moon by the end of the decade, only the visionaries dreamed of actually exploring other worlds. Science fiction television and films were largely confined to the B-movie category, known for their bad scripts, bad sets, and bad acting. Children and teenagers might be entertained by it, but no one with mental images of the theatrical *Buck Rogers* or the televised *Lost in Space* could begin to take science fiction seriously as commentary on anything except the prevalence of mindless bad taste.

Not yet embracing science fiction films as an art form or as a medium for social comment, American society yawned at *Star Trek*. In retrospect, *Star Trek's* creator and contributors appear in many respects to have been unsung heroes, bravely saying through poetry what few others were saying in prose. Much of it fell on deaf ears, except for the ears of the young and impressionable, for whom *Star Trek* was more than entertainment. To them, *Star Trek* was *real. Star Trek meant* something. *Star Trek* spoke *the truth.* Kirk, Spock, and McCoy were not two-dimensional cardboard cutouts. They were flesh and blood people who could serve as role models. The *Enterprise* was not merely a huge metallic spacecraft. It was modern humanity on a thrilling journey toward the unknown. Intergalactic conflicts were not contests over vague ideologies but fights for human rights, human freedom, and human destiny.

Yet *Star Trek* could also disquiet, disturb, and deconstruct. Its episodes repeatedly challenged unthinking submission to authority, whether that authority was political, economic, social, or religious. *Star Trek* stood for diversity, pluralism, tolerance, non-conformity, and individualism when these traits were not necessarily considered virtues by the masses. *Star Trek* represented rebellion against authoritarianism, rejection of ethnocentrism, and resistance to the status quo. In thinly veiled parables the series addressed diverse issues such as war, slavery, drug abuse, overpopulation, dehumanization, bigotry, ecology, and the misuse of power. Hence, "*Star Trek* was more than a TV show, it was a crusade" (Pringle 1996: 139).

On a Friday evening in 1967, "Who Mourns for Adonais?" was for most viewers little more than an interesting bit of space opera. The plot seemed straightforward enough. The starship *Enterprise* encounters a giant hand in space, which seizes the ship. A male head and face, crowned with laurel leaves, comes on the viewing screen demanding that a landing party beam down to the planet Pollux IV, but without Mr. Spock, who is normally included in such excursions. To the surprise and disbelief of the *Enterprise* crew, they meet the Greek god Apollo, who millennia ago had been worshipped on Earth.[2] In this case, however, he is no myth, but an immortal who once was regarded as a god.[3] According to Apollo, the Greco-Roman gods were actually space travelers who left Earth when the ancient world forsook them. All but Apollo finally gave up their godhood and became part of the Infinite. But Apollo had waited many long centuries for humanity to find him again when they ventured out into space.

Apollo demands worship. But humanity has lost its need for gods. Kirk and company defiantly resist Apollo, risking his wrath. He is no longer a god to them; they have outgrown him and no longer believe he offers anything they do not possess in themselves. Nevertheless, Apollo is able to win over the sole female in the landing party, Lieutenant Carolyn Palamas, by impressive displays of power and flattery, much to the chagrin of Mr. Scott, who is infatuated with her. The *Enterprise* is immobilized in orbit, communication devices won't work, and Apollo seems invincible and invulnerable.

Kirk's only recourse is to try to convince Lieutenant Palamas to reject Apollo's advances. By doing so, Kirk reasons, Apollo will fly into a rage, expending energy that is already taxed by his hold over ship and crew. The ruse works. As a furious Apollo attempts to rape Lieutenant Palamas, Spock finds weaknesses in Apollo's force field through which to shoot phasers. Targeting his temple, the source of Apollo's power, the *Enterprise* concentrates a steady stream of phasers on the structure. Apollo, knowing that the *Enterprise* can mean his destruction, shoots lightning bolts at the ship, but to no avail. Apollo's temple melts into oblivion and with it evaporates his power base.

Shocked and saddened, Apollo realizes that "the time is past; there is no room for gods." With tears streaming down his face, he reproaches Lieutenant Palamas and the landing party for his tragic fate, and then offers himself up to the cosmos. He fades from sight, calling on the ancient deities, "Take me." As the echo of his plea dwindles away, Kirk expresses regret that it came to this and muses: "Would it have hurt us, I wonder, just to have gathered a few laurel leaves?"

APOLLO AND ADONIS IN GREEK MYTHOLOGY

In Greek mythology Apollo was the offspring of the philanderous Zeus, king of the gods, and Leto, a daughter of the ancient Titans. Apollo was a master musician who delighted the Olympians when he played his golden lyre, which had been made by Hermes. He was also the archer-god, lord of the silver bow. He was the healer who first taught humanity the healing art, though later his son Asclepius took over this role. Apollo was the god of light and truth. At Delphi, a city in Phocis, Greece, an oracle—a sacred place where deities were consulted—belonged to Apollo. Apollo was a beneficent link between the gods and human beings, guiding them to know the divine will, showing them how to make peace with the gods, and even cleansing them from guilt. Rituals of purification and expiation were an important part of his worship (Burkert 1985: 143–49).

Apollo's counsel was sought on commercial ventures, political issues, and personal problems. He was known for his moral earnestness and the seriousness with which his advice should be taken. Though he could send destructive plagues or illnesses in retribution for sacrilege, he could also ward off evil. As a vegetation deity he guarded against mice, grasshoppers, and plant diseases. As a god of herds, he offered protection against predators. After Zeus, therefore, Apollo was the most important god in the Greek pantheon, and his cult was prominent in the Mediterranean world. Yet for all of his beneficence, Apollo remained at some distance from humanity (Danker 1992 :297–98).

Apollo was capable of enormous compassion. When his best friend, Hyacinthus, was accidentally struck in the head by a discus thrown by Apollo, the god knelt beside his dead body and wept: "Oh, if I could give my life for yours, or die with you."

But Apollo could be pitiless and cruel. Along with his twin sister, Artemis, Apollo struck down fourteen children of a woman who had defied the gods by daring to compare herself to Apollo's mother. During the Trojan War, Apollo killed many in the Greek army because Agamemnon refused to release the daughter of Apollo's priest. When Midas, king of Phrygia, was chosen as an umpire in a musical contest between Apollo and Pan, Midas stupidly decided in favor of Pan. Insulted, Apollo gave Midas the ears of an ass. On another occasion Apollo flayed a satyr named Marsyas who dared to challenge him to a flute contest.

Apollo yearned for many women. Cassandra, to whom he had given the gift of prophecy, spurned Apollo. In retaliation, Apollo saw to it that no one ever believed her word. He was also rejected by a beautiful maiden, Coronis of Thessaly, whom he killed in revenge. He raped a young girl named Creusa. Daphne, an independent and athletic young woman, fled Apollo's attack until saved by her father, the river god Peneus, who to prevent her rape, turned her into a laurel tree. Apollo pursued a mortal woman named Marpessa who was married to Idas, an Argonaut. She was saved from Apollo only by Zeus' intervention, who gave her the right to choose lovers. Wisely, she chose against the philandering god. Apollo's history of rejection by women is not an insignificant detail in the rage he experiences when rejected by Lieutenant Carolyn Palamas in "Who Mourns for Adonais?"

Adonis, on the other hand, was a young man loved by Aphrodite, the goddess of love. Loving him from his birth, she gave him to Persephone, the goddess of the underworld, to take charge of him for her. But Persephone also fell in love with Adonis. Neither goddess would yield claim to him, so Zeus decreed that Adonis would spend the autumn and winter with the queen of the dead and the spring and summer with the goddess of love and beauty.

One day while hunting alone, Adonis speared a wild boar. Mad with pain, the boar rushed Adonis and gored him. Aphrodite rushed to his side and kissed him as he died. Every year thereafter Greek girls mourned for Adonis, but rejoiced when his flower, the blood-red anemone, bloomed again. The annual ritual of mourning for Adonis received its very name from him: the Adonia.

"WHO MOURNS FOR ADONAIS?" AS GREEK TRAGEDY

"Who Mourns for Adonais?" story writer Gilbert A. Ralston confessed: "Immodestly, I'm an expert in Grecian history" (Gross and Altman 1995: 54). This appears to be no overstatement in regard to his accurate representation of the mythological Apollo. With the help of scriptwriter Gene L. Coon, the character development of Apollo concurs with Greek legend. Michael Forest magnetically portrays Apollo with emotions covering the gamut from rage to resignation. As in the Greek myth, his Apollo is both sensitive and insistent, compassionate and lustful, fatherly and intolerant. Above all, he is lonely and tragic. His plight evokes our pity.

The title for this *Star Trek* episode contains a variant spelling of the word Adonis. Adonais is a word coined by Percy Bysshe Shelley (1792–1822) for his 1821 poem, "Adonais: An Elegy on the Death of John Keats." The title line, "Who Mourns for Adonais?" is taken directly from Shelley's poem.[4] The poet altered the spelling of Adonis for stylistic and euphonic reasons (King-Hele 1963: 305) but the basic theme—a goddess mourning the untimely death of a gifted mortal—seems perfectly suited for the loss of Apollo by Lieutenant Palamas.

"Who Mourns for Adonais?" fits the qualifications for a Greek tragedy. The tragedy, first conceived in Greek literature in the sixth century B.C.E., is a story that has an unhappy ending brought about by its central character, who is impelled by fate to final disaster. There are several features in this *Star Trek* episode that perfectly correlate to classic tragedy (Bergman and Epstein 1987: 912–15).

Tragedy arouses fear and pity. Fear is awakened by seeing our likeness to the central character. It is particularly fear-inspiring when someone falls from a position of high rank or power. Pity is evoked when the central character suffers more than he deserves. Tragic heroes do not have to be totally guiltless; indeed, they must not be pure victims. It is, rather, some fatal flaw that contributes to his or her undoing that arouses feelings of pity.

Apollo is all of these things. He is humanoid. Apart from the tremendous power he wields, the only thing that distinguishes him physically from human beings is an extra organ in his chest. Even though he is petulant and grandiose, he is not an evil being. Apollo "knows so much of love," as Lieutenant Palamas comments. If Apollo has some central flaw, it is simply that he is, through no fault of his own, an anachronism.

Apollo is radically isolated. Long ago the other gods and goddesses had given themselves up to oblivion. Apollo waited for humanity to find him again. Yet when this occurs, humanity has changed. Apollo discovers to his dismay the futility of his wait and, worse still, his own sudden irrelevance. If "tragedy's one essential is a soul that can feel greatly" (Hamilton 1964: 142), then Apollo is a tragic figure of titanic proportions.

Recognition and reversal are features of classic tragedy. Recognition is the awakening awareness of one's impending destiny and/or the weaknesses in one's character that have caused a catastrophic predicament. Reversal is the process by which good fortune becomes bad. This often takes place in conspicuous or violent ways. Reversal is particularly moving when the character's action has an opposite effect from what he or she intended. This is known as tragic irony.

Apollo is startled by the resistance he encounters in the *Enterprise* crew. Instead of simple shepherds he meets scientists; instead of naive devotees he finds critical thinkers. His reaction to the landing party's resistance is to use tactics that unintentionally create greater defiance. Apollo is unable to respond with a new game plan for a new humanity. Only at the end does he realize that threats and violence are ineffective against those who wield god-like powers themselves. Instead of creating worshippers he creates enemies. Reversal takes place in counter-violence. Just as Apollo threatened to crush the *Enterprise,* he is crushed by rejection. Apollo hurls his thunderbolts into the sky; phasers come down from the sky to destroy his temple. Only when it is too late does he realize his mistakes. Apollo is a victim of his own hubris. The arrogance rising from his pride and passion is his undoing.

Catharsis is the experience of relief that comes when the tragedy transpires. Since we know it is coming, we are not surprised when it occurs, yet our feelings in response to it are mixed. There is an emphatic sadness for the character, but there is also reassurance that though the worst has happened we are still alive, if not better off for what we have vicariously participated in.

The viewer is relieved when the *Enterprise* crew is safe again. Ultimately, we knew Apollo would be defeated, yet we feel sorry for Apollo. We also identify with the landing party. Through them we have defeated a force that threatened our autonomy, progress as a species, and science. Released from an antiquated relic from the past, we are cleansed of a pernicious superstition. Humankind is free again. We experience catharsis.

In the encounter with Apollo we have cut the last cord to a pre-scientific understanding of the cosmos with its myths of the gods. Nevertheless, something in the back of our minds is unsettled and unsatisfied. At the corners of consciousness we sense that the cosmos is colder than it was before. Some nameless dread, some angst, crowds unwelcomed into our psyche. We are not reassured; we are disquieted. This anxiety is an interpretive key to the symbolic meaning of "Who Mourns for Adonais?"

THE DAY GOD DIED

The April 8, 1966, cover of *Time* magazine blared out the startling three words: "Is God Dead?" American society of the 1960s had reason to wonder if God were dead. Many Americans remember the 1960s as "years of hope, days of rage" (Gitlin 1987). Traditional values, norms, mores, beliefs, and institutions were under attack by young minds. The Church was assailed. The young wanted to know how, where, and whether the Church was relevant. For that matter, did God exist at all? Where was God in the race riots, in the oppression of the poor, in the napalm bombing of civilians? Where was God to be found in the megapolis with its anonymity, depersonalization, and dehumanization? Thus, the cover of *Time* was a sign of the times.

The 1960s were dominated by the secular spirit. Secularism is the conviction that this world, whose nature is known by the methods of the natural sciences, is the only world that matters. Anything beyond that which is knowable by reason and sense perception is unknowable at best or illusory at worst (Ferm 1981: 21). Historian Martin E. Marty (1966: 138) states:

Secularism permits no transcendent reference, no witness to the activity of God in history, no possibility of 'belief *that*' he is or 'belief *in*' his actions or belief in the witness to himself in the human sphere. It is self-contained, self-explanatory, self-enclosed. It can very well be the real religion of the modern world, incorporating most elements of what belonged to life in historic religions.

The expression "God is dead" first occurred in an orthodox Lutheran hymn to describe the death of Christ. It then was used by German philosopher Georg W. F. Hegel (1770–1831) to describe the spirit of modern times. It was later utilized by Friedrich W. Nietzsche (1844–1900), who announced to the world: "God is dead! God remains dead! And we have killed him" (in Kung 1980:138).

By the early 1960s, Protestant theologian Gabriel Vahanian (1961) of Syracuse University used "death of God" metaphorically for the Western world's slide into a post-Christian era. For Vahanian, Christianity had degenerated into mere religiosity, modern culture was losing the identifying marks of the very religion that had brought it into being and shaped it, and tolerance was becoming religious syncretism. The transcendent was becoming reduced to the imminent. The sacred was being lost to the secular.

The spirit of secularism impacted the theological community. One response was a spate of books and articles that accepted secularism as a given, criticized institutional religion as too other-worldly, and dismissed most God-language as meaningless.

The early harbinger of theological secularism was German theologian and martyr Dietrich Bonhoeffer (1906–1945), who believed that the world had "come of age" and that human beings had learned to get along without any God-hypothesis. Modern persons must abandon false notions about God and become "religionless." This would create a "Christian worldliness" in which "before God and with God we live without God" (Bonhoeffer 1974: 360).

Borrowing Bonhoeffer's cryptic catch-phrases, though probably not his actual ideas (Macquarrie 1967: 29–42), English theologian John A. T. Robinson wrote *Honest to God* in 1963, which called into question all thinking of God as "up there" or "out there." God was instead "the ground of being" who was immanent in the world (Robinson 1963; Edwards 1963). A related note was sounded by Harvard theologian Harvey Cox, who believed that the process of secularization had liberated moderns from the old supernaturalism, so that "politics replaces metaphysics as the language of theology" (Cox 1966: 223; Callahan 1966).

Extreme positions followed that wanted to correlate God and secularity in more novel ways. William Hamilton of Colgate Rochester Divinity School seemed undecided whether God had actually died objectively in the cosmos or subjectively in human experience (Hamilton 1961; Hamilton and Altizer 1966). Thomas J. J. Altizer of Emory University argued that God annihilated himself when he became embodied in Jesus Christ. There could be no more traditional God-talk, for God as transcendent was dead. The good news of the gospel was this "Christian atheism" (Altizer 1966). Paul M. van Buren of Temple University insisted that the word "God" had no clear meaning, and thus there could be no valid discussion about God or anything transcendent at all. Still, if theological language induced personal liberation and interpersonal reconciliation, then one had found "the secular meaning of the gospel" (van Buren 1963). What van Buren offered was "an imminent Jesus without a transcendent God" (Ferm 1981: 34).

Jewish theologian Richard Rubenstein proclaimed the death of God because theodicy—the problem of evil—had long tormented the Jewish community. Rubenstein (1966: 142, 143), author of *After Auschwitz*, wrote in a review:

> If there is a God of history, He is the ultimate author of Auschwitz. I am willing to believe in God the Holy Nothingness Who is our source and our final destiny, but never again in a God of history. . . . What the death-of-God theologians depict is an indubitable cultural fact in our times: God is totally unavailable as a source of meaning or value. There is no vertical transcendence. Our problem is not how we shall think of God in a secular way. It is how men can best share the decisive crises of life, given the cold, unfeeling, indifferent cosmos that surrounds us and given the fact that God the Holy Nothingness offers us only dissolution and death as the way out of the dilemmas of earthly existence.

The "death of God" theologies created excitement more as a momentary media event than as a serious theological movement. Collectively, these theologies seemed to want an absolute immanence that abolished transcendence, and a negation of the sacred by the secular. They wished to take this world so seriously that every other world was denied, and to kill God in order that humankind might live (Schilling 1969: 113–14; Murchland 1967; Ice and Carey 1967). By the end of the decade such notions had been thoroughly critiqued and largely abandoned, and theologians were calling for a "renewal of God-language" (Gilkey 1969). But the "death of God" theologies reflected some loss of the sense of God that profoundly troubled Americans.

"WHO MOURNS FOR ADONAIS?" AS THEOLOGY

Classic *Star Trek*, like American society at that time, was haunted by God and God-questions. In the original series biblical allusions abound in names such as Adam, Eve, Abraham, Isak (Isaac), Gideon, Lazarus, Methuselah, Moses; in themes such as death and rebirth, eternity and immortality, sacrifice and worship, good and evil; and in specific concepts such as sin, sacrilege, the devil, heaven, hell, and purgatory (Caprio 1978). Theological motifs appear: the wrongful usurpation of god-like powers by mortals ("Where No Man Has Gone Before" [1966]), atonement by death for guilt ("The Ultimate Computer" [1968]), the authority of sacred writings ("The Omega Glory" [1968]), redemptive vicarious suffering ("The Empath" [1968]), and the struggle of good versus evil in the human soul ("The Enemy Within" [1966]). Episode titles reflect an uneasy conscience about the God-question: "The Way to Eden" (1969), "This Side of Paradise" (1967), "Whom Gods Destroy" (1969), "The Paradise Syndrome" (1968). Christ is even specifically mentioned once by name ("Bread and Circuses" [1967]).

This preoccupation continues in the movies based on the original series. In *Star Trek: The Motion Picture* (1979) a created being is in search of its creator. In *Star Trek II: The Wrath of Khan* (1982) and *Star Trek III: The Search for Spock* (1984), the Christian story of Jesus' death and resurrection for the salvation of others is dramatically reenacted with Spock as a Christ-figure. *Star Trek V: The Final Frontier* (1989) has the *Enterprise* crew looking for God at the center of the galaxy. It would appear that classic *Star Trek* is quite absorbed with the God-question.

Early in "Who Mourns for Adonais?" Apollo invites all but Mr. Spock to beam down to Pollux IV.[5] Apollo does not want Spock to join the landing party because Spock reminds Apollo of Pan, "and Pan," Apollo comments, "always bored me." In Greek mythology, Pan was the chief of the lesser gods of earth. The son of Hermes, he was a noisy, merry god with goat's horns on his head and a goat's hoofs instead of feet. He was the shepherds' god and the companion of the woodland nymphs when they danced. His home was all the wild places such as thickets, forests, and mountains. Known as a wonderful musician, he played sweet melodies with his reed pipes. Pan was always in love with one nymph or another, but continually rejected because of his ugliness. Strange sounds heard in the wilderness at night by trembling travelers were supposedly made by him, creating *pan*ic.

Thus, Pan was decidedly unlike Spock, merrily dancing with nymphs, perennially falling in love, and engaging in devilment. Apollo has covert reasons for not wanting Spock to join the landing party, which have nothing to do with his Pan-like looks.[6] The real threat Spock represents is that he cannot be manipulated emotionally, and Apollo is a past master at such manipulation. Out of earlier generations of humans Apollo had successfully wheedled mindless adoration, servile submission, and cringing dependence. The worship of Apollo had been based upon motives of greed (promise of reward) or fear (threat of punishment). Spock is immune to such appeals. Indeed, Apollo has ample reason to fear Spock. Spock sees Apollo as a technical problem to be solved, not a god who inspires awe. On Pollux IV McCoy says dryly of the ship's engineer: "Scotty doesn't believe in gods." Neither, it would seem, does Spock.

To Spock ultimately goes the credit for destroying Apollo's power. In an arresting but brief scene, while Apollo is hurling his lightening bolts at the Enterprise, Spock is seen calmly in the captain's chair, his hands clasped nonchalantly. He knows technology will triumph over Apollo. Apollo awakens defiance and hostility in Kirk, anger and jealousy in Scotty, sarcasm and contempt in Chekov, fear and loathing in McCoy, and adoration and hero-worship in Palamas. For Spock, Apollo evokes no emotion, except perhaps a hidden anxiety for his friends. To him, Apollo is a curious life-form, albeit a dangerous one, but nothing more. The implication seems clear: to rational, scientifically grounded persons, gods are passé, representing neither promise nor threat.

Lieutenant Palamas, on the other hand, responds to Apollo with intense emotion. Forgetting her professionalism and reacting with the infatuation of a schoolgirl, she may seem stereotypically pre-feminist. In the *Star Trek* universe, we may surmise, she would have been put on report for her behavior on Pollux IV. Yet Apollo knows how to seduce—and how to abuse power. He flatters, promises, and persuades. He dresses her in stunning elegance and walks her through the Garden of Eden. He pushes every button in her psyche: physically handsome and intelligent, he appeals to her needs for love, reassurance, romance, power, importance, immortality, and progeny. His speech to Palamas is striking in its overwhelming guarantees: Because you have the sensitivity to understand,

I offer you more than your wildest dreams have ever imagined. You'll become the mother of a new race of gods. You'll inspire the universe. All men will revere you almost as a god yourself. And I shall love you for time without end, worlds without end. You shall complete me, and I you."

In this episode, Palamas symbolically incarnates the presumed core of religious devotion: dependence, submission, conformity, compliance, passivity, subservience, and unquestioning loyalty. Thus, religion is rooted in affect, not reason. The stereotyping of gender behavior, so common in *Star Trek* (Rose 1990), is present here as well. The men, representing rationality, reject Apollo. The woman, representing emotion, is swept away by Apollo's charisma. Only when Palamas follows her duty (logic) rather than her heart (feelings) does she succeed in breaking free from Apollo's mesmerizing embrace. The equation: feelings = faith.

Contrary to Apollo's initial reassurances, everyone loses in this encounter. Although Palamas rehabilitates herself professionally by her rejection of Apollo, she is traumatized by love lost as well as by rape.[7] Kirk and McCoy are sorry for what they've done. Mr. Scott, paling in comparison to Apollo, no doubt lost Palamas. But Apollo loses the most: his worshippers have outgrown him and have no more need of him. "Even for a god there's a point of no return," Apollo says. His raison d'être gone, his existence has become meaningless and his continued life pointless. He evaporates into the cosmos to join his fellow gods.

After Apollo yields himself up to the cosmos, McCoy says almost tritely: "I wish we hadn't had to do this." Kirk responds by acknowledging that civilization had a historical and cultural debt to the worship of the Greek gods.[8] Perhaps they should have gathered a few leaves of homage from the laurel, Apollo's tree.

"Who Mourns for Adonais?" may be interpreted as a parable about the death of God, not as a theological fad but as a cultural mood that became particularly visible in the 1960s. God, personified in Apollo, is dead. Apollo is a superficially impressive but ultimately pitiable charlatan masquerading as a god. A belief in an Apollo-like God, or any god, is a nuisance at best and a hindrance at worst in the age of science. Even if the loss of the Transcendent is painful and sad, it must be accepted by a humanity come of age. This theme occurs many times both overtly and covertly in *Star Trek* episodes. "Who Mourns for Adonais?" is only the most blatant.

If Apollo represents the God of the Bible (or the Qur'an), the message of "Who Mourns for Adonais?" is that God is an anachronism, an outmoded belief, a hopelessly dated myth. Religious faith is grounded in pre-scientific irrationality. Kirk puts it succinctly to Apollo: "We've out-grown you. You ask for something we can no longer give." Kirk's wistful concession to Apollo's historical significance parallels a comment by Jean-Paul Sartre (1905–1980), French existentialist and atheist:

> I needed God. "He was given to me. I received Him without realiz-ing that I was seeking Him. Failing to take root in my heart, He veg-etated in me for a while, then He died. Whenever anyone speaks to me about Him today, I say, with the easy amusement of an old beau who meets a former belle: "Fifty years ago, had it not been for that misunderstanding, that mistake, the accident that separated us, there might have been something between us." (Sartre 1964: 102–3)

Thus, contrary to some interpreters (Devereaux 1990; Caprio 1978), the mere presence of many biblical allusions, concepts, themes, and motifs in *Star Trek* do not add up to theism for the *Star Trek* universe. Rather, the traditional idea of God found in Western religion suffers a sig-nificant pummeling in Classic *Star Trek*. Even if the existence of God is not categorically denied in a literal way, God is still denied symbolically and pragmatically. Symbolically, god-figures are consistently disappoint-ing, decadent, and/or dangerous.[9] Pragmatically, God does not function in any clear or meaningful way in the *Star Trek* universe or in the lives of Federation members.[10] Despite Kirk's brief comment to Apollo that "we find the one [God] quite adequate," in the twenty-third century the God of traditional Western theism is dead. There is no transcendent, personal Deity who exists independently of humanity.

It is true, as indicated earlier, that in the movie versions of classic *Star Trek*, the God-question rises as a celestial spectre. Though panned by critics and fans alike, *Star Trek: The Motion Picture* is about a creature (V-ger) in search of its creator. Repeating themes found in the television episode "The Changeling" (1967), the script underlying this movie was originally entitled *The God Thing* and then *In Thy Image* before it became the familiar film (Shatner 1994: 44–60; Sackett and Roddenberry 1980: 54–71). In *Star Trek V: The Final Frontier* the *Enterprise* is explicitly off in search of God at the center of the galaxy.

Upon closer examination, however, both movies implicitly protest against classical theism. Though near god-like in mechanical perfection and knowledge, V-ger discovers that mere mortals made it originally. Its true God for whom it seeks, therefore, is humanity. When united with a man, the machine moves up the evolutionary ladder in an odd, unintentional parallel to the Christology of the Chalcedonian Creed (451 C.E.): "truly machine, truly man, united in one person."

Sybok's search for God in *Star Trek V: The Final Frontier* results in tragedy. Sybok's god is devilish. In this connection a comment by Gene Roddenberry, who held great sway over the content of the original series, is suggestive. When the script for *Star Trek V: The Final Frontier* was in process, Roddenberry argued that *Star Trek* should avoid specific religious themes such as the *Enterprise* actually encountering God: "I didn't object to it being an alien claiming to be God, but there was too much in it that an audience could have thought was really God or really the devil, and I very strongly resist believing in either. I do not perceive this as a universe that's divided between good and evil. I see it as a universe that is divided between many ideas of what is" (Gross and Altman 1995: 130).

At the end of the same movie, McCoy asks Kirk if God is really "out there." Kirk responds by saying: "Maybe God is here—the human heart." While this ambiguous comment could be taken to mean *in* the human heart, the collective history of Classic *Star Trek* suggests that God *is* (or, is no more than) the human heart.[11] Once more, Gene Roddenberry speaks to the issue:

> As nearly as I can concentrate on the question today, I believe I am God; certainly you are, I think we intelligent beings on this planet are all a piece of God, are becoming God. In some sort of cyclical non-time thing we have to become God, so that we can end up creating ourselves, so that we can be in the first place. . . . My own feeling is that relation to God as a person is a petty, superstitious approach to the All, the Infinite. (Alexander 1994: 618, 620)[12]

"Bread and Circuses" may seem to be a clear exception to this rule. The pacifistic "children of the sun/Son" are destined to repeat Earth history by taking over the twentieth-century Roman Empire that exists on Planet 892–IV. Rejecting Roman decadence and living in hiding, these "sun/Son worshippers"[13] believe that the only true religion is their own and that no compromise with paganism is possible. Dr. McCoy, however, states flatly that the the United Federation of Planets represents "many beliefs." Later he describes Christianity as "a *philosophy* of total love and total brotherhood."[14] When Kirk mouths words about the wonder of watching Christianity conquer a world again, it somehow seems both unconvincing and discordant with the Kirk we know otherwise as a rambunctious idol-smasher. Kirk may admire Jesus' *ethic*, but that is a far cry from embracing Christian *faith*.

"Who Mourns for Adonais?" is therefore paradigmatic of *Star Trek's* cosmology, encapsulating a recurring theme: a God-hypothesis stands in the way of the maturation of humanity. The *Enterprise* crew members essentially are non-theists,[15] rejecting God because a deity is unnecessary and irrelevant to their existence. They are simple humanists, which Kirk states pointedly to Palamas as the rationale for rejecting Apollo:

> We're the same. We share the same history, the same heritage, the same lives. We're tied together beyond any untying. Man or woman, it makes no difference—we're human. We couldn't escape from each other even if we wanted to. That's how you do it, Lieutenant, by remembering who and what you are: a bit of flesh and blood afloat in a universe without end, and the only thing that's truly yours is the rest of humanity.

It may be no more than mere coincidence, though no doubt Mr. Spock would find it a fascinating one, that Shelley, whose poem provided the title for this episode, was himself a bitter opponent of orthodox religion and embraced a form of pantheism (Baker 1961: 239–54; Clark 1966). Perhaps it is no less interesting that Shelley's "Adonais" bears a striking likeness to the word *Adonai*—one of the most common names for God in the Hebrew Bible—with the only difference being an English *s* attached as a termination (Woodman 1964: 160). For the *Star Trek* universe, Apollo is God and God is dead.

Consequently, the episode title, "Who Mourns for Adonais?" may be considered a question arising directly out of the socio-religious turbulence of the 1960s and addressed to modern humanity: who mourns for a dead God? In the original context of Shelley's poem, the question refers to Keats and is a call to hope, for "the soul of Adonais, like a star, beacons from the abode where the Eternal are." In this *Star Trek* episode, however, the question refers to God and is a call to courageous non-theism. In the poem, no one should mourn because *Keats* is better off without *us*. In the episode, no one should mourn because *we* are better off without God. Without God or god-figures, humanity is free to be itself, under the unspoken assumption that human nature is basically good, especially when made wise by science. *Star Trek* thus trumpets an optimistic view of human nature and the inevitability of human progress.

THE WAY TO EDEN?

Classic *Star Trek* has almost unbounded confidence in the powers of human rationality and science. In this regard, *Star Trek* reflects the intellectual foundations of the Enlightenment, an eighteenth-century philosophical movement characterized by rationalism (trust in reason), empiricism (trust in the senses), and skepticism (trust in mistrust—refusing to believe in anything without good evidence). Enlightenment thinkers assumed that any knowledge that resulted from these principles was certain, objective, and good. Furthermore, anything that infringed on the process of obtaining knowledge was suspect. Reason, observation, and experience had to be unfettered from external authorities and extrinsic curtailments.

Mr. Spock is the personification par excellence of the sober, rational, objective scientist. Thus, he is the ideal man of the Enlightenment with his emotions in check, dispassionately analyzing situations and prescribing reasonable solutions (Grenz 1994: 26). When he slips and does something emotional/human, he declares that it is "logical" to do so, even when he sacrifices his own life in *Star Trek II: The Wrath of Khan*—an act that his comrades must have seen as motivated more by love than logic. In the end, nevertheless, all problems are rational and require rational resolution, making Spock not only the perfect dramatic foil to Dr. McCoy's emotionalism, but also the prime spokesperson for the nature of Being itself.

In "Who Mourns for Adonais?" Mr. Spock's cool, calculated logic finds a way to puncture Apollo's force field and obliterate his base of operations. Spock knows that the laws of physics apply to Apollo, his claims to godhood notwithstanding. At the same time, Kirk logically deduces that Apollo is not and cannot be a god and thus is finite. By exploiting Apollo's finitude, they demystify his deity. This is a typical pattern in Classic *Star Trek*: the gods—humanoid, mechanical, or incorporeal—wither under sober analysis. There are no gods, only pretenders to the throne.

Star Trek intimates, furthermore, that any belief in God has a retarding effect on human progress, human tolerance, and human freedom. In almost every *Star Trek* episode where religion exists in some form, it is represented as intolerant, anti-intellectual, subversive of progress, and inimical to a scientific view of the world. In "Who Mourns for Adonais?" this attitude is unmistakable. Apollo offers life in paradise. "What else," Apollo asks rhetorically, "does mankind demand of its gods?" In exchange, the *Enterprise* crew must give him ritual worship. One thing, however, must be sacrificed—the *Enterprise,* whose empty hull Apollo will crush. A god cannot tolerate technological science, which represents both a challenge to his power and freedom from his dominion. As in "This Side of Paradise," where Kirk proudly asserts that humanity has walked out of a second Eden under its own power, so in "Who Mourns for Adonais?" the choice is mindless subservience to authority or manly assertion of autonomy. The options are religion or science.

Classic *Star Trek* seems to view religion as an entrenched, reactionary social power and that, conversely, atheism stands for science and progress (Ebeling 1968: 80–81). Historically, however, what allowed the emancipation of empirical science from entrenched cultural and ecclesiastical authoritarianism was not the rejection of *theology* but the intellectual overthrow of the *philosophy* of Aristotle and Ptolemy, an overthrow which began in the sixteenth century. But "as far as the origins of modern science are concerned, the notion of a conflict between science and religion is one of the myths of history" (Richardson 1961: 23).

Incarnated in Spock, "the scientific method" becomes the Arbiter of All Truth.[16] This is, of course, scient*ism*, a belief that if something is not knowable by science, it does not exist (Peters 1997: 650). Natural science normally assumes naturalism—the philosophical belief that the universe is a closed continuum of natural cause and effect. Yet naturalism is a working hypothesis, a "leap of faith" (Rust 1967: 38–84) that cannot be proven beyond doubt by rational or empirical means. Certainly anything that can be scientifically verified is significant, but one may not flatly assert that anything scientifically unverifiable is insignificant. If a Supreme Being exists who is unlike anything else, then such a Being could not be discovered by methods used to validate the existence of anything else (Hordern 1973: 250–51).[17] The "atheism" of the natural sciences is a methodological procedure that intentionally disregards God because God, by classical definition, cannot be discovered by turning the Deity into an empirical Object (Bultmann 1965: 85).[18]

To convert science into an intrinsically benevolent goddess who holds in her hand the key to a golden future, as *Star Trek* seems to do, is fundamentally naive. It is the *use* which humanity makes of scientific knowledge that will determine whether any given scientific discovery is a blessing or a curse to current or future generations. Humankind thus faces two problems: how to win control over nature to do humanity's bidding without destroying nature or humankind in the process, and how to overcome the destructive tendencies in humankind itself (Richardson 1950:

21–22). *Star Trek* assumes that both problems have been solved by the twenty-third century without recourse to any traditional religious faith. Theologically speaking, *Star Trek* has an implicit *eschaton* (end) without an explicit eschatology (talk about how the end will come).

BY ANY OTHER NAME

Star Trek clearly is not functioning merely as entertaining myth when its fans can blind themselves to its scientific blunders and troublesome technobabble (Krauss 1995; Goswami 1983). It is not simply a television/film phenomenon when it spawns thousands of books and magazines a year, dominates hundreds of fan clubs and conventions annually, governs moral ideals and personal values, and seems to defy explanation by academics. Although the primary goal of the original contributors was to create a hit television series and not a comprehensive worldview,[19] *Star Trek* offers far more for many fans. Perhaps the central myth, common to much science fiction, is the inevitability of progress (Kreuziger 1986: 84). But it also offers a faith in the innate goodness and unity of humanity, a sense of egalitarian community transcending racial and cultural boundaries, and a supreme confidence that science and technology will produce some form of near-utopia. *Star Trek* has thereby created a sizeable subculture that qualifies as a distinct social movement, if not some form of religious phenomenon (Jindra 1994).[20] For a significant subculture, this visionary brand of science fiction has become "the last source of a personal mythology for us" (Caprio 1978: 126).[21]

For *Star Trek* humanity is not only "the measure of all things," but is on its way to a kind of technological godhood.[22] This optimistic view of humanity's future parallels the sentiments of English biologist Julian Huxley (1887–1975), who said: "My faith is in the possibilities of man" (Huxley 1957: 212). Hence, one of *Star Trek's* great ironies may be that in rejecting traditional theism it has founded its own "religion" with twin deities of science and humanism. Its temple is a starship. Its altar is a computer screen. Its Golden Rule is the Prime Directive. And its creed is the scientific method.

Yet *Star Trek*'s optimism about human nature and human potential is called into question by depth psychology—itself a product of modernity. If Sigmund Freud (1856–1939) did anything for modern self-understanding, he uprooted overbelief in conscious motivation and underscored the unconscious roots of our proneness to evade, deny, rationalize, and excuse our self-serving behavior.[23] Psychologist David E. Myers (1980: 47) comments: "Freud unmasked our hypocrisies, our phoney ideals, our rationalizations, our vanities, and our chicaneries, and not all the efforts of humanists and rationalists will restore the mask." Even scientific rationality can be compromised by irrational prejudices and fixations, wishful thinking and emotional reasoning, denial and repression, and unresolved neurotic disturbances.[24]

Star Trek's non-theistic cosmology seems more a psychological matter of negative fusion than an ontological matter of considered worldview. Negative fusion is emotional bondage to that which one consciously repudiates. The negatively fused person is still controlled by that which he or she rejects, only in reverse, rebelliously reacting against belief and finding identity in anti-belief.[25] The repetitive way in which Classic *Star Trek* can't seem to leave religion alone suggests that it is bedeviled by the divine. A theist might argue that this preoccupation itself is a "signal of transcendence" (Berger 1970), a sign that God has a way of appearing as a guest incognito, even when the divine is unwelcome and the setting is radically secularized.

THIS SIDE OF SCIENTISM

Classic *Star Trek*, like the radical theologians of the 1960s, declared that God was dead and enthroned science in the place of the Deity. By the end of the 1960s, the death of God had itself died, for "one could never weep for a dead god. A god who can die deserves no tears" (Cox 1967: 253). "Who Mourns for Adonais?" is a parable of that revolutionary time, mirroring who and what we were.

The generation that was most influenced by *Star Trek*, the baby boomers, jettisoned institutional religion in record numbers, though many continued to seek a sense of spirituality in their lives. While this repudiation of Church and synagogue can hardly be laid at the door of a television drama, *Star Trek*'s religious iconoclasm correlated with the rejection of many accepted social values of the time. For this generation, television became, according to sociologist Wade Clark Roofe (1993: 54), "the major source of information shaping their definitions of reality, exceeding that of books, newspapers, teachers, religious leaders, perhaps even supplanting the family itself."[26] *Star Trek*'s mistrust of religion and religious authority figures must have struck some responsive chord in that generation.

In the decades since *Star Trek* first aired on television, alternative religions and various New Age amalgams have rushed in to fill the void left by the cultural death of God. Psychologist Christopher Evans (1973: 10) states:

> In their heart of hearts most people still want some fairly simply, reasonably logical answers to the questions that human beings have always asked—answers which will ease the chill which we have all felt when, in the small hours of the morning, we wonder about life and death, time and space, creation and destruction. These gaps, we will have to agree, need plugging. And if science and present-day philosophy—currently obsessed with semantics and linguistics—are unprepared to help, while the great world religions offer only outdated, timeworn and implausible concepts, then the field is ripe as never before for stop-gap systems, pseudo-scientific philosophies, quasi-technological cults and new Messiahs to emerge. They are, in fact, already here, and there is evidence that their strength is growing.[27]

Later incarnations of *Star Trek* (*The Next Generation, Deep Space Nine, Voyager*), apparently influenced by post-modernism,[28] seem less self-assured about the omnipotence of science and the non-existence of the spiritual. If post-modern thought continues to change our cultural presuppositions, Classic *Star Trek*'s scientism may one day appear to be as authoritarian and antiquated as the theism-caricature it condescendingly rejected. Perhaps this confirms philosopher George Santayana's (1863–1952) observation that those who wed themselves to the spirit of their times are destined to be widowers in the next generation (Ferm 1981: 35). Nevertheless, as theologian Hans Kung (1980: 35) observes: "Not every step away from scientific credulity is a step toward theistic piety. Skepticism toward science and technology is far from being a foundation for belief in God."

Even though the death of God has often been declared in one form or another, somehow the corpse never stays put. Who, then, mourns for Adonais? Perhaps Mark Twain's response to newspapers who printed his obituary prematurely would be that of the Almighty: "The reports of my death are greatly exaggerated."

NOTES

1. This discussion will only be concerned with the seventy-nine original televised *Star Trek* episodes and the six movies that utilized the original crew. This

is widely referred to as Classic *Star Trek* to distinguish it from later television and theatrical incarnations. No attempt is made to dialogue with the voluminous material mushrooming out of the original series (*TOS*) that may be found in novels, the animated series, comic books, and similar sources. *Star Trek* fans debate what should and should not be considered part of the "canon" of *Star Trek*, i.e. what ought to be regarded as authoritative for the basic myth. A narrow definition of canon excludes everything not authorized by Gene Roddenberry or his successive representatives, which means the canon is confined to the four television series and the movies. But there is no unanimity among fans on the parameters of the canon.

2. Apollo's reference to 5000 years since he was worshipped on Earth is misleading. If *Star Trek* is set in the twenty-third century C.E., this would demand a date of around 2800 B.C.E. for the beginning of the Greek myths. Yet very little is known of this Early Minoan period. Polytheism certainly existed in early Mycenaean culture (1600–1400 B.C.E.), but the stories of the Greek gods developed greatly during the Dorian invasions (1100 B.C.E.) (Burkert 1985: 10–52; Swain and Armstrong 1959: 151–73).

3. "Who Mourns for Adonais" seems to endorse the idea that aliens had visited earth and were responsible for architectural and religious phenomena in the ancient world. This notion was circulating in the UFO subculture of the 1960s long before Erich von Daniken sensationalized it in the 1970s with his *Chariots of the Gods?*, *Gods from Outer Space*, *Gold of the Gods*, and *In Search of Ancient Gods*. Although selling over thirty-six million copies, von Daniken's "research" has been scathingly shredded by historians, archaeologists, and scientists (Ridpath 1978).

4. I am indebted to Ms. Cindy Ellis, Adjunct Instructor of English, Oakland City University, Oakland City, Indiana, for alerting me to this literary reference.

5. In a plot oversight, Spock seems to know who this superbeing is despite the fact that Apollo doesn't reveal his exact identity until the landing party beams down, without Spock (Ferrand 1994: 130). This difficulty is lessened somewhat if we assume that Apollo's initial appearance and historical references were clues to Spock, who then deduced his probable identity.

6. While Spock's "unlucky in love" history and his skill as a musician form interesting parallels with Pan, they are too subtle to be significant here. Mr. Spock's repressed sexuality is a much discussed topic among *Star Trek* fans. An interpretation is offered by Harvey R. Greenberg (1990).

7. Though there is some ambiguity in the televised version, the looming figure of Apollo, the shrieks by Palamas, and her subsequent numbed and disheveled appearance suggest the rape was completed. In the original story Pala-

mas conceived by Apollo. This is explicitly stated in the novel adaptation based on the original script (Blish 1991: 112–13).

8. Within the *Star Trek* universe, Apollo's return to the cosmos is as much loss as gain. As fan author Allan Asherman explains: "The United Federation of Planets governs itself by laws that owe much to the teachings of Apollo and his companions left on Earth. Mr. Spock would surely have realized this and tried his best to communicate peacefully with Apollo, had the alien not attacked the *Enterprise*, making instant enemies of Kirk and Spock and setting the stage for his own defeat. Apollo's destruction leaves Kirk stunned, and Carolyn in a state of shock; no one benefits from the *Enterprise*'s "victory" over the immortal. The Federation loses a powerful ally, to say nothing of his unfulfilled potential to become the greatest historian in the galaxy" (1986: 73).

9. When figures with god-like powers or abilities appear in *Star Trek*, they generally prove to be disappointments if not devils. Most beings who could be classed as supranormal in nature behave rather badly, whether by using humanoids as playthings for personal amusement ("The Gamesters of Triskelion" [1968]), or as unwitting stooges in the service of malevolence ("And the Children Shall Lead" [1968]), or as pawns of hate and violence ("The Day of the Dove" [1968]). Perhaps the most despicable is Redjac ("Wolf in the Fold" [1967]), who takes sadistic delight in murder and terror. Among such beings, only the Organians ("Errand of Mercy" [1967]) and, somewhat less absolutely, the Companion ("Metamorphosis" [1967]), seem divinely benign.

Humanoids who have god-like attributes are usually amoral. In "The Menagerie" [1966] (and "The Cage" [1964] before it) the Talosians of Talos IV are deceptive, manipulative, and self-serving, using their telepathic capabilities as a weapon against their inmates. Their compassion for Captain Pike after his debilitating accident notwithstanding, the Talosians are hardly kindly Keepers. Trelane ("The Squire of Gothos" [1967]), a godling, wields tremendous power but is actually a spoiled brat run amok. Though a far more sympathetic character, "Charlie X" (1966) is similar in that he is dangerously immature in his use of power. Sargon ("Tomorrow is Yesterday" [1967]) exists in a near-spiritual state and wields power benevolently, but only because he is a repentant being who dared once to think of himself as a god. His counterpart, Henoch, is neither benign nor repentant. Even Sargon's wife, Thalassa, acts irresponsibly when provoked.

Other powerful humanoids illustrate the same theme. Lal and Thann ("The Empath" [1968]) seem like Nazi death-camp doctors, brutalizing Federation personnel in a bizarre attempt to ascertain whether Gem's race is "worthy" of being saved from a disaster about to engulf her planet's solar system. The inhabitants of Plotinus ("Plato's Stepchildren" [1968]) are telekinetics whose cruelty is only exceeded by their conceit. When a mere man, Gary Mitchell ("Where No Man Has Gone Before" [1966]), acquires god-like knowledge and abilities, absolute power corrupts him absolutely. This theme is continued on a colossal scale in *Star Trek V: The Final Frontier* (1984), where "God" turns out to be an ill-tempered imposter.

10. One exception to this is found in "Balance of Terror" (1966) where Specialist Angela Martine prays before and after the death of her fiancé. Her faith seems to be indulged kindly by Kirk, but not affirmed. Although he offers a vacuous bit of pop-theology to her after Tomlinson's death ("It never makes any sense. We both have to know that there was a reason"), his half-quizzical sidelong glance at the chapel platform (and whom it represents) before he turns and strides out without looking back suggests that Kirk's attitude, at least, is dismissive of religion.

Dr. McCoy's "Lord, forgive me" before he phasers the salt-vampire in "The Man Trap" (1966) could express belief in God or be no more than an exclamation of horror at what he is about to do. The Companion in "Metamorphosis" (1967) expresses a belief in "the Maker of all things," but the content of that belief is left vague. The sum total of clear references to religion in Classic *Star Trek* are succinctly listed by Bjo Trimble (1995: 231–32).

11. See Shatner's comments on the theology of this movie in his *Star Trek Movie Memories* (1994: 220–68; cf. Lisabeth Shatner 1989: 34–72). In a personal appearance with Leonard Nimoy at the UIC Pavilion in Chicago, Illinois, on May 15, 1992, William Shatner was asked by an audience member what he personally believed about the existence of God. His response endorsed pantheism— that God is everything.

12. After noting that "the real villain is *religion*" as practiced by violent people, Roddenberry adds in a letter to a cousin in 1984: "I've elected to believe in a God which is so far beyond our conception and real understanding that it would be nonsense to do anything in its name other than perhaps to revere all life as being part of that unfathomable greatness" (Alexander 1994: 522). Given these premises, Gene Roddenberry's refusal to cast a chaplain among the *Enterprise* crew in the original series (Nichols 1994: 280–81) is more than understandable. Paul Harrison (1996: 82) states: "In *Star Trek*, religious mythologies and supernatural phenomena almost always have scientific explanations. Alien gods are never *really* supernatural—their powers are always explained by exo-biology or by mechanical devices. Indeed 'gods' are often malevolent or egotistical. When they are benevolent, they usually turn their worshippers into mindless or childlike zombies. . . . It is clear that Roddenberry felt a fairly deep hostility to organized religions, to transcendental gods and supernatural powers. . . . However, it's equally clear that Roddenberry really was a pantheist, of an unsystematized but intelligence-centered kind verging on the pan-psychic variety." Martin E. Marty makes the observation that "Americans, if they deviate from historic Christian norms, exchange them for other theisms or for pantheism and not for atheism."

13. Dr. McCoy makes a glaring historical error in his claim that ancient Rome had no sun worshippers (an error Spock should gladly have pointed out to him). Sun worship was a significant religion from the days of the Roman republic to the time of Constantine (Ferguson 1970: 44–56).

14. While some of the early Church fathers referred to Christianity as a "philosophy," it is not in the modern sense of the term which Dr. McCoy assumes. Christian apologists described Christian faith as a philosophy to indicate that it was spiritual, non-magical, and non-superstitious, and hence the all-embracing truth about the meaning of existence itself. Apologists found the term "philosophy" useful to assert the truth-claim of their religion among the educated (Tillich 1968: 27).

15. The term "theism" generally is used for a belief in a personal God who is the transcendent Creator of the universe and yet is imminent in its processes. Pantheism is the belief that God is All, i.e, identical with the universe. A variation on pantheism is panentheism, which is the belief that All is God, i.e. the universe is Deity. The difference between the latter two may be put in this manner: God is ALL (pantheism), GOD is all (panentheism). Atheism is the denial of God in any form. Because of its many pejorative connotations in popular usage, it may be unwise to call the *Star Trek* universe atheistic. But it clearly protests against classical theism and thus at best is pantheistic, or perhaps deistic—believing in a transcendent God who administers creation through natural law but remains remote and essentially unknowable in any personal terms. Regardless, "neither understanding of God qualifies as 'theistic' in the sense important to the main stream of Western religious thought" (Ferre 1967: 122).

16. The phrase "the scientific method" is commonly used to describe generally accepted rules of scientific investigation and interpretation. These rules traditionally have insisted that science should be objective (free of personal bias), empirical (based on data available to the senses), and rational (wholly logical). Yet "the term 'scientific method,' if applied to scientific investigation in general or to something allegedly embodied in the practice of every branch of science, can only refer to the lowest common denominator of a range of methods designed to cope with problems as diverse as classifying stars and curing diseases. If such a lowest common denominator exists . . . it can amount to little more than fidelity to empirical evidence and simplicity of logical formulation. . . . [But] the search for a unique scientific method seems less urgent than it once did, because by now it is clear that in general it has already been discovered, while in detail there is no such thing" (Caws 1967: 339, 343). Moreover, the majority of scientists acknowledge that subjective, non-empirical, and non-rational factors influence scientific interpretation and that "pure" science is a myth (Barbour 1971: 137–270).

17. The "two-language theory" is one of the most common ways of making peace between theology and science, as explained by Gilkey (1959: 34): "The

inquiries of the physical sciences and those of theology are now seen to be asking fundamentally different kinds of questions, in totally different areas of thought and experience. Consequently the answers to these questions, the hypotheses of science, and the affirmations or doctrines of theology, cannot and do not conflict. Religious myth has finally become that for which it was most aptly fitted: a symbolic story expressing the religious answer to man's ultimate questions. This was always its most significant function." More recent theorists, however, are proposing a new model of "hypothetical consonance" where both theology and science are identifying common domains of question-asking and "the God question can be honestly asked from within scientific reasoning" (Peters 1997: 652).

18. Tippler (1994: 10, 17, 339) posits the obviously controversial thesis that "theology simply *must* become a branch of physics if it is to survive" and that "theology is nothing but physical cosmology" from the viewpoint of physics. Therefore, in claiming that rational arguments can be used to prove the existence of God and the promise of future resurrection, he asserts that "religion is now part of science." But cf. Barbour (1971: 290): "It is 'misplaced concreteness' to take the abstractions of any theory, old or new, as an all-inclusive clue to reality. Neither classical nor modern physics—nor any other specialized science—can do justice to all aspects of human experience or provide a comprehensive worldview. The most we should expect from physics is a modest contribution to a view of nature at one limited level." Peters (1997: 650) calls Tippler's view "scientific imperialism."

19. Herbert F. Solow, the executive in charge of production of the original series, reminisces: "It's important to understand that, first and foremost, *Star Trek* was not created or developed as a critical study of truth, life's fundamental principles, or concepts of reasoned doctrines. We just wanted a hit series. The basic *Star Trek* philosophy was developed by its producers and writers during its production. However, a profound and metaphysical overlay was superimposed over the years as popularity begat popularity and viewers saw and defined a subjective something that validated and increased their appreciation of the show. The fact that so many fans saw, and continue to see, so much more in *Star Trek* than we ever realized was there makes me happy and proud beyond belief" (Solow and Justman 1996: 431).

20. Robert Short (1983: 15) states: "Space fantasy or 'science fiction' may never even mention anything 'religious' in the ordinary sense of the word. But whenever this fiction tries to help people find ultimate meaning for their lives, then it is—by definition—*religious*. As a religious fiction it will often display a very sensitive and accurate intuition of what all people basically are hungering and thirsting for."

21. Cf. *Star Trek* script contributor David Gerrold (1973: 48): "*Star Trek* is *not* pure science fiction. It is not predictive science fiction, and it is not accu-

rate science fiction. It was never meant to be. . . . What *Star Trek* is, is a set of fables—morality plays, entertainments, and diversions about contemporary man, but set against a science fiction background. *The background is subordinate to the fable*" (italics in original).

22. One fascinating feature of *Star Trek*'s optimistic humanism is that it also expressly denies to humanity the qualities traditionally ascribed to God such as immortality, omniscience, and omnipotence. In a curious parallel to Genesis 2–3, these are clearly forbidden zones for human beings in the *Star Trek* universe, regardless of their technological progress.

23. Even if traditional Freudianism or neo-Freudianism represents only a minority in the psychological community today, the point is still valid. Freud's atheism has often been commented on, of course, though its general contours were not original to him, it was not fundamental to his psychoanalytic theory, it was not supported by the scientific method he so valued, and he was not joined in this view by many of his disciples (Kung 1980: 262–339).

24. Dr. McCoy is a remarkable, but no doubt unintentional, example of this very point. Even as a man of science in the twenty-third century, he reveals racial prejudice (against Vulcans), engages in tirades against technology (especially the transporter), and frequently reacts to new situations with fear and trembling. There is a veritable parade of twenty-third century humans and humanoids, some of them Federation personnel, who waltz through the *Star Trek* universe creating havoc due directly to their twentieth-century-style psychological maladjustments. A partial list would include Harry Mudd ("Mudd's Women" [1966]; "I, Mudd" [1967]), Dr. Robert Crater ("The Man Trap" [1966]), Dr. Tristan Adams ("Dagger of the Mind" [1966]), Anton and Lenore Karidian ("The Conscience of the King"]1966]), Commodore Matthew Decker ("The Doomsday Machine" [1967]), John Gill ("Patterns of Force" 1968]), Dr. Richard Daystrom ("The Ultimate Computer" 1968]), Lawrence Marvick ("Is There in Truth No Beauty?" [1968]), Lokai and Bele ("Let That Be Your Last Battlefield" [1969]), Captain Garth ("Whom Gods Destroy" 1969]), Dr. Sevrin ("The Way to Eden" [1969]), and Dr. Janice Lester ("Turnabout Intruder" [1969]).

25. Andrew M. Greeley lamented in a 1976 *New York Times* editorial that American film directors do not raise the God-question enough because, being alienated from religion themselves, they do not consider it worthwhile as a subject for film. John R. May responds that the reason is elsewhere: it is more in the cultural tradition of America to raise the question of the demonic as evil within us or as a force rampant within our social institutions, but *not* as an independent persona, despite films such as *The Exorcist* (1973). With the notable exception of "The Enemy Within" (1966), *Star Trek* seems generally quite certain that evil is located in independent personas, usually in the gods or god-figures of authoritarianism. But May (1983: 83) states: "Our most compelling [film] directors

have avoided the demon as persona in favor of the demon in men's hearts and the loosing of Satan as confidence man. The reason, I feel, is as simple as this: artistic sensibility has never been too far removed from genuine religious sensibility to fall for that most subtle of all 'demonic' ploys that someone else is the source of the problem. The tendency to locate evil outside of man is a characteristic of primitive religions whereas the singular blessing of the world's great religions has been their persistent determination to interiorize evil. It is encouraging to recall that the earliest Judaeo-Christian evidence concerning belief in the origin of evil, the Jahwist tradition of the fall in Genesis, makes the unequivocal point that evil enters the world through man, and, regardless of how one interprets the role of the serpent, the narrative is equally clear that blaming the serpent is passing the buck."

26. "While *Star Trek* limped along for three years in the Nielsens before expiring, *over twenty million people* watched the Starship *Enterprise* on its five-year mission to explore the galaxy every week, and a whole generation grew up on its endless reruns. More people saw *Star Trek* every day than read a work of literary S[cience] F[iction] in five years. *Star Trek* imprinted the imagery of science fiction on mass public consciousness, where it had never been before, opening, thereby, the languages and concerns of science fiction to a mass audience for the very first time." (Spinrad 1990: 79).

27. "The spectacular achievements of science have begotten an age of anxiety about man's survival, man's integrity and wholeness, and man's compatibility with the natural universe. Dead is the dream of a scientific utopia. Few now believe that *faster, bigger, stronger, surer, more efficient, more intricate*, and *more amazing* will cure the spiritual malaise of the aging twentieth century. . . . It would appear that a better world will not evolve from any number of blastings off, pluggings in, switchings on, and startings up" (Berger 1976: 200).

28. Post–modernism is difficult to define, but it suggests an intellectual and cultural movement away from the assumptions of modernism, which stresses unity, order, the absolute, and the rational, to an appreciation of paradox, ambiguity, irony, indeterminacy, and contingency (Natoli and Hutcheon 1993).

4

Religion and Science in *Star Trek: The Next Generation*

God, Q, and Evolutionary Eschatology on the Final Frontier

GREGORY PETERSON

S cience and religion are at war. At least, that is the impression one might get from a casual viewing of *Star Trek: The Next Generation* (*TNG*). From the very first episode, "Encounter at FarPoint" (1987), to the final season, the viewer repeatedly sees the intrepid crew of the *Enterprise* using the twin beacons of science and reason to break others free from the dark thrall of ignorance and superstition. Those who pretend to hold the keys to the supernatural are, time after time, revealed to hold nothing more than, as Jean-Luc Picard would say, "a magician's bag of tricks" ("Devil's Due," 1991). Those who rely on science and reason can, time after time, be seen to offer the truest and best solution to any problem plaguing the crew or the civilizations that they encounter.

A closer examination of the content of the series, however, reveals a more complex situation. In *Star Trek: The Next Generation*, belief in supernatural beings is consistently subjected to withering attack, yet *TNG*'s universe is populated with immortal entities that possess god-like powers. In several episodes, Captain Picard goes to great lengths to prove the falsity of a religious claim, yet he appears to treat the religious beliefs of Klingons and Vulcans with a great deal of respect. And while no human member of the crew adheres to any known religion, the crew collectively exhibits a confidence in reason, science, and evolutionary progress that in many ways seems religious in character. What should be made of this?

One option is to assume that these apparent contradictions are the typical result of composite authorship which bedevils any television series, where screenwriters, directors, producers, and network executives all can and do contribute to forming a final product. A more compelling option, however, is to see *TNG*'s many statements regarding science and religion as the result of a deeply systematic worldview that informs the actions of the primary characters throughout the show. Despite the different parties involved in the production of the series, a single, coherent perspective does emerge. In this worldview, science and reason are the basis of knowledge and moral action. Religion, based on supernatural revelation and faith, is an impediment to scientific and cultural progress that must be dealt with from time to time. Furthermore, science and reason fulfill many of the functions that religion purports to fill. Specifically, science and reason inform an evolutionary eschatology in which individuals contribute to their species' evolutionary progression toward higher and more benevolent life forms.

To show this, four aspects of the portrayal of science and religion in *TNG* will be considered: 1. the relationship of science and religion generally 2. the religious persecution of science and scientific debunking of religion 3. the religious and mystical beliefs of advanced aliens who are "culturally other," and 4. how science builds an evolutionary eschatology that replaces traditional religious accounts of salvation with its own naturalistic account of the future of the human species.

SCIENCE AND RELIGION: CONFLICTING MODES OF THOUGHT

It would, of course, be a mistake to assume that *TNG* is a philosophical tract, intent on persuading the world through sustained argumentation of a single thesis. As a television series, *TNG* had a seven-year run that included storylines from the humorous to the tragic and, in addition to themes regarding science and religion, dealt with such issues as genetic engineering in "Unnatural Selection" (1989), gender and sexuality in "The Outcast" (1992), and life from the viewpoint of an android in "Data's Day" (1991). Of these episodes, only a minority deal explicitly with religion. Yet these episodes are often dramatically important because they inform us of the philosophical perspective of the series and (therefore) the crew of the *Enterprise,* which in turn informs the crew members actions in many of the other episodes.

Science is integral not only to the mission of the *Enterprise,* but to the conception of the entire series. Every episode begins with the well known charter to "Explore strange, new worlds. . . ." It is repeatedly affirmed that the *Enterprise* is not a ship of war (although it can be such) but a ship of exploration (e.g. Data to Ishara Yar in "Legacy," 1990). The scientific emphasis of the *Enterprise's* mission is the basis or pretext of a great many storylines, from "Home Soil" (1988) to "Masks" (1994).

The role of science in *TNG,* however, goes far beyond the happenstance of the *Enterprise's* mission. New technologies, the handmaiden of scientific discovery, often provide the occasion for wrestling with deep moral or philosophical issues. The novel technology that produced Data and the discovery of possible intelligence in servo-robots spark discussions on the nature of life and self-hood ("The Measure of Man," 1987; "The Quality of Life," 1992). The ability to clone and to genetically alter offspring likewise provoke debate on the appropriate uses of technology ("Unnatural Selection," 1989; "Up the Long Ladder," 1989).

From this concern with ethical consequences, one might conclude that *TNG* negatively portrays the role of science and technology in society. Nothing could be further from the truth. More often than not, scientific discovery and new technological solutions provide the solution to any number of dilemmas, even to those produced by technology in the first place. In "Unnatural Selection," for example, the abuse of genetic engineering creates a crisis, but it is a further technological fix that helps to provide the answer. Frequently one finds the solution to an urgent crisis to be a new scientific/technological discovery or a technological innovation on the *Enterprise* itself, from the warp core to the sensor array, explained in appropriately sounding technological jargon incomprehensible enough to sound authentic to the average listener. In this we see, in a very minor way, something of the salvific role of science. Science and technology often provide the way out of a problem, even a moral problem. Science and technology make us healthier, help us live longer, and provide many of the creature comforts and entertainments that help us to be happy.

The role of science, however, does not stop with providing technological solutions. In *TNG,* science and reason are the basis of knowledge and, perhaps, the sole basis of knowledge. From knowledge, comes progress. Those left in ignorance, by contrast, are lost to a life of suffering and brutality. It is here that the conflict *TNG* presupposes between science and religion emerges. Science, in *TNG*, is rational knowledge based on the gathering of evidence. Hypotheses are accepted or rejected based upon discoveries made through the process of scientific reasoning. *TNG* does not provide a full-fledged philosophy of science, yet these assumptions about the nature of science come through clearly enough in many episodes. "Evolution" (1989) and "Half a Life" (1991), among others, provide examples of scientists doing research in this very fashion. Members of the crew are often portrayed as engaged in scientific discovery or innovation using this method of reason based inquiry. Beverly Crusher thus engages in biological experiments ("Cause and Effect," 1992), Captain Picard pursues the study of archaeology ("The Chase," 1993), Geordi La Forge refines the engineering of the Enterprise ("Booby Trap," 1989), and Wesley Crusher, among other things, experiments with nanites (a type of microscopic machine) ("Evolution," 1989).

In *TNG*, religion is portrayed as the principle in opposition to science. Whereas science is based upon reason, religion is based on faith. Faith, typically, is placed in one or more supernatural figures who dictate commandments to be followed slavishly and without thought to their rationality. It is the "irrational" behavior (as seen from *TNG*'s version of the scientific worldview) prompted or commanded by religious authority which often serves as the basis of dramatic conflict between science and religion ("Justice," 1987; "Who Watches the Watchers," 1989; "Devil's Due," 1991).

Several examples may serve to highlight this conflict more readily. In "Rightful Heir" (1993), Worf, the Klingon officer on board the *Enterprise,* believes that the Klingon prophet Kahless has returned from the dead. The following interchange between Worf and Data, the precisely logical android, ensues:

DATA: May I ask a question? In the absence of empirical data, how will you determine whether or not this is the real Kahless?

WORF: It is not an empirical matter. It is a matter of faith.

DATA: Faith—then you do believe Kahless may have supernatural attributes. As an android, I am unable to accept that which cannot be proven through rational means. I would appreciate hearing your insight on this matter.

WORF: Perhaps some other time, commander. I do not believe I can provide much insight at this moment.

Worf never does provide the insight, since it turns out that his faith is misplaced. We can note, however, the way faith and reason are treated in this exchange. They are opposites that are in conflict. Faith believes (necessarily) in the absence of evidence. Reason (and science) holds only to that which can be verified by the scientific method. When reason establishes the false identity of the returned Kahless, Worf's faith is substantially shaken.[1]

An even clearer enunciation of the radical opposition of science and religion occurs in the episode "Who Watches the Watchers." In this episode, human anthropologists are studying the Mintakans, a primitive "proto-Vulcan" society engaged in a largely pastoral way of life. This race has "evolved" beyond the religion stage until a reactor failure in the anthropologist's blind reveals them to the Mintakans. One of the Mintakans, Liko, falls and severely injures himself while investigating the incident. Just in time, Dr. Crusher arrives to rescue the anthropologists, and seeing the injured Mintakan near death, brings him along for treatment to the *Enterprise*. There, Liko remains unconscious most of the time, but wakes briefly to see someone talking to Picard by name. Liko is then returned to the planet. Thinking that he has been miraculously healed and has been granted a vision of the "Great Picard," Liko starts a religious revival among his people, with the Picard-deity at its center. The chief anthropologist, Dr. Barron, suggests that since the damage has been done, this religious belief should be encouraged. Picard replies, "Dr. Barron, your report describes how rational these people are. Millennia ago they abandoned their belief in the supernatural. Now you are asking me to sabotage that achievement? To send them back into the dark ages of superstition and ignorance and fear? No!"

Again we see the conflict between science and religion. The rationality of the people is connected to their abandonment of faith in the supernatural. The encouraging of religious belief, by contrast, entails a return to the dark ages. This contrast between religion and rationality is doubly emphasized by the fact that Mintakans are a proto-Vulcan race, for the Vulcans in *TNG* (as in the rest of the *Star Trek* franchise) are the epitome of rational action and behavior.

These and other episodes indicate how science and reason are portrayed in relation to religion and faith. Science is the basis of knowledge. Religion, which is based on faith, stands only in the absence of knowledge. Science explains in terms of the natural. Religion explains in terms of the supernatural. For *TNG*, science and religion represent opposite ends of a spectrum moving from the rational to the irrational and, since they are opposites, it is only natural that they come into conflict.

RELIGION AND SCIENCE AT WAR:
PERSECUTION AND DEBUNKING

This conflict between religion and science in *TNG* is not, however, portrayed simply as a clash of ideas but as a clash between modes of life. The mode of life associated with science is one of progress, harmony, and happiness. The mode of life associated with religion is one of war, intolerance, and ignorance.

This association of religion with negative consequences is apparent already in "Encounter at Far Point" (1987). In this first episode, Q, a super-evolutionary being with apparently unlimited powers, asserts that humanity is a savage race and that humans have "murdered each other over quarrels over tribal god-images." Q goes on to describe human history as a series of self-inflicted barbaric atrocities that the human species now threatens to unleash upon other worlds. The implication is that religion has had no small part to play in these events.

In "Who Watches the Watchers," we find the same association. In the key meeting during which the crew must decide what to do with the new Mintakan religion, the following exchange ensues:

> DR. BARRON: Like it or not, we have rekindled the Mintakans belief in the Overseer.
>
> RIKER: And are you saying this belief will eventually become a religion?
>
> DR. BARRON: It's inevitable. And without guidance, that religion could degenerate into inquisitions, holy wars, chaos!
>
> PICARD: Horrifying!

Dr. Barron's assumption, from which Picard and Riker do not dissent, is that religion, left unchecked, naturally devolves into the worst of atrocities. Indeed, any religious claim to have positive effects seems misguided. In "Devil's Due," we find a civilization, the Ventaxians, which believes that long ago it had made a pact with the devil Ardra for one thousand years of peace, a clean environment, and prosperity. The one thousand years has passed and now someone claiming to be the devil has returned to collect her due. Picard challenges the validity of Ardra's contract with the Ventaxians and, in true dramatic fashion, a court battle ensues. Among other tactics, Picard challenges Ardra's claim to have actually helped the Ventaxians. He calls Jared, leader of the Ventaxians, to the stand and cross-examines him.

PICARD: Did Ardra simply snap her fingers and transform the planet into this?

JARED: No, the changes occurred gradually over a long period of time.

PICARD: Did she personally form the government that so peacefully ruled over the planet for a millennium?

JARED: No, historical records indicate a council was convened to assess our options. They drew up a new constitution, which the population later ratified.

PICARD: I see, so she advised the council?

Jared: No.

PICARD: No? Then she must have destroyed all the weapons on the planet.

JARED: No, our leaders did that. And they signed a treaty of nonaggression.

And so the cross-examination continues, until it becomes clear that Ardra isn't responsible for the positive changes that took place at all and that all of them emerged from the people themselves. The religious beliefs of the Ventaxians had no role in the positive developments that occurred. If anything, religion has a negative effect since it causes panic and allows the Ventaxians to be duped by, as Picard establishes, a woman only pretending to be Ardra. As with "Who Watches the Watchers," no good comes of their religious beliefs.

When science directly clashes with religion in the *TNG* universe, it seems that one of two things can happen. The first and most familiar may be described as the "Galileo mode" of conflict, where a famous scientist or theory is persecuted by religious authorities. There seems to be a hint of this behind Q's diatribe against "savage humanity" in "Encounter at FarPoint." This is probably also behind the references to inquisitions and such in "Who Watches the Watchers." Surprisingly, however, this mode of conflict does not seem to be played out directly within the *TNG* series. The closest analog occurs in "Half a Life" (1991), where Dr. Timicin, a well-respected scientist of the planet Kaelon II, is near to making a discovery that will save his civilization from immanent destruction. Tragically, the scientist is about to approach the age of sixty, when all members of his society ritually kill themselves, resulting in a moral dilemma over what should take place. Should the scientist break the revered tradition or save his civilization? While religious justifications or references are absent from the ensuing debate, the episode follows this "Galileo mode" of science-religion warfare. The cultural mandate for death at sixty is given no satisfactory reason for its existence beyond adherence to tradition, giving it an irrational flavor that *TNG* seems to generally associate with religion. In the end, the scientist bows to social pressure, not only bringing an end to scientific discovery but to his entire civilization as well.

By far the more prevalent form of science-religion conflict to appear in *TNG* is the "debunking mode." Here science, in the hands of the technologically more sophisticated crew of the *Enterprise,* is used to prove the falsity of any number of religious tenets. In several of the episodes already discussed, this is the primary mode of conflict that takes place. To return once again to "Who Watches the Watchers," Captain Picard is so mortified at the thought of inadvertently starting a new religion, that he goes to great lengths to reverse the effects. Even though Federation policy, in terms of the Prime Directive, forbids direct interference with other less-developed cultures, Picard feels so strongly that the effects of religion are deleterious that he is willing to do anything to prevent its spread. In violation of the Prime Directive, Picard meets the Mintakans and allows himself to be shot with an arrow, thereby proving his frail humanity through rational, empirical means. Religion is stopped in its tracks.

We find this same pattern in "Devil's Due." As soon as Picard hears of the appearance of Ardra, he immediately sets out on a course of debunking her authenticity, even though this was not part of the original mission and the *Enterprise* has (at least initially) no stake in the matter. By finding the source of her apparently magical powers in advanced technology hidden in a spaceship, Picard once again demonstrates the falsity of religious belief.

This debunking motif occurs as well in "Justice" (1987), where Wesley Crusher is to be executed because he was quite unaware of a rather irrational law. When it is discovered that the law is alleged to have divine origins, the crew of the *Enterprise* sets out to debunk the deity's authenticity. In this case, the crew discovers that those actions which the civilization had falsely attributed to God in fact stem from a complex orbiting computer. Their religion's claims proved false, the irrational laws become irrelevant and Wesley is spared his life.

It may be useful, at this point, to reiterate the common denominators necessary for this warfare to take place. The religions with which the crew of the *Enterprise* come into conflict are characterized by appeals to faith in the absence of reason, the institution of apparently arbitrary laws or rites of worship and appeal to supernatural beings. The consequences of the religions, as seen from *TNG*'s perspective, are uniformly negative. Furthermore, when these religions encounter the scientific worldview promoted by the members of the *Enterprise*, the religions are proven to be false in their claims and expectations. The model of the relation of religion and science that *TNG* gives is one of conflict, a conflict that religion cannot win.

RELIGION AND SCIENCE AT WAR II:
THE PROBLEM OF PLURALISM AND THE CULTURAL OTHER

Despite the many diatribes against religion that occur in *TNG*, not all religions suffer equally at the bar of *TNG*'s version of the scientific worldview. Throughout the series, one finds occasional references to humanity's "barbarous past," which clearly includes the evils of religion. One also finds conflict between the *Enterprise* and the religious beliefs of "lesser developed" civilizations, such as the Mintakans. Among the human crew of the *Enterprise*, religious belief, as *TNG* conceives of it, is noticeably absent. It is not even possible for conflict between science and religion to occur here.

When one turns to the other advanced alien races of the *TNG* universe whose level of technology is on a par with the Federation, the treatment of religion becomes more complex. There appear to be two primary reasons for this. One reason is a commitment by the series to the notion of cultural pluralism, most clearly embodied in the principle of the Prime Directive, by which members of Starfleet are forbidden to interfere in the affairs of less developed cultures. If the Prime Directive compels a hands off policy toward less developed cultures, then all beliefs, including religious ones, should be allowed to follow their natural development. As we have seen, however, the Prime Directive doesn't seem to fully apply when religion is involved. But if the religions of less developed cultures are treated with scorn, why are the religions of advanced civilizations such as the Klingons and Vulcans (where the Prime Directive is not in effect) accorded any respect?

The answer to this question may lie in a reason different from the commitment to cultural pluralism: the mode of religion that is practiced. Klingon religion and rituals are given the greatest attention of any alien culture in *TNG*. Klingon life, in contrast to the portrayal of human life, remains highly ritualized in the twenty-fourth century, including rituals for everything from adoption ("The Bonding, 1989) to suicide ("Ethics," 1992) and sex ("The Emissary," 1989). Underlying these rituals is the warrior's code of honor, in which the highest good is to die in the line of duty, preferably in hand-to-hand combat. These warrior's values in turn are derived from the founding documents of Klingon culture, scriptures and lawbooks based on the sayings of Kahless, who is prophesied to return from the dead. The Klingons even have a belief in the afterlife. Yet, while the Klingons have a devil ("Devil's Due") there appears to be no God or gods, and indeed, references to the supernatural are minimal. In contrast, Worf, the only Klingon member of the *Enterprise* crew, is frequently shown to be engaged in Klingon meditation (a sort of t'ai ch'i) or in rituals that seem designed to induce trance or vision states (most prominently in "Rightful Heir," 1993).

Vulcan religion, if it may be called such, is similarly non-theistic. Although Vulcan religion is most fully developed elsewhere (especially *Star Trek III: The Search for Spock*, 1984), the *TNG* portrayal of Vulcan religion is strongly synonymous with the rest of the *Star Trek* universe. Whereas the Klingons emphasize honor, Vulcans emphasize the role of logic as the guiding principle in life, a principle that has saved them from their own barbarous past. Like the Klingons, the Vulcans have their own rituals, most notably the mind-meld before death where the thoughts and memories of an individual are passed on to the next generation. In *TNG*, Spock appears more or less as an apostle to this cause in the two-part episode, "Unification" (1991), where he perceives a need to spread the word of Vulcan ways to their sister-race, the Romulans. This is the rare instance where what may be described as religious proselytizing is portrayed in a positive light in *TNG*. In the context of the episode, Spock may well have other (particularly political) motivations for contacting the Romulans, but the spreading of the Vulcan "message" is certainly prominent.

Interestingly enough, Native American beliefs are given this same degree of respect in "Journey's End" (1994) and, it would appear, for similar reasons. The Native Americans, as portrayed in the episode, practice a spirituality largely devoid of references to supernatural entities or resulting in irrational commandments. For the Western-biased *TNG* crew, Native Americans are, disturbingly, as alien as Klingons. This parallel between Native American religion and the religions of the Klingons and Vulcans may reflect, in fact, the role that these advanced aliens do play in the series. Many of the alien races encountered serve as a mirror for humanity's own foibles and dilemmas. By projecting our problems onto an alien civilization, as *TNG* did with gangs in "Legacy" (1990), drug addiction in "Symbiosis" (1988), and homosexuality in "The Outcast" (1992), science fiction can provide new ways of examining contemporary problems. The space-faring alien, however, can also serve as the cultural Other by exposing us to novel and unusual beliefs and customs. Arguably, Vulcans and Klingons provide *TNG*'s universe with a vision of the religious Other. In these cultures, we find religions devoid of supernatural beings, prayer, or (it would appear) arbitrary commandments. These are modes of religion largely alien to the Western mind as well as to the human crew of the *Enterprise*, evoking a fascination with the unusual. In this, we can see some analog with the West's own encounter with Eastern religions, which are likewise seen as devoid of God or appeals to faith. Just as the secular West has displayed curiosity and fascination for Zen Buddhism and other Eastern traditions, so too does *TNG* seem to display curiosity and fascination with the radically different beliefs of the Klingons and Vulcans. Also, like portrayals of Eastern religions to the West, the religions of the Klingons and Vulcans are portrayed as being devoid of the most objectionable elements usually associated with religion: ignorance, superstition, and irrationality.

Nevertheless, alien religion, even that of advanced alien cultures, remains in a certain tension with the primary vision of the series. This is most prominently seen in the episode, "Rightful Heir," where Worf, suffering from a spiritual crisis, travels to the spiritual center of the Klingon Empire to meditate and receive a vision of Kahless, the lawgiver. Kahless does appear, though not as a vision but as a real being. Klingon priests immediately proclaim the long-awaited second coming of Kahless, and even Worf is "duped" for awhile, before the debunking motif once again asserts itself. Kahless is found to be a clone, duplicated from DNA recovered from the blood of the original Kahless and engineered with memories derived from the original Klingon law books. Technology once again holds the upper hand, yet the episode is left curiously unresolved. The evidence convinces Worf that he has been duped. Worf cannot deny his religious beliefs, but neither can he accept them as they were.

Debunking occurs again in a different context, this time in "The Next Phase" (1992). Ensign Ro Laren, a Bajoran, and Geordi La Forge, one of the central human characters, undergo a transformation that makes them, for all practical purposes, ghosts, invisible to their comrades and able to pass through normally solid objects. Ensign Ro, in accordance with traditional Bajoran beliefs, assumes she is dead. Geordi assumes that they are alive and works toward a scientific solution to the problem.

Geordi turns out to be correct and, as with Worf in "Rightful Heir," Ensign Ro's beliefs are left battered and unresolved.

The fact that in both of these cases the faith of the alien (Worf in "Rightful Heir," Ensign Ro in "The Next Phase") is left unresolved is perhaps telling of *TNG*'s approach to alien religious claims. It would appear that religions of advanced aliens are allowed a certain provisional status and respect. As long as these religions portray a non-Western mode of religious belief and practice, they remain objects of interest and respect. Other cultures show us alternative ways of thinking, believing, and acting. But when these religions incorporate styles of belief that are typically Western (as with Worf's belief in a returned prophet Kahless and Ensign Ro's belief in the afterlife), the conflict mode returns and for apparently the same reasons and in the same fashion as with other human and lesser alien religions.

Moreover, alien religion is always for aliens. True, humans may on occasion be intrigued by the practice and occasionally participate (as with Worf's t'ai ch'i), but the religions of the Other are explicitly for the Other; they are not for us. In the end, this may be because *TNG* has its own religious vision, one that is based on and extrapolated from the sciences and which, in its own way, attempts to fulfill many of the needs traditionally accorded to religion.

RELIGION AND SCIENCE AT PEACE: EVOLUTIONARY ESCHATOLOGY AS THE RELIGION OF *STAR TREK: THE NEXT GENERATION*

If religion, as traditionally conceived, is at war with science, and if humans need a framework for the acting out of life, then science, or some interpretation of it, must ultimately provide that framework in place of religion. This seems to be the logic behind the philosophical perspective that emerges in *TNG*. If science provides us with the truth, then we must frame our hopes and aspirations within the framework that science gives us.

It becomes clear as the series develops that what may be called an evolutionary eschatology is being advocated. True, *TNG* disparages religion as such, but it replaces traditional religious beliefs with a competing religious vision of its own, purportedly based upon a rational understanding of science, human nature, and evolution. What makes this vision a religious vision, moreover, is that it offers salvation and provides a rationale for the motivation and actions of the primary characters.

This evolutionary eschatology is apparent at the beginning of the series with the pilot episode, "Encounter at FarPoint" (1987). The first mission of the new *Enterprise* and its crew involves negotiating the entry of a new world into the Federation, of which Earth is a primary member. On the way, however, they are held up by a representative of the Q Continuum. The Continuum is a collective of very highly evolved creatures. Their powers, conventionally speaking, are unlimited. While the Continuum is plural, it acts as one, and now it has sent one of its kind, simply referred to as Q, to stop the *Enterprise* specifically as the beginning of a more general effort to stop the spread of humanity, the "savage race." Captain Picard, bound to his duty first and his fear of mortality last, ignores the order and proceeds on his original mission. Q then puts humanity on trial, with the crew of the *Enterprise* as its representatives. Q asserts that humanity is a savage race and that its history has, in general, been a series of self-inflicted barbaric atrocities, which it now threatens to unleash upon other worlds. Picard's response to these charges is key. Picard first denies that human history has been savage. Under pressure from Q, however, he admits that humans have committed grievous atrocities in the past. Picard then makes another argument: while it is true that humans were that way in the past, he asserts that we are no longer, that in the twenty-fourth century humanity has changed such that these barbarous attitudes are no longer a part of our nature. We have, so to speak, evolved beyond them. In another episode, "The Neutral Zone" (1988), the same point is made to travelers from the twentieth century recently resuscitated from cryogenic suspension. In the twenty-fourth century, there is no war, no poverty, not even money. Drugs and violence are a thing of the past. People apparently work out of conviction, not out of need.

It should be stressed here that evolution in *TNG* is synonymous with progress. Evolution is not simply a random process but has a definite arrow toward increased intelligence and more sophisticated life forms. The evolution of human life is seen within this broader framework. Note, for instance, this interchange between Picard and Q in "Hide and Q" (1987):

> PICARD: I know Hamlet and what he might say with irony, I say with conviction. "What a piece of work is man, how noble in reason, how infinite in faculty. In form, in moving, how express and admirable. In action, how like an angel, in apprehension, how like a god!"

Q: Surely, you don't see your species like that, do you?

PICARD: I see us one day becoming that. Is it that which concerns you?

In this framework, moral and biological evolution go hand in hand. When Picard replies to Q that the evils of the barbarous past are no longer a part of human nature, he seems to be implying that it is not even part of our biological make-up. Humans are no longer capable of that sort of behavior. As a species evolves physically, it learns how to use technology, which also requires it to evolve morally at the peril of destroying itself through nuclear war, environmental catastrophe or any one of a number of calamities. Increased mastery of technology, in turn, allows it to modify itself biologically.

We see something of this process in the "Nth Degree (1993)." The unassuming Lieutenant Barclay is subjected to the effects of an alien device, which causes him to go through a fantastic rewiring of his brain that results not only in vastly increased intelligence but in making him a better person. Whereas Barclay was clumsy, ineffectual, and withdrawn before, after the transformation he becomes thoughtful, assertive, and emotionally balanced. In the end, Barclay takes the ship to a distant part of the galaxy where the crew is examined by benevolent and apparently omnipotent and all-knowing beings. Through them, we see the potential future and salvation of humankind. Salvation in *TNG* is not salvation for the individual (except inasmuch as one reaps the fruits of science and technology), but salvation for one's descendants in the species line, who for all practical purposes will be immortal, omnipotent, and omniscient. One might rephrase the Mormon dictum: "What God was, humankind now is. What God is, humankind shall become." This phrase is an appropriate characterization of *TNG* eschatology. Eventually we, or at least our descendants, may become like gods.

Of course, not every species or civilization makes it that far. Salvation, as in the typical Western understanding of religion, is contingent and even highly evolved races (such as the benevolent progenitors in "The Chase," 1993) can die out. And while moral and biological evolution generally go hand in hand, this may not always be the case. The Borg, for instance, represent a technologically more advanced society and morally repugnant one. It is unclear, however, whether this is an exception or not. The Borg, because they rely on collective intelligence, are treated more like a virus than a being with its own intelligence. It even remains unclear whether they produced their own technology or stole it. But through the Borg's conquest of other civilizations, we see the contigency of evolutionary advancement and, therefore, salvation.

More interesting is the case of the Q who, as indicated earlier, are all-powerful, eternal, and all-knowing. The Q Continuum are the most prominent god-like beings in the show, typically appearing once a season as well as in the beginning and final episodes. They also play the most ambivalent moral role of any characters to appear on the series. Initially, at least, they appear hostile to humans and seemingly indifferent to the pain and suffering of lesser beings. In the episode, "Hide and Q" (1987), it appears that they dislike humanity not only because of its rapid spread throughout the galaxy, but also because humanity, as it evolves, may one day pose a threat to the Q Continuum itself. At other times, the Q seem to simply serve as a *deus ex machina*, a plot device to allow otherwise impossible scenarios. Rarely is it the case, however, that the Q are ever in the final result malicious, although their methods leave something to be desired. Rarely do their actions directly cause death and in some cases they work for the good. In one episode, "Tapestry" (1993), Q grants Picard a second chance at life after learning a rather painful lesson about the past. In another, Q guides a member of the crew who is unaware of her powers to her proper home with the Q Continuum ("True-Q," 1992).

Is it simply that the Q were never really integrated into the moral and religious universe that Gene Roddenberry had built? Or is it a statement regarding the limitations of our own understanding, that just as our actions are so beyond the mind of an ant, so too is the rationality of the Q Continuum beyond us? Either way, Q serves the purpose of *TNG*'s evolutionary eschatology. Q shows that humanity too may become like gods. By evolutionary development, aided by scientific advance, a bright and beatific future awaits us. How is this known? Because the Q continuum, like many other species, has already done it. They have achieved a state where death is unheard of and whose power is, in practical terms, limitless. It becomes clear that *TNG*, in the end, attempts to integrate science and religion into a synthesis. Salvation, such as it is in the *TNG*'s universe, is naturalized salvation. Deity, if one may speak of such, is naturalized deity, seemingly immortal and all-powerful, but still (allegedly) within the confines and explanation of natural laws. In the end, there is no room for supernatural religions because they have been replaced by a naturalized one.

CONCLUSION

The viewpoint of *TNG* on the relationship between science and religion should now be clear, forming a complex but coherent whole. Religion and science, faith and reason are placed on opposite poles that imply, by their very definition, conflict. *TNG* incorporates a critique of human religion on the basis of its association with humanity's "barbarous past." Alien religions that bear these features (belief in supernatural beings, appeals to faith, demands to follow irrational laws) are treated in the same manner. The religions of advanced aliens receive some respect because of their non-Western modes of expression. But while alien religion fascinates, it does not satisfy and even it must give way to the bar of scientific reasoning. Instead, *TNG* provides its own religious viewpoint in terms of an evolutionary eschatology, wherein the species as a whole is saved inasmuch as it reaches the highest echelon of evolutionary being.

This claim should be put into context. *TNG* is not primarily a series about religion, nor is its sole purpose to disparage existing religions and replace them with one of its own. Nevertheless, the religious motifs of the *TNG* form a consistent whole, and the view of traditional religion found therein is not favorable, replaced by its own, sometimes monolithic, religious system. There are a number of ways that the science and religion relationship could have been played out. Warfare is certainly one of them. But religion can also encourage scientific discovery, where the Book of Nature is as revelatory of the Divine as scripture. Religion may even be supposed to occupy a totally separate realm of inquiry from science that exists in harmonious relationship.

Consistently, however, this is not the way that religions are portrayed in the series. Every time a religious issue presents itself in *TNG*, we find the same patterns occurring. The only viable religion for the crew of the *Enterprise* seems to be one founded on science, and a particular interpretation of science at that. In one of the few television series of its time to openly champion the wisdom of diversity and tolerance, the approach of *TNG* to religion represents a missed opportunity.

NOTE

1. Interestingly, at the end of the episode, Data does allow some place for faith, but in the context of the show, it is clear that faith must always give way to empirical evidence and that usually such empirical evidence is against the tenor of any kind of faith.

5

Deeds of Power

Respect for Religion in
Star Trek: Deep Space Nine

PETER LINFORD

If we don't start living together and respecting one another we're not going to make it to the age of *Star Trek.*

—Gene Roddenberry

The kingdom of God depends not on talk but on power.

—1 Corinthians 4:20

Star Trek: Deep Space Nine (*DS9*) is the third series in the *Star Trek* television franchise, and it is the first of the *Star Trek* series to address the question of religion in any serious depth. The Bajoran religion described in *DS9* is a fiction, and while this may seem an obvious point it is one worth making. We should not fall into the trap of discussing it as though it were real. In the following analysis, it is not the religion itself as portrayed in *DS9* that will provide the focus for argument, but the way in which religion is treated by the characters within the series. *DS9* attempts a more sophisticated and positive view of religion than that traditionally found within the genre of science fiction. The subtle implications of the series, however, often contradict this apparent intention. In doing so, the series also contradicts the underlying ethos of tolerance and openness often ascribed to *Star Trek* as a whole.

FAITH

DS9 informs us that the Bajoran faith is many thousands of years old. According to the character of Kai Opaka, the spiritual leader of the Bajoran people in the episode "Emissary" (1993), the first of the orbs through which wisdom is revealed to the Bajorans arrived some 10,000 years ago. Eight more orbs followed. Each of the orbs, she says, have allowed the Prophets to teach the Bajorans and shape their theology.

About this theology and institution we are told very little in this first episode. Bajorans have something called a *pagh,* a term which apparently describes those personal characteristics which support an individual mentally and spiritually. Vedeks, the senior members of religious orders whose junior members are described as monks, can sense the *pagh* of others through touch. This ability is also ascribed to the Prophets themselves. The leader of the Bajoran faith is called the *Kai,* to which office he or she is elected by an assembly of Vedeks. Beyond these details, little about the Bajoran faith is revealed in "Emissary," so we must turn to other episodes to piece together a more complete picture of it.

The Bajoran faith as presented shows little evidence of being a personal one. The Prophets, too, are always spoken of collectively. Although it is said that the Bajorans worship the wormhole aliens as Prophets, we rarely see them doing so. Apart from a scene at the opening of "The Homecoming" (1993), where Major Kira appears to be involved in a ritual act before a private altar, it is not until "Accession" (1996) that there is strong evidence of regular worship. Later, in "Ties of Blood and Water" (1997) Major Kira is seen to pray. Other facets that we might expect to see in a religion are more clearly absent. There is, for example, no creativity attributed to the Prophets. Nor is there any soteriology. There is, in fact, little reason given for the Prophets to be worshipped. It is never said, for example as it might be (although it is once implied), that upon a Bajoran's death he is taken to the Celestial Temple, as the Bajorans regard the wormhole. The content of the Bajoran prophecies is rarely discussed. When it is they appear to be prophecies in the most literal sense. The opening of the wormhole is foretold, as are Cardassian experiments with it. The prophecies do not seem to offer moral teaching, myths, or eschatology.

It could be argued that in making these objections we are attempting to define Bajoran religion in terms of the prevailing Western model of Christianity, and it is to the series' credit that the religion it presents has few such obvious parallels. While this is true in one respect, it is also true that if the Bajoran religion is a faith, as it is described as being, then Bajorans must be seen to have 'faith in' or 'faith that' something, but the series does not make clear what either might be. Given that the Prophets are reported to have the ability both to sense and replenish a person's *pagh*, we might take it that the faith is in this replenishment, given certain conditions. There is a possible connection between this expectation and the burning of "renewal" scrolls, on which are written a person's woes, during the Gratitude Festival witnessed in the episode "Fascination" (1994). Again, however, this conclusion is made at the risk of imposing our Judaeo-Christian contractual model of faith upon the fictional Bajoran religion. The more general impression given by the series is that the Bajorans have faith that the Prophets will work for their best interests. Kai Winn repeatedly refers to "the will of the Prophets" as being her guide for action.

The will of the Prophets for the Bajoran people is communicated apparently in two ways. First, there is a large volume of scripture, the Prophecies, which may be interpreted in varying ways. Where there is theological discourse, it seems to be on matters of the interpretation of this scripture. Thus, disputes such as occur in "Destiny" (1995) over the Tricor Prophecies, or over such major issues as whether Sisko is or is not the Emissary, may take place. What is not made clear is how the writers of these prophecies came by them. In "Destiny" the Tricor prophecies seem to be ascribed directly to him but it is not implied that Tricor was himself one of the Prophets. There are only tenuous grounds for claiming names for an individual Prophet. Presumably, these Prophecies are ascribed to Tricor only because it was he who wrote them down, or possibly because he received them through the orbs.

Second, communication takes place on an individual basis through the use of the orbs. As noted, Tricor's prophetic writings may have been made following an orb encounter, though this interpretation is unconfirmed by the episode. Such encounters seem to be rare. Much is made on several occasions of the privilege implied by such an encounter, which is seen to have lasting effects. The Bajoran Vedeks seek to guard, protect, and restrict the use of the orbs, but the orbs are not limited in their efficacy to the Bajorans, which suggests, within religious reasoning at any rate, that the Prophets' interest in guiding the affairs of others may extend beyond Bajor. This, as we shall see, is significant for the model of the divine that the series proposes.

The Bajorans do not use the word "gods" to described the aliens, but we shall take it that divinity is ascribed to them. The nature of this divinity will be discussed in the final part of our analysis and will constitute the most significant part of our claim that, while in many ways a step forward, *DS9* is also introducing ideas which serve to present religion in a negative light. Religion becomes a minority issue in which, as in previous *Star Trek* series, believers are shown to be interpreting in a religious fashion events and relationships that may have an alternative, non-religious explanation.

ANALYSIS

One notable example among the many analyses that have been performed of religion in science fiction is that of Adam Frisch and Joseph Martos (1985), who discern a three-fold model for the use of religion by science fiction writers. Their conclusions are aimed more at describing what is revealed about the writers by the religious content of their work rather than vice versa, but their model is interesting and useful to us nonetheless.

First, Frisch and Martos suggest that all religions, real or fictional, have comprehensive cosmologies, and so must reduce reality to fundamental images. Religion is not adept at coping with complexity or the possibility that in all areas of life there are, in addition to black and white, also shades of grey. This is called fundamentalising, which is characterised by the inclination to dichotomic thinking, believing that a thing is either one or the other but never neither or both. The religion will describe basic realities, such as, to use Frisch and Martos' (1985: 11) examples "god/devil, or creation/duration/destruction." The utopian Roddenberry vision for the original series (*TOS*) to some extent exhibited this trait, most notably in the episode "Let That Be Your Last Battlefield" (1969), where the characters of Bele and Lokai are, both ideologically and physically, with their half-black, half-white faces, mirror images of each other. By the final *TOS* film, Kirk is starting to realize the difficulty of this approach. As he confesses to Spock: "You're a great one for logic. I'm a great one for rushing in where angels fear to tread. We're both extremists. Reality is probably somewhere in between." *DS9*'s murky, less clear-cut universe is a significant step forward in this respect.

Second, according to Frisch and Martos, religion is primarily concerned with meanings of life and existence, hence the habit of ultimatising, characterised by an inward-looking preoccupation with values and the underlying meaning of events. Frisch and Martos (1985: 17) cite *Star Trek* as a series that addressed ultimate values in the conflict between "Spock's reliance on rationality and Kirk's affectivity," a conflict commented on directly by the characters themselves in the scene from *The Undiscovered Country* (1991) quoted earlier. A religion likewise lays down before its adherents a view of those things that are most important.

Finally, negotiation between the first two traits, according to Frisch and Martos, leads to moralising and the preoccupation with how people should respond to the realities, both internal and external, and the ultimate values the religion describes. *Star Trek* is particularly adept at this, one particularly notable example being the closing speech given by Picard in the film *Generations* (1994), in which Picard ultimatises the nature of Time and then moralises about our response: "Someone once told me that Time was a predator that stalked us all our lives, but I rather believe that Time is a companion who goes with us on the journey; reminds us to cherish every moment, because they'll never come again. What we leave behind isn't as important as how we've lived."

In religions, according to Frisch and Martos, it is this moralising trait that is apt to cause religious belief to become religiosity—the phenomenon by which behavior becomes more important than belief. The rituals and procedures of the religion overcome those understandings about the world that originally gave rise to them and become simplified into dogmas and idols. Frisch and Martos make two conclusions from their analysis. The first is that religious science fiction writing is indicative of a deep, if often unrecognized, religious belief. The second is that when science fiction is critical of religion, it is not religion per se but religiosity, which is the target.

This latter claim is supported by the results of Norman Beswick's survey of religion in science fiction, which appears in the journal *Foundation*. Beswick (1991: 26) describes the so-called Golden Age of science fiction (roughly the early 1940s to mid-1950s) as a period in which "religious institutions [were used] as symbols of reaction and obscurantism, contrasted with the progressive openness of science." This is hardly an original observation, but Beswick's survey of the phenomenon is thorough. What is interesting about both the Beswick study and the Frisch/Martos analysis is that they share with the writers of science fiction a tendency, if not indeed a preoccupation, to detach religion from God. The religiosity of the writers of science fiction is matched by a religiosity on the part of those who comment upon it. Frisch and Martos, Norman Beswick, and others discuss the structures of the imagined religion rather than the imagined gods. In many cases this is entirely appropriate, but in the case of *DS9*, the nature of the gods themselves is at least as important as the practices surrounding them. It is this striking model of the divine that sets *DS9* apart from other religious science fiction, but it also leads to a problematic model of respect for religion.

UTOPIA

The original *Star Trek* series bore witness to a belief on Roddenberry's part that moral and technological development would run in parallel, leading to an interplanetary age in which war, crime, and other of humankind's less attractive impulses would be eliminated. This vision has been referred to by fans as "the optimism effect" (Lichtenberg et al. 1975: 106 ff.), and is the key to our analysis of the way in which *Star Trek* in general, and *DS9* in particular, treats religion. It will be seen that *Star Trek* implicitly (and *TNG* explicitly) places religious belief among those traits which give way to the enlightened age of the Federation. *DS9* presents a more sophisticated and detailed examination of religion, yet although apparently taking a more positive attitude, in the end *DS9* takes the same stance.[1]

Star Trek Lives! (Lichtenberg et al. 1975), written in the interval between the original series and the release of *Star Trek: The Motion Picture* (1979) (the animated series notwithstanding) eulogises about this vision to a considerable extent. Lichtenberg et al., writing as fans, suggest that the key word for an understanding of *Star Trek* is optimism, and that it is this "optimism effect" which attracted such a large audience to the show, especially against the background of the Vietnam War. Story editor Dorothy Fontana is quoted as saying that the message communicated by *Star Trek* is that "we've survived this irrational and pretty illogical time of our development and have gone on, gotten past that danger to be better human beings" (1975: 108).

Other participants in the original series have also lent support to this view, and they all credit Roddenberry as being the man who gave *Star Trek* this utopian appeal. Gene Roddenberry, it seems, was a man whose great faith in a better future, and whose iron grip on his creation, inspired and uplifted many of his series' viewers with the assurance that however bad the current situation may be, things are bound to improve. Media studies scholars John Tulloch and Henry Jenkins (1995: 44) certainly see it in this way and describe *Star Trek* as having both an "ideological project" and a "utopian mission."

For Darko Suvin, prolific writer on science fiction, the genre of science fiction and the genre of utopia are closely linked. Suvin regards utopia as being inherently non-religious, even though the father of the genre, Thomas More, died for his faith and became a saint of the Roman Catholic Church. More's *Utopia* devotes a lengthy concluding section to the description of an imagined religion, so More clearly believed that, whether it be Christianity or not, some form of religion was an essential or inevitable component of any utopian society. For Suvin (1988: 34), however, in his *Positions and Presuppositions in Science Fiction*, a utopia cannot include Christianity or any other faith, because utopian societies must, by definition, be established by humanity's own efforts:

> As different from religious ideas about other worlds such as Paradise or Hell, utopia is an historically alternative wishful construct. Its islands, valleys, communities or worlds are constructed by natural intelligent beings—human or humanoid—by their own forces, without transcendental support or intervention. Utopia is Other World immanent to the world of human or at least psychozoic endeavour, dominion and hypothetic possibility—and not transcendental in a religious sense.

Suvin suggests that science fiction and utopian fiction begin from the same point. Both transpose their characters and their relationships into radically different locations. Both devise unique communities because both are bearing witness to the desire for alternative possibilities for the world and its people. Both require the reader (or the viewer) to grasp not only new ideas but new means of conveying such ideas.

If we accept Suvin's definition, we can confidently place *Star Trek*, as envisioned by Gene Roddenberry, into the genre of utopia. *Star Trek* imagines a world separated, in this case by time, from our own, where those things that make our own world imperfect and that we would wish to change have ceased to trouble us. Races mingle together; technology is our servant (and when it is not it is swiftly vanquished); peace reigns; there is no poverty, no famine, very little crime, and as Suvin would expect, no religion. It is also, as Suvin insists that it should be, an historical proposition. It is presented as a world built from our own world.

Following the death of Gene Roddenberry in October 1991 this utopian vision of the Federation has passed. Certainly, toward the end of

Star Trek: The Next Generation (*TNG*), Captain Picard had become an island of virtue in a sea of corrupt or compromised Starfleet admirals. The pre-publicity for *DS9*, a series with which Roddenberry had almost no involvement, declared that it would be an altogether more serious and "gritty" series. This has proven to be the case. The enlightened optimism of *TOS* and early *TNG* has given way to a more brutal universe rife with subterfuge and hidden agendas. That *DS9* is rewriting the Roddenberry schema becomes most clear in the episode unsubtly titled "Paradise Lost" (1996), wherein the Federation is repeatedly described, without a hint of irony, as "paradise." In this episode, feuding officers accuse each other of trying to undermine the Federation by exposing it to the threat of infiltration by the Dominion, an empire of shape-shifting aliens from the other side of the Bajoran wormhole. The truth, it is revealed, is that "paradise" is being destroyed not from without but from within and has ceased to be anything of the kind. By this point in the series even the peace treaty between the Federation and the Klingon Empire, the crowning achievement of the Roddenberry vision, suggesting that even the deadliest of enemies can get along with each other, gives way to war. It is into this background that religion first becomes prominent in the *Star Trek* universe.

The Suvinian pairing of science fiction and utopia suggests a reason why religion becomes prominent only once "paradise" is lost. In *Star Trek's* early days Starfleet, as imagined by Roddenberry, represented a highly technological culture in which all needs were met by manufactured devices. Where all human need is met by technology, God is no longer a necessity; the world is created and controlled by mortals. As Suvin suggests, such a utopian vision is inherently non-religious, if not anti-religious, as borne out by the tenor of *TOS* and *TNG*. There is no place in this "paradise" for religion.

In distinction to the utopian tenor of *TOS* and *TNG*, in *DS9* a number of characters are critical of Starfleet as an environment which makes humanity dependent on technology to the extent that it has dulled instinct and sensitivity. *DS9* thus begins to move away from *Star Trek's* early Roddenberry-inspired utopian vision by suggesting that humanity/Starfleet can no longer rely entirely on its own works to sustain it. With the decline of the utopia, something more is needed. What emerges, in *DS9*, is religion.

The acceptance of religion as a legitimate endeavour in *DS9* is contrary not only to *Star Trek's* own history but to that of science fiction in general. As a matter of literary history, science fiction has been hostile to religion, and *TOS* continued this tradition. One of science fiction's early principles was that science would explain those mysteries hitherto accounted for by faith. Roddenberry's utopian vision of humanity developing its technology into a future where all needs are provided for affirms this view by juxtaposing technological sophistication with human contentment and harmony. Roddenberry was reportedly not a religious man, although he was raised a Baptist (Harrison et al. 1996). *TOS* reflects Roddenberry's hostility to religion, and there are several episodes in which Captain Kirk and his crew liberate the locals from the shackles of their religious belief. This "liberation" is accomplished in one of two ways: either by demonstrating to them that their religion is false ("Return of the Archons" 1967) or by persuading them that it is unnecessary ("The Apple" 1967). That Kirk and, in *TNG*, Picard (e.g. "Justice," 1987) reveal religion to be false and unnecessary clearly places religion alongside warmongering in the realm of primitive practices that the Federation has grown beyond. It is significant that, when religions do arise in *Star Trek*, they are not religions that have been practiced on Earth. Earth's religions, we may assume, passed away as humans moved into the enlightenment of the Federation, which was then carried to the stars.

Thirty years after *TOS,* the circumstances under which *Star Trek* is being produced and broadcast are quite differen,t and this is bound to affect the content of the programme. If the original series was borne of the liberal climate of the 1960s, *DS9* has a very different social pedigree, which it nevertheless tries to blend with the Roddenberry optimism, a necessary survival strategy, according to Jim McClellan (1996) writing in the British newspaper, *The Guardian Review*:

> *Star Trek* championed liberalism, optimism and tolerance. It took on board the ideas of the civil rights movement and the Space Race. Launched from the heart of the American century, it seemed to suggest that we were all headed onwards and upwards. The strength of that original idea is its weakness today. In times of political cynicism and diminished social ambition, *Star Trek's* faith in big (interplanetary) government looks rather dated, especially when set against the anti-government paranoia of *The X Files*.

DS9's more sophisticated approach to religion may be a result of this less confident social background and the quite different premise necessitated by it. The model of enlightened, liberating humans works properly only in the context of *TOS* because the scenario of that series is much more limited than that of *DS9*. Kirk and his crew were largely complementary to the universe, like the detached visitor who arrives in utopia and reports upon it. They were the ones who travelled, and the Federation and the Klingons were like opposing tribes roaming a desert of isolated communities, seeking to assimilate them. *TNG* then began the process in which representatives of other cultures could participate in the ongoing narrative to a much greater extent. A large multi-species cast of characters is now seen to populate the Federation, and many of these alien races play recurring roles. In this pluralistic environment it is much less possible for the Federation to drop by, sow its own ideas among alien species, and then move on without regard to consequences, as happens in *TOS*. Although some of the original series' episodes explore such consequences, in general the question of the Federation's impact on other peoples does not arise. In *DS9*, however, the situation is almost reversed: the space station *DS9* is stationary, offering other species the chance to bring new ideas to Starfleet personnel. Indeed, Sisko initially receives from the wormhole aliens treatment similar to that received by the "primitive" alien cultures visited by Kirk. He is brought from his own limited understanding of the universe to a broader and more enlightened one.

It was clear from the opening episode of *DS9*, "Emissary" (1993), that the religious aspect of the series was to be a major one, and the groundwork was laid for future development of religious issues. This development takes place over many episodes, and given that the series is still in production, we should be mindful that new episodes may enhance or overturn earlier assumptions about the faith. As *DS9* has progressed, attention has been paid to the Bajoran religion less often, and episodes dealing with it have become more peripeteian. So, for example, in "Accession" (1996) and in "Rapture" (1997) major shifts in our perception of Sisko's role in the religion have taken place. The status of Captain Sisko within the Bajoran religion, his response to the Bajoran faith, and his own role within it, become the focus for understanding the portrayal and treatment of religion in *DS9*.

MESSIAH

The role of Captain Sisko is central both to *DS9* as a narrative and to our argument that the series takes steps both forward and back in the treatment of religion by science fiction. We have already seen that *DS9* rewrites the earlier *Star Trek* mythos in order that a perfect society should give way to a more morally and politically uncertain world whose people once again have recourse to find answers to spiritual questions. The inter-action between the culture of Starfleet and Bajoran spirituality proves no less problematic than the increased political and military confrontations with which Sisko also has to deal.

As the characters in *DS9* grapple with religious issues, so too does the series itself. The transitions the series undergoes with respect to religion take place in both Sisko's own words and actions as a character, and in the nature of the relationship between him and the wormhole aliens who are worshipped by the Bajorans. This latter relationship is the most significant part of our claim that the series undermines its own intentions to present a more sophisticated religious debate. What follows is an examination of how the character of Sisko came to be invested with religious status, and what his response to this status tells us about *DS9*'s position on faith.

In *DS9*'s opening episode Sisko discovers a "stable wormhole" and communicates directly with the aliens within it. The wormhole and the aliens are regarded by the Bajorans as the Celestial Temple and the Prophets, respectively. The worship and terminology surrounding the aliens equates their status as prophets with divinity. In discovering the wormhole, Sisko fulfils ancient Bajoran prophecies and takes his place as a central figure in Bajoran religion known as "the Emissary." His subse-quent twofold status as Starfleet officer and religious leader is one of the series' continuing tensions and first becomes a serious issue in the episode "In the Hands of the Prophets" (1993). It is here that the series first grap-ples with the conflicts which may arise between a fundamentally spiritual people and a secular authority such as Starfleet.

The episode "In the Hands of the Prophets" (1993) opens with Keiko O'Brien, the wife of a Starfleet officer, being interrupted in the multi-racial school she has opened on Deep Space Nine by Vedek Winn during a lecture on the wormhole. Winn interrupts the lesson to contra-dict Mrs O'Brien's scientific account of the phenomenon with a religious one. The following exchange ensues:

WINN: Do you believe that the Celestial Temple of the Prophets exists within the passage?

KEIKO: I respect that the Bajoran people believe that it does.

WINN: But that's not what you teach.

KEIKO: No. I don't teach Bajoran spiritual beliefs. That's your job. Mine is to open the children's minds to history, to literature, to mathematics, to science.

There are a number of things happening in this exchange, which encapsulate both the attempt by *DS9* to take a more sophisticated approach to religious issues, and the re-enforcement of the separation between secular and religious systems in which this model of religion is, we shall find, bound to result.

Keiko O'Brien is teaching within the utopia of the Federation. This means that for her the religious perspective is not "open-minded" and lies outside the boundaries of an academic point of view. Nevertheless, she accepts that there are those within her tutelage who are not yet fully participant in the utopia and may not, therefore, fully appreciate her standpoint. By so doing she actively attempts to accommodate both Bajoran and Starfleet perspectives, but she declines to take a second step when she states that it is not her responsibility to address the alternative (religious) view.

Partitioning the scientific and religious approaches to the study of the wormhole may be considered appropriate to the extent that it is an application of *Star Trek's* Prime Directive (the principle that Federation officers should not interfere with the development of other cultures). Where the practice becomes more questionable is in Mrs. O'Brien's stated view that the alternative (religious) perspective is to be totally absent from the classroom. As she says: "That's your job." The Federation, she implies, has moved beyond religion to the extent that religion is no longer part of public consciousness, and hence does not enter the curriculum. Religion is a private interest and may only be taught as such, regardless of the fact that the school in question exists within a culture where religious belief plays a major role, and includes children from that culture.

This point about the cultural context of the school is made by Major Kira, the character who bridges the Federation ("tolerant" atheist utopia) and Bajoran ("primitive" religious culture) perspectives and who takes the Bajoran side in this dispute. Fictionally, this is what one would expect her, as a Bajoran, to do. However, it is a shock to the expectations of the *Star Trek* viewer to see a character who has, over many episodes, been consistently seen within a Starfleet environment and so become identified with the Starfleet utopia, side against Starfleet outside the usual context of becoming an enemy agent, as happens, for example, in "The Maquis" (1994) and *Star Trek: Voyager's* "State of Flux" (1995).

That Major Kira sides against Sisko on the school issue is crucial for the exploration of Sisko's status as the Emissary, which takes place in this and subsequent episodes. Kira's argument is that the Bajoran context of the school makes a revision of the curriculum to include the Bajoran faith appropriate. Mrs. O'Brien's response—that she is teaching science—is consistent with the early *Star Trek* position and the tradition of the fathers of science fiction which holds that science is supreme. Science offers answers that may not be questioned. This position is affirmed by Mrs. O'Brien's subsequent suggestion that philosophy is to be taught outside the classroom, and it is at this point that Sisko states his own position. "My philosophy," he says, "is that there is room for all philosophies on this station." Sisko will later contradict this statement, first in favor of Starfleet ("Destiny"), and later in favor of the Bajorans ("Rapture").[2]

By *DS9*'s fourth season, war is on the horizon, and the apparent utopia of the Federation may be less perfect than it seems. The actions and the ideals Sisko professes are inconsistent, and Kira's assertion that there may be no solution to the problem of Deep Space Nine's school is correct. When Sisko meets with Vedek Winn, he flatly contradicts her by denying that he is the Emissary. At this point in the proceedings there is no compromise to be had, either within the narrative or within the series. On the one hand, Sisko states that there is "room for all philosophies" on the station, and on the other hand, he actively discourages the Bajoran belief that he is their Emissary to the Prophets. Steps forward and back are taken in more or less equal measure. The series reveals both a willingness to address the religious perspective, but also an unwillingness to let the religious perspective govern events.

"In the Hands of the Prophets" is being more cautious than the later episode "Destiny" in that the former blends with its mature exploration of the conflict between secular and religious culture the implication that Vedek Winn and, at this point, Vedek Bareil are power-mongering. To this extent the debate is undermined by the ascription of an ulterior motive to some of the players. It is these hidden motives that enable Sisko to be seen to be in dispute with Vedek Winn without being critical of the Bajoran faith, and the honour of his position is reinforced by the speeches of tolerance that he delivers to others. He tells his son Jake that religion is a "matter of interpretation" and the fact that Jake holds a different view from someone else does not make the other's view wrong. Nevertheless, Sisko's conversations with Vedek Winn in this and subsequent episodes make it clear that he does not share her beliefs, and in "In the Hands of the Prophets" he does his best to ensure that these beliefs are not propagated in the station school. That the cultural conflict is really one of interpretation is also the point put to Sisko himself by Kira in "Destiny" after he is confronted by an ex-Vedek who tells him that a prophecy is about to be fulfilled that could destroy the wormhole. At this point Sisko's ideals of tolerance break down, despite his continued profession of them. Furthermore, in "Destiny" Sisko also argues that it is the lack of a religious dimension to the relationships on the station hitherto that has enabled the Starfleet personnel and the Bajorans to come closer together. Yet, with Bajoran society so steeped in religion, it is a dimension Sisko is foolish to ignore, as he starts to recognize in "Destiny" when he consults the prophecies concerning the Emissary and faces the fact that they may indeed refer to himself.

"Destiny" begins with a team of Cardassian scientists who wish to conduct an experiment with the wormhole to enable communication through it. Yarka, an excommunicated Vedek, tells Sisko of a prophecy which appears to indicate that such an action will be calamitous. Nevertheless, Sisko permits the experiment to proceed. It appears at first that the prophecy is to be fulfilled and that the wormhole will collapse, but Sisko is able to prevent the disaster and both he and Yarka realize that the prophecy has been fulfilled in a way that neither expected.

Throughout "Destiny" Sisko denies, as until this point he has always sought to do, that he is the Emissary. He also denies, or at best refuses to consider, the prophecy about which he has been warned. It has, he says, "no place on the bridge of the *Defiant*" (the *Defiant* being the Federation battleship attached to Deep Space Nine). Implied by this statement is the conviction that the only legitimate place for religion is in the temple or church, where it cannot affect "real-life" decisions not wholly connected with the religion itself. That this is Sisko's view is also made clear by his discussion with Yarka at the beginning of the episode:

YARKA: That is why I came to you, Emissary, because I have faith in you. I know that you will do what must be done.

SISKO: Vedek, I have the utmost respect for your beliefs but I have no intention of calling this project off.

YARKA: I hope that you will reconsider, Emissary. My followers and I will remain on the station and pray that you change your mind.

SISKO: You are free to do that, of course.

Reasonable as this approach of Sisko's appears to be, the moment after Yarka has left, Sisko orders Kira to have him investigated and to ensure that he and his followers do not cause trouble while the Cardassian scientists are aboard the station. This in itself is hardly an act of respect for the Vedek's faith and suggests that Sisko's words are just for show. Furthermore, Sisko refuses not only to act upon but also even to consider the warning given to him. The Vedek's belief and the prophecy itself have no impact on Sisko's world. He does not need to act upon them because they have no reality for him. His perception of events is different, as he says: "Where you see a Sword of Stars I see a comet. Where you see Vipers I see three scientists and where you see the Emissary I see a Starfleet Officer." His respect for the prophecy is seen to be limited to, and limiting of, the environment in which it is discussed, and this is symptomatic of the way in which such respect works. Sisko is willing to respect the beliefs of the Bajorans only to the extent that they are not allowed to affect or intersect with the operation of the space station. Effectively he is denying that religion makes claims about reality.

This is the same approach as that taken in the episode "In the Hands of the Prophets" by Mrs. O'Brien, whose conversation with Vedek Winn has the same effect. Her statement that teaching about the beliefs of the Bajorans is Winn's job indicates that it has no place in school, just as the prophecy Yarka delivers has no place on the bridge of the *Defiant*. While both Sisko and Mrs. O'Brien state that they respect Bajoran beliefs, they are in fact placing a barrier between religious belief and the world. By stating that the prophecy has no place on the bridge of the *Defiant* Sisko is attempting to make religious belief a thing which affects only those who hold it. This view does not recognize what religious belief actually is, as it suggests that belief is unconcerned with life decisions and the course of history. As presented, religion is no more significant than culinary practices—strictly a matter of taste. However, it is in the nature of faith that it cannot be only an internal preoccupation. Religion, and faith in it, makes claims to truth and knowledge that reach beyond the individual believer.

RESPECT

Frisch and Martos describe this inward-looking tendency as ultimatising, and in terms of their analysis, the Bajoran faith exhibits most strongly this second of the three traits (fundamentalising, ultimatising and moralising) that they identify as central to science fiction portrayals of religion. This trait, possibly as a result of the series' early spiritual focus, gives *DS9* as a whole a much more introspective and cerebral atmosphere than the rest of the *Star Trek* franchise. The Bajoran Vedeks are not prone to fundamentalising. They speak of the wormhole and the Prophets not in terms of universal significance but in the specific context relevant to them. When Vedek Yarka, in "Destiny," exhorts Sisko to prevent the Cardassian experiments, he does not foretell cosmic devastation or the end of time. He is concerned with particular events and particular moments in time, and most importantly for the argument to come, his concern is specific to Bajor. The Bajoran faith may have prophecies and doctrines about the beginning and end of time, but we do not hear (or have not yet heard) about them. Belief in the Prophecies is regarded as important not for an understanding of the universe, but as a mechanism by which Bajoran lives are given meaning. It is in these terms that the use of the faith as a support through the occupation of Bajor by the Cardassians makes sense.

This approach to religion is a clear step forward from the Frisch/Martos model in which dogmatic believers characterise each and every event in terms of their belief system. Nevertheless, there is an important way in which the approach taken in *DS9* also upholds that model. As presented in *DS9*, the Bajoran faith must be regarded as a paradigm for religious belief as a whole: this is what religion is, and this is what religious people do. Frisch and Martos, as well as Norman Beswick, observed a tendency among science fiction writers to portray religion as religiosity. In this sense, the religion is not portrayed as a system of belief but as a pattern of behaviour. Where religion is present in a text in order to be criticised, it is this model of religion that is easiest to attack. Whereas on Earth there are many different religions, on Bajor there is only one, and it is offered to the viewer as a model comprising many, though not all, of those elements we take to make up a religion. Bajoran religion has its own sects, its own offices, its own festivals and its own scriptures. One thing that it does not have is the problem of interacting with other faiths. Instead, it must interact with a secular Starfleet. Just as a country seeking membership of the European Union or a member state wishing to join the single currency must fulfill certain criteria, so must a planet seeking to join the Federation match the Federation's standards. It is not, of course, the case that the Federation insists upon the abandonment of religion, but we are repeatedly shown how religious conflict interferes with Starfleet's ability to do its job. It is possible that Sisko could see his role in assisting the Bajoran Provisional Government and preparing Bajor for membership in the Federation as including weaning the Bajorans from their religious beliefs. In "Accession," for example, Sisko makes it clear that the Federation will not accept the reintroduction of a caste system which Sisko's replacement as Emissary demands. Thus, even if the religion itself is not rejected, it seems that its teaching might be.[3]

It is this fact that makes the *DS9* approach to religion problematic. In the context of the model of the divine, which we shall discuss later, it will be seen to have most serious consequences. Religions make claims about the nature of the universe and of the obligations of the people within it. Religions also usually require their adherents to encourage others to believe as they do. This is why, if Sisko and *DS9* genuinely attempt to "respect" religious belief, the approach taken is not only inadequate but achieves the opposite of the intended effect. Respecting religious belief becomes, in *DS9*, less an exercise in addressing the insights and perspectives that faith has to offer, and more a means of maintaining public order. This is clear from Sisko's stated desire to prevent Yarka from creating trouble on the space station in "Destiny" and from the events in the episode "In the Hands of the Prophets," as well as in the trilogy of episodes that opens the series' second season, in which a nationalist movement and a religious order form a political alliance that causes violent civil unrest. If Sisko achieves the respect that he describes, then he will have peace on the space station, but he will also be denying the Bajorans the opportunity to spread their faith, if this is what they wish to do. Those they seek to convert will place the wall of respect between them, accepting that this is what religious people do, and that they as non-religious people need not be affected by it. It is akin to accepting that one's colleague likes the music of Strauss when personally one prefers Bartok. One is content that they should listen to Strauss provided that they do not force others to listen to it. In return one will not force Bartok upon those who prefer not to hear it. Treating religious belief as a choice no more significant than this one is not merely rejecting, but not even acknowledging, the claims religion makes. Believers must first convince others that it is necessary to have belief, and then that their own beliefs are the correct ones.

In the case of "Destiny" the marginalization of religious truth claims may not matter, because the prophecy is fulfilled despite Sisko's attempts to ignore it. It made no difference whether Sisko believed in the prophecy or not, for he fulfilled the role the Bajorans believe was allotted to him. What we shall find to be problematic is the nature of this fulfilment. While initially it may appear that the episode is placing the sceptics who denied the validity of the prophecy in the wrong, the reverse is actually the case. The fulfilment of the prophecy ultimately depends upon scientific intercession—upon, in other words, "something Starfleet." Religious writings may have foreseen events, the episode informs us, but the events themselves are scientifically explicable.[4]

The tension between Sisko's perspectives as Emissary and as Starfleet officer become their most stark in the episode "Accession," where a number of new aspects of the Bajoran faith are introduced, and where we discover that Sisko has been quietly mellowing in his attitude to his status as Emissary. While he appears content to offer blessings to Bajorans when requested to do so, it is nevertheless clear from what he says to Dax that he still does not believe he is the foretold Emissary, and he is delighted to relinquish the title when given the opportunity to do so. "No more ceremonies to attend," he says. "No more blessings to give. No more prophecies to fulfil. I'm just a Starfleet Officer again. All I have to worry about are the Klingons, the Dominion and the Maquis. I feel like I'm on vacation." Whereas Kira and others see the return to the old ways introduced by the new Emissary as a matter of faith, Sisko insists, as he does in "Destiny," on seeing it in terms of his mission as a Starfleet officer. If the new Emissary succeeds in reintroducing the caste system, Bajor will not be allowed to join the Federation and Sisko will have failed in his mission. As in "The Circle" (1993) and "The Siege" (1993), what is for the Bajorans a spiritual upheaval is for Sisko an issue of public order. In the case of both "Accession" and "Destiny" the solution to problems which arise from religious conflict is shown to be the appropriation of contested religious issues into a secular context . Ultimately, the model of the divine that *DS9* proposes does this for religion as a whole.

Sisko's initial reluctance to take on the role of Emissary results from his fear that he will become, as Kira puts it, "a religious icon." He has no similar qualms about adopting the role of the social revolutionary Gabriel Bell in the two-part episode "Past Tense" (1994–1995) because the cause involved is one in which he believes. His reticence to adopt the role of Emissary is indicative of the fact that, no matter how much he may respect the beliefs of the Bajorans, he is not willing to address these beliefs on their own terms. His admission in "Destiny" that the prophecy appeared to be coming true is made with great reluctance, and when speaking with Kira he insists that any interpretation of her beliefs that would persuade him to consider the prophecy must be a scientific one. "Something concrete," he insists. "Something Starfleet." This view echoes the *Star Trek* franchise's original emphasis on a civilised scientific utopia bringing reason to primitives. When the prophecy is fulfilled at the end of "Destiny" it comes true in an unexpected way, through the use of sophisticated technology. It is therefore fulfilled, as Sisko had hoped, by "something Starfleet." Starfleet secularises religious beliefs by contextualizing them within a reductionistic scientific and technological framework.

Thus, Sisko can continue with his respect but distance himself from Bajoran religious beliefs. This allows him to continue to put primary emphasis on his position as a Starfleet officer and to minimize his role as the Emissary.

A similar situation emerges in the episode "Accession." Although Sisko has apparently internalized the lessons of "Destiny" and settled into his role as Emissary, he nonetheless takes the opportunity to use the Prophecies to demonstrate that he is not the Emissary once a Bajoran candidate for the role arrives. When he seeks to wrest the role back it is not because he has become convinced of the truth of his position as the true Emissary, but because he is concerned about losing a potential new member of the Federation. His motivations are still contextualized within his role as a Starfleet officer, and not within his religious role. When, in "Rapture" Sisko appears at last fully to accept that he has been chosen by the Prophets, his acceptance of this role takes place as the result of a technological accident, the effects of which are medically counteracted at the end of the episode. Even here, where Sisko comes to fully accept and embrace his religious role as the Emissary, the scientific and technological emphasis of Starfleet is used to counteract the religious perspective.

"Rapture" progresses logically from where "Accession" left off. At the beginning of the episode Sisko admits that he is again, as in "Accession," taking advantage of his status as Emissary to achieve personal ends, albeit in this case in a very minor way, to gain private access to a religious artifact. Although he began to reflect upon his role as Emissary in the episode "Destiny," the results of this reflection appear to be a willingness only to play the role, rather than to accept it fully. Having defended his position as Emissary in "Accession," Sisko is more open to it than in the past. By the end of "Rapture" there can be little doubt that he has fully accepted the responsibilities of the position. He makes prophecies of his own, greets adoring crowds, sides with the Bajorans against Starfleet, and re-enforces his position as Emissary by following up his discovery of the Celestial Temple with finding B'hala, the Sacred Lost City of Bajor. This done, even the formerly sceptical Kai Winn apparently accepts him as Emissary.

"Rapture" is significant for our argument in three respects. First, the episode presents a new dimension of Sisko's role as Emissary. Second, it further highlights the conflict between secular and religious cultures by relocating a character from a secular to a spiritual framework. Finally, the episode offers the possibility that the same set of events can legitimately be contextualized within both secular and religious terms. This last point will form the final part of our discussion, and provide the most curious model of respect.

In "Rapture" Sisko starts using religious language and those around him—his officers—find themselves bound to defend him to his own superiors. Dr. Bashir seems to accept that his own medical explanation for Sisko's "visions" may not be the only legitimate one, and Worf says to Kira: "Your gods have granted the Captain a powerful vision." Sisko himself now seems to think that the Prophets, or wormhole aliens, may indeed be using him for their own purposes. The possibility that Sisko has developed a faith in the Bajoran religion is sufficient to worry Admiral Whatley, who sees Sisko's status among the Bajorans as problematic for Starfleet. When Sisko lurches into the conference room to prevent the seal being put on Bajoran membership in the Federation the Admiral's fears seem borne out. Sisko has finally acted fully from within his religious role as the Emissary, rather than from within his role as a Starfleet officer.

Sisko's acceptance of the role of Emissary stems from the visions he has been receiving from the Prophets since the accident that initiated his changed relationship to the role. The visions Sisko receives from the Prophets, however, come to threaten his life. The situation is ultimately resolved with the secular Starfleet pattern; a medical rather than a spiritual solution saves Sisko's life. What has changed is the gloss put on this fact. Dr. Bashir is not dogmatic about what it is that is happening to Sisko. He merely states that he can put a stop to it using medical technology, regardless of the cause. The episode maintains an escape clause whereby the event is to be seen in a purely secular context, but it also reveals more willingness to allow either the secular or the religious context to be legitimated.

MODELS

This brings us to the final part of our analysis. In "Rapture" the most significant statement is Worf's comment, quoted earlier, regarding the Prophets. His description of them as "your gods," can be interpreted in either of two ways. First, there is the now familiar interpretation that implies: "The beings whom you worship as gods." An alternative interpretation, and the one this chapter suggests is implied by the series, is: "The beings whom to you are gods."

These apparently similar statements are in fact loaded with differences. It is characteristic of gods in science fiction television that they have parochial concerns. Such gods are frequently shown to limit their interest to a single race. Their interest in other races is constrained by the extent to which those other races interact with the primary race. In *DS9* the wormhole aliens are seen to exist in a different relationship to the universe from the beings around them. The wormhole aliens, for example, have no conception of "linear time." The problems Sisko encounters in conversing with them devolve from this fact. This fact also enables Kira to attempt a justification of her faith to Sisko in "Destiny" and Sisko to justify his defence of the faith to Jake in "In the Hands of the Prophets," as discussed later in this chapter. Since the aliens have a different relationship to time from other life forms in the series, they are able simultaneously to see the past, the present, and the future. So it is that they may be described as, or capable of being, prophets. On the series' terms it may also be sufficient to credit them with divinity. If it is, then the implications are considerable.

As we have seen, the aliens in *DS9* communicate, or are believed to communicate, with the Bajorans by means of the orbs. Sisko is the first person known to have communicated with them directly. It is this fact, and the brokering by him of an agreement to allow the passage of ships through the wormhole, which causes Sisko to be designated the Emissary. Given that the aliens have knowledge of past and future events they must have made a choice, or have known, that it would be Sisko who would initiate these events. In this sense they are directly participating in Bajoran history in a way favorable to the Bajorans. They, and no one else, have the power to make these things happen. Similarly, in "Prophet Motive" (1995), the aliens are seen to intercede in the affairs of another race, the Ferengi, in a radical and hugely significant way. They take it upon themselves to alter the nature of a whole race by changing the personality of the Ferengi Grand Nagus Zek, "the financial leader of [the Ferengi] people," as he is described. They and no one else have the power to do this, and it is an awesome power. Quark, another Ferengi, and Sisko can do nothing more than argue their cases for survival in the face of it. That both are successful indicates a benevolence on the part of the aliens.

This benevolence is emphasised by the aliens' behaviour vis-à-vis the orbs. The claim of the Bajorans that they are sent by the Prophets is never explicitly substantiated, but there is a clear link between the orbs and the aliens established both in "Emissary" and "Prophet Motive." At the very least the aliens are content for the Bajorans to have the orbs. The experiences of those who look into them and those who enter (rather than pass through) the wormhole are similar and at least one orb, described by

Vedek Bareil as "the Third Orb—the Orb of Prophecy and Change," enables those who look into it to see, in a limited and vague way, into the future.

If it is the case that the aliens have allowed the Bajorans to hold and to use the orbs and that they have communicated to them information about their future by this means, then we might infer that they possess and exercise a proprietorial interest over the Bajorans and their affairs. Weight is given to this view by their actions in "Accession," when Sisko invites them to arbitrate in a dispute nominally about whether he or Akorum is the Emissary. In fact, the dispute is about the future development of Bajor, and the aliens clearly take a partial view. Similarly, albeit less clearly, in "Rapture" the aliens seem to guide Sisko toward the discovery of the lost city of B'hala and warn against membership in the Federation. Why the aliens should do this is not clear, but the fact that they do so— and more importantly, the fact that they have the power to enforce their decisions—places a unique significance on the nature of the relationship between the wormhole aliens and the Bajorans. It is this relationship that is being described by the series as divinity.

The relationship is one of a disequilibrium of empowerment. The implication inherent in this relationship is that it is not the ontology of, but the relationship between, participants which defines the nature of the beings involved. Beings are gods not in and of themselves but only in relationship to others of less ability, knowledge, or power. This is a tremendously important claim to be making in any circumstances, but in the particular circumstances of *DS9* it gives support to the view that religious belief is a local and private matter. If the relationship between the Bajorans and the wormhole aliens is the heart of the religion, then it is perfectly in order for Starfleet to leave the Bajorans to their religion because Starfleet's own relationship with the wormhole aliens is quite different. Thus Captain Sisko, in "Rapture," can tell Admiral Whatley that he will work for the admission of the Bajorans to the Federation both in his capacity as a Starfleet officer and as the Emissary.

The wormhole aliens in *DS9* have the power to guide the development of the Bajorans in the direction they choose by giving knowledge to them. They also, as we see in "Accession," make choices on the Bajoran's behalf and appear, as we see in "Rapture," genuinely to be using Sisko to facilitate their decisions. The result of the decision, and the stated disequilibrium in the relationship between the Bajorans and the aliens, Starfleet and the aliens, and the Bajorans and Starfleet, is to affirm the original position that one race, by being in a relationship that defines another race as gods, is in a lesser state of development than other races, because with greater intellectual or technological sophistication the relationship could instead be one nearer to parity. The Bajoran religion, therefore, is revealed to have a tangible basis in fact. Their gods are real and powerful. Their prophecies are seen to be accurate. Having created within the formerly non-religious framework of *Star Trek* an environment in which religion can be a significant aspect of the narrative, the series does not, as might have been the case in the past, simply introduce a hero who reveals to believers the error of their ways. Rather, the hero (Sisko) supports the continuation of the religious tradition. We have seen, however, that these actions are not in all ways performed in the interests of the faith. Sisko uses the faith for his own (non-religious) ends. He also pursues policies to contain the faith and keep it separate from non-religious activities on the space station.

The series establishes a narrative justification for this, in the form of the legitimately different relationships between the Bajorans and the aliens and Starfleet and the aliens, but then undermines the forward-looking opportunities of the series' premise. The cumulative effect of the actions of the characters and framework of the series is to re-enforce the notion that religion is significant only to the extent that it impacts upon the believer. Rather than presenting this view dogmatically, the series uses interaction between Starfleet and Bajoran cultures to present a working model of localised religion, divorcing religion from any universal significance. The position *DS9* finally holds is that where religion exists, then so be it. Where it is absent, so much the better. While beginning with an obvious attempt at a more sophisticated religious debate, *DS9* ends up entrenching the very view with which science fiction began.

NOTES

1. *DS9*'s concern with religious issues is apparent from the opening episode, in which the lead character, Benjamin Sisko, is established as a religious figure. That the tension caused by his reluctance to accept this role is a major dynamic in the framework of the series sets it apart from its predecessors and contemporaries and stakes its claim to be undertaking a more thoughtful exploration of religion than has been made, certainly by science fiction television, in the past.

2. We should note that this noble ideal is a huge leap for a series which has hitherto made it clear that its own society is the model to which all others

should aspire. This model, as we have seen, is one that excluded religious belief and practice. Previously *Star Trek* implied that the Federation had solved all of humankind's problems. As it is rather smugly said in *TNG*'s "Time's Arrow" (1992): "Poverty was eliminated on Earth a long time ago and a lot of things disappeared with it—hopelessness, despair, cruelty." If this wonderful truth is so, then it would be quite in order for other societies, especially one such as the Bajoran society, which is riven with strife, to be guided toward this Federation ideal, Prime Directive or no Prime Directive. This, of course, is overstating the case, but the stirring speeches Captain Picard was known to make about human progress in *TNG*, for example in "Hide and Q" (1987), where he quotes *Hamlet*—"what a piece of work is man"—are conspicuously absent from *DS9*.

3. This is consistent with other *Star Trek* episodes that reject particular religious teachings while upholding the freedom to choose, in principle. See, for example, "Justice," (1987) and "Devil's Due" (1991).

4. It is, of course, true that for many years religious events have been interpreted scientifically. The miracles of Christ have been attributed to various natural, if unusual, causes. The response to such arguments is either to say that religious believers are misguided or that the divine is making use of natural events to further its own ends. *DS9* at this point leaves the question open, but by raising it at all seems to be hedging its bets.

6

(Re)Covering Sacred Ground

New Age Spirituality in
Star Trek: Voyager

DARCEE L. McLAREN
AND JENNIFER E. PORTER

Since *Star Trek*, the original series, first aired in 1966, the worldview portrayed in the series and its three spinoffs has been dominated by science and rational humanism. Issues of religion have typically been marginalized in the *Star Trek* franchise. Although characters such as Spock from the original series (*TOS*), Lieutenant Worf from *Star Trek: The Next Generation* (*TNG*) and Major Kira Nerys from *Star Trek: Deep Space Nine* (*DS9*) have been shown to adhere to spiritual or religious beliefs, religious perspectives are continually superseded by scientific explanations of the universe. All four *Star Trek* series have portrayed a rationalized, demythologized world. With the 1996–1997 season, however, episodes within both *DS9* and *Voyager* have attempted a more nuanced treatment of religion.

In the fourth series, *Voyager,* issues of religion are less marginalized and have been more fully integrated into the series. In episodes such as "The Cloud" (1995), "Cathexis" (1995), "Initiations" (1995), and "Basics, Part I" (1996), religion is portrayed as part of the daily lives of the characters. In these instances, the storylines themselves are not concerned with issues of religion; religion is integrated with the characters'—

particularly Chakotay's—lives and concerns. In other episodes, such as "Tattoo" (1996) and "Sacred Ground" (1996), religion is the focus of the plot. The spirituality portrayed in *Voyager* is individualistic, humanistic, and rationalized, revealing a New Age emphasis. Furthermore, as we will show, this New Age spirituality is compatible with the scientistic and rational humanistic worldview of *Star Trek*. Within the parameters established for the *Star Trek* universe, *Voyager* offers a nuanced portrayal of religion in which science and spirituality are both compatible and legitimate.

The relationship between science and spirituality is explored in *Voyager* through the characters of Captain Kathryn Janeway and her Native American first officer, Commander Chakotay.[1] In *Voyager's* first season, spirituality is confined almost solely to the person of Commander Chakotay. Within the context of the four *Star Trek* series, Chakotay is the first human character shown to have religious faith. In earlier series, characters such as Spock, Worf, and Kira—characters with distinct spiritual beliefs and practices—were always non-human, alien, and distinctly Other[2] Insofar as Chakotay is human, his religious faith is more mainstream and approachable than that of Spock, Worf, or Kira. At the same time, insofar as Chakotay is Native American, his religious faith is marginal, exotic, and also distinctly Other. As historian Daniel Francis (1992: 8) has noted, "non-Natives in North America have long defined themselves in relation to the Other in the form of the Indian." Furthermore, as an intentionally generic Native American, the character of Chakotay is an "imaginary Indian," a white, European representation of what it means to be Native.[3] Like other imagined Indians, Chakotay is a standard against which we measure ourselves (Francis 1992: 8).

The form of spirituality in which Chakotay is seen to engage in *Voyager* portrays a positive standard for a renewed religious practice. Chakotay's religion exemplifies New Age ideals for an individualized and ecologically aware spirituality. According to religious studies scholar James R. Lewis (1992: 10), the idealization and emulation of Native American spirituality represents increasingly dominant trend within the New Age movement. The version of Native spirituality expressed in *Voyager,* including spirit guides, vision quests, soul travel, healing rituals and environmental concern, epitomizes a New Age vision of generic Native American spirituality.[4] Spirit guides are first introduced in the episode "The Cloud" (1995). In this episode, Commander Chakotay teaches Captain Janeway how to contact her own animal spirit guide.[5] From the perspective of the New Age influence, it is interesting to note that these animal spirit guides, or "power animals" as they are called in the New Age context, are contacted with the aid of a technological meditation device.[6] As sociologist Michael York notes (1995: 165), New Agers express a "desire to be close both to nature and to spirit and [to] the changes that advanced technology allows on this score." The juxtaposition of meditation technology and animal spirit guides in this episode is characteristic of New Age spirituality.

In the episode "Cathexis" (1995), two more characteristics of the New Age form of Native spirituality are portrayed: soul travel and healing rituals. Commander Chakotay is rendered comatose, and the episode explores both the biomedical and the psycho-spiritual models of diagnosis and treatment. In articulating a biomedical model, the Doctor observes that Chakotay has been rendered "brain dead" following the extraction of his "bio-neural energy." An alternative psycho-spiritual explanation is offered by Lieutenant Torres, however, who performs a Medicine Wheel ritual intended to lead Chakotay's lost soul back to his comatose body.[7] In accordance with the New Age emphasis on holistic healing techniques that treat body, mind, and spirit, the Doctor shows himself to be conversant with the Medicine Wheel ritual as part of his familiarity with "a variety of medical treatments, including those based on psycho-spiritual beliefs." Neither model provides an immediately effective treatment for Chakotay, however, and as the plot unfolds, it becomes apparent that Chakotay's soul has become disembodied.

Continuing the juxtaposition between scientific and religious models, Chakotay's soul is first assumed to be an "unknown alien entity" possessing the minds of crew members. While the medical model suggests that "there's just not enough left of [Chakotay's] mind to work with," the religious model suggested in the paradigm of the Medicine Wheel leaves open the possibility that the "unknown entity" is Chakotay's disembodied soul. Soul travel, or spirit walking, is considered both possible and natural within the context of the New Age movement.[8] According to anthropologist Paul C. Johnson (1995: 173), the idea of soul travel or loss is used within the context of New Age shamanism to explain illness or the effects of trauma. Anthropologist David Hess (1993: 118–19) suggests that while traditional science rejects the possibility of disembodied consciousness because consciousness is understood as the product of the body, New Agers have "a concern with relations between mind and body" not reducible to physicality. In "Cathexis," the religious model and the medical/scientific model ultimately coexist, as the empirical evidence overwhelmingly suggests that Chakotay's consciousness was disembodied. The New Age emphasis on the soul and the possibility of spirit walking is maintained.

Two final examples of the way in which religion is integrated into the daily life of a character are found in the episodes "Initiations" (1995) and "Basics, Part I" (1996). "Initiations" opens and closes with Chakotay performing "Pakra," a ritual marking the anniversary of his father's death. This ritual is represented as reminiscent of a vision quest, in which Chakotay leaves the familiar surroundings of the ship, taking his medicine bundle to meditate and commune with the spirit of his dead father. In "Basics, Part I," Chakotay is seen communicating more directly with the spirit of his father. Troubled and needing guidance, Chakotay meditates with the aid of items from his medicine bundle, and prays that the spirit of his father will "find" him. The next scene shows Chakotay in a natural, forest setting, with the spirit of his father awaiting him. Chakotay listens to his father's advice, and subsequently acts on it. Like the animal spirit guides, the healing rituals, and the spirit walk, communing with the spirits of one's ancestors is an integral component of New Age versions of Native American spirituality (Churchill 1994: 212).[9]

In addition to the inclusion of spirituality into Chakotay's everyday life as portrayed in the described episodes, religion is also the primary focus of several *Voyager* episodes. In the second-season episode "Tattoo" (1996),[10] the entire plot revolves around Chakotay and his religious beliefs. The story establishes a parallel between the site of a *Voyager* mission to procure a vital mineral and a trip Chakotay took as a teenager with his father to the South American rainforest in search of their ancestral roots. Chakotay learns that the myths of his people which tell of the Sky Spirits have a basis in reality. A race of people from a planet 70,000 light years from Earth visited Chakotay's ancestors 45,000 years in the past and selected them "so they might thrive and protect your world [Earth]." The episode, by juxtaposing flashbacks of the teenage Chakotay with the adult's experience, establishes the ambivalence Chakotay had long felt toward the traditional religion of his people. As a teenager, Chakotay had emphasised the importance of technology and science and chose to leave his tribe to join Starfleet, despite his father's misgivings. The young Chakotay says to his father, "Our tribe lives in the past, a past of fantasy and myth. Other tribes have learned to accept the twenty-fourth century. Why can't ours?" As an adult, Chakotay's practice of the traditional rituals of his people takes on renewed significance for him after meeting the people he calls the Sky Spirits. At the end of the episode, Chakotay sees a hawk circling above him and hears his father's voice say, "Listen to him Chakotay. Do you hear what he says to you?" Chakotay's reply indicates his altered point of view when he says, "Yes, Father, I hear him, I finally hear him."

Through the course of the episode, Chakotay learns that, contrary to what he thought as a child, science and religion are not necessarily opposed and that his life and beliefs may be informed by both. In discovering a rational and empirical basis for ancestral myth, Chakotay is able to reconcile his Starfleet training with his traditional upbringing. The religious or spiritual explanation of his people's origins has been rationalized; that is, it has been framed in the language of science in which events have natural, rather than supernatural explanations (Weber 1952). Nonetheless, the ancient truths of his people have been affirmed for Chakotay. He has discovered an extraterrestrial connection to his people's origin myths.

According to David Hess (1993: 22), incorporation of extraterrestrials as spiritual figures within the New Age movement is one expression of the transformation of "the otherworldly discourse of spirits and apparitions into . . . somewhat more rationalized form[s]." Like the Indian, extraterrestrials provide an exotic Other in which to locate spiritual wisdom. The fusion of Indian and alien in this episode is characteristic of one aspect of New Age spirituality, in which Native American elders and nonnative New Agers explore the extraterrestrial heritage of indigenous peoples.[11] This heritage, which is understood to include "their origin from the stars, [and] the influence of *Star People* visitors on the formation of their culture and their spiritual beliefs and ceremonies," is closely connected to the insistence that UFOs and extraterrestrials are scientifically legitimate.[12] As scientifically legitimated figures of spiritual authority, extraterrestrials can therefore mediate between religion and science, for while many orthodox scientists discount the possibility of the existence of spirits, the possibility of extraterrestrials' existence is given some scientific credence (Porter 1996). For Chakotay, this transformation of discourse from Sky Spirits to Aliens allows him to integrate his religious beliefs with his scientific view of the universe.

The final connection to New Age spirituality made in this episode occurs when the Sky Spirit/extraterrestrial spokesman tells Chakotay the story of the first meeting between Chakotay's ancestors and his own people. Within the New Age context, both Indians and Aliens are understood to be concerned with environmental issues (Saliba 1995: 48–49; York 1995; Melton 1992; Bowman 1995). In "Tattoo," the Sky Spirit spokesman explains that Chakotay's ancestors were chosen to become the caretakers of the Earth because of their "respect for the land, [and] for other living creatures." In reward for this concern, Chakotay's ancestors were given a genetic bond with their extraterrestrial visitors. This theme also mirrors that of the Native American/Extraterrestrial component of the New Age movement, for according to New Age Native speaker Standing Elk, "Star People and Indians have the same DNA." (Boylan 1996a: 6).[13] The New Age link between Indians, Aliens and environmentalism is also mirrored in "Tattoo" in the hesitancy of the Sky Spirit people to contact the *Voyager* crewmembers due to humanity's heritage of environmental destructiveness. The Sky Spirit spokesman tells Chakotay: "We were taught your world had been ravaged by those with no respect for life or land." Finally, despite their great need, the Sky Spirit people refuse to allow the *Voyager* crew to take all the mineral they need from the planet, allowing only as much as can be taken without damage to the environment. In his association with Indians and Aliens, the Sky Spirit/extraterrestrial is both definitively Other and ultimately authoritative. As a consequence, he is ideally situated to speak on environmental issues within the context of New Age spirituality.

As Commander Chakotay is shown to reconcile his traditional beliefs with his scientific worldview, Captain Kathryn Janeway is shown to reconcile her scientific beliefs with spiritual experience. As established in the episode "Coda" (1997), Janeway was raised with a worldview based in sceptical rationalism.[14] She was trained by Starfleet as a science officer (Okuda and Okuda, 1996: 281), and she continues to be a scientist at heart. Consequently, when confronted with challenges or questions, Janeway approaches them from a scientific perspective and seeks rational and empirical explanations. In the episode "Resolutions" (1996), for example, when she and Commander Chakotay are infected with an illness that has no apparent cure, she continues to search for a scientific solution long after Chakotay has reconciled himself to exile. Janeway's view of the world is therefore thoroughly and unambiguously secular and scientific.

In representing a rational, scientific worldview, Janeway is Us as Chakotay is Other. According to theologian and philosopher of science Langdon Gilkey (1987: 167), "We live in an advanced scientific culture. The first implication of this is that science is now thoroughly established . . . and thus does the society unquestionably support it, pay its bills, and revere it. . . . Science permeates down to and shapes all the levels of modern society."

As a scientist and as Captain of *Voyager*, Janeway is therefore ultimately representative of authority. She provides a model of normative behaviour for American society.[15] Furthermore, she is also normative and authoritative within the *Star Trek* universe. Her scientific rationalism epitomizes the rational and scientific worldview of *Star Trek*. Janeway is thus recognizable as Us—a familiar figure who represents and portrays the scientific worldview of modern society.

The third season episode "Sacred Ground" (1996), therefore, represents a dramatic departure for the character of Captain Janeway as she is confronted with the possibility that her scientific view of the world may be inadequate. In certain circumstances, she learns, faith may be more important than science. In this episode, one of the *Voyager* crew (Kes) is critically injured by coming into contact with a "biogenic" field, and the only hope that Captain Janeway has of saving her crewmember's life rests in going through a ritual to plead with the Nakoni ancestral spirits. Janeway approaches the ritual from her rationalist, scientific perspective. When Chakotay notes that she has "never been one to put much trust in religious ceremonies," Janeway agrees.

> JANEWAY: If you're asking whether I expect to speak to the ancestral spirits—no, of course not. But something happens to the monks when they go through the ritual. Something that allows them to withstand the effects of the biogenic field. I want to find out what that is, it might provide clues to a treatment.
>
> CHAKOTAY: Some kind of physiological change, maybe . . .
>
> JANEWAY: That's what I'm guessing . . .
>
> CHAKOTAY: Of course, there is always the possibility that the ancestral spirits really do control what happens in the shrine.
>
> JANEWAY: To each his own, Commander. But I imagine if we scratch deep enough we'd find a scientific basis for most religious doctrines.

Janeway thus undertakes the ritual on the assumption that the scientific data she can accumulate by doing so will provide the information necessary to cure Kes. As she states, "I didn't come here for personal enlightenment, I'm trying to save a member of my crew." After enduring a number of ordeals, Janeway is forced to realize that the ritual, as she has conceived it, is ultimately meaningless. The data she has collected is inexplicably insufficient to effect a cure, and Janeway must return to the shrine to try again. With her scientific worldview thrown into question, Janeway must approach the ritual as a spiritual quest rather than a scientific inquiry. When her spiritual advisor at the shrine notes that Janeway has come back to "seek the spirits," Janeway responds "I don't know what I'm seeking." Her scientific and rationalist preconceptions have not yielded the results she expected, and thus she is somewhat at a loss as to how to proceed. Before Janeway can genuinely attempt to approach the ancestral spirits, she must shed her preconceptions and expectations about the nature of the ritual. Janeway had initially entered the ritual with the expectation that it would be like any number of other initiatory rituals in the Federation database. Thus, she endures trials of strength and stamina, a hallucinogenic episode, and a death-like experience. When these ritual experiences fail to provide the information necessary to cure Kes, she asks her spiritual advisor why.

> JANEWAY: I did everything you asked of me. You led me to believe that would allow me to help Kes.
>
> ADVISOR: I haven't led you anywhere, Kathryn. You've taken me along, wherever you wanted to go. This was your ritual.

The suggestion in "Sacred Ground" that the ritual Janeway undergoes has no formal structure but is instead determined by her own needs and expectations is illustrative of New Age spirituality. Within the context of the New Age movement, there is no single spiritual path or set of rituals; each individual is responsible for finding their own spiritual path (Bowman 1995: 146; Hess 1993: 14; Melton 1992: 171–72). Furthermore, within the New Age context, reality itself is often seen as subjective. According to sociologist Roy Wallis (1975), these two characteristics are definitive of the New Age "cultic milieu":

> First, there prevails in the milieu an attitude of "epistemological individualism," that is, a belief that the individual is the ultimate locus for the determination of truth. Secondly, there prevails an ideology of "revelational indeterminacy," that is, a belief that the truth may be revealed in diverse ways and through diverse agents. No individual or collectivity possesses a monopoly of the truth.[16]

In "Sacred Ground," Janeway's realization that her own expectations have determined the shape of her ritual, and her spiritual advisor's insistence that the specific ritual details were "meaningless," exemplify the New Age belief that spiritual experiences are a response to individual spiritual needs and interpretations. As one New Ager expresses this point, "Whatever you believe—that the advisor [met during an altered state of consciousness during a religious ritual] is a spirit, a guardian angel, a messenger from God, a hallucination, a communication from your right brain to your left, or a symbolic representation of inner wisdom—is all right.[17]

The goal of spiritual experience within the New Age movement is "one of radical mystical transformation on an individual level" (Melton 1992: 172). Although Janeway initially denies that she is seeking "personal enlightenment," she must ultimately confront the inadequacy of science and make a leap of faith which cannot be rationalized. Within the ritual, Janeway is shown that her faith in science is in itself a belief system.

> GUIDE 1: You'll find all the answers eventually, with enough time and study, and the right sort of tools. That's what you believe, isn't it, as a scientist?
>
> GUIDE 3: Be honest.
>
> JANEWAY: Yes, that's what I have always believed.
>
> GUIDE 2: Even when her science fails right before her eyes, she still has full confidence in it. Now there's a leap of faith.

Acknowledging the limits of science is Janeway's first step in letting go of her reliance on fact and accepting that some things must be taken on faith. Against all scientific reason, Janeway is told that, in order to cure Kes, she must take her back into the shrine which injured her.

> GUIDE 3: Your orbital scans and medical research have given you the facts, and they tell you the biogenic field is lethal.
>
> GUIDE 1: If you believe the facts.
>
> GUIDE 2: Let all of that go, Kathryn. Take Kes back into the shrine, and trust the spirits to return her soul.
>
> JANEWAY: . . . how could either of us be ready to go through the field?
>
> GUIDE 2: If you believe you are ready, then you are. There is no more to it than that.

The ritual guides in the episode challenge Janeway to put faith in something in addition to science, something that cannot be seen or touched or tested. Janeway's willingness to accept the challenge of faith indicates a transformation of her worldview to include spiritual awareness in addition to scientific rationality. This transformation is established in the final two scenes of the episode. First, despite the fears of her first officer, Janeway does take Kes into the shrine. When Chakotay appeals to her, saying "Captain, I don't understand this," Janeway responds "Neither do I. That's the challenge." Second, when the Doctor provides a scientific rationale for Kes' recovery, Janeway acknowledges that "its a perfectly sound explanation, Doctor. Very—scientific." However, by her expression and by her delivery of this comment, it is clear that she is uncomfortable with this scientific explanation of her very personal experience. By the end of the episode, Janeway has a new understanding of the value of religious mystery. As Chakotay noted earlier in reference to himself and the Nakoni, Janeway has "chosen not to lose the mystery [of the ritual]." While she accepts the validity of the Doctor's scientific explanation, she nonetheless believes, from her own experience, that faith, as well as science, played a part in Kes's cure.

The religious practices and experiences of Chakotay and Janeway take place within the dual context of demythologized *Star Trek* rationalism and New Age spirituality. Spirituality as conceived within the New Age context is individualistic, humanistic, eclectic, and rationalized and is understood to be integrated within, rather than opposed to, science (Kyle 1995; Hess 1993; Lewis 1992; Porter 1995, 1996). The *Star Trek* worldview is also conceived as individualistic, humanistic, pluralistic, and rational, although also thoroughly secular.

Individualism is a key component of the American worldview (Hess 1993: 89) of which both *Star Trek* and the New Age movement are representative. Within the New Age context, this is expressed in an appreciation for each individual's unique spiritual path. As religious studies scholar Marian Bowman (1995: 146) writes, within the New Age movement "each person must take responsibility for his or her spiritual life, using whatever tools seem right for the individual on their inner journey." Within the *Star Trek* context, individualism is expressed through the democratic ideal and the philosophy of the Prime Directive which maintains that every society, and by extension, each individual, must find their own way in the universe without external interference.[18]

Humanism is also a key component in both New Age spirituality and the *Star Trek* worldview. According to some New Age scholars (Melton 1992; York 1995; Kyle 1995), the New Age movement grew out of the transpersonal psychology and the Human Potential movement, and the emphasis placed on human potential and the optimistic vision of human nature within these systems has been maintained within New Age spirituality. As Richard Kyle (1995: 146) notes, this results in a New Age worldview that places "great confidence in human evolution and Western optimism. As a result, humanity has unlimited potential and is capable of a self-awareness that places individuals in touch with their divinity." Within *Star Trek*, the future and progress are conceived of in terms of human potential. This view is embedded in the *Star Trek* universe and reinforced by the view of *Star Trek*'s creator, Gene Roddenberry. Roddenberry was a member of the American Humanist Association (Jindra 1994: 34) and known to be vehemently opposed to anything which he believed curtailed human potential. In *The Last Conversation* (Fern 1996: 67), Roddenberry is quoted as saying, "God, to me, is intrinsic to humanity. To the imaginative principle. To what we create, and think. He—or I should say It—is a source, yes, but more an involvement with the unknown. God is like the leap outside oneself, something that has no discernible source, but is a source." For both the New Age movement and *Star Trek*, therefore, humanism is intimately linked to the idea that God, or divinity, is not "out there" but dwells in the human heart.

Eclecticism is a third intrinsic element of New Age spirituality, insofar as it encourages multiple and inclusive approaches to spiritual enlightenment. As Marian Bowman notes (1995: 146), the New Age movement encompasses a "collage approach to religion and cultural traditions" (see also Melton 1992: 171–72). Similarly, the *Star Trek* philosophy of IDIC (infinite diversity in infinite combination) stresses pluralism and tolerance for all beliefs.[19] Although the collage spirituality of the New Age and the IDIC philosophy are not identical, they are not incompatible. Whereas doctrinal religious approaches can be seen as incompatible with a worldview emphasizing infinite diversity, New Age spiritual eclecticism encourages an acceptance of the plurality of human experience. The IDIC philosophy can encompass New Age spirituality, and New Age spirituality does not violate *Star Trek* principles.

Rationalism is also a concept that the New Age movement and *Star Trek* philosophy share. Within the New Age movement, spirituality is understood as a rational rather than irrational response to human experience. Science, therefore, in its "true" form of "scientific holism" (Kyle 1995: 98; Peters 1991: 133), is compatible with, rather than opposed to, spirituality for spirituality is understood to be natural rather than supernatural. As David Hess notes (1993: 68), New Agers "share a belief that theirs is the open-minded, rational system that is grounded in some notion of 'factuality' . . . or experiential evidence." Rationality in *Star Trek* is conceived of in terms of an empirical understanding of the universe in which all things can be seen to operate according to natural laws.[20] All events have a rational explanation; it is not necessary to resort to supernatural forces to understand the universe. The rationalism of the New

Age and of *Star Trek* is experiential, based upon natural laws and coupled with the conviction that humans can know the truth about the universe.

The compatibility of New Age spirituality and the *Star Trek* world-view permits *Voyager* to include religion and religious ideas in its characters and plots while remaining within the philosophical system established for the *Star Trek* universe. The similarities found in the concepts of rationality, pluralism or eclecticism, humanism, and individualism between New Age and *Star Trek* perspectives provide points of contact for religious ideas within *Star Trek* stories. The relationship between religion and science continues to be portrayed as a dichotomy within *Voyager*, yet the dichotomy has been muted. The emphasis has shifted to the potential and the promise of the relationship between science and spirituality and away from issues of conflict and claims to absolute truth. As seen in the characters of Commander Chakotay and Captain Janeway, New Age spiritual ideals can be effectively explored without denying or falsifying the basic precepts of *Star Trek*. The exotic otherness of Chakotay's spirituality becomes a model to be admired and emulated, and the startling introduction of spirituality into Janeway's scientific worldview suggests that spirituality is of immediate personal concern not simply for the Other,but also for Us. The congruence between New Age spirituality and *Star Trek* consequently permits a more nuanced and positive treatment of religion than the *Star Trek* franchise has previously attempted.

NOTES

1. In the fourth season episode "The Omega Directive," (1998) the character of Seven of Nine is also shown to experience a religious awareness. As a Borg character, Seven of Nine represents a fusion of humanity and technology. She experiences a mystical, noetic awareness while engaged in the practice of science. While gazing at an "Omega" molecule, understood by the Borg to symbolize ultimate complexity in ultimate harmony, Seven of Nine experiences something that transcends the bounds of her understanding. Seven of Nine's mystical experience maintains the emphasis within *Voyager* on the compatibility, rather than conflict, between science and religion. "The Omega Directive" was broadcast only after this volume was submitted for publication, and so could not be more fully discussed here.

2. Spock is half-Vulcan, Worf is Klingon, and Kira is Bajoran. All three practice the traditional spirituality of their peoples. In the original series episode "Balance of Terror" (1966) a human woman was shown praying in the ship's chapel. However, there were no identifying characteristics to establish the nature

of her beliefs, and the chapel was never seen again. The ship in *Star Trek: The Next Generation*, the USS *Enterprise* 1701–D, does not have a chapel.

3. The creators of *Voyager* deliberately avoided associating the character of Chakotay with any particular native people. This was done to minimize issues of accuracy with regard to specific ritual and cultural practices. In his book, *The White Man's Indian: Images of the American Indian from Columbus to the Present*, historian Robert Berkhofer, Jr. (1978) notes that this tendency to generalize about the nature of the Indian has a long history in Euro-American cultures. He writes, "Not only does the general term Indian continue from Columbus to the present day, but so also does the tendency to speak of one tribe as exemplary of all Indians and conversely to comprehend a specific tribe according to the characteristics ascribed to all Indians" (26). For a discussion of the historical precedents of European representations of the Indian as Other and as foil, see Berkhofer (1978), Francis (1992), and Clifton (1990).

4. See, e.g. Paul C. Johnson's (1995) comparison of New Age shamanism and the shamanism of the indigenous people of Ecuador.

5. Janeway is not the first person that Chakotay has taught to contact his or her spirit guide. In this episode, we learn that Lieutenant B'Elanna Torres has also learned to see her spirit guide.

6. See Johnson (1995) for a discussion of power animals, and the use of technology to induce alternate states of consciousness and visionary experiences.

7. The ritual, we are informed, was taught to Torres by Chakotay himself, in case he should ever be seriously wounded.

8. See, e.g. York (1995: 59, 60).

9. Ed McGaa (1990) provides a manual for non-natives wishing to practice a New Age form of native spirituality. Included in his list of rituals are: (1) a peace pipe ceremony, (2) a sweat lodge ceremony, (3) a vision quest ritual, (4) a Sioux Sun Dance ceremony, (5) a spirit-calling ceremony, (6) a blood-brother/sister ceremony, and (7) a give-away ceremony, in which gifts are given and received. These rituals all focus on healing, spirit (animal, ancestral, and natural) communication, communal bonding, and environmentalism.

10. The name of the episode, "Tattoo," refers to the mark Chakotay wears on his forehead, above his left eye. Part of the purpose of the episode would thus seem to be to explain the significance of the mark. Chakotay states, "I wear [the tattoo] to honor my father. He wore it to honor his ancestors."

11. Since 1996, there have been at least four conferences organized to discuss the links between Indigenous peoples' religions and extraterrestrial influences. These include the Star Knowledge Conference held on the Yankton Sioux Reservation in South Dakota, June 12–16, 1996; the Star Visions Conference,

held in Fort Collins, Colorado, November 7–11, 1996; the Star Family Conference held in San Diego, California, March 13–16, 1997; and the Star Council Conference of Native American Elders and other Star People Specialists, held in Rapid City, South Dakota, June 11–14, 1997. For reports on the Star Visions and Star Knowledge conferences, see Boylan (1996a, 1996b).

12. Boylan (1996a: 1). According to Boylan (1996b: 6), "government officials [are working] through the National Science Foundation to spread the word to American scientists that UFOs and extraterrestrials are now legitimate topics for scientific discussion."

13. In Boylan (1996a: 5–6),. Standing Elk is described as "Lakota Keeper of the Six-Pointed Star nation Altar." Further parallels to the *Voyager* episode are apparent in Standing Elk's claim that the ancestral spiritual language of the Sioux was intended as a form of communication with extraterrestrials (in "Tattoo," Chakotay's people also spoke the language of their alien visitors)˙and in his claim that the Star Peoples have been in contact with Native American peoples because of their concern for the world's environment (Boylan 1996a: 2).

14. In "Coda" (1997), an alien impersonating her father tells Janeway, "I raised you to be a doubter and a sceptic, to look at the world with a scientist's eye." Janeway accepts this as a valid statement on the nature of her upbringing.

15. While it has often been argued that women and children are represented as marginal in media presentations (see Hess 1993: 120–41), Janeway is not a marginal character. When the series *Voyager* was created, a deliberate choice was made to cast a woman as captain. in order to show a woman authority figure as normative. Challenging gender roles is in keeping with the *Star Trek* tradition of breaking racial and gender stereotypes.

16. Cited in Lewis (1992: 7). This point is further supported by sociologist Richard Kyle (1995: 76), who suggests that for New Agers, "final authority resides in experience and intuition. 'Truth is intensely personal and entirely subjective.'"

17. Quoted in Johnson (1995: 173).

18. Emphasis on the value of the individual can be seen in such episodes as "Mirror, Mirror" (*TOS*: 1967), "Return of the Archons" (*TOS*: 1967), "The Measure of a Man" (*TNG*: 1989), and "Best of Both Worlds, Parts I and II" (*TNG*: 1990). The New Age individualism of Janeway's religious experience is apparent in her spiritual guide's insistence that it was Janeway herself who dictated the form and content of her religious ritual. There was no single correct way to approach the ritual or to communicate with the spirits, only the way appropriate to the individual seeker. Janeway's Starfleet individualism is apparent in her adherence to the Prime Directive of non-interference and her explicit mention of "to each his own" in response to Chakotay's question of religious belief. For

Chakotay, his practice of Native American spirituality is characteristically New Age in its individualist emphasis. Anthropologist Paul C. Johnson (1995: 174–75) suggests that New Age versions of shamanism differ from their indigenous counterparts in their universalized, individualized, and psychologized emphasis: one can be a shaman, in the New Age context, while embedded in the individualistic, pluralistic, and fragmented context of modernity. One does not need a clan, or a tribe, or an indigenous peoples' cultural milieu, in order to practice New Age spirituality.

19. See, e.g. "Is There In Truth no Beauty?" (*TOS*: 1968);. also Okuda et al. (1994: 134) and Lichtenburg et al. (1975: 119).

20. This attitude can be seen in episodes such as "Who Mourns for Adonais?" (*TOS*: 1967), "Who Watches the Watchers?" (*TNG*: 1989) and "Devil's Due" (*TNG*: 1991).

PART II

Religious and Mythic Themes

7

Intimations of Immortality

Death/Life Mediations
in Star Trek[1]

JON WAGNER

One of the reasons for *Star Trek's* popularity is that it does the work of myth, exploring the contradictions, ambivalences, and paradoxes of human experience in a way that provides some sense of illumination and reconciliation. By confronting through narrative those problems that are among the most unmanageable in ordinary life, myth opens a space for creativity within the irreconcilable polarities of our existence.

The present chapter will consider the ways in which *Star Trek*, as a contemporary humanist mythology, employs secular narratives set in a hypothetical future to address the problem of human mortality. Awareness of our mortality is not only a hallmark of the human condition, but it is also a subject addressed in most mythologies. At the same time, one of the characteristics that distinguishes *Star Trek* from most traditional myths, or even from such science fiction narratives as the *Star Wars* cinema trilogy with its New Age mysticism and its hints of an afterlife, is that *Star Trek* bears the imprint of a stridently rationalist humanism that was established initially by its creator Gene Roddenberry. Thus, although *Star Trek* may engage in a creative recycling of traditional motifs like spirit migration, reincarnation, resurrection, and the like, it ultimately strives to reframe such elements in natural terms. *Star Trek* does not construct the sort of mythos in which human mortality is overruled by a supernatural or spiritual doctrine of life after death; rather, *Trek* operates within the discursive realm of science and natural law to pose narrative strategies for mediating and destabilizing the boundary between life and death.

The other notable feature of *Star Trek* that sets it apart from traditional myths is its use of a future rather than a primordial setting. Traditional mythic narratives are usually set outside the flow of mundane events in a time before ordinary time, when beings and events were profoundly different from those in secular history (Bascom 1965). The unique ahistoricity of primordial time bestows on mythic events a privileged freedom from the demands of ordinary plausibility, and it allows for what Eliade (1954) characterized as an "eternal return" to the ever-present mythic time through ritual retellings and reenactments. In a pluralistic society like ours, however, the primordial past is contested insofar as any particular account of primordial events may, if taken literally, contradict other primordial narratives. Thus, primal myths tend to set particular religious (and scientific) subcultures apart from one another. The imagined future, on the other hand, offers a narrative venue capable of appealing to a wide range of religious and secular subcultures. Like the primal past but unlike overtly fictional settings, a hypothetical future can be thought of as "real" in some sense, yet to its advantage, a futuristic narrative can never be more than a provisional truth, a hypothetical possibility that diverse North American subcultures may be able to entertain without entering the contested areas of particular creation accounts or eschatological metaphysics. In short, if contemporary North American society is at all capable of accommodating a broadly shared mythology, the kind of secular, future-oriented narratives seen in *Star Trek* may offer some crucial advantages.

The rise of structuralist approaches from the 1950s through the 1970s focused attention upon the role of myth in expressing and mediating a culture's salient oppositions. For structuralists like Claude Lévi-Strauss (1955) and Edmund Leach (1967), the object of studying myth is to go beyond surface meanings in order to discover the underlying grammar or structure of thought inherent in a given mythology, a given culture, and ultimately, the human mind itself. These structures take the form of binary oppositions, which myths seek to mediate by transforming them into parallel oppositions more amenable to synthesis by a third element.

Noting that the "antinomy of life and death" is one of the most universal of the oppositions that myth seeks to mediate, structural anthropologist Edmund Leach (1967: 3) points out that Judeo-Christian scripture mediates this opposition, in part, through the concept of "a land of the dead where life is perpetual." Pueblo myths, on the other hand, pursue the mediation of the "antimony of life and death" by setting up narrative structures in which these apparently irreconcilable categories, transmuted into the opposition of agriculture (a means to life) and war (a means to death), are mediated by hunting (a means to life through killing). In other Pueblo myths, herbivores (which do not kill to eat) and predators (which must kill to eat) are mediated by carrion-eaters that eat meat but do not kill. This mythic mediation, says Leach, "serves to imply that life and death are *not* just the back and the front of the same penny, that death is *not* the necessary consequence of life" (Leach (1967:4–5, italics in original)

The approach of the present chapter shares structuralism's general interest in mythic mediation, as well as its particular concern with the mediation of the death/life antinomy. The emphasis here, however, is not upon the graceful cognitive geometry of structuralist analyses but rather the down-and-dirty, emotionally laden, amorphous, and ambiguous mediations of fluent human creativity. We suggest that if myths seek meaning and resolution, they seek a different kind from that revealed in elegant structural diagrams or that codified in doctrines, theologies, and catechisms. The strength of complex mythic narrative certainly does not lie in its ability to erase ambiguity—dogma is far better suited to that purpose. Rather, myth excels in probing life's ambiguities in a way that preserves an appreciation of their subtlety and poignancy, while penetrating to a deeper level of understanding and imparting a sense of empowerment. As the novelist and critic Marilynne Robinson (1993: 136) puts it:

I consider myths to be complex narratives in which human cultures stabilize and encode their deepest ambivalence. They give a form to contradiction that has the appearance of resolution. . . . Myth is never plausible narrative. It asks for another kind of assent. To anyone for whom it does not strike an important equipoise, it seems absurd. The myth of the Fall makes it possible to think of humankind and the world as at the same time intrinsically good and intrinsically evil. Those to whom this vision is not compelling grumble about the apple and the snake.

I speculate that the attraction of the mind to myth comes from a sense that experience really is more complex than we can articulate by any ordinary means. . . . We know from physics that contrary things can be true at the same time, and we seem also to know this intuitively. I would suggest that the power of myth lies in the fact that it arrests ambivalence. I would suggest also that myths are coined continuously, usually in very small denominations, and that lesser myths are related to greater ones as a penny is related to a gold mine.

Not surprisingly, mythic reconciliation differs from worldly reconciliation; its methods are narrative rather than doctrinal or practical. Myth need not, for example, provide an explicit logical alternative to the certainty of death; rather, it may simply provide ways of thinking about the death/life opposition that serve to destabilize the boundary between the two, a boundary that in everyday experience seems so distressingly absolute and impenetrable. One of the advantages of mythic mediation is that, since it need not offer an explicit death-denying doctrine but rather seeks to destabilize the conceptual boundaries by which death and life are opposed, it is able to approach its project from a number of different directions without being constrained by strong requirements of self-consistency. *Star Trek* makes use of numerous devices that scarcely add up to anything doctrinally but that allow for diverse possibilities for re-visioning the familiar antinomy of death/life. These strategies include raising rational doubts about the categorical denial of life after death, the deconstruction of firm logical boundaries between mortal/immortal or living/nonliving, a rich diversity of metaphors on the theme of resurrection, and a valorization of the possibility of death as an energizing presence.

DEATH, THE UNDISCOVERED COUNTRY

One of *Star Trek*'s textual strategies for dealing with the life/death antinomy is to stress the provisional nature of our metaphysical knowledge. In order to appreciate this point fully, we must consider some of the defining premises of the *Star Trek* universe as laid down in the original series (*TOS*) and elaborated early in *Star Trek: The Next Generation* (*TNG*). Although *Star Trek* narratives are the product of a highly complex and shifting authorship, *Trek*'s original creator, Gene Roddenberry, outspokenly proclaimed as his guiding values a love of humanity and an optimism concerning the human prospect (Fern 1996). It might be said of Roddenberry that he was a militant agnostic, strongly opposed to humanity's penchant for overvaluing its current state of knowledge, and that he was awed by the magnitude of all that humankind has yet to learn. Thanks to Roddenberry, the ideals of growth and discovery were, and remain, central to the creed of *Star Trek*. *Star Trek*'s agnosticism about final truths is extended to the metaphysics of death in a way that leaves room for a variety of interpretations, suggesting that even in the scientifically advanced twenty-third and twenty-fourth centuries, we will not have explained away, or finally ruled upon, the possibility of death-transcending planes of existence.

Nowhere is the openness toward diverse views on life after death more succinctly expressed than in *TNG*'s episode "Where Silence Has Lease" (1988). The alien being Nagilum, having confronted the crew of the *Enterprise* with immanent death in order to "study" their response, takes the form of the innocently curious android Lieutenant Commander Data and asks Captain Picard the perennial question: What is death? Picard's answer is most instructive. Some people, he says, believe that we continue to live forever in an incorporeal form and that "the purpose of the universe is to maintain that form in an earth-like garden, which will give delight and pleasure through all eternity." "On the other hand," Picard continues, "There are those who hold to the idea of our blinking into nothingness—that all of our experiences, and hopes, and dreams [are] merely a delusion." Asked which of these he believes, Picard pauses thoughtfully, then muses:

> Considering the marvelous complexity of the universe, its clockwork perfection, its balances of this against that—matter, energy, gravitation, time, dimension—I believe that our existence must be more than either of these philosophies; that what we are goes beyond Euclidean or other practical measuring systems, and that our existence is part of a reality beyond what we understand now as reality.

Thus, according to Picard, the reality of what happens to us after death may go far beyond our present limited conceptions. Picard, like Hamlet, seems to suggest that death is the ultimate "undiscovered country." While this kind of agnosticism obviously does not establish any positive doctrine about life after death, it allows room for the contemplation of immortality by aligning that hope with an essentially humanist appeal to the expansion of our horizons of understanding. It also establishes a rationally legitimized domain of doubt within which *Trek* narratives can employ various other strategies for destabilizing the death/life opposition.

IMMORTAL, MORE OR LESS

Another of *Star Trek's* narrative strategies for dealing with mortality is to propose that the universe's diverse humanoids could, in principle, have variable—even indefinite—life spans, which in turn would suggest that death is a contingent rather than a necessary aspect of life. Within *Star Trek's* narrative frame of reference, it is not always easy to place life forms into the categories of mortal or immortal. The extradimensional superbeing Q, first introduced in the *TNG's* episode "Encounter at Farpoint" (1987), characterizes himself as immortal, yet the *Star Trek: Voyager* episode "The Q and the Grey" (1996) reveals that members of the Q continuum sometimes kill one another in their wars. The highly advanced "pure energy" inhabitants of Organia, portrayed in the original series (TOS) episode "Errand of Mercy" (1967), do not explicitly claim to be immortal, but they say that no one has died on their planet in "countless thousands of years." In *TOS's* "This Side of Paradise" (1967), the members of the *Enterprise* crew are offered the opportunity to join with the colonists of Omicron Ceti III, who under the influence of mind-altering spores, can live indefinitely in a state of paradisal bliss (a state that, as it turns out, the *Enterprise* heroes and even the colonists finally reject as inauthentic). Apollo and the other godlike aliens of *TOS's* "Who Mourns for Adonais?" (1967) may be immortal or nearly so, but if they are deprived of worship their corporeal form fades "on the wings of the wind." At the other extreme, the Ocampa, depicted in *Voyager*, live for only nine years. The lifespan of *Trek's* Terrans is, from all indications, not much different from our own, somewhat augmented by Starfleet's advanced medicine and its healthy lifestyle. The serene, disciplined Vulcans, however, may live for centuries. Mr. Flint, of the *TOS's* "Requiem for Methuselah" (1969), was born on earth several thousand years ago with an extraordinary natural ability to regenerate his body, and would have been for all practical purposes immortal had he not chosen to leave earth for another planet.

TNG's "The Host" (1991) introduces an extraordinarily ambiguous case of longevity in the Trill, humanoids who pair up with sluglike "symbionts" whose personalities and memories are blended with those of their individual hosts. Trill hosts apparently have lifespans comparable to those of humans, but the symbionts are extraordinarily long-lived, and their passing from host to host provides a continuity not only for the symbiont, but also for earlier hosts whose memories merge with those of the symbiont and the later hosts. In the series *Star Trek: Deep Space Nine* (*DS9*),

Captain Benjamin Sisko refers to his science officer, a young Trill woman named Jadzia Dax, as "Old Man." The reference is to Sisko's old friend Curzon Dax, the composite of the Dax symbiont with an earlier host. Curzon is dead, and yet "he" can reminisce with Sisko about old times!

As these examples illustrate, *Star Trek* represents the longevity of humanoid and other intelligent life-forms as a complex matter entailing an enormous range of variations and twists. Beings that are immortal are ambiguously so; even for them, death is possible under certain circumstances. The difference seems surprisingly unimportant to most of these beings; the various species each go on with their lives in more or less the same manner. *Star Trek* represents mortality and immortality as points along a spectrum, and it blurs the absoluteness of immortality even as it proposes the possibility, thus reframing mortality/immortality as a contingent variable. A simple twist of fate can, as with Flint or the Omicron Ceti colonists, turn a mortal human into an immortal, just as other contingencies (or even voluntary choices) may work an opposite change for these same people. All this serves to imply that, to borrow Leach's phrase quoted earlier, "death is not the necessary consequence of life."

"HE'S NOT DEAD, JIM": TALES OF RESURRECTION

Few people would deny that death is, from all outward appearances, the most absolute and irreversible of human transitions. Yet the archeological record of funerary customs over tens of thousands of years (grave goods, sacrificial offerings, mortuary cosmetics, funerary inscriptions and the like) hint that our species has long been engaged in an attempt to transcend death and to envision possibilities for the continuation or regeneration of life. In its most explicit form, this project sustains the idea of resurrection, the restoration of the life of the individual person after death. Despite its adherence to a material frame of reference, *Star Trek* manifests the ancient theme of resurrection in a variety of ways.

Star Trek's greatest story of resurrection spans the two feature films *Star Trek II: The Wrath of Khan* in 1982 and *Star Trek III: The Search for Spock* in 1984). The storyline of these two films weaves an elaborate, multilayered metaphor that portrays time and aging as a process that moves in two directions, placing mortality within a larger pattern of ebb and flow that also entails renewal and rebirth. *The Wrath of Khan* opens on a battle scene in which we witness the death of Spock and most of the original *Trek* crew. They snap back to life, however, when Admiral Kirk enters the scene, which was in fact a training simulation for the young Vulcan officer Saavik. When Saavik protests that this training program offers no way to avoid the simulated "death" of the crew, Kirk lectures her that "How we deal with death is at least as important as how we deal with life." When Kirk next sees Spock he asks, jokingly, "Aren't you dead?"

The action of the film centers on the Federation's Genesis project, whose purpose is to create "life from lifelessness" by instantaneously reorganizing matter, so that a sterile planet is able not only to support life but to nurture the "evolution" of life-forms at an accelerated rate. Beaming down to verify that the target planet Ceti Alpha V is indeed lifeless (Genesis would destroy existing life during its creative process), officers of the Starship *Reliant* are captured by the genetically engineered superman Khan, who was unwittingly entombed on the dying planet by Captain Kirk in *TOS*'s "Space Seed" (1967). Khan, obsessed with vengeance against Kirk, commandeers the *Reliant* and proceeds toward the Regula science station with the intention of stealing the Genesis device. After Kirk's old flame, chief Genesis scientist Dr. Carol Marcus, alerts him to the threat, Kirk takes command of the refitted *Enterprise*, then on a training mission, and heads for Regula. Arriving on the station to find most of its staff murdered by the rampaging Khan, Kirk follows Carol into an underground chamber on the nearby asteroid Regula, where he meets the son he never knew, Dr. David Marcus. Khan, close behind, beams up the Genesis device and leaves Kirk and the others, as he wickedly gloats, "buried alive." Kirk, idle for once, broods about the family life he gave up for his Starfleet career and confesses that he feels "old and worn out," but Carol Marcus offers to show him something that will make him feel "young as when the earth was new"—the Edenic world created by Genesis deep within the asteroid. The supposedly disabled *Enterprise* soon arrives to rescue them, as previously arranged in a coded message to Spock. Khan, ignoring the pleas of his own followers, pursues the *Enterprise* into a battle that cripples his ship and kills all those aboard but himself, and in his despair he sets the Genesis device to explode and destroy both ships.

Knowing that the crippled *Enterprise* cannot escape without warp drive, Spock silently resolves to sacrifice his life by entering the radioactive warp chamber and making the needed repairs. In Spock's death scene, after the *Enterprise* is saved, Spock tells Kirk not to grieve, for "the needs of the many outweigh the needs of the few, or the one." In his eulogy, Kirk says that his friend's death takes place "in the sunrise of a new world," that is, the Genesis planet formed when the Genesis device was detonated. Spock's funerary pod sails toward the planet to the accompaniment of Scotty's bagpipes playing "Amazing Grace," a hymn to redemption and eternal life, which is taken up by the orchestral sound track. Among the many portents of renewal that follow is Dr. McCoy's inversion of his most trademark line,"He's dead, Jim." "He's really not dead," muses the Doctor, "as long as we remember him." Kirk, who admits that he has always cheated death rather than facing it, must now confront the death of his friend. But amid this grief is the theme of renewal, as expressed in Kirk's healing reconciliation with his son David, in his suddenly restored sense of youth and vitality, and in his promise to return to the Genesis planet for the sake of the friend he leaves behind. The closing shot of the film shows Spock's coffin, unharmed, on the verdant new planet.

In the beginning of the sequel film *The Search for Spock*, Kirk finds himself still feeling the "emptiness of this vessel," owing to a sense of having "left the best part of myself back there on that newborn planet." Soon enough, other events distract Kirk from his own troubles: Doctor McCoy begins acting strangely, and Spock's father, Sarek, shows up wanting to know whether Kirk has been the recipient of the customary last-minute Vulcan mind-meld. They come to the realization that Doctor McCoy has been implanted with Spock's memories, which Kirk refers to as Spock's "immortal soul." When stodgy Starfleet bureaucrats deny Kirk permission to embark on a quest to recover Spock's body, Kirk and his old companions, Sulu, Uhura, and Scott, steal the *Enterprise* and make a daring escape from the space dock. Their quest takes place amid a running battle with the Klingons, who want to steal the Genesis design for its destructive potential. In the course of this struggle David gives his life to save Kirk's *Enterprise* companions, and Kirk destroys the *Enterprise* to keep it from falling into Klingon hands. Meanwhile, Spock has been found roaming the Genesis planet as a mindless boy whose painful and spasmodic growth is somehow linked with the accelerated, convulsive geological and biological processes of the planet itself.

After a climactic battle in which Captain Kirk kicks the unregenerate Klingon leader into the hellish fires of the Genesis planet, Kirk brings Spock to Mount Seleya on Vulcan for a perilous ritual of "re-fusion." McCoy agrees to risk his life in the hope of restoring Spock, and the successful re-fusion leaves Spock's body and mind once again united. Even before he begins the long process of regaining his knowledge and memories, Spock approaches Kirk with a dawning recognition. Why, he asks, did Kirk risk everything to save him? "Because," Kirk explains, "The needs of the one outweigh the needs of the many." Spock then utters the line that marks the beginning and end of each of these two adventures: "I have been, and ever shall be, your friend."

The strength of this tale of resurrection lies not only in the literal rebirth of Spock, but in the weaving of this theme into a larger tapestry wherein the oppositions of death/life, aging/rejuvenation, and decay/restoration are portrayed as complementary aspects of a reciprocal movement or cycle. In this way, the seemingly irreconcilable opposition of life and death is assimilated to other oppositions that lend themselves to reversibility and dual movement. By the same process that restores Spock to life, Captain Kirk, who in the opening scenes is preoccupied with his own aging, is restored to youth.

Roth (1987) suggests on the basis of the first film that Spock is Kirk's spirit double, representing and facilitating Kirk's inner process of renewal, and the sequel film *The Search for Spock* seems to provide further support for this interpretation. By juxtaposing the theme of resurrection from death with the secular American ideal of perpetual rejuvenation, the narrative of these two films implicitly assimilates the two processes. The theme of rejuvenation might also apply to the decadent Starfleet, whose smug bureaucrats, jaded officers, and smart-aleck youngsters are portrayed as lacking in the "youthful" qualities of courage and wonder that Kirk and his aging companions ultimately exemplify, and which finally triumphs. The Genesis Project itself, with its dual qualities of life-destruction (the feature that appealed to the Klingons) and life-creation, also resonates the motif of dual motion toward and away from decay and death.

The theme of sacrificial love plays a central role in these processes of renewal: Spock's and David's sacrifice of their lives and McCoy's willingness to risk his life for Spock; Kirk's sacrifice of his ship (the symbol of all he had lived for) and his son (representing another source of life and immortality that has more recently presented itself to him); Scott, Sulu, and Uhura's jeopardizing of their Starfleet careers by their decision to join Kirk in his act of mutiny; and Kirk's offer to trade his own life for the safety of his crew when Khan has the *Enterprise* cornered in *The Wrath of Khan.* When McCoy says "He's not really dead as long as we remember him," he seems to be speaking figuratively of love as an avenue by which to transcend death, but his words point the way to a literal avenue of rebirth as well. The link between resurrection, sacrifice, and love is also developed through the mythic theme of a hero's descent into the underworld as part of a quest to rescue life from the realm of the dead. Kirk is "buried alive" in the asteroid Regula but returns to save his friends and to foster the birth of a planet; later he descends to the unstable fiery Genesis planet to retrieve Spock. Spock climbs down a series of ladders into the warp chamber (perhaps the only scene in all of *Trek* in which movement toward this part of the ship is so explicitly depicted as a descent), where he is consumed by its radioactive fires in order to bring the ship back to life and save his shipmates from certain doom.

Although *The Wrath of Khan* and *The Search for Spock* constitute *Trek's* most sustained treatment of the resurrection theme, it is by no means the only one. In *TOS's* "Amok Time" (1967), Captain Kirk is placed in a state of simulated death to rescue Spock from an impossible situation in which the two friends are bound by Vulcan custom to fight to the death. In *TNG's* replay of this strategy in "Code of Honor" (1987), the combatant, Yareena, really does die and is afterward revived by Doctor Crusher. In *TNG's* "Tapestry" (1993), Picard dies during surgery and enters the after-life to find himself in the company of the godlike Q, who eventually restores him to life on Doctor Crusher's operating table. In *Voyager's* "Coda" (1997) Captain Kathryn Janeway dies on a mission to a remote planet, and an incorporeal being posing as her father's ghost tries to coax her disem-bodied spirit into the "afterworld." After Janeway's soul firmly refuses to enter the realm of the dead, she is able to re-enter her body, thus allowing her companions to revive her. In *DS9's* "The Visitor" (1995), young Jake Sisko witnesses a terrible accident in which his father dematerializes, and for the rest of his life remains obsessed with the recurrent apparition of his father's ghost. The ghost turns out to be Captain Sisko trapped in another dimensional reality, and the aging Jake Sisko sacrifices his life so that the "normal" course of events, and with it Captain Sisko's life, can be restored.

In a figurative echo of the resurrection theme, persons defined as dead may unexpectedly turn up alive. In Voyager's episode "The 37's" (1995), Amelia Earhart and other humans abducted from earth in the year 1937 turn up alive and well on a planet in the Delta Quadrant. According to the film *Star Trek: Generations* (1994), Captain Kirk is pre-sumed to have died when he was blown into space during an accident aboard the *Enterprise*; a century later, however, he is discovered by Cap-tain Picard to be living in a time aberration called the Nexus.

It is a considerable jump from the explicit resurrection story of Spock's rebirth on the Genesis planet to the figurative resurrection in Kirk's rescue from the Nexus, to the metaphorical assimilation of death-reversal with the secular American themes of rejuvenation and spiritual renewal. Yet through these diverse strategies, *Trek* presents resurrection in a variety of refigurings, transforming mortality from an essential fact of life to an elusive one while remaining within the discursive frame of secular humanism.

ONE LIFE TO LIVE?

While such death-transcending motifs as resurrection after death show clear parallels with traditional religious beliefs, there are other death-reconciling strategies to which science fiction is more uniquely suited. This is particularly true of the theme of multiple parallel existences that can allow the "same" person to die and yet remain alive. *Star Trek* often portrays alternate universes that contain points of reference (like recognizable characters or places) in common with our familiar universe but which are different enough that a person who is dead in one "reality" or "timeline" might well be alive in another. Thus, Benjamin Sisko visits a "mirror universe" in *DS9*'s "Through the Looking Glass" (1995) and "Shattered Mirror" (1996) where his deceased wife, Jennifer, is still alive. Chief Engineer Miles O'Brien dies in *DS9*'s "Visionary" (1995), but he is soon replaced by another version of himself from another timeline just a few hours into the future (a world whose own O'Brien, presumably, disappears permanently, raising the question of whether that O'Brien has, in effect, "died"). Ensign Harry Kim's death is similarly repealed in the *Voyager* episode "Deadlock" (1996). Although security Officer Natasha Yar is killed during a mission to the planet Vagra II (*TNG*'s "Skin of Evil," 1988), she is encountered in a later episode (*TNG*'s "Yesterday's Enterprise," 1990) when another *Enterprise* from an "alternative timeline" unexpectedly appears. Yar returns to this other timeline, where she does not die on Vagra but gives birth to a daughter Sela (*TNG*'s "Redemption, Part II," 1991), and is eventually killed in the year 2349, which in the *Trek* narrative timeline is fifteen years before her death in *TNG*'s "Skin of Evil."

The alternate universe is only one of the *Star Trek* narrative devices by which a person can have more than one existence and, hence, be both dead and alive. Another, equally effective textual strategy for giving a person more than one existence is the frequently encountered theme of the double or clone. Examples and variations of the double theme in *Star Trek* are too numerous even to list, and the doubles run the gamut from selective opposites such as an "evil twin" (*TOS*'s "The Enemy Within," 1966) to exact replicas in which both entities have an equal claim on the same personal identity. As an example of the latter, *TNG*'s "Second Chances" (1993) reveals that Commander William Riker had been duplicated in a transporter malfunction seven years earlier, which created two identical and equally "real" copies of Riker; one aboard the Starship and the other marooned on a remote planet. In the ensuing years, the two developed into distinct persons who can each lay equal claim to being the "authentic" Will Riker.

If the same person exists as two or more duplicates, can that person die and yet remain alive? In *DS9*'s "Whispers" (1994), we experience the final hours and moments of Miles O'Brien's life as he is hunted down and killed by his Starfleet companions, who seem to have gone altogether mad. In the end we learn what the central character did not know—that he is a duplicate of the "real" Chief O'Brien, subliminally programmed to commit acts of terrorism. The clone believes that he is O'Brien and there-fore experiences O'Brien's death (as does the audience), yet O'Brien lives. A similar textual use of the clone motif appears in *TNG*'s "Rightful Heir" (1993), when Commander Worf must assess his religious faith after he comes face to face with the mythic Klingon culture hero Kahless the Unforgettable, who lived more than a millennium earlier and whose return is prophesied in Klingon lore. It is revealed that this Kahless is actually a clone created by the priests from the original prophet's DNA and programmed with all that is known of his life and memories; thus, the clone actually believes himself to be Kahless.

Although Worf is aware that this individual was created by cloning, he sides with those who recognize the clone's claim to the identity of Kah-less, thus acknowledging that, at least in this case, cloning amounts to res-urrection. In *DS9*'s "Ties of Blood and Water" (1997), the Vorta are said to be such experts in cloning that they routinely make copies of them-selves as a hedge against death—a practice amounting to what Captain Sisko rather disdainfully calls "immortality."

While the notion of a personal double is sometimes encountered in traditional belief (as in German folklore the ghostly twin, or *Doppel-gänger*), the idea of a person having multiple existences is developed at rel-atively great length in *Star Trek*, thanks to a burgeoning technology of information pattern reproduction and a growing acceptance of such notions as multiple realities. Insofar as we can seriously contemplate the existence of multiple selves in different realities, the finitude and mortal-ity of the individual become highly problematic, and the possibilities for deconstructing the distinction between being dead and being alive are profoundly expanded.

LIFE OF THE MIND

The idea of duplicating people through the reproduction of information patterns opens the door to a related theme: the unlimited preservation of the human mind. In our age of information technology, we are increasingly inclined to label the intangible aspects of the person as "mind" (a term with connotations somewhat different from "soul"). The mind, in turn, is often characterized as a complex set of information patterns. We are well-accustomed to the idea of the rapid, massive transfer of information as invisible currents flowing through tiny circuits or even through empty space; hence, the premise that the mental aspects of a human being might be instantly transferred to a new physical location is not an unreasonable extrapolation from phenomena we already accept as routine. If the mental element could be transferred from one physical location to another, this phenomenon would be reminiscent of the transmigration of souls that various religious traditions have associated with life beyond death.

There is, in fact, a great abundance of *Trek* stories that employ the principle of transmittable "minds" or "patterns" in ways that parallel the traditional motifs of spirit migration. *TOS*'s "The Lights of Zetar" (1969), for example, tells of mental energy beings, the last remains of the inhabitants of the planet Zetar, who possess a passenger on the *Enterprise* and must be driven away by placing the victim in a pressurized atmospheric environment. In *TOS*'s "Return to Tomorrow" (1968), three alien minds "borrow" the bodies of Kirk, Spock, and a visiting scientist while they make android bodies, but they then become involved in intrigues and rivalries that almost get our heroes killed. *TOS*'s "A Wolf in the Fold" (1967) depicts a murderous demonic being called Redjac, who once took the form of Jack the Ripper. Cornered on the *Enterprise*, he transmigrates from one human body to another in a futile attempt to escape justice. Human bodies are also inhabited by interloping minds in *TOS*'s "Operation: Annihilate" (1967), "By Any Other Name" (1968), and "Turnabout Intruder" (1969). Spock's ability to mind-meld with another person or being, and thus have its memories exist in him, is another sort of transmigration, which operates in reverse when he inserts his consciousness into the unsuspecting Dr. McCoy in *The Wrath of Khan* (1982).

The Next Generation episode "The Schizoid Man" (1989) concerns a doomed human, Dr. Ira Graves, who takes over Data's android body to prolong his life. Finally, realizing that he hasn't the self-control necessary to manage such superhuman powers, he places his memories into a computer. To the extent that the mind defines the person, Dr. Graves is potentially immortal whether his mind resides in Data or in the computer. The transfer of a human mind into a potentially immortal android body is also central to *TOS*'s "Requiem for Methuselah" and "Return to Tomorrow," discussed earlier, as well as *TOS*'s "What are Little Girls Made Of?"

(1966). In *TNG*'s "Inheritance" (1993), Data encounters his "mother" Dr. Juliana Tainer, the former wife and scientific co-worker of Data's creator Dr. Noonien Soong. Eventually, Data discovers a secret about Tainer that even she does not know: Noonien Soong transferred his wife's mind from her dying organic body into an android one. Data does not tell Tainer this, but chooses to let her go on believing that she is organic. Although the android Juliana Tainer has been programmed to age as an organic being would, Soong could presumably have chosen to make her as immortal as her "son" Data.

Androids are not the only imaginable vehicle by which the information patterns that make up the "mind" could join with an artificial human form. The three later *Trek* series regularly feature the phenomenon of "holographic projections," quasi-solid three-dimensional emanations from a computer. In *DS9*'s "Doctor Bashir, I Presume" (1997), Starfleet's Doctor Zimmerman (the model for *Voyager*'s holographic Doctor) recruits Bashir as the personality prototype for a new and more realistic hologram, assuring Bashir that it offers him "a shot at immortality." Bashir does not, in the end, become the pattern for a hologram, but the theoretical possibility of a person attaining immortality in this manner, once raised, remains a part of *Trek*'s imaginal reality.

Holographic programs, like androids, sometimes serve as receptacles for storing a person's patterns of mental information in order to rescue the mind from death. In *DS9*'s "Our Man Bashir" (1995), several crewmembers' lives are preserved after a transporter malfunction by storing their "body" patterns in one part of the ship's computer system while their "minds" enter the holodeck's computer to become actors in Bashir's spy-thriller holographic program. In this particular story, the indefinite existence of human minds in holographic bodies is ruled out by the fact that their patterns are deteriorating, and luckily, they are restored to their human bodies just in the nick of time. But one might easily see this barrier as a mere technicality that could be overcome. In that case, would the holographic projections, which contain the memories and thoughts of given people, become heirs to their personhood, and might not those persons thereby be exempted from the usual human fate of old age and death?

THE IMMORTAL MACHINE

While *Star Trek*, as myth, is conspicuous for the absence of animals, or of nature in general, among its symbolic elements, it gives considerable attention to the sentient machine and its implications for our traditional definition of living versus nonliving things. In the 1979 film *Star Trek: The Motion Picture* (*TMP*), the unmanned Terran space probe *Voyager* has, through interactions with other free-ranging machines, developed into the immensely powerful artificial being V-ger, whose intelligence has grown so far that it is experiencing existential angst and is on a quest to find and merge with its creator in order to discover the purpose of its existence.

Might a machine-being with an artificial intelligence cross the boundary from nonlife to life by acquiring feelings, a sense of self, a quest for moral purpose, and a will to live? Where is the line that must be crossed for the machine to become a living thing? Is the boundary crisp and definitive, or is it gradual and ambiguous? The android Data is, to say the very least, close to this transition. In *TNG*'s "The Measure of a Man" (1989), Picard defends Data against those who would objectify him as a thing, arguing that no one can confidently deny that Data has a soul. It is noteworthy that Picard does not claim Data has crossed a definitive boundary, but chooses instead to emphasize the ambiguity—perhaps even the obsolescence—of that boundary in the *Trek* universe. Since Data is supposedly immortal, the hypothesis that he might be considered alive (perhaps even a "person") calls into question the logical link between life and mortality.

We have already discussed the recurrent *Trek* theme of placing human minds into potentially immortal holographic "bodies," but this process is one that may operate in the other direction as well. Holodecks and holosuites can be made to concoct virtual people who behave as generic types—headwaiters, martial opponents, detective-fiction gangsters, and so on—or even as specific people made to order or based on biographical information. In *TNG*'s "Descent, Part I" (1993), Data programs holodeck simulations that enable the projections of three physicists of past centuries—Isaac Newton, Albert Einstein, and Stephen Hawking (played by Hawking himself)—to converse with one another. Sometimes (e.g. *TNG*'s "The Big Goodbye," 1988; "Elementary Dear Data," 1988; and "Ship in a Bottle," 1993) these projections show evidence of self-awareness and a will to live. The *Star Trek Voyager* series has a holographic projection (the Emergency Medical Hologram, a.k.a. the Doctor) among its regular central characters. The Doctor, who has been modeled on the "real" Doctor Louis Zimmerman, seems to possess a sense of personhood that is in no way less (and in some ways more) "human" than that of others on the crew. If an artificial being with no finite lifespan has the mental qualities of a human, and perhaps even believes itself to be a person, does it then follow that a "human" (at least by this expanded definition) can, under these circumstances, be immortal?

Star Trek—and this is part of its genius—does not offer unequivocal answers to such questions. It does not provide a royal road to the transcendence of human limitations through our merger with the machine, but neither does it provide an easy path out of this somewhat unsettling prospect. At times, Star Trek raises the possibility that the human spirit contains something not reducible to information and thus (perhaps) in principle not replicable and preservable; at other times, it raises the opposite possibility. Data, for all his magnificent powers of memory and reason, cannot get a joke or feel jealousy—but then, neither can Spock, and Spock is certainly a living, mortal (and half-human) individual. Other androids including Data's "brother" Lore (TNG's "Brothers," 1990, and "Datalore," 1988) and his "mother" Juliana Tainer (TNG's "Inheritance," 1993), have emotions, and so does Data once he installs his "emotion chip" in Generations. Holographic projections sometimes (but not always) seem capable of self-awareness, emotion, and the desire to perpetuate and even enhance their own existence—as Captain Picard learns when a holographic Dr. Moriarty from Data's "Sherlock Holmes" holodeck adventure outgrows his programming and demands to be set free from his limited holographic existence (TNG's "Elementary, Dear Data," 1988, and "Ship in a Bottle," 1993).

In this and the previous section, we have examined Trek's narrative deconstruction of the boundaries between human and thing, living and dead, mortal and immortal, both from the perspective of the human mind entering a machine and the sentient machine developing an essentially human intelligence. In each case the result is similar: a "human" consciousness residing in a potentially immortal vessel. Such a possibility tends, at least at the narrative level, to uncouple life from mortality. The human or humanlike mind residing in an infinitely restorable artificial body need no longer be thought of as, to use Yeats' imagery (1956), a soul "fastened to a dying animal."

AMIABLE SWEET DEATH: NORMALIZING MORTALITY

Traditional myths often posit the appropriateness of death by showing why the Creator(s) saw fit to originate it. According to some Native American myths, for example, the primordial beings introduced death because of their recognition that, without it, the world would become too crowded (Erdoes and Ortiz 1984: 67, 470–71). Similarly, *TOS*'s "The Mark of Gideon" (1969), depicts the inhabitants of the planet Gideon who, having prolonged human life through technological advances, are now desperate to introduce epidemic disease to their miserably over-crowded planet. This story pursues a strategy of "normalizing" death—that is, of framing mortality as a normal and even beneficial aspect of life. Mr. Flint in *TOS*'s "Requiem for Methuselah," mentioned previously, who has lived many illustrious lives in such identities as Brahms and Da Vinci, becomes bored with it all and migrates to the planet Holberg 917G where his powers of endless self-regeneration are negated and he can die in peace. The virtually omnipotent and immortal superbeing being Q shows up on *Voyager* in "Death Wish" (1996) as a refugee from the Q Continuum, seeking the Continuum's permission to become mortal so that he can end the tedium of his existence.

Star Trek's tale of three death-cheating Terrans from the late twenti-eth century (*TNG*'s "The Neutral Zone," 1988) is a parable on the folly of fearing and denying death. After the cryogenically frozen corpses are rescued from a deteriorating module adrift in space, Doctor Crusher is able to reverse their terminal medical conditions and restore them to life. In the course of explaining twentieth-century "cryonics," the dialogue treats that era's fear of death as a cultural trait every bit as quaint and out-moded as the notion of having one's corpse frozen. As it turns out, this unnatural extension of life is not satisfying for its intended beneficiaries, who are out of place in this changed world. Only the young woman, whose husband's denial of her death had apparently led to her involun-tary preservation, seems to appreciate the profundity of their situation, and this makes her the most unhappy of the three but also the most con-structive in dealing with her situation. This cautionary tale suggests that the denial of death is a symptom of the denial of life, and that the forced prolongation of life is no substitute for living courageously and insight-fully.

In *TNG*'s "Time's Arrow" (1992), Data confronts his own death when the *Enterprise* team finds his disembodied head preserved among the remnants of nineteenth-century San Francisco. Although this death is later erased in one of those time-paradox escapades for which *Trek* is noted, Data in the meantime has an opportunity to consider the mean-ing of his death. Rather than being troubled by the prospect of mortality, he is comforted by the thought that this brings him closer to humanity and relieves him of the bleak prospect of outliving every human friend he makes. Thus Data, whose striving for humanity is an enduring central motive, finds signs of his mortality not frightening but consoling.

The theme of mortality as a humanizing influence appears in the *Voyager* episode "Real Life" (1997), when *Voyager*'s holographic Doctor programs himself a holographic family in order to help him to understand his human patients. The plan begins to work in earnest only after his picture-perfect "family" is reprogrammed to be slightly dysfunctional, largely out of his control and, as he tragically discovers, mortal. Faced with the impending death of his virtual daughter Belle, the Doctor must choose either to end the program and spare himself the grief of losing someone he has come to think of as his child, or to run the program to its conclusion and experience the death of the child (who is also, of course, a being more like himself than are the other crewmembers). In the end, he chooses to do the latter because the experience will bring him closer to an appreciation of life and an understanding of humanity.

Through its narrative strategy of "normalization," *Star Trek* defines death—or rather the presence and possibility of death—not as an evil but as a boon, an energizing aspect of the human condition. It is no accident that people who live in Edenic "paradises" like that of Omicron Ceti III, where mortality does not seem to rear its ugly head, are depicted as anesthetized and stagnated. The philosophical climax of the feature film *Star Trek: Generations* comes when James T. Kirk, living in a timeless, euphoric state within a temporal disruption called the Nexus, suddenly realizes that this existence is not "real" because it is guaranteed for eternity—because there is no risk of death, and hence "no danger." Kirk's immediate response to this awakening is to join Jean-Luc Picard in a clearly dangerous undertaking that, indeed, brings about Kirk's heroic death. Given the choice between an eternity of bland, safe existence and a life of risk and heroism where death is at least a possibility, *Trek* suggests that the latter is more authentic and humanizing.

Trek does not try to persuade us that death is good; rather, it casts a veil of ambiguity over death by showing that an existence where death is impossible might be, in some respects, an impoverished one. Our conventional way of thinking about death within a secular framework goes something like this: it might be nice if we could live forever, but unfortunately all living things must die. In the *Star Trek* universe, the deconstruction of mortality as an essential concomitant of life, combined with an ambiguous valorization of mortality, suggests a reversal of the commonsense view: Immortality may indeed be possible, but it is not necessarily desirable.

CONCLUSION

In its role as a secular humanist mythology, *Star Trek* has developed narrative strategies for addressing mortality—strategies that include the normalization of death, the cultivation of a rationally based agnosticism about the afterlife, and the deconstruction of death as a stable category through narratives of resurrection, transmigration of mind, and the merger of human sentience with the immortal machine. These devices do not boil down to any coherent doctrine or argument, convincing or otherwise, but instead employ a set of suggestive metaphors and images that allow us to re-envision death.

It would be too much to expect that myth in general, much less *Star Trek* as a contemporary secular mythology, be able to arrest the emotional and cognitive distress that results from the clash of our species' awareness of mortality with our will to live. What *Star Trek* can and does do, it has been argued here, is to use the specifically narrative means at its disposal to blur and destabilize the sometimes distressingly stark boundaries and emotional valences of life/death. *Star Trek*'s mythic power enables us, from within a framework of secular rationalism, to valorize mortality, imbue it with mystery (and thus with hope), and to recuperate in a humanist context the ancient themes of resurrection and the immortality of the human soul. While *Star Trek* does not have one overarching approach toward destabilizing the life/death opposition, it makes use of narrative strategies that reframe death as veiled, malleable, and reversible, rather than naked, immovable, and final.

NOTE

1. This article expands on material in pages 75–79 of the book *Deep Space and Sacred Time: Star Trek in the American Mythos* by Jon Wagner and Jan Lundeen (Westport, Conn.: Praeger Publishers, 1998). I am indebted to my coauthor for her ideas, and to Praeger and the Greenwood Publishing Group for their permission to adapt and expand material from our book.

8

Suffering, Sacrifice and Redemption

Biblical Imagery in Star Trek

LARRY KREITZER

Colin Morris (1984: 170), former head of religious broadcasting at the British Broadcasting Corporation (BBC), once wrote: "Television is the most potent source of myth and symbol for increasing numbers of people. It weaves a web of accessible imagery which those outside the charmed circle of formal religion can draw upon to feed the life of the spirit."[1] It is clear that *Star Trek* has a key role in myth-making for millions of people the world over, helping to weave that "web of accessible imagery" of which Morris speaks. The genius of *Star Trek* is that it has managed to tap into certain ideas and concepts readily understood in Western cultures, particularly as they fall under the sway of American values and ideals which are spread internationally by means of such visual media. In this regard, we should not fail to note that, notwithstanding its worldwide success, *Star Trek* espouses an essentially *American* vision of life, *American* hopes and dreams and obsessions. There are many key ideas, operating at a mythological level, which make *Star Trek* the force that it is today within the entertainment business. Certain presuppositions about the moral value of a market economy, about the role of the family in society, gender roles, human sexuality, and so on are all to be found here.

At the same time, included within this rich mythological tapestry are many important theological declarations from the Judeo-Christian heritage. One needs only to consider the centrality of the Garden of Eden story within many of the *Star Trek* episodes, or the centrality of the Genesis Project within *Star Trek II: The Wrath of Khan* (1982) and *Star Trek III : The Search for Spock* (1984), to see how important the Bible is as a background against which the drama of the world of *Star Trek* is played out.[2] And *Star Trek V: The Final Frontier* (1989) was deliberately constructed to raise the issue of the existence of both God and Eden. Despite the fact that the film's promotional materials rather gratuitously proclaimed the story as one in which "the crew of the *Enterprise* go in search of God," there is much theological insight to be gained from an attentive viewing of this piece. Indeed, William Shatner, who directed it and was partly responsible for the screenplay, is on record as saying that the idea of Sybok, the religious fanatic who is convinced that God has spoken to him, was inspired by watching American TV evangelists at work (Shatner 1989: 34–38; Shatner 1994: 220–21).

Our task within this chapter is to examine briefly some of the ways in which biblical texts, as well as key theological themes and ideas, have been used within the mythological world of *Star Trek*. We will restrict our investigation to the classic *Star Trek* of the original series (*TOS*) and portions of the first six feature films which concentrate on Kirk, Spock, and McCoy as the three principal actors. However, an investigation into the place that religion and sacred texts or ideas have in *Star Trek* could usefully be extended to the other three subsequent series as well, the hallowed rites of Klingons and Bajorans in *Star Trek: The Next Generation* (*TNG*) and *Star Trek: Deep Space Nine* (*DS9*), together with the American Indian beliefs and customs of Chakotay in *Star Trek: Voyager*, to cite but a few obvious examples, offer much for consideration along these lines, as some of the other contributions in this volume amply demonstrate. Our task here is more mainstream, and we shall concentrate on themes central to the Judeo-Christian tradition. Our study can be divided into two parts: (1) we shall first examine one particular episode of the original *Star Trek* series and focus on how it develops the ideas of self-sacrifice and substitutionary suffering, (2) then we shall turn our attention to the *Star Trek* feature films and discuss the way in which Spock is represented as a Christ-figure, particularly as he surrenders his life for the sake of the *Enterprise* crew and then is brought back from the dead.[3]

DYING FOR OTHERS:
CHRISTIAN THEOLOGY IN "THE EMPATH"

It is difficult to think of a more succinct description of the theological core of the Christian faith than the words of Jesus recorded in John 15:13. Embedded within a discussion on the nature of true love, which he hopes the disciples will embody, Jesus declares: "Greater love has no man than this, that a man lay down his life for his friends." Indeed, discipleship is frequently defined within the New Testament gospels in terms of the willingness to follow Christ's lead and risk the loss of one's life for the Lord and the message he preached. Thus, Mark 8:34–35 has Jesus declare, in words suggestive of the fate that awaited him at Calvary: "If any man would come after me, let him deny himself and take up his cross and follow me. For whoever would save his life will lose it. and whoever loses his life for my sake and the gospel's will save it."

The idea of "taking up one's cross" is a powerful metaphor of Christian discipleship and is picked up in a number of writings within the New Testament. Luke's version of the saying from Jesus is an even more explicit call to discipleship, with the gospel writer adding the critical word "daily" to the saying (9:23): "If any man would come after me, let him deny himself and take up his cross daily and follow me." Paul the Apostle uses similar imagery in describing his own sense of personal identity and Christian calling when he says in Galatians 2:20: "I have been crucified with Christ; it is no longer I who live, but Christ who lives in me. And the life I now live in the flesh I live by faith in the Son of God, who loved me and gave himself for me."

Such a mystical vision of the Christian life, in which Christians are mystically united with the crucified Christ and have the power of the resurrection energizing their lives, is also found in Romans 6:3–5:

> Do you not know that all of us who have been baptized into Christ Jesus were baptized into his death? We were buried therefore with him by baptism into death, so that as Christ was raised from the dead by the glory of the Father, we too might walk in newness of life. For if we have been united with him in a death like his, we shall certainly be united with him in a resurrection like his.

At the heart of such statements lies the close interconnection of crucifixion and resurrection; one blends into the other. Crucifixion and the death it brings are overturned by resurrection; rising from the dead stands as a vindication of the selfless surrender on the cross of Calvary. In terms of theological understanding, from the vantage point of the cross, one looks forward with a sense of anticipation to the empty tomb; from the vantage point of the empty tomb, one looks backward with a sense of fulfilment to the cross. The power self-evidently contained within declarations such as those of Jesus and Paul (previously mentioned), will inevitably cause its influence to spread to places strictly outside the confines of Christianity. In the case of Gene Roddenberry's imaginative world of *Star Trek,* the seeds of Christian belief in such sacrificial self-offering have found a fertile ground, and they have yielded a rich harvest. Why is this so? The answer, in part, has to do with the fact that *Star Trek* unashamedly attempts to address the deeper philosophical questions of human existence—questions of purpose and meaning, life and death, creation and fulfilment. It discusses issues concerned with death and dying and does so within a dramatic framework of human relationships and deeply felt friendships. Thus, *Star Trek* fan writer Joyce Tullock (1981: 105) hits upon a key point when she says: "There is not a single *Star Trek* episode that does not have, as its most basic building block, the simple human fear of death."

Yet, when this all-too-human fear of death clashes with the desire to surrender one's life for the sake of others, particularly those one loves and cares for, a profoundly theological principle is brought into play. We see in these situations the notion of willing self-sacrifice borne out of love. As Captain Kirk says of The Companion in *TOS*'s "Metamorphosis" (1967), "Love sometimes expresses itself in sacrifice." With this sentiment Jesus no doubt would have agreed.

Nowhere is this theme of self-sacrifice more evident in the world of *Star Trek* than in an episode from the third season of *TOS*'s, "The Empath," arguably one of the best of the final season. "The Empath" was written by Joyce Muskat and directed by John Erman and was first aired on December 6, 1968. If the episode from the second season entitled "Bread and Circuses" (1968) could be described as exploring the *historical* aspects of Christianity,[4] then "The Empath" strikes at the heart of the *theological* dimension of the faith, namely, the sacrificial death of Jesus Christ on behalf of others. "The Empath" has been variously described as: "classic *Star Trek*" (Johnston 1986: 135),[5] "*Star Trek*'s Passion play" (Tullock 1980: 11), and "one of the most intensely emotional episodes of the series" (Tullock 1980: 97); there is much evidence to support these as accurate first soundings.

"The Empath" is also one of the most important *Star Trek* episodes for establishing the relationship between the triumvirate: Kirk, Spock, and McCoy. Within this episode we see not only the depths of commitment that the three have for one another, but the lengths to which they will go in demonstrating their concern for each other. One fan describes the central theme of self-giving love, which lies at the heart of this episode, in this way: "While 'The Empath' is not overwhelming in plot detail, it is still extraordinary because it displays the great love that each of the three have for each other; it is a love so intense that it causes each of the three to offer their lives so that their friends will live" (Kusik 1988. 74). Insofar as Kirk, Spock, and McCoy, each in turn, willingly offers his life so that the other two companions might live, they demonstrate the love Jesus spoke of, and which Christian theology, on the strength of his example, has identified as central to its beliefs.

The storyline of "The Empath" begins with Spock, McCoy, and Kirk beaming down to the second planet in the Minarva system, where the Federation has a science station monitoring the imminent collapse and transition of the Minarvan star to nova phase. On the surface of the planet they discover two members of a strange race of beings, known as the Vians, who capture them and begin to conduct a bizarre experiment on them that involves a female member of another humanoid species: she is known simply as Gem (played by Kathryn Hays). The plot revolves around the Vians' attempt to induce Gem to learn the meaning of self-sacrifice for the sake of others so that she might become the instrument of salvation for her own planet. Kirk, Spock, and McCoy become, in effect, her teachers for this lesson of commitment and self-sacrifice for others, under the rather unscrupulous gaze of the two Vians, named Lai and Thann. The dilemma faced by the Vians is the fact that they can save only one race from extinction when the sun goes nova, and they are attempting to see if Gem's race exhibits the needed sense of compassion and self-sacrifice to warrant their selection. She must learn from watching how the *Enterprise* triumvirate interact with one another when they are subjected to torture by the Vians, how they demonstrate their care for one another, and so gain this instinct to put herself in the service of others, and if need be, sacrifice herself for her people. As one of the Vians says, her "instinct for self-sacrifice must be stronger than her instinct for self-preservation."

However, it is not until late in the episode that the viewing audience is allowed to learn this true reason for the torture of the *Enterprise* crew by the Vians. Kirk's plea to the Vians as he is first subjected to their cruelty, suspended by his wrists in chains, echoes our own desire for an understanding of what is going on in the experiment. Kirk begs them, with the words. "if my death is to have any meaning, at least tell me what I'm dying for!" Predictably, the deep concern of the *Enterprise* trio for one another eventually wins the day, not the least because McCoy renders both Kirk and Spock unconscious with a hypo from his medical kit and goes on to face the final segment of the Vians' torture experiment alone. In the end his willingness to sacrifice his own life for his companions is enough to teach Gem the value of such concern for others. In fact, McCoy's sacrifice is the third attempt to free the *Enterprise* trio from their predicament: both Kirk and Spock had made similar attempts to free their two other comrades. The final statement by the Vians to Kirk, Spock, and McCoy concerning Gem reveals all: "You were her teachers— the will to survive, love of life, passion to know. Everything that is truest and best in all species of beings has been revealed by you."

To apply the statement to our theme of Christian self-sacrifice, we could say that the example of Jesus Christ is ideally taken up by all who call themselves his disciples: he is, in this sense, their teacher. So, too, Kirk, Spock, and McCoy are Gem's teachers, demonstrating to her in their interactions with one another, the nobler values of life she needs to learn in order that her people might survive.

In addition, several important biblical themes and motifs can be said to underlie the story contained in "The Empath," notably the use of crucifixion imagery and Suffering Servant imagery.[6] Let us examine both of these in more detail for they add significantly to the rich theological tapestry woven within this episode.

Crucifixion Imagery

Two images contained within the episode "The Empath" might be taken to be reflective of the crucifixion of Jesus of Nazareth, thus echoing concepts that lie at the heart of the Christian faith. The first comes in the form of the table, or bed, which appears at several points in the story. The first time we encounter it is also the first time that we see the character Gem: she is lying on this prop, which is roughly the shape of a body-sized cross, with two cross-beams for extended arms along a longer horizontal plank.

The second image, much more graphic in its expression, is the fact that both Kirk and McCoy, each in his own turn, is tortured by the Vians by being suspended from chains in a typical crucifixion pose, with arms outstretched and (in the case of Kirk) the upper body exposed. Many who watch this scene find their imaginations wandering to images of Jesus

Christ being suspended from the cross of Calvary in a similar scene of passion, an image deeply embedded within our culture and reinforced by countless examples from Christian art.[7] The idea of Christ willingly submitting to the pain and agony of crucifixion at the hands of Roman authorities is central to the Christian story. By undergoing crucifixion, Jesus Christ not only *speaks about* friends being willing to give their lives for others they love, but *demonstrates* it with his own life. In this regard, the idea of one voluntarily offering himself for others, so central to the plot of "The Empath," is interwoven with powerful visual images suggestive of the crucifixion of Jesus Christ. All of this supports our contention that "The Empath" builds upon ideas and images central to the Christian story, namely, the self-offering of Jesus Christ on behalf of others and his crucifixion on a Roman cross. The imaginative world of *Star Trek* is thus building upon established Christian mythology and is developing a new mythology based upon it, one that has a theological dimension buried deep within.

Suffering Servant Imagery

At several points, the presentation of the character Gem bears remarkable similarities to the biblical text of Isaiah 53, which contains the fourth so-called Suffering Servant song, which has been hugely influential in the history of the Christian church. It is clear that early on in the life of the Christian church these passages were interpreted messianically and applied to Jesus of Nazareth who had suffered and died at Golgotha (North 1948; Herbert 1975; Sawyer 1996: 83–89).[8] Such a messianic interpretation takes place even within the New Testament itself. For example, Isaiah 53:4 is cited in Matthew 8:17 in connection with Jesus' healing of the demon-possessed and ill who were brought to him. The suggestion made by Matthew is that such exorcisms and hearings were made possible because Jesus had taken upon himself the infirmities and diseases of the afflicted. Similarly, Isaiah 53:7 is quoted by the apostle Philip in Acts 8:30–35 as the apostle expounds the meaning of the prophecy to the Ethiopian eunuch. In essence, he relates the Old Testament passage to the life and ministry of Jesus Christ, thereby interpreting the meaning of the prophecy for his Ethiopian questioner. The same holds true for the writer of 1 Peter, who applies Isaiah 53:5 to his understanding of Christ's sacrificial death on the cross when he says in 2:24: "By his wounds you have been healed."

This is all well and good, but how does it relate to Jesus' own thoughts on the subject? The debate about whether Jesus himself saw his

own ministry as a fulfilment of the prophecy of the Suffering Servant continues apace. The so-called ransom saying of Mark 10:45 is a *crux inter-
pretum* in this regard, with scholars divided about whether this is a deliberate allusion to Isaiah 53 on the part of Jesus (Barrett 1959, 1972;
Zimmerli and Jeremias 1965; Moulder 1977–78; Stuhlmacher 1986:
16–29; Page 1992).

Two particular features of the storyline in "The Empath" demonstrate striking parallels to the prophecy contained in Isaiah 53. The first of
these allusions to Isaiah's prophecy involves the fact that Gem is, in fact, a
mute, and that throughout the episode she never has a line of dialogue.[9] In
the *Star Trek* episode this is explained as due to the fact that her race apparently evolved without the development of vocal cords. This is a convenient
explanation as far as the plot of the episode is concerned, and it does provide ample opportunity for dramatic development. The viewer sympathetically identifies with the character Gem and is drawn more deeply into
the story as a result. Gem's consistent silence does, at the same time, provide an important connection to the passage from Isaiah. One of the most
remarkable features of the Suffering Servant song is the description of the
Servant's silence. The writer of the song uses an image that would have
been familiar to the people of ancient Israel, particularly in view of the cultic sacrificial system which was an integral part of their religion. Thus we
read in Isaiah 53:7: "He was oppressed, and he was afflicted, yet he opened
not his mouth, like a lamb that is led to the slaughter, and like a sheep that
before its shearers is dumb, so he opened not his mouth."

The provocative image of the silence of the lamb was not overlooked by the early Christians. The silence of Christ in the face of his
accusers during the trial before the Sanhedrin is explicitly mentioned by
both Matthew (26:63) and Mark (14:61). At the same time, the idea that
Christ is like a lamb being led to the slaughter is brought out most powerfully within the gospel of John 1:29 beginning with the declaration
made by John the Baptist when he first sees Jesus coming toward him in
order to be baptized: "Behold, the Lamb of God, who takes away the sin
of the world!" This Lamb of God theme is also carried through in the way
that John's gospel presents the story of Christ's passion and crucifixion. In
fact, within his narrative John creatively moves the actual day of the crucifixion backward twenty-four hours, from the Friday to the Thursday, in
order to have Jesus' death take place at the same time that the Jews were
slaughtering the lambs for the Passover celebrations."[10]

One final adaptation of the sheep-lamb metaphor within John's
gospel is also worth mentioning briefly. This occurs within the parable of

the Good Shepherd. Here the image is considerably adapted, so that the disciples whom Jesus loves and cares for become, within the bounds of the illustration, the sheep, while he himself is said to be the Good Shepherd who takes care of them. The depth of this care is explicitly said to include his willingness to give his life up for them, as we see in John 10:11, 14–15: "I am the good shepherd. The good shepherd lays down his life for the sheep. I am the good shepherd; I know my own and my own know me, as the Father knows me and I know the Father,. and I lay down my life for the sheep." Within this same parable we also find a further declaration by Jesus that his willing self-sacrifice for the "sheep" he loves is to be followed by the "taking up of his life" again, a veiled reference to the resurrection. This occurs in John 10:17–18: "For this reason the Father loves me, because I lay down my life, that I may take it again. No one takes it from me, but I lay it down of my own accord. I have power to lay it down, and I have power to take it again."

To return to the storyline of "The Empath": the second interesting connection between "The Empath" and Isaiah 53 concerns the way in which suffering is transferred between Gem and the trio of Kirk, Spock, and McCoy. In short, at several key points in the story Gem takes on the suffering of the *Enterprise* crew and makes it her own, actually embodying their physical pains and afflictions, while risking her own life in the process. She does this, for instance, when touching Kirk's head wound and relieving him of a nasty gash on his forehead by taking it onto her own person. Similarly, later on in the episode, she saves Kirk from even greater trauma by empathizing with him following his torture by the Vians and taking upon herself his bodily afflictions, including the wrist gashes caused by his suspension by chains. Most importantly, she empathizes with McCoy as he is near death following his torture at the hands of the Vians, saving him from death by assuming all of his pain and agony, taking all of his internal and external injuries into her own body. These include, most significantly, the battered and bruised countenance that McCoy bears as a result of the torture, an appearance and an interchange remarkably reminiscent of the well-known verse from Isaiah 53:5: "But he was wounded for our transgressions, he was bruised for our iniquities; upon him was the chastisement that made us whole, and with his stripes we are healed."

The point is that Gem takes the sufferings and physical afflictions of McCoy onto herself, thereby allowing him to recover and be made whole. In this regard Gem stands as the equivalent of the Suffering Servant, whose wounds and bruises are taken to be the healing and salvation of the nation Israel. The prophecy of Isaiah 53, with its provocative image of the Suffering Servant who takes upon himself the sins of the nation Israel, readily lends itself to such use. The passage stands as something of a common ground, where the world of the early Christians and the world of *Star Trek* meet and construct theological myths. Not only does the Old Testament passage serve as a lens through which the early Christians interpreted the significance of the passion and death of Jesus of Nazareth, but it also provides a further focal point for the world of *Star Trek* to explore these profound theological matters as well. Gem is to Kirk, Spock, and McCoy what Jesus Christ was to the world—the means whereby pain, suffering and death are empathetically absorbed and healing and salvation effected for others.

We are never told what finally becomes of Gem or of the Vians, or if the attempt to instill the principle of self-surrender to Gem's world by the Vians was successful. Ultimately, this is unimportant. "The Empath" presents us with a subtle, yet provocative, story about the nature of self-sacrifice and the willingness to accept the pain and suffering of others onto oneself. In this sense, "The Empath" stands as something of a parable of Christ's substitutionary death on the cross of Calvary for the sake of humanity. In short, the world of *Star Trek* might be said to have borrowed the biblical imagery and creatively used it in constructing its own modern theological myth, a mythology that unashamedly addresses issues concerned with human pain, suffering and salvation. The emotive text from Isaiah 53 is an ideal vehicle in this regard. It contains graphic visual images of suffering for the sake of others, imagery traditionally associated with the crucifixion of Jesus Christ, but at the same time, an imagery that also yields much fruit in the fictional setting of *Star Trek*'s twenty-third century.

SPOCK AS CHRIST-FIGURE: GIVING HIS LIFE FOR OTHERS AND RISING FROM THE DEAD

For many, the character of Spock has been a special focal point for comparisons with Christianity. Incidental parallels between Spock and Jesus Christ abound, with interested Christian viewers of *Star Trek* keenly identifying and suggesting more and more of them all the time.[11] Here we have a classic example of a recent trend within science fiction cinema as a whole, the appearance of what cinematic studies scholar Hugh Ruppersberg (1990: 32–38) has called "the Alien Messiah," in which a saviour-figure from another world comes to earth to help humanity.[12] Such mythical substitution is an important feature of what religio-cultural studies scholars Robert Jewett and John Shelton Lawrence (1977: xx) have described as "the American monomyth." As they put it, this new mythology "secularizes the Judeo-redemption dramas that have arisen on American soil, combining elements from the selfless servant who impassively gives his life for others and the zealous crusader who destroys evil. The supersaviors in pop culture function are replacements for the Christ figure."

The death of Spock at the end of *Star Trek II: The Wrath of Khan* offers one of the most interesting parallels along these lines, incorporating, as it does a space-age reversal of a well-known maxim about the value of the one over against the value of the many. In *The Wrath of Khan*, Spock's death is powerfully presented as an affirmation of the many at the expense of the one, for it is by means of his death that the *Enterprise* and her crew are saved from the destructive force of the on-rushing Genesis wave. In the eyes of some fans this is taken as a veiled reference to Jesus' substitutionary death for the world, developing imagery associated with the crucifixion and the Suffering Servant, which we already noted are at the heart of the storyline in "The Empath." But such concentration on the passion of Christ is not the end of the matter, for Spock's self-sacrifice is followed by a thinly disguised promise of his "resurrection"—an even greater example of theological mythmaking and reliance upon biblical imagery, given that the resurrection of Jesus Christ might legitimately be described as the central theological declaration within the New Testament.[13] Little wonder then that Spock has become something of a Christ-figure among many fans of *Star Trek*. Since the film borrowed, as it were, two key planks from the Christian faith, it is hardly surprising that there has been a reaction against *The Wrath of Khan* and its sequel *Star Trek III: The Search for Spock* among some conservative Christian circles (MacDonald 1991: 27–29).[14]

These two key motifs, the willing self-sacrifice of oneself for others and the resurrection from the dead, are worth closer examination. Each in its own way provides us with another example of theological mythmaking in the *Star Trek* world. Together they allow us to show how the theological trajectory, which we noted was pivotal to the plot of "The Empath," is followed through within the feature films.

The Sacrificial Surrender of the One for the Many

Our central contention here is that the idea of the sacrificial surrender of the one for the many is a theme of paramount importance within the

New Testament and that this idea is picked up and creatively developed in the mythology of *Star Trek*. Clearly, Christ's willingness to go to the cross and surrender his life there is crucial for any understanding how the early Christians understood the significance of the death of Jesus. In this regard, the assessment of Jesus Christ's death, certainly in terms of its beneficial effects on others, is a *theological interpretation of the historical event*. To drive the essential point home, we would do well to remember that according to all four gospel accounts there were *three* men crucified on that Friday afternoon. And yet it is only the man on the middle cross whose death has come to be invested with salvific value, the other men on either side of Jesus Christ are not even given the dignity of being identified by name. No doubt the importance of the death of Jesus is due in no small measure to the fact that, according to the gospel accounts, his crucifixion was followed by his resurrection from the dead three days later. Understandably, Christ's rising from the dead was seen by the early Christians not only as a reward for his selfless sacrifice, but as divine vindication for his innocent death. All of which serves to illustrate that the bond between Jesus' self-offering on the cross and his resurrection from the dead three days later is theologically indissoluble. Before we move to discuss how such ideas are developed within the mythological world of *Star Trek*, it is worth noting that opinions other than the theological interpretation of Christ's death are also made.

Even within the pages of the New Testament the death of Jesus is variously assessed, and to this extent other understandings of how the "needs of the many outweigh the needs of the one" can be found. A good illustration of this is found in John 11:49–50 where we have what might be described as a *political interpretation* of the need for Jesus of Nazareth to be put to death. This suggestion is expressed by the High Priest Caiaphas, as he gives the Jewish Council his evaluation of how to handle the troublesome prophet Jesus. According to the gospel of John, the High Priest says to the Sanhedrin: "You know nothing at all, you do not understand that it is expedient for you that one man should die for the people, and that the whole nation should not perish."[15]

It seems that Caiaphas is arguing that the death of the one man, Jesus, was necessary in order to avoid a military confrontation with the Roman authorities. The political scene at the time was quite volatile, with a considerable section of the Jewish population harboring a seething resentment of the Roman presence in Judaea. In this sense, the death of the one (Jesus) would ensure the continuing survival of the many (the Jewish people at large). In the end, the clash between the Roman occupiers of Judaea and Jewish nationalist forces did indeed take place, and the so-called First Jewish Revolt makes Caiaphas' attempt to forestall the death of the nation futile. However, the crucial point (for our considerations) remains valid nonetheless. In short, from the standpoint of some of the Jewish leaders of the day, the death of the one man Jesus would benefit the *whole* of the nation, at least in political terms.

But what are we to make of Jesus' own understanding of the *possibility* (*if not probability!*) of his death at the hands of violent forces? To what extent might we say that Jesus' own life, ministry, and teaching was governed by the idea that the one should be willing, in love, to sacrifice himself for the many? One of the most forthright statements made by Jesus addresses precisely this point. The remark is recorded as having taken place on the road to Caesarea Philippi and marks a turning point in the gospel narrative. From here Jesus moves inexorably toward the cross and his date with destiny. Jesus responds to a question about status and rank that has arisen among his followers and offers them a vision of discipleship which stresses self-sacrifice. He says: "The Son of Man came not to be served but to serve, and to give his life as a ransom for many" (Mark 10:45 and Matthew 20:28).

How unique is such a declaration? It is by no means completely without precedent, and we deceive ourselves if we think that Jesus Christ was the first to suggest such a thing. Similar statements about the surrender of the individual for the group are also to be found within other religious traditions and within the writings of many great philosophers down through the ages. The English philosopher Jeremy Bentham (1748–1832) is a case in point. His famous summary of economic strategy, popularly expressed in the maxim "the greatest good for the greatest number," is well known and in some ways might be said to parallel Jesus' declaration about giving his life for the many.[16]

This philosophical principle, which Bentham took to be the foundation for morals and legislation in society, is made much of within *The Wrath of Khan* and *The Search for Spock*, particularly in connection with the death of Spock. And yet there is a crucial difference between the way in which the one and the many are handled within Jesus' teaching and the way they are treated within the thought of Bentham. It is quite true that the results may be the same (the many benefit at the expense of the one), but there are also important differences between these two ways of seeing how the one and the many interrelate. The willingness to surrender one's life for those whom one loves, an idea which, as the declaration cited above demonstrates, lies close to the heart of Jesus Christ's life and teaching, becomes reduced to a social and economic axiom within Bentham's philosophy. It is this matter of love for another that motivates willing self-sacrifice in Christ's teaching, effectively injecting a personal dimension within the equation which is difficult to quantify, or even account for, within Bentham's philosophical system. And it is precisely this personal dimension we see coming through so clearly in the world of *Star Trek*, especially when the one, for whom the many (the crew of the *Enterprise*) are willing to risk their lives, is a character as beloved and as central to the plot of the films as Mr. Spock. Let us explore how this idea of the one'and the many is developed with regard to Spock's death.

The idea of the one and the many is a theme first picked up in an exchange between Spock and Kirk early in *The Wrath of Khan*. The two are discussing the danger of their impending mission and Spock graciously concedes control of the *Enterprise* to Kirk, brushing aside any suggestion that he is offended by Kirk's taking over his command.

> SPOCK: Logic clearly dictates that the needs of the many outweigh the needs of the few.
> KIRK: Or the one.

Dramatically, this simple exchange serves as a foretaste of the much more weighty declarations that follow. Next we note the sombre exchange between Spock and Kirk in the reactor room of the engineering section of the *Enterprise* following the battle with Khan, who had been commanding the stolen *Reliant*. Here we have the second version of this "discourse on the needs of the many." Spock has just willingly entered the fuel chambers of the ship in order to restore the warp drive and save the ship, but at the cost of exposing himself to a fatal dose of radiation, his death is imminent. Spock's famous death soliloquy follows, and it includes the critical expressions, although this time they are redistributed between the two characters.

> SPOCK: Don't grieve, Admiral. It is logical. The needs of the many outweigh . . .
> KIRK: . . . the needs of the few.
> SPOCK: . . . or the one.

The exact same lines of dialogue are repeated at one point in *The Search for Spock*. In this scene Spock's father Sarek mind-melds with Kirk in an attempt to find out about the death of his son. Toward the end of the film, after the successful re-fusion of Spock's *katra* with his rejuvenated (resurrected?) body, another version of these words also appears. This happens during an exchange between Kirk and Spock on Mount Seleya. Note the inversion of the relative value of the one and the many within Kirk's reply to Spock's question; here Spock becomes the one which the rest of the *Enterprise* crew value so much that they are willing to risk themselves for him:

> SPOCK: My father says that you have been my friend. You came back for me.
> KIRK: You would have done the same for me.
> SPOCK: Why would you do this?
> KIRK: Because the needs of the one outweigh the needs of the many.

Leonard Nimoy rightly picks up on the centrality of the theme of sacrifice within *The Wrath of Khan*, and at the same time notes how *The Search for Spock* (which he directed) deliberately changes the spin on the relationship between the one and he many. Speaking of the possibilities that *The Search for Spock* provided, he writes: "Clearly the theme of *Star Trek II* centered around sacrifice, and the notion that 'the good of the many outweighed the good of the few . . . or the one.' Was it possible that, this time, the good of the one might outweigh the good of the few, or the many?" (Nimoy 1995: 223).

And just to make certain that the audience understands the importance of the exchange on Mount Seleya between Kirk and Spock, the scene is used within the pre-credits introduction to *Star Trek IV: The Voyage Home* (1986). This film (*TVH*), which was also directed by Nimoy, features a further conversation between Spock and his mother Amanda, which is relevant to our topic. She interrupts her son as he is retraining on a complex computer console and questions him about his understanding of what has happened to him. She wonders if Spock fully appreciates what Kirk and the others have done in rescuing him from the Genesis Planet:

> AMANDA: Spock, does the good of the many outweigh the good of the one?
> SPOCK: I would accept that as an axiom.
> AMANDA: Then you stand here, alive, because of a mistake made by your flawed, feeling human friends. They have sacrificed their futures because they believed that the good of the one—you—was more important to them.

There seems little doubt that this discourse on needs takes on an almost philosophical role within the feature films, standing as a summary of all that is valuable and important within love and friendship. At the same time it is recognized throughout that friendship of this caliber, love of this depth, often requires risk, perhaps even sacrifice of life. Thus, as we noted in our discussion of "The Empath" where McCoy endures suffering and willingly sacrifices himself so that his friends Kirk and Spock might be allowed to live, so, too, here we have a creative juxtaposition of the one and the many in which friendship is worked out in terms of self-sacrifice. In going back to the Genesis planet, the crew of the *Enterprise* risk everything, not only their careers within *Starfleet* but also their very lives, in order to rescue Spock. It is worth stressing that in the latter two citations of the discourse on needs cited above, the one and the many appear deliberately reversed, as the focus shifts from the needs of the *many* crew members of the *Enterprise* to the needs of the *one* crew member Spock. Indeed, this could be interpreted as an ironic challenge to the prevailing spirit of Bentham's philosophy, deliberately turning the notion of the value of the group, over against the value of the individual, on its head.

In summary, the willing self-surrender of one's life for the sake of those whom one loves is deeply embedded within the Judeo-Christian tradition, and certainly formed an essential component of Jesus' own thinking. His own sacrificial death on the cross is quickly interpreted by early Christians along these lines and self-sacrifice for friends becomes a mark of true Christian discipleship. The mythological world of *Star Trek* is quick to develop its own version of such self-sacrifice, particularly in the feature films which concentrate on the death of Spock. This is so much so that we might indeed describe *The Wrath of Khan* and *The Search for Spock* as an extended two-part parable on the relative needs and values of the one as set over against those of the many. The Vulcan's willingness to give up his life so that Kirk, McCoy and the rest of the crew of the *Enterprise* might live is a desperate act, but it is one that is born out of love. So, too, are the reciprocal actions on the part of the crew as they return to the Genesis planet for Spock, In both cases, while the language used to express this interchange of love is vaguely reminiscent of the philosopher Jeremy Bentham's moral maxim ("the greatest good for the greatest number"), the motivation behind it is well in keeping with the words and actions of Jesus Christ himself. *Star Trek* here has beautifully adapted one of the central themes of the New Testament and has made it its own; this is theological myth-making at its best.

Spock's Resurrection from the Dead

There are several points at which *The Wrath of Khan* appears to cross over into quasi-religious territory, territory generally accepted as holy ground within Christianity. Nowhere is this more clear than in the way that the idea of Spock's resurrection from the dead was eventually worked into the storyline of the film and subsequently developed more fully in *The Search for Spock*. The reluctance of Leonard Nimoy to continue playing the role of Spock ad infinitum is well known, and it is generally acknowledged that he only agreed to participate in *The Wrath of Khan* because the script included a strong death scene for Spock. And yet, *how* the death of the character was to be achieved is something that developed in the course of the filming of the movie itself, and several key ingredients for the version of Spock's denouement that eventually made it to the big-screen took place rather late in the production and editing of the film. The early versions of the film did not have the scenes of Spock's coffin being jettisoned from the *Enterprise* and landing on the Genesis planet nor the final scene on board the ship where Kirk, McCoy, and Carol Marcus discuss the loss of their friend. Indeed, the president of Paramount pictures at the time, Michael Eisner, in a executive meeting that followed the first public screening of the test film to a sample audience, is on record as saying: "What we don't have here is resurrection. We have the death scene, we have Good Friday, but we don't have Easter morning. We need the garden of Gethsemane" (Shatner 1994: 144).[17]

The film was thus re-edited, with these key scenes (just described) added. As a result, *The Wrath of Khan* contains its own versions of Good Friday and a hint of the Easter Sunday to come, as well as its equivalent of the Last Supper, the symbolic meal that anticipated the impending death of Jesus. All three components have their counterparts within the storyline of the film. Not only is Spock's act of self-sacrifice to save the ship presented in such a way that it echoes with Christ's surrender for others on the cross at Calvary, but the shot of Spock's coffin landing on the Genesis planet hints at the possibilities of a future resurrection. In addition, the scene in which Spock transfers his "katra" to McCoy by means of the Vulcan mind-meld is also rich in symbolic significance and might be said to have its own parallel within the biblical narrative. Spock's exhortation that McCoy should "Remember!" is reminiscent of the command issued by Jesus Christ to his disciples at the Last Supper, "Do this in *remembrance* of me." (recorded in Luke 22:19 and 1 Corinthians 11:24). The two stories (the narrative world of Jesus in the New Testament and the imaginative world of *Star Trek*) are united in that they contain an all-important call by the one who is to die (Spock in *Star Trek* and Christ in the New Testament) to the one(s) who are left behind (McCoy in *Star Trek* and the twelve Apostles in the New Testament) that they are to *remember* and not forget. It appears that a great deal of theological myth-making is in evidence here.

What of other parallels between the New Testament narratives and the depiction of Spock's death and resurrection? Other intriguing examples are also to be found. For example, Kirk's emotional eulogy over his friend Spock is given with the words: "Of my friend I can only say this: Of all the souls I have met, his was the most . . . human."

This statement might be likened to the declaration of the Roman centurion at the foot of the cross of Christ: "Truly this man was God's Son!" (Mark 15:37). This is especially so when we recall that the declaration of Jesus as the Son of God was not so much a statement about his *deity*, as it was a statement about his humanity, at least as far as the first-century context is concerned. In other words, the all-too-casual assumption that to affirm Jesus Christ as *the Son of God* is identical to affirming him as *God the Son*, is inaccurate (at least as far as we are able to determine the thought of the writers of the New Testament). The declaration that Jesus was the Son of God was above all an affirmation of his being God's chosen Messiah, the human agent and representative of God Almighty. Thus, when Kirk offers his eulogy over Spock, he is emphasizing the true humanity of the Vulcan in a manner similar to the way in which the Roman centurion eulogizes over the crucified Jesus. The sacrificial self-offering on the part of Jesus Christ opens the door for a fresh evaluation of him as the Vindicated One, the man who had given voluntarily himself on behalf of others and was resurrected as a reward.

Even Spock's funeral service on board the *Enterprise* is somewhat Christianized. As the photon torpedo tube bearing his body is ceremoniously ejected from the ship, we hear the sounds of John Newton's famous hymn "Amazing Grace" being played on the bagpipes. This hymn, perhaps more than any single other, symbolizes one branch of Christianity, namely the evangelical wing of Protestantism.[18] The sound of Newton's hymn may not seem much in itself, although it does appear to justify the claim that *The Wrath of Khan* is deliberately borrowing from a hymn from a popular expression of Christianity in its portrayal of Spock's end. Nevertheless, the inclusion of "Amazing Grace," a traditional Scottish funeral tune, does stand as somewhat incongruous to the fictional occasion. Why was a Vulcan hymn not used? Certainly it was not beyond the imagination of the production crew to have a suitable Vulcan anthem composed for the film. Similar musical creations were made for the Klingons in *Star Trek: The Motion Picture* (1979).[19] It is likely that "Amazing Grace" was used because it was thought to be instantly recognizable to many in the audience as music that sounds appropriate for a funeral. Regardless, the presence of such an established Christian hymn within the film does add an essentially "religious" atmosphere to the scene.[20] Perhaps it is thus entirely fitting that the hymn was played by two bagpipers at Gene Roddenberry's own funeral in Los Angeles in November of 1991.

Even more evocative in *The Wrath of Khan* is Dr. McCoy's line about Spock's death at the end of the film. As McCoy, Kirk, and Carol Marcus (Kirk's former lover) all gather on the bridge of the *Enterprise* following the burial of Spock on the Genesis planet, McCoy looks into the camera and says, as if to us: "You know, he's really not dead . . . as long as we remember him." Like the final scenes of Spock's coffin landing in the greenery of the Eden-like Genesis planet, this also was a scene added late in the editing and production of *The Wrath of Khan*. It too arose in part as a result of the remarks noted earlier made by Michael Eisner about the need to have an Easter Sunday scene as a dramatic counterpart to the Good Friday scene of Spock's death. Indeed, William Shatner describes the added line spoken by McCoy as a "foreshadowing" of Spock's resurrection and rightly notes: "Those few simple lines gave the end of the picture an entirely different feeling, one that allowed audiences to begin pondering what might happen in the future" (Shatner 1994: 146).

How significant is the idea of remembering? And how does remembering relate to a belief in a deceased one's abiding presence, if not his or her actual resurrection from the dead? The New Testament accounts of Jesus' post-Easter appearances tie together the idea of his resurrection from the dead and the disciples' remembering of him in striking fashion. Thus Luke 24:13–32 tells the story of how two of the disciples encountered the risen Lord on the road to Emmaus and were engaged by him in conversation. They discussed the meaning of the crucifixion and the resurrection of Jesus from the dead (which had been reported to the disciples by the women at the tomb). However, it was not until after the disciples had invited Jesus to share an evening meal with them, and he had broke bread with them (presumably in a manner reminiscent of the Last Supper) that they knew it was Jesus himself. In Luke's words (24:30–31): "When he (Jesus) was at table with them, he took the bread and blessed, and broke it, and gave it to them. And their eyes were opened and they recognized him." The description of the blessing of the bread, the breaking of it, and its distribution to the disciples is strikingly reminiscent to Luke's account of the Last Supper. Thus, we read in Luke 22:19, "And he took bread, and when he had given thanks he broke it and gave it to them, saying, 'This is my body which is given for you. Do this *in remembrance* of me.'"[21]

No doubt there is a deliberate bringing together of the two stories on the part of the author of the gospel of Luke. The Last Supper is a prefiguring of the crucifixion wherein Jesus gives his physical body to be broken for his disciples, and the breaking of the bread by the risen Lord Jesus Christ is designed to invoke remembrance of his sacrifice among them. Thus, the sacrament of Holy Communion might rightly be seen as a means of remembering the crucified Christ and encountering him as the risen Lord. Given this creative bundling together of the themes of symbolic meal, sacrificial death by crucifixion, and resurrection, it is hardly surprising that the idea of remembrance[22] has remained an essential part of theological discussions about the meaning of the Eucharist from the earliest days of the Christian church. Remembering the sacrifice of Christ on the cross only makes sense from the perspective of the empty tomb—the significance of Good Friday is made clear by Easter Sunday.

So what are we to make of the death of Spock and the possibility of his resurrection from the dead? Without question, the way in which *The Wrath of Khan* ends leads the viewing audience toward hope in Spock's resurrection. The creative power of the Genesis effect seems duty-bound to raise the Vulcan from the dead and preserve for us one of the essential characters of the *Star Trek* world.[23] It is as if in *The Wrath of Khan* we have two central ideas, whose New Testament parallels are theologically linked, being brought together in highly dramatic fashion. We have, in the form of Spock handing on his "katra" to McCoy, the *Star Trek* equivalent of the Lord's Supper and its command to "Do this in remembrance of me!" We have, in the form of Spock's act of self-sacrifice in the *Enterprise* engine-room, the *Star Trek* equivalent of Christ's sacrificial death on the cross for others. The final scenes of the film contain suggestive hints of resurrection, but nothing more. Something like this appears in the pages of the New Testament where we find Jesus giving hints of his future resurrection from the dead, such as the enigmatic saying about "the sign of Jonah" contained in Matthew 12:40. "For as Jonah was three days and three nights in the belly of the whale, so will the Son of man be three days and three nights in the heart of the earth."

Yet Jesus offers nothing concrete in terms of how his resurrection will take place and what the impact will be on his disciples. As far as the resurrection of Spock is concerned, we had to wait until *The Search for Spock* to see precisely how this was worked out. In the New Testament the gap between the death of Jesus Christ and his resurrection was three days, in the world of *Star Trek* the gap between Spock's death and his resurrection was two years—between the cinematic release of *The Wrath of Khan* in 1982 and the release of *The Search for Spock* in 1984.

CONCLUSION

This study has been concerned with exploring how important biblical imagery is for the mythological world of *Star Trek*. In pursuing this topic, we have concentrated on one particular episode from the third year of the original series, "The Empath," together with two of the feature films, *The Wrath of Khan* and *The Search for Spock* . Through a careful examination of these materials, we have demonstrated some of the ways in which biblical themes and theological ideas have been borrowed from the biblical texts and creatively incorporated within the storyline of *Star Trek*. The manner and extent to which this takes place suggests that *Star Trek*'s mythological world is one that has a significant theological dimension at its heart. In short, *Star Trek* has freely borrowed, and creatively adapted, important mythical ideas from the Judeo-Christian heritage as it has evolved into becoming the dominant science fiction myth of our day. Insofar as it has done this, *Star Trek* has created its own highly original version of a theological myth.

"Myth" and "mythical" are loaded words, particularly in the theological world of Christianity, at least as it is popularly conceived. But they are deliberately chosen for this context, and for good reason. In *A Glossary of Literary Terms* M. H. Abrahms remarks that the term "myth" has come to have another meaning outside of it being a formal definition of a literary genre. Abrahms (1981: 112) says that myth: "is the solidly imagined realm in which a work of fiction is enacted." In this sense I believe it is possible to address the idea of the *Star Trek* myth and I have made some tentative suggestions about the precise religious connections and theological underpinning's that it has. This is hardly an original approach—many others, including fellow contributors to this volume, have described the essentially mythic quality of *Star Trek* (Tyrrell 1977; Jewett and Lawrence 1977; Kreuziger 1982: 188–98; Ellington and Critelli 1983; Hurley 1983). Nevertheless, I hope I have demonstrated the theological undergarment (so to speak) of that myth. In this sense the translation of the Biblical myth into another imaginative universe, albeit one from the realms of science fiction, is complete. *Star Trek* thus stands as a prime example of the "web of accessible imagery" that nurtures the spiritual life, as described by Colin Morris in the quote with which we commenced our study. There is a great deal that may be profitably explored here, particularly when we consider how rarely professional theologians have anything to do with popular science fiction writing. This is much to their own detriment for there is no doubting that for many contemporary people, a worldview created by science fiction functions in precisely the same way within their lives as did the worldview created by religious belief for previous generations.

I close with a quote from Kingsley Amis's (1963: 134) tribute to science fiction, his book entitled *New Maps of Hell*: "One is grateful that we have a form of writing which is interested in the future, which is ready to treat as variables what are usually taken to be constants, which is set on tackling those large, general, speculative questions that ordinary fiction so often avoids." Although Amis is describing science fiction writing here, this could also be a definition of theological thinking at its best, a thinking characterized by an openness to the variables of life, ever seeking, ever questing. Is there any wonder that science fiction remains so popular in our time?

NOTES

1. Also worth reading on the subject are Gregor Goethals (1993) and David George (1995).

2. For a full listing of all of the biblical quotes and allusions in *Star Trek*, see Kreitzer (1996: 9–15). Apart from Shakespeare's plays, the Bible is the work of literature most frequently cited or alluded to in the original *Star Trek* series.

3. The character Kahless, spiritual founder of the Klingons, presents what is perhaps the most intriguing parallel to Jesus Christ. We were first introduced to the character in an episode from the original *Star Trek* series entitled "The Savage Curtain" (1969). However, it is in *Star Trek: The Next Generation* that the spiritual dimensions of Kahless are developed, particularly in the episode entitled "Rightful Heir." Michael Jan Friedman's recent novel *Kahless* (1996) explores this quite thoroughly, setting up a situation in which the legendary exploits of Kahless, indeed his very historical existence, are brought into question by the chance discovery of an ancient scroll that offers an alternative opinion about him. It is easy to see parallels to the kind of doubts and suspicions raised concerning the

historical Jesus by scholars who make similar claims, frequently on the basis of some contentious materials contained within the Dead Sea Scrolls.

4. I have discussed this more fully in a public lecture entitled "'*Bread and Circuses*': Christian History According to the World of *Star Trek*" which was given on January 30, 1997, at Regent's Park College, Oxford, under the auspices of the *Centre for the Study of Christianity and Culture* based at the college.

5. Johnston argues that this episode, more than any other, is true to the Platonic ideal of a virtuous person as one who perfectly balances all aspects of life.

6. It is interesting to note that the British Broadcasting Corporation (BBC) initially screened *Star Trek* in four seasons (from July 12 1969 to December 15, 1971). Three episodes from the third year of production, namely "The Empath" (1968), "Plato's Stepchildren" (1968), and "Whom Gods Destroy" (1968), did not pass the censorship standards of the time and were not aired on British TV. Given that all three deal with the suffering of beings at the hands of capricious "gods," one wonders whether they were all considered by the censor to be too theologically controversial for the British public.

7. This is particularly true in Western art. The iconography of the crucifixion within Eastern Christendom is noticeably different. In the East there is a difference in the shape of the cross (a T-shaped one is generally used), as well as a different presentation of the body of Christ as he is fixed upon it (with the body in more of a Z-shaped design). A good example of this is to be seen in Martin Scorsese's controversial film *The Last Temptation of Christ* (1988), which is based on the novel by the Greek writer Nikos Kazantzakis.

8. The extent to which *pre-Christian Judaism* understood the Suffering Servant in such messianic terms is not so clear though some evidence suggests that the Suffering Servant was considered a national image, rather than an idealized Messiah-figure (Heaton 1977: 111–14). Others have interpreted the passage to refer to an individual figure, such as the prophet of Deutero-Isaiah himself (Whybray 1975: 171–83) or Zerubbabel (Watts 1987: 222–33).

9. Asherman (1989: 115) remarks on this point: "Kathryn Hays (Gem) deserves a great deal of credit for the success of her scenes. She is an excellent mime, and although Gem never utters a single word throughout the story, Ms. Hays's gestures and facial expressions create as sensitive a character as could be created through the use of dialogue."

10. On this point see Kreitzer (1990: 21–24). Paul the Apostle also suggests that Christians early on interpreted the death of Jesus in terms of his being sacrificed like the Passover lambs when he describes Christ in 1 Corinthians 5:7 as "our Passover who has been sacrificed." The letter dates to about 57 C.E.

11. See David (1986), who offers an interesting list of parallels based on the Gospel accounts and the first two *Star Trek* feature films.

12. Ruppersberg (1990: 32) suggests that this feature is so persuasive within science fiction of the past twenty years or so that it might legitimately be described as "a cultural phenomenon."

13. The resurrection is explicitly mentioned or alluded to in twenty out of twenty-seven books of the New Testament. The exceptions are 2 Thessalonians, Titus, Philemon, 3 John, 2 Peter, James and Jude, and in these it might safely be presumed. It is quite striking how frequently the idea of a resurrection/regeneration/rebirth is dealt with in science fiction films. Ruppersberg (1990: 38) cites *The Day the Earth Stood Still, Superman, Cocoon, Star Trek III: The Search for Spock, Starman, Star Wars, The Last Starfighter, E.T.,* and *2010* as examples. We could add the hugely influential *The Terminator* and *Terminator 2: Final Judgment* as further evidence of the same phenomenon.

14. Thus, MacDonald (1991: 29) writes: "As usual, Hollywood is happy to mix elements of Christian tradition with a spoonful of Eastern mysticism to raise one of its characters back to life."

15. Caiaphas' prophecy is again alluded to in John 18:14.

16. The clothed skeleton of the philosopher Bentham is housed in University College in Malet Street, London. It is displayed in a glass case at the top of a flight of stairs within the building. This display, built in accordance with the terms of Bentham's will and known as the "Auto-icon," actually displayed the mummified head of Bentham, suitably poised between his feet, from 1850–1948. The head, perhaps the most macabre possession of the University of London, is now kept in the University College safe.

17. Sharp-eyed critics of the Bible will note, of course, that Eisner has made a mistake here in confusing the garden of Gethsemane with the garden tomb in which, according to the gospel accounts, Jesus was laid and from which he was resurrected. The incident in the garden of Gethsemane was *prior* to the crucifixion and represents Jesus' agonizing struggle with his impending death as the political machinations of the day progressed and brought the likelihood of the cross ever nearer.

18. Newton (1725–1807) himself was an Anglican clergyman, but his hymns have become the anthems of evangelical Protestantism in general and his popularity as a hymn-writer extends far beyond the borders of his own denomination.

19. The composer of music for the film, James Horner, objected to the inclusion of "Amazing Grace" in the funeral sequence; he was overruled in the matter. The hymn is not on the soundtrack for the film available from Crescendo Records, Inc. (1982).

20. James Van Hise (1991: 58–59), reports that originally the film script called for a Christian prayer to be read at Spock's funeral. However, this idea was

dropped following strong objections by Gene Roddenberry who felt it violated the prevailing humanistic philosophy of the *Star Trek* world. Roddenberry's humanism and his views on religion are the focus of an interview he gave to David Alexander (1991: 5–38). These matters are also discussed in William Shatner (1994: 36–38, 229–30); Joel Engel (1995: 3, 234–35); David Alexander (1995: 38–40, 167–68, 459–60, 617–25); and Yvonne Fern (1995: 53–61, 110–14).

21. An almost identical declaration is found in 2 Corinthians 11:23–24. The breaking of bread motif is also carried through several times in Acts (2:42, 46; 20:7, 11; 24:30).

22. The Greek term is *anamnesis*, which has been a key technical term in liturgical discussions ever since.

23. Although Spock dies at the end of *The Wrath of Khan*, there was little doubt among staunch fans that he would somehow be brought back from the dead. It is difficult to imagine *Star Trek* without Spock, so central is he to the heart of the series. As a result, *The Search for Spock* did not come as a complete surprise to loyal followers of *Star Trek*. However, not all fans were happy about the impact of Spock's return. In the words of one concerned Trekkie: "What then are we to make of this return from the dead, this newfound life which has been granted our Vulcan friend? Does his resurrection from a noble death and well-earned rest thus invalidate our treasured conceptions of heroic sacrifice and eternal friendship?" (Blake 1987: 166). Nevertheless, another fan expressed his hope in language that could be taken to be very reminiscent of the New Testament descriptions of Jesus' death and subsequent resurrection: "I must admit that as the camera panned across the Genesis planet at the end of *Wrath of Khan*, I half expected to see the casket open—and footprints leading away from it . . ." (Alfred 1983: 83).

9

The Outward Voyage and the Inward Search

Star Trek *Motion Pictures and the Spiritual Quest*

IAN MAHER

D iscernible within the *Star Trek* films is a parallel between the outward voyage of the *Enterprise* and the inward human search to find meaning and purpose in a vast and sometimes frightening universe. Amid the triumph of science and technology there remain fundamental questions to be answered. What is the purpose of life? What does it mean to be human? Where does humanity fit into the broader scheme of things? Is there a "God" behind it all? These are questions that belong to all of us and resonate with something deep within ourselves. At one level, *Star Trek* can be understood as an entertaining adventure, and at another level it connects with the human spiritual quest.

The *Star Trek* films portray a number of the overarching themes inherent in this human spiritual quest including the yearning to know where we come from and where we are going, human responsibility and relatedness to the created order, spiritual hunger and the longing to know that death is not the end, the search for true peace and reconciliation and the essence of being human. Reflecting its influence on the formation of the Western culture out of which *Star Trek* emerged, the lens through which these themes will be addressed is that of the Judeo-Christian tradition.

STAR TREK: THE MOTION PICTURE

In *Star Trek: The Motion Picture* (1979), the USS *Enterprise* is sent to intercept a deadly vessel headed toward earth from deep space and destroying all before it. At first the origins of the vessel seem to be alien, its intent malign. But as Captain James T. Kirk (William Shatner) and his crew discover in the ensuing drama the vessel is not primarily an offensive weapon. It has a name, V-ger, and having killed one of the *Enterprise's* crew, Lieutenant Ilia (Persis Khambatta), it sends a probe in her image to the *Enterprise* and dialogue is initiated. At this stage, Vejur perceives the *Enterprise* as a living entity and its crew merely as an infestation of "carbon-based units." In a novel twist on the human presuppositions of what constitutes life, Vejur, a machine, cannot conceive of organic beings as capable of intelligence.

Faced with the infinitely more advanced technology of V-ger, Kirk and his crew are left to think their way out of a hopeless situation. The film draws toward a climax when Mr. Spock (Leonard Nimoy) mindmelds with V-ger and discovers its intent to return home. He also experiences the desperate barrenness within the machine's consciousness and recognizes the question, "Is this all that I am?" Kirk, in customary fashion, then senses a way forward. He demands of the Ilia probe that he be allowed to speak with V-ger. The probe agrees and Kirk, Spock, Dr. McCoy (DeForest Kelley), and Commander Decker (Stephen Collins) end up in a direct encounter with V-ger.

At the heart of the alien vessel they discover, to their amazement, a relic from the past. The core of V-ger is in fact *Voyager 6*, an unmanned craft sent into space by NASA in the twentieth century. Still legible on the hull of *Voyager* are the letters V___GER 6, hence V-ger. The NASA craft had, in the course of its journey, disappeared into a black hole, subsequently emerging on the other side of the galaxy in desperate need of repair. There, it fell into the orbit of a planet populated by sentient machines. These living machines read the programming of *Voyager* which, in essence, was to gather information and return the information to its "creator," i.e. NASA. *Voyager* was thus repaired and set at the heart of a vessel of immense power, equipped to cross the galaxy and complete its mission and capable of overcoming with deadly force any obstacles that hindered its journey homeward.

Voyager 6, with the help of the machine beings, had become a conscious, living entity. What was once a piece of technological hardware responding simply through its computerized software to the instructions of its builders became self-aware. V-ger became able to make choices and decisions as it sought to complete its primary task of gathering and returning information to its source. No longer held within the confines of its programming, V-ger was curious to know about its origin and ultimate purpose. V-ger's quest can therefore been seen as analogous to the deep-seated need of humanity to reach out and search for answers to the fundamental questions of existence. Meanings are often found by going back to roots. It was the very nature of V-ger to return to its creator, and it could not and would not be complete until its mission was fulfilled. Returning to the creator was its prime motivation.

Humans throughout history and across the globe have striven to find their origins, to discover the "mind" behind the universe and to understand our place within it. Human beings have an inbuilt desire to respond to the source of their existence—in Christian terms, to worship the creator. Writing in *The Independent* (London) newspaper (January 18, 1997) about worship and the search for a sense of wonder, Dr. Peter Forster, the Anglican bishop of Chester, commented:

> "It is, I believe, innate in all human beings to have a sense of transcendence and of wonder. It is experienced in many ways, including, but not limited to, religious contexts. It may be when you fall in love, and suddenly the whole world is transformed. It may be to hold a new-born child, or key moments in family life. It can be true when you are present with someone as their life slips away. It can be the beauty of a sunrise or sunset. These moments, when the world is transfigured with special meaning, illustrate and embody the human potential to know God."

Within the Judeo-Christian tradition the longing for human relationship with the Creator is evident within its scriptures and also from the lived experience of the community of faith. The Bible is, from Genesis to Revelation, the story of a people created by God who become alienated from their creator, yet who know that they are incomplete until they can, in effect, return and restore their relationship with God. St. Augustine of Hippo (354–450 C.E.) has described this spiritual quest as follows: "Thou awakest us to delight in Thy praises; for Thou madest us for Thyself, and our heart is restless, until it repose in Thee" (Appleton, 1985:64). From a Christian perspective, it was not possible for humanity to find this rest on its own. The human fall from grace could not be undone through human effort no matter how sincere or noble. It required God to reach out in the person of Christ and provide a way back.

Clearly, there are limits to how far parallels can be made with respect to the story of V-ger's journey across the vastness of space and the human search of the heart for the Creator, but there is certainly some resonance present within the plot of *Star Trek: The Motion Picture*. Despite the incalculable wealth of knowledge accumulated during its journey, V-ger's consciousness and self-awareness led it to confront existential questions that could not be answered by scientific methods. This challenge to confront existential questions is accentuated for V-ger when Ilia is killed and her memories, emotions, and feelings are assimilated by the probe. At last V-ger perceives the possibility of an existence beyond that of the mechanical acquisition of knowledge. Put another way, V-ger is brought to a recognition of something more than the physical universe. Ilia's death, in this sense, brings a much fuller life to V-ger than the purely functional consciousness given to it by the intelligent machines on the far side of the galaxy. The spiritual and relational dimension of Ilia lives on in V-ger, and V-ger experiences the nature of the love once shared between Decker and Ilia. This is demonstrated in the interaction between the Ilia probe while on the *Enterprise* and Decker.

Although the Ilia probe was created by V-ger simply to make dialogue between it and the *Enterprise* crew easier, it is clear that some vestiges of the real Ilia remain. The Ilia probe and Decker have a rapport that does not exist between it and any other crew members. Ultimately, it is this unconquerable resilience of the spirit, love transcending death, which saves the earth from destruction. For upon failing to receive an answer to its radio messages, V-ger sets into orbit devices with the potential to cleanse earth of its "infestation of carbon-based units," and it is only Decker's love for Ilia, and his subsequent decision to merge with V-ger, that saves the earth and allows V-ger to evolve to the next stage of its existence.

Star Trek: The Motion Picture is very much a modern parable. As humankind stands on the brink of a new millennium it does so at the end of a century that has witnessed incredible scientific and technological advances. A microchip the size of a fingernail can now carry more information than computers that once occupied entire floors of buildings. From our living rooms it is now possible to access information on an infinite number of subjects from any part of the globe. Advances in medicine break new frontiers almost daily. Yet humankind remains faced with the specter of war, poverty, and disease. Somehow, despite the apparently limitless potential of human beings to acquire knowledge, something is lacking. There is a need that remains unmet despite the onward march of science and technology. Christians and many people from other faiths recognize this as a spiritual need. V-ger's self-awareness resulted in a desperate loneliness and the need to somehow make contact with its creator. This is a poignant reminder that meaning and purpose are to be found only in relationships and, in particular, in relationship with the Other.

Within the Christian tradition emphasis on the relationship with the Other is apparent through the belief that humankind is created in the image of a relational God. The doctrine of the Trinity is an expression of that belief. At one level, the Trinity is considered an unfathomable mystery, yet at another, it gives the clearest possible clues as to why it is only in relationship with each other and with the Creator that human beings can make sense of our existence. Summarized, the Christian understanding of God as Trinity is as follows, and it is from this that all else flows. God, from all eternity, is a community of Persons revealed in the Bible as Father, Son, and Holy Spirit. Completely self-sufficient and existing in a perfect community of love, God chose to create out of love a people with whom to be in relation. The Genesis stories tell how humankind turned away from this love, becoming unable to find its way back to God. Only through the coming of Jesus Christ—when one Person of the Holy Trinity became human, suffered, and died and was then raised from the dead—was the relationship restored and direct access to the Godhead made possible (e.g. McGrath 1987; Pinnock and Brow, 1994: 45–54).

It is the relationship with the Creator that provides a reason for existence that knowledge alone can never manage. The parable of V-ger reflects a paradox of the Western high-tech culture within which *Star Trek* in particular and the science fiction genre in general have flourished. Scientific progress has been phenomenal in the space of a few short decades and for a while it seemed that it was only a matter of time before science solved all the problems that beset humankind. Such promise has not been fulfilled, and increasingly, it seems that answers to the fundamental questions of purpose and meaning will not be found in isolation from issues of spirituality.

For human beings to even begin to make sense of the universe requires an awareness of our place within it and our relationship to each other. In *Star Trek: The Motion Picture*, as soon as V-ger became self-aware, its pure-science task of gathering data became meaningless in itself. Only through the experience of love and the relational dimension that this brought to V-ger's existence did the universe make sense.

STAR TREK V: THE FINAL FRONTIER

The theme of the spiritual quest evident in *Star Trek: The Motion Picture* becomes far more explicit in *Star Trek V: The Final Frontier* (1989), Spock's half-brother, Sybok (Laurence Luckinbill), is portrayed in this film as a fanatical mystic on a single-minded religious quest. Under his leadership a devoted band of followers help to hijack the *Enterprise* and travel to the center of the galaxy seeking the planet that Sybok believes to be the home of God. Sybok has a gift of somehow being able to tap into the deep-seated spiritual hunger not only of the humans whom he encounters but also the members of a variety of alien races. Each race has its own understanding of God. Humans, Klingons, Romulans, Vulcans, and others all perceive God through the cultural lenses of their respective societies, but the concept of God, together with the notion of a heaven, is presented in the film as universal.

In the hands of its rebel crew the *Enterprise* speeds toward the center of the galaxy and Kirk, powerless to control his ship, is left to ponder the question, "what if they do find God across that final frontier?" When the *Enterprise* breaks the barrier at the center of the galaxy and assumes orbit above the planet Sybok believes to be Sha Ka Ree to the Vulcans and to humans, Eden, an assorted band including Kirk, Spock, and McCoy do apparently encounter God. With a sense of standing on holy ground at the end of a long pilgrimage, they come face to face with a being who manifests itself in guises drawn from the religious myths of the various cultures represented in the landing party. The human image of God is a reflection of the Western stereotype: a white, venerable, bearded male. It is only in the ensuing dialogue that the being's true identity is revealed. Far from being divine, this being is an immensely powerful alien seeking the technology of a starship to escape across the barrier trapping it at the center of the galaxy. This becomes apparent following the alien's violent response to Kirk's lack of reverence in questioning it. The image of a deity that hurls thunderbolts does have some currency, however, in the popular mind.

A frightening, judgmental God has held a place within Christianity at various times throughout history and hellfire-and-brimstone preaching and theology persist even in the present day. Kirk and his human companions, with wise theological insight, see through the alien's pretense of divinity. The image on which they draw is that of the Christian God who would not impose his power upon his people. Comments made in *The Final Frontier* by members of the landing party when attacked illustrate this point:

McCoy: I doubt any God who inflicts pain for his own pleasure.

Sybok: Stop. The God of Sha Ka Ree would not do this.

Love, not violence, is God's abiding quality. God reaches out and longs for relationship, open to the consequences of the free will given to his creatures and all the risks entailed in such openness (Pinnock et al. 1994).

The malevolent self-interest of this alien leads even Sybok to recognize his mistake and to see the evil nature of the being who claims to be God. He comes to the awful realization that somehow, this creature has manipulated his own genuine spiritual search. Sybok subsequently sacrifices himself to provide the rest of the landing part with a chance to escape. Sybok's sincerity had never been in doubt, but he had been deceived, realizing the deception only when it was too late.

Within the spiritual quest are inherent dangers of deceit and manipulation. The Christian church is littered with the tragic debris of embarking upon similar journeys in the name of sincerely held, but false, images of God. The Crusades stand as an exemplar of what happens when a distorted image of God is acted upon. God was recreated in the image of humankind with all its egocentric weaknesses and failings. This continues to be so wherever religious bigotry raises its ugly head. Yet the God revealed in the Bible, and ultimately in the Person of Jesus Christ, is a God of compassion—a God who stands beside his people in the midst of all their struggles and never over them as a fearsome tyrant. The symbol of God for the Christian is not a sword but a Cross. The greatest victory of all, removing the barrier between God and his people, is achieved not through force but by an act of love in which God experienced to the utmost the suffering of those he had created. "Christian faith stands and falls with the knowledge of the crucified Christ, that is, with the knowledge of God in the crucified Christ, or, to use Luther's even bolder phrase, with the knowledge of the 'crucified God'" (Moltmann 1974: 65).

Even if God needed technology to cross the galaxy, *The Final Frontier*, in keeping with nature of the Christian God, suggests his very nature would not allow him to take by force that which was not freely given. The film also alludes to belief in a God that does not need to be sought on a distant planet. He is not remote in the heavens but finds his home within the human heart. This portrayal of God echoes the words of Jesus to the Samaritan woman recorded in the John's Gospel: "Believe me, woman, a time is coming when you will worship the Father neither on this mountain nor in Jerusalem. . . . God is spirit, and his worshipers must worship in spirit and in truth" (John 4:21–24). In *The Final Frontier*, the need to look inward for God is suggested in the following exchange:

KIRK: (to McCoy and Spock) Cosmic thoughts gentlemen?

McCOY: We were speculating. Is God really out there?

KIRK: Maybe not out there, Bones. Maybe he's right here . . . human heart.

The "outward" voyage of Sybok and the *Enterprise* leads to the realization that there is no need to seek God beyond the stars. God is already present within the heart. The only barrier to human beings discovering their spiritual home is the distortion arising from the folly of attempting to create God in the image of humankind. Sybok ironically stole a starship and traveled to the center of the galaxy to find the God who was "out there." He never thought to look inward, to the undiscovered reaches of his own heart.

STAR TREK: THE WRATH OF KHAN

While *The Motion Picture* and *The Final Frontier* connect with the theme of reaching for the transcendent, other films in the series draw attention to the place of humanity in relation to the rest of the created order. *Star Trek II: The Wrath of Khan* (1982) and *Star Trek IV: The Voyage Home* (1986) raise a number of issues in this respect. In *The Wrath of Khan*, the genetically engineered villain, Khan Singh (Ricardo Montalban), and his followers embark on a mission of revenge against Captain Kirk. In an encounter with Kirk some fifteen years earlier, Khan was defeated and exiled with his crew for their crimes to an uninhabited, though pleasant and life-sustaining planet (Ceti Alpha V) orbited by a huge satellite moon (Ceti Alpha VI). The moon itself was lifeless and desolate. Unknown to the Federation, soon after Khan's exile the moon exploded causing the planet to tilt on its axis with devastating climatic changes resulting. An easy exile on Ceti Alpha V had thus for years been a struggle against the odds for survival, made possible only by Khan's massive, engineered intellect.

The research vessel *Reliant,* arrives at what it believes to be the uninhabited moon and two members of the crew, Captain Terrell (Paul Winfield) and Commander Chekov (Walter Koenig) beam down to the surface. They are captured by Khan and his followers, discovering to their cost that they are in fact on Ceti Alpha V. Khan then forces Terrell and Chekov to assist him in gaining access to and control of the *Reliant*, where he takes command and sets out to wreak havoc on Captain Kirk. For Khan, discovery of the Genesis Project is an added bonus, providing him with the potential for inflicting massive destruction upon any worlds that refuse to capitulate to his demands. Whereas to a desolate world, a Genesis device could bring life from nothing, on a populated planet it would result in devastation.

The story unfolds with Khan's thirst for vengeance upon Kirk becoming all-consuming. Defeated and near death following a battle with the *Enterprise*, Khan starts the countdown to set off the Genesis device. The resulting cataclysm would engulf both Khan's ship and the *Enterprise*, and would allow Khan in death to visit vengeance upon Kirk. Only Spock's self-sacrifice provides the means of escape for the crippled *Enterprise* as he enters a massively irradiated chamber in order to restore power to the ship.

In a world where genetic engineering and experimentation is progressing at an alarming rate, *The Wrath of Khan* is a reminder of some inherent dangers. Intended to be a perfect human specimen, Khan exemplifies the Darwinian notion of the survival of the fittest. For Khan, the claim to genetic superiority meant the exercise of power and domination over others irrespective of the misery and suffering that might result. The weak were pushed aside and trampled upon and those who stood in his way were destroyed. It was for such crimes on Earth that Khan was exiled by Kirk following their first encounter. Khan's genetically enhanced physical and mental capabilities did enable him to accomplish incredible feats, not least ensuring the survival of himself and his followers in the nearly impossible conditions of Ceti Alpha V. What Khan did not possess, however, was the ability to appreciate either the sanctity of life or the equality of all people. Those who did not serve his needs or who challenged him in any way were considered expendable. The story in *The Wrath of Khan* in relation to the person of Khan, acts as a reminder of the dangers in tampering with genetics outside of a moral framework. The inquisitive nature of human beings results in pushing the limits of discovery ever further. There is a tendency to take that extra step as soon as it becomes possible. This sense of reaching out beyond current capabilities is an aspect of the spiritual quest with consequences that can be both exhilarating and dangerous. Life can be enhanced or diminished depending upon the direction of the quest and the motivation that lies behind it.

In one respect, Khan epitomizes the consequences of an amoral approach to genetic engineering that essentially adopts a "building blocks" approach. The "perfect" human being, from this perspective, is simply the product of assembling the necessary genetic materials that ensure a fitter, faster, stronger, and intellectually more capable human being. Yet such an approach is fundamentally flawed, a fact to which John Habgood (1993: 79), a former Archbishop of York and also a trained scientist, draws attention: "One of the most striking characteristics of human life, as actually lived and experienced, is its open-endedness. To be human is to be unfinished and free."

In the Christian view, being human is to exist not as a finished product but as life that is still becoming. A life that will not be perfected until the other side of death. "It does not yet appear what we shall be, but we know that when he (Jesus) appears we shall be like him for we shall see him as he is" (1 John 3:2). Christians believe that human perfection is intrinsically related to becoming Christ-like. It is a process that has its beginning in this life and grows in relationship with God and with other human beings. Perfection is not, therefore, about flawless bodies and towering intellects, but rather it is linked to reflecting and identifying with the crucified Christ in the world. In *The Wrath of Khan*, Khan epitomized the very opposite. For him power was something to be seized by any means necessary. Only the strong should survive, and qualities such as compassion and forgiveness were simply signs of weakness.

The Wrath of Khan also highlights, in the different approaches toward the Genesis Project held by its developers and Khan, how the morality of science is determined by its use. For the former, the Genesis Project represented the opportunity to bring life where there was none; for the latter, it was a potential weapon to be used to destroy life. The Federation was aware of the dangers of its misuse; Khan had no qualms whatsoever about utilizing its destructive potential for his own ends. Somewhat disturbingly, the use of science is not always discernable as good or bad. The best intentions sometimes produce the most appalling results. The splitting of the atom, for example, opened up huge potential for good. It also laid waste to Nagasaki and Hiroshima. This dilemma is something picked up in *Star Trek III: The Search for Spock* (1984) when the scientists responsible for developing the Genesis Project realize too late that the attempt to create life is, in fact, taking science one step too far. Miracle turns to nightmare as the newly formed Genesis planet destroys itself.

When boundaries of discovery are seen as limitless, without adequate consideration for the effect upon others, sorrow and pain are never far away. The paradox is that as humankind becomes more god-like in terms of capability at a scientific and technological level it moves further away from reflecting the image of the Christian God as portrayed in the Bible. The Sermon on the Mount (Matthew 5) and the Magnificat (Luke 1:46–55) reveal a very different order of things. Those at the very bottom of the pile are in fact precious to God. Many would in fact argue that God has a "bias to the poor" (e.g. Gutierrez 1988; Sheppard, 1983). They are not insignificant pawns at the disposal of the mighty to be sacrificed upon the altars of the laboratory in the name of scientific advancement. Khan represented the very antithesis of such Christian qualities in his approach to life.

The words of Jesus in Matthew 25:31–46 draw attention to the true measure of humanity and it amounts to neither power and gain nor genetic "perfection" nor scientific miracles. To be truly human in the Christian sense means recognizing our brothers and sisters in the hungry and the homeless, the sick and the imprisoned, those regarded as the least important in our society. Such a spirituality provides a potential yardstick by which all human projects can be measured.

STAR TREK IV: THE VOYAGE HOME

In *Star Trek IV: The Voyage Home* (1986), the key issue raised is the relationship of humanity to the rest of life on this planet. Kirk and his crew are approaching Earth in a captured Klingon Bird-of-Prey vessel following the events of *Star Trek III: The Search for Spock* in which the *Enterprise* was lost (considered later). As they head homeward they discover that an immensely powerful alien probe has taken up position above the earth and is threatening life on the planet by vaporizing great quantities of the earth's oceans.

Spock subsequently discovers that the alien probe is seeking to reestablish contact with the humpback whales which once lived in abundance in the oceans of the world. Hunted to extinction by the twenty-third century setting of the film, there were no whales left in the oceans to respond to the probe's communication. Kirk suggests time travel as the only possible solution, traveling back to the past to somehow bring a pair of humpback whales forward to the twenty-third century and thereby enable a response to the probe. Bringing these whales forward in time would also reestablish a once extinct species in the earth's oceans. Twentieth-century San Francisco is where the time travelers arrive to carry out their task.

The Earth of Kirk's day is shown in *The Voyage Home* to suffer the bitter legacy left to it by Earth's citizens of the twentieth century. War, poverty, pollution, and the relentless march of human self-interest on Earth had long since been eradicated, but some of the consequences of human folly were far-reaching. Countless species had been wiped out through hunting or pollution and many of the earth's natural resources were lost forever. The humpback whales serve as a contemporary example of a species on the brink because of the actions of humankind.

The scale and immediacy of the environmental destruction of the twentieth century is brought home in some statistics produced by the World Wide Fund for Nature: "Each day between 3 and 50 species of life become extinct. By AD 2000 15–20 per cent of all species on earth may have disappeared due to human activities. That is, about 1,000,000 species will have become extinct" (quoted in Wood 1986: 20). *The Voyage Home* provides a fantasy answer to the restoration of one single extinct species. Time travel is not an option for the real world. There is, in reality, no going back to undo the harm of the past. Extinction is forever, and that is arguably the point of the film. The problem must be addressed in the here and now. The need for the development of a holistic spirituality is a pressing one. For those holding a Christian worldview, the destruction of species is an affront to the belief in a God who is a purposeful Creator. In that respect it is a matter inextricably bound up with the spiritual quest. Life is diminished by anything that disturbs the natural balance of the created order. For those who would place their concern for the planet outside of any spiritual framework, chords are also struck deep within the psyche.

The Voyage Home draws attention directly to environmental and ecological matters. If humanity regards itself in a self-centered way, then the earth's resources—animal, vegetable, and mineral—become no more than commodities to be exploited. This has been the dominant approach in modern times with the result that the planet has, and continues, to be stripped of things that can never be replaced as humanity continues on what seems like a suicidal path. An awakening to the realization that what happens on the earth of today will affect those who come after for good or for ill is desperately needed at all levels. The earth's destruction might not come about as a result of an alien probe but it is within the realms of possibility that the seeds of tomorrow's desolation are being sown in the human short-sightedness of today.

In the *Star Trek* world of the twenty-third century, the interconnectedness of life on the planet has long since been recognized. Destruction of the environment and disturbance of fragile ecosystems are regarded as dark

moments in the history of humankind. There is an implicit holistic spirituality of creation present, reflected elsewhere in the *Star Trek* saga in relation to life on other worlds. All life holds an intrinsic value and is sacred.
Spock's comment in *The Voyage Home:* "To hunt a species to extinction is
illogical" is by then not just Vulcan logic but human commonsense. Long
past is the greed-driven onslaught against the other living species of the
planet. There is respectful approach toward non-human life, whether terrestrial or extra-terrestrial. It is non-judgmental, non-aggressive, tolerant of
difference, and aware of being part of a larger whole. It is a way of being,
an aspect of spirituality, which is already present today in the noblest
expressions of many of the world's religions. Such a spirituality might also
be the best hope for Earth to survive the ecological disaster toward which
it seems to be heading. There is no time-traveling starship that can repair
the damage currently being inflicted upon the earth's ecosystem. The vehicle is instead an approach which recognizes that the answer is not "out
there" but within the human heart. Such a spirituality may, or may not, be
linked to a formal religious system.

Christianity has often manifested an unhealthy anthropocentrism in
relation to the rest of creation, such a distorted relationship is not the
whole picture. Celtic Christianity, for example, was a model of a "creation
spirituality" (e.g. Van de Weyer 1990). The Christian Orthodox Churches
of the East similarly recognize within their liturgies and spiritual tradition, the holiness of the created order (e.g. Lossky 1991; Fedotov 1981;
Wybrew,1989). From the Catholic tradition, St. Francis of Assisi provides
another example of a less human-centered approach to Christianity
(Engelbert 1979). Humankind is understood within such strands of
Christianity to be entrusted by God with the care and wise stewardship
of the earth. In the present day, the theologian and mystic Matthew Fox
has done much to stimulate the Church in the West to return to its roots
in recognizing environmental and ecological issues as essentially spiritual
in nature (Fox 1983). Fox is controversial and has been rejected by the
Dominican order within Roman Catholicism in which he was a priest.
His syncretistic approach and outspoken opinions have proved too much
for some to take. But he does identify clearly within the religions of the
world, including Christianity, a deeply spiritual vein of concern for creation. It may well be that as a secular, materialistic world fails to fulfill its
promises that humankind will look to tap the rich resources of its spiritual traditions. Fox and others like him may be regarded by history as
prophets to their generation. *The Voyage Home* suggests that the recognition of such wisdom will come too late.

STAR TREK III: THE SEARCH FOR SPOCK

Questions about life after death are raised in *Star Trek III: The Search for Spock*. The desolation that loss brings is apparent in the aftermath of Spock's self-sacrifice in saving the *Enterprise* from destruction in *The Wrath of Khan*. It is picked up again at the beginning of *The Search for Spock* with Kirk reflecting upon the death of his friend. There is an aching void that cannot be filled. This is part of the human experience of the death of loved ones. The pain of separation draws attention to thoughts of what lies beyond that final frontier. Is death an end or a beginning? Non-existence or a different kind of existence? Such questions are raised as the plot of this third film of the series unfolds.

Back in space dock following the battle with Khan, the *Enterprise* crew are in the process of disembarking when an intruder is detected in the late Spock's sealed quarters. It turns out to be McCoy who is acting very strangely and resembling Spock in occasional mannerisms and expressions. Kirk attributes this to the stress and grief encountered during the voyage. Later, however, Kirk is challenged by Spock's father, the Vulcan ambassador Sarek (Mark Lenard), as to why he left his son on the Genesis planet. Sarek is insistent that Spock would have found a way to allow his "katra," or soul, to survive beyond death. In Vulcan mysticism, the katra is that which survives the body and can be preserved and stored on Vulcan. The wisdom of the ages is thus never lost. In extreme circumstances, such as those faced by Spock in the emergency on the *Enterprise*, where the normal death ritual is not possible, Vulcan's are able, through touch, to transfer their katra temporarily to another living being.

Kirk, somewhat mystified by Sarek's insistence, replays the ships visual logs that recorded Spock's death. The recording shows that it was to McCoy that Spock transferred his katra, shedding light on the doctor's strange behavior. Sarek urges Kirk to find a way to bring Spock's body from the Genesis planet, on which it was laid to rest, to Vulcan in order that the katra ceremony can take place on his home planet. Permission to take Spock's body home is refused to Kirk on several grounds. First, the *Enterprise* is being decommissioned and the crew reassigned. Second, the planet—created out of the matter produced from Khan's detonation of the Genesis device—has been declared off-limits except to the scientific teams responsible for the project. Undeterred, Kirk and his colleagues steal the *Enterprise* and head for the Genesis planet, where they discover a hostile Klingon presence intent on stealing the Genesis technology.

With the *Enterprise* en route to Genesis, the scientific team orbiting the Genesis planet detect life signs in the photon torpedo casing that served as Spock's coffin. Two members of the team, David Marcus (Merrit Butrick)—who is Kirk's son—and Lieutenant Saavik (Robin Curtis) beam down to the planet to investigate and find the torpedo casing to be empty except for Spock's burial robe. They soon discover nearby a naked Vulcan child. The mystery of the missing body and the identity of the Vulcan child is solved when Marcus and Saavik realize that the Genesis planet effect has somehow regenerated Spock's body. His mind is blank, a *tabula rasa* in effect. The problem facing them, however, is that the Genesis experiment has failed and the planet is aging at an incredible rate. The Spock-child will die rapidly of old age if they remain on the surface. In the meantime, their ship has been destroyed by the Klingons who have also beamed to the planet to capture Marcus and Saavik. In the encounter with the Klingons all three are taken hostage.

Once the *Enterprise* arrives at the planet, the challenge becomes that of taking the "resurrected" body of Spock to Vulcan in order to reunite it with the Spock katra carried in the mind of McCoy. Following conflict with the Klingons, in which Marcus is killed, the *Enterprise* self-destructs, and its crew commandeer the Klingon vessel, Spock—rapidly grown to manhood due to the Genesis effect—is returned to Vulcan. The ceremony to reunite Spock's katra with his body is performed. The very essence of who Spock is, his spirit, has remained intact. Spock is, however, left with the task of re-learning the factual knowledge lost in his death.

One of the metaphors within *The Search for Spock* and expressed through the "resurrection" of Spock is that this life is not all there is. Attention is drawn toward an aspect of individual existence that survives physical death, yet which retains personality. This belief finds a significant place in many of the world's religions. It is a central tenet within Christianity, where the resurrection of Christ from the dead is seen as the assurance of life beyond this life for all believers. There is difference in the form of the individual with the resurrected person no longer limited by the constraints of flesh and blood. There is continuity because that which makes us who we are, our personality, survives. The very heart of the Christian hope is that death is not the end but the beginning of a greater life in the nearer presence of God, made possible through the death and resurrection of Jesus Christ. This resurrected life is continuous with life before death no less than an oak tree is continuous with an acorn. St. Paul explores this theme further in 1 Corinthians 15:35–58:

But some may ask, "How are the dead raised? With what kind of body will they come?" . . . The body that is sown is perishable, it is raised imperishable; it is sown in dishonor, it is raised in glory; it is sown in weakness, it is raised in power; it is sown a natural body, it is raised a spiritual body. . . . For the perishable must clothe itself with the imperishable, and the mortal with immortality. When the perishable has been clothed with the imperishable, and the mortal with immortality, then the saying that is written will come true: "Death has been swallowed up in victory."

Various theories abound within the Christian church as to the nature of resurrection, including bodily resuscitation, bodily transformation, spiritual resurrection and reductive resurrection (Davis 1993: 44, 45; Williams 1972). The theories range from the idea of resurrection being the restoration of life to a dead body, to resurrection as a psychological experience in the minds of those close to the departed. The story of Spock's return from the dead does not fit neatly into any of the above categories. Only due to the freak circumstances arising from his dead body being left on the Genesis planet was there a "bodily" resurrection with which his katra could be reunited. Yet the Vulcan belief in a life that survives death is very different from a reductive theory of resurrection. It is more than the psychological experience of the bereaved and is a portrayal of the mystical continuance of life after death.

There are limits to the level of analogy that can be made between the Spock story and Christian resurrection. Clear differences exist. What *The Search for Spock* does portray is a belief in a spiritual dimension of existence, even though this is embraced more easily by alien races than humans. While it is true that no overarching religion is prevalent, the inner spiritual life is often alluded to and explored within the *Star Trek* saga, usually through the spirituality of non-humans. *The Search for Spock* makes clear the spiritual dimension of Vulcan life. Similarly, there are deep religious undercurrents running through the life of the Bajoran's in the series *Star Trek: Deep Space Nine*.

The exploration of life after death in *The Search for Spock* despite the huge scientific and technological advances achieved by the twenty-third century may well be a reflection of contemporary Western society. At the close of the twentieth century there has been in the West a renaissance of expressed spirituality. There is now a virtual marketplace of alternatives available. In addition to the established religions, all sorts of spiritualities, including those varied beliefs lumped within the New Age category and the proliferation of "new religious movements," are offered. The reasons are complex and varied but include a disillusionment with materialism and a search for meaning within a chaotic world. For Christians it is faith in a God who has overcome the power of death that makes sense of existence and provides hope for the future. Irrespective of whether *The Search for Spock* is viewed through the lens of a specific spirituality or not, a deep resonance is discernible between the events of the film and the human question: "Is this life all there is?"

STAR TREK: THE UNDISCOVERED COUNTRY

Just what the twenty-third century will look like can only be speculation. But as more and more people begin to recognize the link between the outward voyage that pushes back the frontiers of knowledge, and the inward spiritual search that addresses the question of meaning, *Star Trek* might well in the hindsight of the future be regarded as prophetic. However, the journey toward such an enlightened time will be fraught with difficulties. There will always be those for whom self-interest, power, and might will take precedence over the virtues of love and compassion for others. This negative aspect of humanity is projected onto the Klingon race in *Star Trek: The Undiscovered Country* (1991).

The events of the film unfold in the context of a meeting between the Federation and the Klingon Empire, the latter of which is seeking an end to hostilities between the two parties. This move is prompted by a combination of internal pressures and enormous military expenditure, but more than anything by the destruction through overmining of the Klingon Empire's primary energy source. "Hawks" within both the Federation and the Klingon Empire would rather see the matter resolved through war, but the opportunity for peace is seized, and a meeting to formalize a peace treaty is set up. Chancellor Gorkon (David Warner) of the Klingon High Council and Captain Kirk are to be the prime negotiators for the respective sides. The *Enterprise* is despatched to escort Gorkon safely into Federation space. In the events that follow, Gorkon is assassinated with the act engineered to put the blame on the *Enterprise* crew under the command of Kirk.

The Undiscovered Country addresses some of the essential ingredients necessary in any search for a lasting and true peace: a peace that is not merely the absence of conflict but a state of being in which each person wishes all that is best for the other. Within the Jewish tradition this is expressed as shalom. The search for shalom is, in effect, a spiritual search for relationship at the deepest level and includes relationships between humans as well as humans with God. To even approach shalom requires the letting go of past hurts and differences and relinquishing the thirst for vengeance.

In *The Undiscovered Country*, the Klingons had been fierce enemies of the Federation for over 200 years, with much blood shed between them. In addition, at a personal level, Kirk's son David had been murdered by the Klingons on the Genesis planet. All of this somehow needed to be laid aside if the peace negotiations were to succeed. At best, Kirk needed to find forgiveness in his heart toward the Klingons in general. They were not corporately responsible for his son's death, and in fact the particular Klingon responsible had already been killed in a fight with Kirk on the Genesis planet. Yet, understandably, very powerful, human emotions remained within Kirk as he sat at the dinner table with his former arch-enemies.

On the Klingon side, Gorkon represented a movement that was looking for a better way than violence. They wanted to chart "the undiscovered country" represented by a peaceful co-existence with, and possibly within, the Federation. Gorkon recognized the hardships endured by his people simply to maintain the military machinery of the empire when the need for such military strength had long since passed. It was time for change, albeit the desire for change was accentuated by the ecological disaster that would result in the depletion of all Klingon energy reserves within decades. The Klingons faced two options: all-out war with the Federation or negotiations for peace. Events gave Gorkon the leverage he required to pursue the latter. This would mean much soul-searching for the Klingons in coming to terms with the need to relinquish their warrior ambitions in the name of peace. Both sides needed to put aside past differences for the peace negotiations to begin in earnest. There had to be a first step toward forgiveness and reconciliation if shalom was ever to be possible. The assassination of Gorkon, involving collaboration between hawks from both sides, almost derailed the process. Kirk and McCoy had been framed for the crime and were sentenced to life imprisonment on a Klingon penal colony. Eventually they escape, the true culprits are discovered, and the peace process is resumed.

As is often the case within *Star Trek*, human deficiencies are projected onto alien species. Klingons thus become the archetypal warriors, driven by a thirst for battle and conquest. Vulcans represent the cool, collected, rational side of human nature that is peace-loving and free from the influence of emotions. The reality, of course, is that human beings cannot be compartmentalized in such a way. The human condition is complex and contains within it the drive to love and to hate, to save and to destroy, to have compassion or to be merciless. Acceptance of those who are different and forgiveness toward those who have inflicted harm thus become very difficult tasks. Grudges and deep-seated resentments linger, making true reconciliation elusive but not impossible.

At the beginning of *The Undiscovered Country* it is Kirk who is the party reluctant to enter into negotiations with the Klingons. To the Klingons, Kirk has been an arch-enemy and a veteran of numerous conflicts with them. They have a grudging respect for him, which is why they request him to escort them to the negotiations with the Federation. Kirk is adamant that the Klingons cannot be trusted and is, for a while, blinded by the hatred that he harbors for them as a consequence of his son's murder. Spock's logical remonstrations with Kirk appear to have little initial effect and only under protest does Kirk embark upon the mission. He is not alone in his prejudice against the Klingons. At the commencement of negotiations, Gorkon and his entourage are invited to a banquet on the *Enterprise*. Both before and during the meal, members of the *Enterprise* show quite strong racist tendencies in remarks and attitudes toward the Klingons. This is paradoxical when the multi-racial and even multi-species nature of the *Enterprise* crew is considered. The racist attitudes toward the Klingons illustrates the human tendency to locate the enemy "out there." Naked ambition, violence, the thirst for vengeance, ruthlessness—the list goes on—are ugly facets of the human condition that are more easily placed upon someone else than owned. This effectively dehumanizes both subject and object of the process and the cycle of hatred escalates. History is littered with the carnage of the consequences.

Within the Christian tradition—itself so often guilty of the same human failings—is both a mandate and a supreme exemplar of how to break the cycle. Christians see in the person of Jesus a Messiah very different from the military leader anticipated within Judaism who would, with the use of force, sweep away all injustice. The whole teaching of Jesus can be summarized in his response to the question about which is the greatest of the commandments: "Love the Lord your God with all your heart and with all your soul and with all your mind. This is the first and greatest commandment. And the second is like it: Love your neighbor as yourself" (Matthew 23:37–40). The understanding of neighbor in this context is far wider than the popular perception of someone in close proximity or with whom there is common ground. This is apparent from the exhortation of Jesus: "Love your enemies, do good to those who hate you, bless those who curse you, pray for those who ill-treat you" (Luke 6:27, 28). Similarly Paul, in his letter to the Church at Rome, makes a similar exhortation: "Do not be overcome by evil, but overcome evil with good" (Romans 12:21).

Such an approach provides a way out of the cycle of hatred and violence that so easily forms a closed circle. To reach out with the offer of forgiveness and friendship to an enemy is not without risk and to some it would appear as folly. But when accepted, the offer becomes a stepping stone to trust and the transformation of enemies into friends. The death of Jesus Christ on the cross at first looked like defeat, as though once again violent power had triumphed. But even death itself did not triumph and was defeated by the power of love (cf. Matthew 28, Mark 16, Luke 24, and John 20). It was the ultimate expression of God's "unbounded love" (Pinnock and Brow 1994).

While there are no overt religious references within *The Undiscovered Country* there is a clear recognition that for enemies to become friends there must be a laying aside of past hurts. Keeping a score of wrongs is a barrier to reconciliation and ammunition for further conflict. This, however, is no easy path to follow. The Klingon Chancellor Gorkon knew the risks inherent in his quest for peace. He knew that there were those of his race for whom such a quest represented betrayal and who would stop at nothing to sabotage the talks. His stand was to cost him his life. On the Federation side, Kirk was confronted with the need to put behind him his own personal hatred of the Klingons, bound up with his son's murder on the Genesis planet. By the end of the film, a recognition had emerged of a better way forward for Klingons and humans alike, no longer premised upon the suspicion and hatred of past encounters, but on a desire to meet each other as equals for the common good. Perhaps not "unbounded love" for each other, but at least a first step.

STAR TREK: GENERATIONS

Star Trek: Generations (1994) and *Star Trek: First Contact* (1996) both draw attention to what it means to be human. *Generations* brings together and provides a transition point between the characters of the original *Star Trek* television series and those of *Star Trek: The Next Generation*. The film opens with Kirk, Scott (James Doohan), and Chekov being shown around as honored guests on the newly completed *Enterprise B* which is

about to embark upon a short trip around the solar system for the benefit of the press. On the journey, the *Enterprise B* picks up and responds to
a distress call from two freighters carrying refugees caught in an energy
ribbon.

As the drama unfolds one of the freighters explodes and Kirk's
advice is sought. The *Enterprise* is taken closer to the energy ribbon,
which enables at least some of the refugees from the second freighter to
be beamed aboard just before it, too, explodes. One of the survivors,
Tolian Soren (Malcolm McDowell), a character who assumes major significance later in the film, mystifies the *Enterprise* crew in his desperation
to be returned to the danger from which he had just been rescued. So
frantic is Soren that he has to be sedated. By now, the *Enterprise* is itself
trapped in the ribbon's pull and dangerously close to suffering the same
fate as the freighters. A last ditch effort by Kirk which involves him man-
ually re-routing power on a lower deck saves the ship, but not without
cost. The *Enterprise*, seemingly out of danger, is hit by a bolt of energy
that causes a hull breach on the level where Kirk is working. His body is
never recovered and history records his death.

Generations continues some seventy-eight years later with Captain
Jean-Luc Picard (Patrick Stewart) on the bridge of the *Enterprise D*.
Shortly after receiving devastating news from Earth concerning the death
in a fire of his brother and nephew, the *Enterprise* responds to a distress
call from an observatory that is under attack. On arrival the attackers have
long since gone and a party from the *Enterprise* beam across to investigate.
There they discover one survivor—Dr. Tolian Soren. He is an El Aurian,
a race of extreme longevity. This is the same Soren who was rescued from
the energy ribbon by the *Enterprise B* almost eight decades earlier.

At the heart of the story is Soren's desperate desire to expose himself
once again to the mysterious ribbon that he describes as the Nexus. It is
a place where anything that a person wishes can come true. In the Nexus
there is no death or suffering and possibilities are endless. Many years previously Soren's family had been destroyed by the Borg—a merciless race
of part-organic, part-machine beings—and his loss has driven Soren to
the point of insanity. He is prepared to stop at nothing in order to re-enter
the Nexus and fulfill his dream of being reunited with his family. Following a devious plot involving a renegade Klingon ship, Soren and Picard
end up face to face on a planet from which Soren is planning to launch a
missile into the planet's sun. A cataclysmic explosion will result with the
effect of attracting the Nexus close enough to the planet for Soren to
achieve his goal of being caught up in it. The fact that hundreds of mil-

lions of living beings will die as a result of the explosion is of no relevance to Soren.

Picard is unsuccessful in stopping Soren and finds himself caught up in the Nexus. There he finds the opportunity to live as the father that he had never been, a temptation made all the greater by the recent death of his brother and nephew. Picard almost succumbs but cannot shake the memory of the exploding sun. He then realizes that whatever the Nexus is, it is an illusion and he plans a way to somehow go back and prevent Soren from launching the missile. In the Nexus he finds Captain Kirk living out his own wish to be back on his farm on earth. Picard manages to persuade Kirk that the Nexus is not real and that it is a place somehow outside of time into which he was drawn all those years ago when lost on the *Enterprise B*. Picard and Kirk then together take themselves back to the planet just before Soren's missile launch. They prevent the launch with Soren and Kirk dying in the process.

Generations raises the question: "What if you were able to fulfill your deepest wish?" At one level, at least, to be whatever you choose to be, to go wherever you wish to go, to have whatever your heart desires, sounds like a wonderful opportunity. Soren wanted his slaughtered family back and this was what drove him over the edge. But Picard and Kirk were involuntary visitors to the Nexus. For them the experience of paradise came unexpectedly. Suddenly all their dreams could be realized simply by wishing for them. Yet both of them eventually saw through the illusion, largely because of their refusal to put aside the needs of others. Picard could not let go of the memory of the exploding sun and the huge destruction that it represented. Faced with the choice of staying in his ideal world within the Nexus or going back to risk his life for others, there was only one choice to make. Elsewhere in the film he makes the comment that it is "our mortality that defines us." Kirk overcomes the power of the Nexus in his realization that in such a perfect world there is no way to make a difference to the things that really matter. He says to Picard: "Ever since I left Starfleet, I haven't made a difference." The two captains thus unite to return from the Nexus and defeat Soren. Kirk dies smiling, having paid the ultimate price to make a difference.

Within the Christian tradition, to be human is understood as to live in relationship and to be willing to accept responsibility. Human beings do not live in a social vacuum whereby the needs of others can be sacrificed in the pursuit of personal happiness (though much of Western society has operated on that principle in recent history). Soren represents the tragedy of a once sensitive life stripped by pain and suffering of all semblance of morality. For him, the destruction of millions was an acceptable price to pay for the restoration of the family torn away from him by the Borg. Soren demonstrates in an exaggerated way the consequences of chasing the impossible dream of a life free from sorrow and pain. Like the Nexus, such an existence is a deception. For Christians, to be truly human is to live with the paradox of suffering in a world created by a loving God. Picard recognized, while in the Nexus and despite the pain of his own recent bereavement, that escapism was not the answer. While it might dull the pain, it was not a solution. Kirk similarly realized the hollow nature of a life without risk, where everything is perfect and there is no way to "make a difference."

The clue to avoiding the fruitless search for the perfect life is to recognize that, to be truly human, people need to live in relationship with each other. Such relationships are costly and require persons to give of themselves for the sake of others. Love has a hard edge. The Incarnation of God in the person of Christ stands as the ultimate example of selfless love. The glory of heaven was laid aside for a manger in a stable and a cross on a hill. There is no greater expression of love and it provides a clear, religious insight into all that it means to be truly human (Taylor 1992). Across the centuries countless men and women have understood this and made the supreme sacrifice for others, echoing in their actions the words of Jesus: "Greater love has no-one than this that he lay down his life for his friends" (John 15:13).

Innumerable others have demonstrated and continue to demonstrate their humanity in the unsung heroism of their day-to-day existence, where selfless love takes priority over the quest for self-centered personal happiness. They are the Picards and Kirks of this world for whom the escapism of the Nexus in whatever form it might take would be neither sought nor chosen.

One of the greatest causes of despair in the Western world of the late twentieth century is a pervasive sense of meaninglessness (Cotterell 1990). As the frontiers of science are pushed back and knowledge of the universe increases, humankind is increasingly faced with existential questions. What place do birth, life, death on a speck of dust in the immenseness of space have in the grand order of things? Purpose and meaning in life are therefore key components in avoiding a life of quiet desperation. These are spiritual qualities in the broadest sense, whether expressed through particular religious forms or not. Christians would describe the purpose and meaning of their lives in relation to a God who has, out of love for humanity, entered into creation in the most tangible of ways. For

Christians it is that relationship which makes sense of an otherwise chaotic and frightening universe and which provides the blueprint of relationships between human beings. Those of other religions and no religion may offer different frames of reference as to where life's meaning and purpose is to be found, but it is arguably a truism that life will always be diminished if individual self-interest is its only motivating source. In their actions in choosing to leave the paradise of the Nexus, Picard and Kirk reinforce the point.

At the end of *Generations* Picard makes a telling observation to his first officer William Riker (Jonathan Frakes). Refuting a statement made earlier by Soren that referred to time as a predator, something to be feared and escaped, Picard remarks: "Time is a companion that goes with us on the journey, and reminds us to cherish every moment because they will never come again. What we leave behind is not as important as how we have lived." Picard understood that the defining feature of being human is to be found in relationships rather than in achievements. In that sense, how we conduct ourselves in relation to others is more important than our longevity. What it means to be human is alluded to also in *Generations* particularly through the character of Data (Brent Spiner). Data is a sophisticated android seeking to become more human. Following a disastrous attempt at humor he takes the decision to have installed in his "neural net" an emotion chip, believing that it will help him achieve his ambition. In the course of the film Data experiences a wide range of emotions for the first time. He enjoys some of the emotions but finds others extremely difficult to cope with, for example, fear, remorse, and sorrow. At one stage, Data even begs to be deactivated in order to have the chip removed. The point highlighted through the character of Data is that being human by its very nature means being open to a wide range of emotions and feelings. It is not possible to live a life that only experiences happiness, joy, and contentment. Living also means sharing in the pain of others and experiencing loss and despair at various times. Data's longing to become human is also a feature of the last film to be considered.

STAR TREK: FIRST CONTACT

Star Trek: First Contact (1996) brings the crew of the *Enterprise E*, newly under the command of Picard, into conflict with the Federation's most feared enemy, the Borg. Within the *Star Trek* time frame, and portrayed in the *Star Trek: The Next Generation* television series, the Borg were last encountered six years earlier by Picard and the *Enterprise*. In a savage battle the Federation sustained an appalling loss of life before eventually finding a way to destroy the Borg vessel. In that encounter, Picard was captured by the Borg and "assimilated." Borg implants in his body effectively robbed him of his personality, turning him into a drone within the Borg collective. Eventually rescued and restored to normality, the experience remains a living nightmare for Picard and in *First Contact* his worst fears are realized when he is informed that the Borg are once again on the move and heading toward Earth.

The Starfleet authorities of the Federation are reluctant to send the *Enterprise E* into battle with the Borg, believing that Picard's previous assimilation could prove an unstable factor in the equation. However, with the fleet hopelessly outmatched by the Borg, Picard orders the *Enterprise* to set an intercept course at maximum warp. In a fierce conflict the Borg ship is destroyed but manages to launch a smaller vessel from within it. The vessel creates a "temporal vortex" and travels back in time, catching the *Enterprise* in its wake. While still in the wake, the *Enterprise* scans the earth to discover that the entire population is now Borg. Somehow the Borg had traveled through time and assimilated the population of the earth. Picard makes an instant decision to follow the Borg vessel through the vortex and somehow undo the damage wreaked by the Borg upon the earth.

On the other side of the vortex, the *Enterprise* locates and destroys the time-traveling Borg ship which has been firing on the earth. Its target was the site in the United States from which Zefram Cochrane (James Cromwell), the inventor of warp drive, made the first warp speed flight on April 6, 2063. Picard deduces from this choice of target what the Borg plan must have been. The date was April 5, 2063, one day before the flight of Cochrane's ship, the *Phoenix*. History recorded that the flight had been the precipitating factor in Earth's first contact with extraterrestrials. A Vulcan ship passing in range of Earth detected the vessel traveling faster than the speed of light. Recognizing the capability of the inhabitants to now reach distant stars the Vulcans diverted to Earth and made contact. The Borg, in seeking to destroy the *Phoenix*, knew that if that first contact could be prevented, the future would be altered, and there would be no Federation to stand in their way.

With the Borg ship destroyed, a team from the *Enterprise* are beamed down to the planet's surface with the task of finding Cochrane, repairing the damage caused by the Borg attack on the *Phoenix* installation and ensuring that the flight goes ahead the next day. What is soon discovered, however, is that somehow before their ship was destroyed the Borg had managed to beam across to one of the decks aboard the *Enterprise*. From there they begin the process of assimilating the crew of the *Enterprise*. The storyline progresses on two fronts. On the Earth the struggle is to make sure the flight of the *Phoenix* takes place the next day. On the *Enterprise*, Picard and his crew are faced with taking on the Borg at close quarters.

In the course of the struggle on the *Enterprise*, Data is captured by the Borg and encounters the Borg queen (Alice Kriege). It is she who brings order to the collective mind of the Borg, assuming a god-like importance. Data had fed an encryption code into the main computer of the *Enterprise*, preventing the Borg from taking control of the ship from the deck they had occupied. The Borg queen sets about trying to elicit the code from Data. Her strategy is to play on Data's longing to become human, an ironic twist considering that the nature of the Borg is to strip away the individuality of those they assimilate, adding the biological and technological distinctiveness of conquered species to their own. What the Borg queen offers to Data, from the experience of the Borg in fusing organic life with machine is the chance to experience what it means to be a being of flesh and blood. With skin grafted onto his arm Data feels physical sensations for the first time and the Borg queen sets out to seduce Data. As the film draws to a close, it at first looks as though Data has succumbed. He relinquishes the encryption code and on the orders of the Borg queen fires upon the *Phoenix* which in the meantime has attained a successful launch. However, the quantum torpedoes launched by Data miss and it becomes clear that Data's behavior is a ruse. He smashes a container of plasma coolant which liquefies the organic parts of the Borg, thus destroying them.

In a conversation with Picard after the destruction of the Borg on the *Enterprise* Data reveals that he felt a strange sense of sorrow at the death of the Borg queen. She had in some way brought him closer to experiencing what it meant to be human in flesh and blood terms and for a short while (less than a second!) he had been tempted. Yet Data resisted this temptation, placing greater value on the lives of his colleagues and the humanity they represented than on his personal desire as an android to become more human.

The twist, of course, is that Data's actions were far more human than the alternative of aligning himself with the cold and heartless Borg and the experience, albeit diminished, of fleshly life offered to him. For the Borg, other species existed simply to service their own needs as they moved toward "perfection." Their ambition was pursued remorselessly and irrespective of the cost inflicted upon others. In a manner reminiscent of the action of Picard and Kirk making the choice to turn their back on the attractions of the Nexus, Data's choice was a selfless one. His friends mattered more to him.

CONCLUSION

Having considered some of the major themes of the *Star Trek* films, there is some clearly discernible resonance between the outward voyage of the *Enterprise* and the inward spiritual search. Questions of the purpose and meaning in life are addressed in *Star Trek: The Motion Picture* and *The Final Frontier* as are issues of human responsibility and relatedness to the created order in *The Wrath of Khan* and *The Voyage Home*. Considerations about life after death are also present in *The Wrath of Khan* along with the struggles associated with the human condition and the consequences of how they are resolved in *Generations, First Contact,* and *The Undiscovered Country*. The themes are not, of course, exclusively contained within the neat confines of the particular films. They overlap and interact as the saga unfolds, reminiscent of life itself. It would also be wrong to suggest that a comprehensive expression of Christian spirituality can be identified even when all the films are considered together. There are, however, as suggested in this chapter, numerous parallels that can be drawn. That should not be surprising, for what the *Star Trek* films represent is a projection of who we really are and what we long to be.

10

Biblical Interpretation in the *Star Trek* Universe

Going Where Some Have Gone Before

JEFFREY SCOTT LAMP

"*S* tar Trek has indeed become an icon of 20th-century popular culture" (Okuda et al. 1994: iii). In a classic example of understatement, this simple sentence clearly characterizes the phenomenon that is *Star Trek*.[1] Four television series, nine feature films, countless publications, toys, fan clubs, conventions, on-line resources (e.g. web pages and chat rooms), and now this volume all testify to the tremendous impact that this vision has had on our culture.

The use of the term "vision" to describe the *Star Trek* phenomenon may appear to the non-initiate to be an instance of an overinflated estimate of self-importance. Nevertheless, it stands as an accurate label for all that *Star Trek* has attempted to deliver to its audiences. As was frequently mentioned during the commemoration of the twenty-fifth anniversary of the debut of the original series, in the numerous eulogies following the death of *Star Trek* creator Gene Roddenberry in 1991, and recently in the thirtieth anniversary celebration of *Star Trek*, this is more than a succession of media productions and concomitant merchandising campaigns. For the multitudes of its fans, *Star Trek* is a vision for our future, a vision for humanity, a vision indeed for the entire cosmos.

To be sure, the vision had somewhat more modest expressions in its inception. A succinct and pedestrian statement of this vision is found on the back panel of the box containing Mattel's *Barbie & Ken/Star Trek* gift-set, issued in commemoration of the thirtieth anniversary of *Star Trek*: "In the 30 years since it first aired, *Star Trek* has inspired generations of fans with Gene Roddenberry's belief that people of various races, genders, and planetary origins can work together to build a constructive future for all [hu]mankind." Indeed, the original series in many respects served as an "acted parable" extolling the morals of this vision. The bridge crew's ethnic and racial makeup certainly affronted the sensibilities of many. The very notion that Asians, Russians, and Americans could work cooperatively in the midst of the Vietnam and Cold Wars was startling, as was the notion of a black woman serving in a position of prominence in the control center of the ship. Throw in a "half-breed" alien and an interracial kiss and one is left with a society that approximates Dr. Martin Luther King's "I Have a Dream" speech.

But as the mythology of the phenomenon grew, so too did the scope of the vision. This is most easily observed with the advent of *Star Trek: The Next Generation* (*TNG*). The expansion of the United Federation of Planets and contacts with more alien cultures demanded an expanding vision, one that exceeded the limited terran focus of the original series (*TOS*). In this respect, *TNG* was an appellation not just indicative of the passage of time among crews and ships; it was indicative of the need to extend the vision from a global perspective to one of a more cosmic magnitude.

In such a process it was inevitable that the subject of religion would require attention. Before *TNG*, religion was a topic that received comparatively little attention in the construction of the vision. With the second series, the place of religion in the *Star Trek* universe would receive greater consideration, as immediately demonstrated with the appearance of the mysterious figure Q in the pilot, "Encounter at Farpoint" (1987). Yet the inclusion of religion into the fabric of the vision was not simply undertaken out of a desire to achieve a sense of socio-cultural comprehensiveness. The vision has always been more than a vehicle to carry the storylines; it has also contained a strong element of proclamation. As such, it is a vision of aspiration, a vision for humanity's place in the scheme of things, at root a prescriptive vision for how a constructive future may and perhaps should look. The expansion of the vision seeks to move its application from the arena of functional social interactions to the arena of ideas. The vision is no longer just advocacy of a sociological paradigm; it has become advocacy of a worldview, or perhaps more accurately, a cosmology.

Why did this become a concern for the successors of the original series? To state it in overly simplistic terms, the landscape of the "cooperation in diversity" discussion changed in the interim. The 1960s were clearly a time of significant social change in American society, a context to which the vision of the original series was sensitive and prescriptive. From the latter part of the 1970s, issues of religious fundamentalism and intolerance occurring within the matrix of a shift toward postmodern pluralism significantly altered the parameters for defining a cooperative yet diverse social context. In the way the original series addressed its social context, its successor had to come to terms with a milieu in which religion played a significant role.

In this respect, religion must become a topic of utmost importance in the presentation of the *Star Trek* universe. If, after all, Earth is home to numerous religious traditions, how much more the whole of the universe? If the incipient vision extolled the virtues of cooperation within a limited scope of diversity (e.g. ethnic, gender, and species), then the expanded version must seek to integrate the factor of religion into the equation of cooperation. The primary task, then, is to depict a way in which multitudinous religious impulses could be tolerated and celebrated while maintaining a viable framework for the efficient function of a cooperative society. Again, it must be remembered that doing so is not just an exercise of the imagination for a fictitious future society. It is also the presentation of a vision for our socio-cultural context.

This volume offers various interpretations of the impact of *Star Trek* on the field and phenomenology of religion. This enterprise is itself fraught with conceptual and methodological obstacles (Albanese 1996; Chidester 1996). As a biblical scholar, my aim in this chapter will be more modestly focused. The primary question of this inquiry is: How is the interpretation of sacred texts portrayed in the religious framework of the *Star Trek* universe?

We will begin our investigation by defining the religious framework of the *Star Trek* universe. This section will consist of some brief observations culled from an inductive study of episodes from the four television series as well as the eight feature films as of the time of this writing.[2] We will then examine selected episodes of *TNG* and *Star Trek: Deep Space Nine* (*DS9*) in which three issues in biblical interpretation contribute to the storylines: the "demythologization" of the sacred text, the role of narrative in the religious life of a faith community; and the fulfillment and

interpretation of prophetic revelation. The conclusion proffered is that
these episodes suggest ways in which the essential core of religious belief
as preserved in ancient sacred texts might be maintained within the context of an intellectual and cultural framework unsympathetic with a
supernaturalistic worldview, all in keeping with the *Star Trek* vision of
cooperation within diversity.

THE WORLDVIEW OF THE *STAR TREK* UNIVERSE

This review will briefly describe six features of the *Star Trek* universe that
constitute the religious framework within which certain cultural manifes-
tations of religious belief exist.

    1. *The worldview of the Star Trek universe is secular and materialistic.*
This observation is the foundational principle upon which all that follows
is based. To say that the *Star Trek* universe is secular and materialistic is to
assert that the dominant paradigm of the United Federation of Planets,
the primary context in which the *Star Trek* mythology finds expression, is
grounded in a secular and materialistic view of reality. In addition to the
explicit portrayal of the conflict of worldviews between the secular Federation and the religious Bajorans on *DS9* ("In the Hands of the Prophets,"
1993; "Rapture," 1996) there is a veritable mountain of implicit data
affirming the secular orientation of the *Star Trek* universe. In some way,
these features all relate to anthropological issues. Transporter technology
raises the philosophical question, "What is humanity that it can be dis-
sembled, converted into energy, and reassembled elsewhere intact?" Do
issues like "soul," "mind," "personality," "spirit," to name but a few,
reduce to material principles? The secular/materialistic worldview is
espoused in the evolution of humanoid species throughout the galaxy
(*TOS* "The Paradise Syndrome," 1968; *TNG* "The Chase," 1993), the
matter of cryogenic resuscitation (*TNG* "The Neutral Zone," 1988), the
whole matter of time travel and the nature of the space-time continuum,
especially in those instances where individuals encounter themselves at
different points along the timestream (e.g. *TNG* "We'll Always Have
Paris," 1988; "Time Squared," 1989), where they experience alternative
timelines (e.g. *TNG* "Parallels," 1993), or where they encounter different
dimensions (e.g. *TOS* "Mirror, Mirror," 1967). Moreover, the issue of
defining sentient life arises with the unfolding story of the android Data.
Each of these matters implies a secular/materialistic approach to reality,
an approach that establishes the primary heuristic and hermeneutical

principle for addressing those experiences generally regarded as religious or spiritual by some cultures that come into contact with the Federation.

2. *The worldview of the* Star Trek *universe is optimistic.* Following closely with the secular and materialistic orientation of the *Star Trek* universe is the view that human society has a propensity to evolve for the better. Several value judgments are voiced, especially in the early episodes of *TNG*, that assert the superior state of twenty-fourth-century life over against the social conditions of twentieth and twenty-first-century human development (e.g. "Encounter at Farpoint"; "The Neutral Zone").

Another strand of evidence for this assertion is found through an exercise of the imagination. If the chronology of key events in the *Star Trek* mythology is overlaid onto our contemporary socio-cultural context, a sort of Hegelian approach to history suggests itself. Two key dates in the *Star Trek* continuity are significant. One date is 2079, the end of World War III.[3] The aftermath of this war is the setting for the barbaric social breakdown of life on Earth. The other key date is 2061, the date that Zefram Cochrane invents warp drive. This development allows for the future "first contact" with Vulcan explorers in the movie *Star Trek: First Contact* (1996). This contact with the Vulcans launches an era in human history that forces humanity to unite and expand its vision beyond terrestrial concerns, the culmination of which is the vision of the *Star Trek* universe.

If we look at contemporary human history, we see at the end of the twentieth century the emergence of the post-modern period, which is characterized by a deteriorating confidence in authority of all types, including confidence in the promises of modernity. The prevailing attitude is one of pluralism and tolerance, an attitude that posits final authority in the will and desires of individuals and consensual collectivities. If the *Star Trek* chronology is overlaid onto current history, then we may view the social breakdown of the twenty-first century as the death throes of post-modernism. In light of the emergence of a renewed confidence in scientific research to bring a better future for humankind, what the *Star Trek* worldview seems to envision is a post post-modernism, which is the result of a synthesis of modernism (thesis) and post-modernism (antithesis). The scientific secular framework of modernity is revived, while the best of post-modernism, especially tolerance and pluralism, is integrated into the worldview. We will discuss the pluralistic propensity of the *Star Trek* universe below, but for the moment, let it suffice to say that pluralism within secularism is the product of a view of history that sees human development as an evolutionary process resulting in the betterment and social advancement of humanity. Even if this overly simplistic construction of the intellectual history of the *Star Trek* universe is rejected, the assertion that the *Star Trek* universe sees the evolution of human social development in an optimistic light still stands.

3. *The worldview of the* Star Trek *universe understands deity to be a matter of relative superiority.* In several instances, individuals and groups have been likened to gods by others on the basis of either technological advancement (*TOS* "The Paradise Syndrome" 1968; *TNG* "Justice" 1987; "Who Watches the Watchers?" 1989; "Devil's Due" 1991) or evolutionary superiority (*TOS* "Who Mourns for Adonais?" 1967; *Star Trek V: The Final Frontier* (1989). The most striking example of evolutionary superiority is Q. Though appearing to possess godlike capabilities, he exhibits a strange fascination with humanity that may be fueled by the fear that humanity may one day evolve to rival the place of the Q in the cosmos (*TNG* "Hide and Q" 1987). The picture of the *Star Trek* view of divinity is clear, if not stated overtly. In a secular worldview, so-called deities are merely other beings who inhabit the cosmos, beings of perhaps immense power and ability, but co-inhabitants of the universe with humanity and other species. The major distinction between beings is not one of god/not-god, but of gradations in evolutionary or technological development.

4. *The worldview of the* Star Trek *universe views the "supernatural" as "natural."* This assertion is really a corollary to the previous point. If divinity is truly just a matter of technological or evolutionary development, as is consistent with a secular/materialistic worldview, then those experiences deemed supernatural must have natural or rational explanations. The *Star Trek: Voyager's* "Sacred Ground" (1996) and *DS9's* "Rapture" are two episodes in which this aspect of the *Star Trek* worldview is examined in detail. Two conclusions may be drawn from these episodes: First, supernatural phenomena can be explained scientifically. Second, and perhaps more importantly, this does not diminish the spiritual significance of the event to the faithful. What is advanced here is a distinction between nature and significance. The nature of the event in question has a basis in scientific fact. All reality can be explained within a closed universe without appeal to the supernatural. But the significance of the event is a matter of personal preference. This is a key facet of the pluralistic element of the *Star Trek* worldview, as will be discussed below.

5. *The worldview of the* Star Trek *universe views religion as fulfilling a functional social role.* This aspect of the worldview is personified in Captain Benjamin Sisko. Upon his arrival to take command of the space sta-

tion Deep Space 9 ("Emissary" 1993), Sisko discovers a stable wormhole to the Gamma Quadrant and encounters a race of beings who exist outside linear time. Upon his return from this encounter, Sisko is given the designation "Emissary of the Prophets" by the Bajoran people. Sisko is uncomfortable with the role and status of a religious figure, yet Starfleet urges Sisko to respect the Bajoran belief, a policy deemed beneficial for gaining Bajoran admission into the Federation (e.g. "Rapture"). In Sisko is embodied the principle that religion can serve the larger social order regardless of whether the social order is intellectually congruent with the precepts of the religion. From the perspective of the larger social order, claims to religious truth are of secondary importance to the role that religion plays in society. Faithless religious participation by those who have a stake in the maintenance of the social order is justified by the benefits that it can bring to society. So long as religion knows its role and boundaries, it can be permitted free exercise in the social structure.

6. *The worldview of the* Star Trek *is religiously pluralistic.* This is not a logical extension of a secular/materialistic worldview, for the vision of the *Star Trek* universe could just as easily have been antagonistic toward religion. Rather, the religious pluralism of the *Star Trek* universe is a conscious move toward tolerance of cultural values under the umbrella of a cooperative social structure. In the vision of the *Star Trek* universe cultural diversity is celebrated and encouraged, up to the point of imposing one culture's religious or value system on another. So long as the dominant secular/materialistic worldview is maintained, individual expressions of religion are permitted.

This principle is nowhere better developed than in the Prime Directive of the Federation, which mandates that "Starfleet personnel and spacecraft are prohibited from interfering in the normal development of any society, and that any Starfleet vessel or crew member is expendable to prevent violation of this rule" (Okuda et al. 1994: 261). While it is clear that the statement and the application of the Prime Directive are in practice quite often two different matters,[4] the principle still forms the official Federation attitude toward the cultural and social institutions of other races. Indeed, it may be argued that the Prime Directive holds the status of a religious principle in the Federation worldview.

Because of the Prime Directive, alien forms of religious practice are granted freedom of expression within the context of the Federation. On Deep Space 9 there is a Bajoran temple where religious services are held. This example is a physical symbol of the tolerance advocated in the Federation—religion exists within the context of the Federation worldview.

In addition, Lieutenant Worf of *TNG* is permitted the exercise of his Klingon religion on the *Enterprise D*, so long as it does not interfere with his duties as a Starfleet officer (*TNG* "Rightful Heir," 1993).

One final word about the nature of the *Star Trek* universe's view of pluralism and tolerance is in order. The form of pluralism advanced here is very context-specific. A distinction between modern and post-modern pluralism must be made.[5] By modern pluralism is meant a view that in some absolute sense all religious perspectives lead to a knowledge of ultimate truth. Some may be "better" than others, but anyone could pursue any path and end up with a knowledge of the truth. In contrast, post-modern pluralism holds that some religious views are entirely appropriate for a specific cultural context, while perhaps being totally inappropriate for another. The view of reality espoused by the Federation permits the free exercise of religion, undisturbed by the secular/materialistic social structure, within specific cultures as those cultures see fit. No judgment of ontological validity is forthcoming. The Federation's secularism remains the dominant paradigm of the *Star Trek* universe, while specific cultures within or in contact with the Federation are permitted their views of reality, as long as those views do not infringe on the social order maintained by the secular/materialistic worldview of the Federation.

BIBLICAL INTERPRETATION IN THE *STAR TREK* UNIVERSE

Does the *Star Trek* vision for humanity give any insight into how faith traditions should handle the sources of their beliefs so that they might engage cooperatively with others who hold divergent views? Once the worldview of the *Star Trek* universe is defined, is there any hermeneutical guidance that the vision might offer these faith communities so that they might interface and integrate into the secular/materialistic social paradigm of the *Star Trek* universe? It is conceivable that the vision might address faith communities with the edict to go the road alone, to do whatever is necessary on their own to make faith work in this social vision. But the genius of the *Star Trek* vision lies in its attempt to give a working model for such a hermeneutical agenda.

Again, this aspect of the *Star Trek* vision is not included out of a desire for intellectual comprehensiveness. Rather, it is crucial in the attempt to make the *Star Trek* vision prescriptive for contemporary and future human societies. After all, the major religious tradition within which the *Star Trek* universe was conceived and defined is Western Christianity, a faith whose source texts and subsequent credal affirmations espouse a worldview that runs contrary to the religious pluralism of the *Star Trek* universe.[6] Historically, orthodox Christianity, particularly in its North American evangelical and fundamentalist expressions, is an exclusivist tradition whose sacred texts demand the conversion of those outside the tradition in the context of a view of the future that sees the consummation of the kingdom of God coming in a triumphalistic manner over the existing social structure. For the vision of the *Star Trek* universe to gain a hearing among an audience conditioned by this tradition, it must define a plausible way for the truth of such a religion to maintain internal intellectual and spiritual integrity while remaining compatible with the dominant paradigm of the vision. At the root of this effort is the interpretation of sacred texts.

The following review will again be an inductive study of the *Star Trek* universe's position on biblical interpretation. While the principles here may be generalized to address the sacred texts of any faith tradition, the following discussion will focus on Christian Scripture, partly in response to the cultural context of the formation of the *Star Trek* mythology, as already described, and partly in response to my own participation and interest in this faith community.

THE QUEST FOR THE "DEMYTHOLOGIZED" KAHLESS

Arguably the most widely pursued and hotly debated subject in post-Enlightenment critical biblical scholarship is the search for the historical Jesus. Do the Gospels present an accurate portrait of Jesus, or do they show signs, at least in part, of embellishment undertaken by disciples of the Nazarene to present this teacher as God's Messiah? If the pre-critical dogmatic assertions about Jesus are set aside, is there a picture of the historical Jesus that can be discerned through application of critical, scientific, naturalistic, positivistic methodologies? And if so, it might be rightly asked, is there anything left on which to build any semblance of Christian faith?

The history of scholarship on this issue is extensive and has produced a voluminous bibliography.[7] At the risk of gross over-generalization, I submit that many critical/liberal constructions of the historical Jesus, birthed out of a skeptical view of the supernatural elements in the Gospel pictures, have produced a Jesus who was an itinerant philosopher or sage devoid of messianic features. Some have even gone so far as to state

202 JEFFREY SCOTT LAMP

that knowledge of a historical Jesus is impossible given the evidence in the Gospels, and to attempt to find a historical Jesus as the basis of faith is impossible and even misguided (e.g. Bultmann 1934; Johnson 1996). Other, frequently more conservative, positions argue that the notions of historical and supernatural need not be mutually exclusive, and that the Gospels do indeed give an accurate picture of the Jesus of history (Wilkens and Moreland 1995). The debate rages on.

For the most part, this debate has been carried on within the confines of academia. But the convening of the "Jesus Seminar" in 1985 drastically changed the parameters of the debate. The Jesus Seminar is a group of scholars and thinkers from a variety of faith traditions whose aim is to examine the canonical Gospels and some extra-canonical sources with the tools of critical scholarship in order to determine the authenticity of the sayings traditionally attributed to Jesus. What makes the Jesus Seminar noteworthy is not the focus of its undertaking, but rather the dissemination of the fruits of its research. No longer would the results of academic research into the life and sayings of Jesus to remain confined to the ivory tower; they would be proliferated in the public media. What makes the Jesus Seminar somewhat anomalous in the current state of scholarly discussion, and yet quite pertinent for our discussion, is that the worldview largely espoused by the Jesus Seminar is that of post-Enlightenment historical-critical scholarship, especially that of the nineteenth and early twentieth centuries. The rather secular worldview adopted by the Jesus Seminar is essentially a wholesale adoption of the scientific, naturalistic, positivistic worldview of a century ago, adopted without any serious interaction with the philosophical and scientific discussion of the past fifty years in which the presuppositions and validity of this worldview are seriously questioned (Wilkens and Moreland 1995: 1–14).

Another especially prominent feature of this worldview is that the picture of Jesus put forth is one in which Jesus is assessed apart from his historical and social context. Such a picture is also anomalous with current research in Jesus studies, which seeks to understand Jesus in his own context (Witherington 1995: 42–57). This approach has led to an application of the "criteria of authenticity" that yield a picture of Jesus as "a sage, but not a very Jewish one, and, perhaps most notably, a noneschatological sage" (Witherington 1995: 50).

This is not the place to enter into a critique of the Jesus Seminar's portrait of Jesus. Rather, we are interested in observing a few key features that assist with our task of understanding biblical interpretation in the *Star Trek* universe. First, we note that both the Jesus Seminar and the *Star*

Trek universe adopt similar worldviews—secular. But there is a further similarity in this respect. Both have returned to a worldview that had been left behind in their respective intellectual histories. As noted above, the Jesus Seminar's position is one that has been largely rejected in modern biblical and philosophical circles, while the *Star Trek* universe's worldview, as suggested earlier, is the re-adoption of modernity tempered by postmodernism. No argument is made here that the Jesus Seminar and *Star Trek* are in some sense dependent on one another, only that there are similarities that may prove suggestive in understanding biblical interpretation in the *Star Trek* universe.

A second feature of the Jesus Seminar that may help illumine our inquiry is the agenda with which the Jesus Seminar has engaged in its program. The Jesus Seminar has determined to make its findings known in the popular media, "to update and then make the legacy of two hundred years of research and debate a matter of public record" (Funk et al. 1993: 1). Robert Funk has stated, "We want to liberate Jesus. The only Jesus most people know is the mythic one. They don't want the real Jesus, they want the one they can worship. The cultic Jesus" (Rourke 1994: E1, E5). The purpose of the Jesus Seminar, as it is in liberal Protestantism at large, is to craft a picture of Jesus that is consonant with a naturalistic worldview while at the same time speaking meaningfully to the contemporary Christian community. This may be characterized as a program of demythologization of the biblical text's portrayal of Jesus. The attempt here appears to be one that maintains partial credibility of the ancient written sources of the faith community while making them congruent with a modern scientific worldview.

In *TNG*'s "Rightful Heir" (1993), the interpretation of ancient Klingon sacred texts is given a similar treatment. In the aftermath of his encounter with a group of Klingons held prisoner on a Romulan prison planet following the Battle of Khitomer (cf. "Birthright," 1993), Worf begins to doubt his own faith in Klingon beliefs. Having gone to this planet to find his father, Worf is captured, learns his father is indeed dead, and discovers a younger generation of Klingons who have not been schooled in Klingon culture and beliefs. Worf takes the task of teaching the ancient stories of Klingon faith, including the promise of Sto-Vo-Kor as the abode for the honored dead, a place where Kahless the Unforgettable awaited them. Worf also tells the story of how Kahless promised to return to the Klingons. The response of the youths to these tales is inspiring, causing Worf to wonder in retrospect if he has the faith he had relayed to the young Klingons ("Rightful Heir").

In his quarters on the *Enterprise* Worf tries to summon a vision of Kahless, causing him to be late for his assigned duty. Picard reprimands Worf for this, but also sympathizes with Worf's plight, ordering him to take leave to search for the answers to his questions. Worf goes to Borath, home to a group of clerics who await the return of Kahless. Following several days of ritual, Worf begins to get restless. After being urged to continue with an open mind, Worf soon gets not only a vision of Kahless but witnesses the presence of Kahless, who has now returned.

Even after most of the others are convinced that Kahless has indeed returned, Worf remains skeptical. Only after tests performed on the *Enterprise* show that this Klingon's genetic material matched the blood-stain on a knife purportedly belonging to Kahless does Worf exclaim, "Kahless has returned."

The Klingon Emperor Gowron, who has come to witness this event, persists in his belief that this is an imposter, part of a plot by the cleric Koroth to seize control of the empire. Following a battle between Gowron and Kahless, which Gowron wins, it is revealed that this version of Kahless is a clone of Kahless formed from genetic material taken from the knife. He had been implanted with some experiences and memories drawn from sacred texts.

Gowron's initial fear, that news of Kahless's return would spark a religious and civil war throughout the empire, is confirmed by Worf, who notes that despite the fact that this is a clone, and not Kahless returned, some would still believe in this Kahless and fight. Finally, a compromise is forged in which Gowron would retain civil authority in the empire while Kahless would stand as a figurehead emperor and a desperately needed moral leader in the empire. As Kahless prepares to leave the *Enterprise*, he tells Worf that in reality it may not matter if the true Kahless ever returns or not, but "what is important is that we follow his teachings" ("Rightful Heir").

Several features of this sketch arguably correspond with the conclusions and agenda of the Jesus Seminar. The overarching correlation is found in the manner in which a resolution is reached within a community of faith that must in turn exist within a secularized framework of reality.[8] But what of the substance of this resolution? Within the boundaries of a faith community exist a variety of convictions. As Worf notes, despite the fact that this "miracle" of Kahless's return could be explained rationally (i.e. without appeal to the supernatural), there would be those who would reject this explanation of the miracle. What is needed is a way in which the integrity of belief in the faith community is maintained while feeding the spiritual needs of that community and permitting functionality within the larger secular view of reality. The resolution of the Klingons, and the resolution of the *Star Trek* universe for those who wish to retain religious beliefs in a dominant secular worldview, is to divert focus from the supernatural claims of sacred scripture and focus on the ethical. In other words, the resolution is to demythologize the sacred texts. This serves a two-fold purpose. First, it allows the faith community to focus on a block of material that forms the practical core of the religious message of the community and its texts. Second, in focusing on this component of the faith, the larger social context benefits from the moral and ethical teachings of the community.

This hermeneutic, *from the perspective of the dominant secular worldview,* is the ideal situation. It produces a functional benefit from the fruits of religion practiced and not just dogmatized, it allows for the possibility of individuals and communities of faith to hold to the substance of their particular faiths while cooperating in the larger social arena, and it provides the criteria for discerning between the natural and so-called supernatural components of sacred tradition. In many ways, this aspect of the *Star Trek* hermeneutic parallels the output of the Jesus Seminar, for in both is propagated a vision for integrating legitimate, if significantly pared, religious belief into a dominant secular worldview.

IT'S A KLINGON THING

Mention has already been made of *TNG*'s "Birthright" in the previous section. This episode not only provides the catalyst for Worf's own spiritual quest, which in turn leads to the later formulation of one of the interpretive principles of the *Star Trek* universe's views of sacred texts, but it also provides in itself another such interpretive principle. This principle is the application of a narrative approach to a text in the formulation of the religious and cultural identity of a community.

In Worf's search for his father, he comes to a Romulan prison planet, on which are being held prisoner the Klingon survivors of the Battle of Khitomer. In failing to find his father, Worf becomes a captive in the compound, but he discovers that the Klingons and the Romulans have developed into a functioning, unified society. As Worf discovers, however, the cost for this peaceful existence is the Klingons' cultural and religious identity.

This is especially evident in the second-generation Klingons. Worf witnesses Klingon children using Klingon weapons as gardening tools and as equipment for playing games. He also hears Klingon girls singing a war song as a lullaby. Having been foiled in his attempts to escape, Worf sets out to educate the Klingon children of their lost heritage. He does so by practicing Klingon meditation rituals in their presence, by showing them the proper use for their misused weapons, and by relating to them the stories of their Klingon heritage.

It is in this last effort that we see the principle of a narrative approach to sacred texts portrayed. In one scene, Worf sits with several children around a fire and tells them the story of Kahless' sword. At one point he relates part of the legend in which Kahless, distraught over having the sword of his father cast into the sea, weeps so much that his tears fill the ocean and flood the shores. At this, Toq, an impetuous Klingon boy, cries out, "That is impossible!" "For you, maybe, but not for Kahless, for he was a great warrior," is Worf's response. Toq retorts, "You're making this up." Worf replies, "No. These are our stories. They tell us who we are."

In the next scene, after the children have been sent off to bed by their elders, Ba'el, a half-Romulan, half-Klingon girl to whom Worf is attracted, approaches Worf and asks him, "The stories that you tell—are they true?" Worf answers, "I have studied them all of my life, and find new truths in them every time."

These scenes illustrate a narrative approach to sacred texts that is frequently employed in several literary approaches in modern biblical interpretation (e.g. Alter 1981; Berlin 1983; Sternberg 1985). In many presentations of narrative criticism, the tendency is to treat the stories of the biblical text as ahistorical. In this regard, the message of the story is conveyed not in the actual historical referents of the text, but in such literary features as plot, characterization, and so on. Meaning is derived by reading the story with an eye toward the artistic or poetic presentation of the story, often leading to the treatment and interpretation of the text as a fiction. As a result, quite often the text is seen as radically autonomous, independent of any historical anchor or of any consideration of authorial intent.

In Worf's conversation with Ba'el we see this aspect of narrative especially highlighted. To Ba'el's question of the historical truthfulness of Worf's stories, Worf replies with an affirmation of the narrative truthfulness of the accounts, a position that allows for fresh communication of meaning with each reading encounter. As placed on the lips of Worf, the *Star Trek* universe's proposition here is that meaning need not be bound to actual historical events, but is rather discerned in the power that religious stories have in shaping reality and imparting meaning to those who read them. In this respect, this understanding parallels the argument of the previous section concerning the demythologizing of the sacred text. It is not important in terms of religious value that the accounts be accurate in terms of referring to actual historical events; it is important that the stories communicate a message that brings meaning to life.

In the case of Worf's interchange with Toq we see another aspect of the power of narrative: the power to shape the religious and cultural identity of those who read and preserve the stories as a community. When Toq questions Worf concerning the origin of the Kahless story, Worf's reply is telling: "These are our stories. They tell us who we are." To Worf, knowing and owning these stories is the definition of what it is to be Klingon. Mere genetics is not enough—Toq is clearly a Klingon. But without a sense of the community narrative, Toq is no more a true Klingon than are his Romulan captors. Such is the power of Worf's response to Toq's charge that it was impossible for Kahless' tears to cause the ocean to flood the shores. If Toq were a true Klingon, familiar with the Klingon heritage like the great warrior Kahless, the story would make all too much sense.

One further observation regarding the narrative approach to biblical interpretation is found in this episode, one that relates especially to the worldview of the *Star Trek* universe. This is the appropriateness of a narrative world to a particular community. In our treatment of the pluralistic perspective of the *Star Trek* universe we labeled this "post-modern pluralism." By this we understand that not only are all religious viewpoints tolerated and validated within the larger social structure, but also that they may be appropriate only for certain subgroups of the larger society.

In an encounter with the Romulan caretaker of the prison colony, Worf charges Tokath with robbing the Klingons of who they were as a people and dishonoring them by taking them captive and holding them prisoner. Tokath, incredulous, responds, "By not slitting their throats when we found them unconscious?" To this Worf growls, "I do not expect you to understand. You are a Romulan."

Worf has effectively stated that Tokath cannot understand why such would be dishonoring and identity-robbing because Tokath is incapable of entering into the narrative world of the Klingons. Even Tokath's creation of a peaceful environment for Klingons and Romulans, in Worf's eyes, does not change the fact that something has been taken from the Klingon captives that is essential in defining them as a people. Stripping the captured Klingons of their honor and keeping the community narrative from their offspring is tantamount to cultural and religious genocide.

Klingons, to be Klingons, must be permitted their community narrative. And while this narrative is appropriate for Klingons, and applauded as such in the *Star Trek* universe, it is exclusively their story. Romulans could no more live by the Klingon narrative than could a Cardassian live by the Bajoran narrative. Each of these groups has a community narrative that is appropriate for each in light of the history, cultural development, and worldview of each.

To summarize, "Birthright" affirms reading scripture as a narrative that need not have an anchor in historical reality. The motivation for suggesting this as an approach for biblical interpretation in the *Star Trek* vision for humanity is clear. If one religious community could lay claim to the historical veracity of its scriptural claims, then there might be justification for evangelistic or proselytizing activities among those who do not accept these claims, and such would violate the pluralistic vision of the *Star Trek* worldview. If, however, scriptural stories can be interpreted so as to conserve religious meaning and identity for a faith community without asserting that such must be accepted by all subgroups in society, then scripture can be regarded as authoritative in a relativistic sense. Each religious community in the human family may still find truth in their ancient texts while living in cooperative co-existence with all other faith communities.[9]

DOOMSDAY COMETH, DOESN'T IT?

As a new millennium approaches, it is not surprising that various religious groups search their sacred writings for understandings concerning the meaning of the approaching landmark. As concerns certain groups within fundamentalist and evangelical Christianity, one need not scan the popular Christian media very long before encountering mountains of literature and a constant stream of broadcasts claiming that items in the day's news correspond perfectly with prophetic predictions in the Bible concerning the end of this world. While much of this type of biblical interpretation and speculation is conducted apart from serious scholarly work on the texts in question, it nevertheless exerts tremendous pressure in the Christian community to anticipate the Parousia of Jesus Christ, the moment that will dramatically bring about the end of this age and usher in the messianic kingdom of God.[10]

The common thread to many such speculations, diverse though they may be, is that they all portray a rather cataclysmic conclusion to this phase of human history that is in some sense connected to the year 2000.[11] This "millenarian hysteria," as it is frequently called, results in a rather narrow interpretive approach to prophetic texts, one that basically proves what it set out to prove. The interesting feature of these interpretations is that they speak with such confidence concerning the meaning of language that is highly figurative and symbolic.

DS9's "Destiny" (1995) explores this phenomenon, but with a different hermeneutical presupposition. Perhaps not all prophecy speaks of Doomsday through its highly symbolic language, but rather predicts the betterment of humanity via its own efforts. In "Destiny," Sisko is presented with an interpretation of a Bajoran prophecy that warns of the destruction of the wormhole if Sisko proceeds with a joint effort with the Cardassians to deploy a subspace communications relay in the Gamma Quadrant, a project that would permit communication through the wormhole for the first time. According to the prophecy, three "vipers" will return to their "nest" in the sky. Vedek Yarka interprets the prophecy to refer to the three Cardassian scientists, the vipers, who are to return to the former Cardassian space station, the nest. Initially, fears are eased when only two Cardassian scientists arrive and are quite friendly in demeanor. However, tensions rise at the announcement of a third scientist to arrive. Kira begins to believe the prophecy to be true, but she refuses to let her personal belief interfere with her duties. When Kira accompanies Sisko, Dax, and two Cardassian scientists to the Gamma Quadrant, they discover a rogue comet, which Kira interprets to be the "sword of the stars" predicted in the prophecy.

When Kira confronts Sisko, the Emissary of the Prophets, with her belief that the prophecy is coming to pass, she tells Sisko that he must make a decision on how to proceed, a decision that was also foretold in the prophecy. He decides to proceed with the project. When they attempt to send a signal through the wormhole, it causes the wormhole to react violently with the effect of pulling the comet toward it. If the comet enters the wormhole, its composition would cause the wormhole to close permanently, also in accordance with the prophecy. An attempt to vaporize the comet with a phaser blast only causes it to split into three pieces, all of which continue to head toward the wormhole. Sisko and Kira enter a shuttle craft in the attempt to create a subspace field around the fragments and guide them through the wormhole into the Alpha Quadrant. In so doing, the small amount of material that emanated from the comet forms a subspace filament that allows for communications to pass through the wormhole.

Reflection on these events causes Kira to realize that the prophecy came true, but that the symbolism was misinterpreted. In reality, the comet fragments were the "vipers" and the filament trail actually wedged open the "temple gates" of the wormhole. Moreover, Sisko gains a new appreciation for Bajoran prophecy and his role in it as Emissary.

The change in perspective in interpreting prophecy, as depicted in this episode, clearly reflects the optimistic mindset of the *Star Trek* vision. The model proposed does not deprecate a faith community's right and responsibility to interpret the sources of its faith, but rather suggests an open-mindedness when interpreting symbolic and figurative language. Moreover, such an interpretive shift greatly benefits the function of the larger society. If prophecy were seen as constructive rather than destructive or cataclysmic, then the faith community would certainly work in accordance with prophetic utterance for the betterment of conditions for all of human society. In this respect, the *Star Trek* vision can be seen to advocate the handling of prophecy in a manner similar to that of a significant portion of mainline Christianity as it pursues the agenda of the "social gospel," the outworking of the social and ethical content of biblical texts apart from acceptance of the supernatural claims and worldview of these texts.

CONCLUSION

We began this discussion by acknowledging the existence of a *Star Trek* vision, a vision that offers an optimistic hope for the future for humankind, a vision that in turn calls contemporary society to pursue its promises. In short, it is a vision that urges cooperation within diversity toward the attainment of a functional society. We further observed in this vision an expanding sphere of concern that includes religion within the scope of its address. In order to understand the place of religious belief in the *Star Trek* vision, we noted several features of the worldview within which the vision is defined. A synthetic summary of these features might be that the *Star Trek* worldview conceives of reality from a secular and materialistic perspective while fostering a tolerant and pluralistic acceptance of cultural and religious diversity so long as the diversity does not hinder, from the perspective of the larger social context, the function of the larger social order.

From here we turned our attention to the particular focus of this chapter: the interpretation of the sacred texts of religious communities within the parameters of the *Star Trek* vision. Our survey of select episodes from *TNG* and *DS9* revealed a partial hermeneutical program for religious communities to follow, a program that suggests models for approaching scriptural texts in a manner that is faithful to the essential core of the religious message of the text while remaining congruent with the vision's aims for the larger social order. We identified approaches that emphasize demythologizing, dehistoricizing, and optimistic interpretations of the text. Such approaches, we suggested, allow for faith communities to mine the ancient sources of their belief for meaning and truth while permitting other groups to do the same within their faith traditions as they all strive toward the goal of achieving and maintaining an orderly, functional, and unified society.

We have also seen that these components of the *Star Trek* hermeneutic are not entirely of its own creation. Rather, as the title of this chapter asserts, the framers of the vision are "going where some have gone before." Observable parallels to the interpretive program of the vision are found in several trends within Christian biblical interpretation. In this respect, very little is offered in the way of innovation.

Indeed, this is the path of wisdom. Were the preachers of the vision to propagate a hermeneutic of their own invention, that would smack of religious imperialism and chauvinism. Rather, the vision borrows from the very traditions that the vision may seek to influence in order to suggest ways in which religious belief can exist with consistency and integrity within a secular and pluralistic worldview. Truly those scholars and theologians who have devoted their energies to the creation of the interpretive approaches highlighted here have tread similar ground as those who put forth the *Star Trek* vision. How can ancient sources of religious faith be interpreted so as to remain consistent with a secular and materialistic worldview and, at the same time, legitimately be called "Christian?" Addressing this question is the task of much biblical and theological inquiry within many strands of the Christian tradition. It is a crucial question for those who craft the *Star Trek* vision for humanity as well.

Having said all of this regarding the worldview and scriptural hermeneutic of the *Star Trek* vision, it must be stated that the vision is not presented with utopian naïveté. The framers of the vision clearly acknowledge the fact that there will inevitably be ideological conflicts among those subcultures existing within the larger social order. Among instances already cited, while Picard demonstrates sympathy and tolerance toward Worf in "Rightful Heir," it is equally clear that Picard considers Worf's ritual practice inappropriate on board the *Enterprise* and better observed in a context more conducive to Klingon spirituality. Moreover, in "Birthright" the interchange between Worf and Tokath shows that an apparently insurmountable obstacle exists between Klingons and Romulans at the level of cultural and religious values and worldviews. In another instance not yet mentioned, in *TNG*'s "Ethics" (1992) Worf's spine is shattered in an accident, and rather than face the prospect of life as a paralytic, he asks Riker to assist him in Klingon ritual suicide. Riker refuses to do so. While this practice is perfectly acceptable within Klingon culture, Riker's refusal to participate, despite his own familiarity with and participation in other aspects of Klingon life ("A Matter of Honor," 1989), illustrates not only that certain religious worldviews are appropriate only in their specific cultural contexts, but also that tensions will frequently arise between cultural subgroups and between these subgroups and the larger social order.

In light of the passion with which religious values are held, it may be rightly asked whether the *Star Trek* vision of pluralism, tolerance, and cooperation is possible. If the beliefs held by the various subgroups within the larger social order are self-designated as ultimately authoritative for ordering existence in the universe, then how might they be subjugated to the will of the larger social order and its secularly based directive of tolerant co-existence and cooperation among often widely divergent subgroups? The tack of the vision seems to be one of acknowledgment of the potential tensions while prescribing an approach to reality that allows for cooperation within diversity and for potential mutual cultural enrichment, all with an eye toward the well-being and advancement of the larger social order. Admittedly, this is an approach that is proffered from the perspective of the dominant secular worldview of the larger social order. As such, it is a view that will be far more palatable to the larger social order than to those whose very outlooks on reality are far more exclusivistic. The view of the *Star Trek* vision is apparently that the attainment of cooperation within diversity on the larger social scale is sufficiently worthy of the aspiration of all for those subgroups with more narrowly defined exclusivistic worldviews to compromise their dogmatic claims of absolute truth. It is toward achieving such a compromise that the aforementioned hermeneutical guidelines are offered.

Accordingly, assessment of the hermeneutical program of the *Star Trek* vision will vary, and with perhaps more passion, for the ground covered here is indeed sacred ground and will be defended with much tenacity. After all, very few will disagree with the basic goal of the *Star Trek* vision, that of a cooperative human society. Many will disagree with the secular and pluralistic worldview that is suggested as the framework for attaining the vision, especially those within faith communities who have their own visions for the fulfillment of human destiny. Nevertheless, the courage to go boldly into unfamiliar and potentially dangerous territories, a courage that epitomizes the vision of the *Star Trek* universe, is evident in this foray into a sensitive area of human existence. And at the end of the day, whether this aspect of the vision, or indeed the whole vision itself, will ever come to full implementation is fodder for the futurists.

But then again, *Star Trek* may be just a TV show.[12]

NOTES

1. Though the title *Star Trek* is properly the title of the original television series (*TOS*), it is commonly used as convenient nomenclature for the entirety of productions, merchandise, and events spawned by the original series, and so will be used in this chapter.

2. Clearly there is a wealth of additional resources from which such observations might be made, such as the animated series (1973), novels, and comic books. For the purposes of this chapter the television episodes and feature films are viewed as definitive of the *Star Trek* mythology while the other resources are somewhat derivative. This is by no means a judgment on their entertainment value or usefulness. It is simply a methodological judgment designed to establish a minimal yet sufficient body of authoritative data from which observations and tendencies might be identified.

3. These dates are drawn from Okuda and Okuda (1993).

4. Take, for example, *TNG*'s "Justice," where Picard must decide whether to allow Wesley Crusher to face execution for a seemingly arbitrary offense (from the Federation perspective) or to rescue Wesley, in accordance with the wishes of Wesley's mother, Dr. Crusher, and in doing so violate the Prime Directive. The interchange between Picard and Dr. Crusher on the virtues of the Prime Directive is instructive background for all such instances where application of the Prime Directive is fraught with moral difficulties.

5. I am indebted here to the position advanced by Grenz (1995). A thorough study of pluralism in the context of Christianity is found in Carson (1996).

6. To many, this may appear to be a rather narrowly conceived depiction of Western Christianity. The rather obvious observation of contemporary Western Christianity is that there are many rather diverse expressions of this tradition in the current North American religious milieu. The statement made here is defensible by virtue of its rather limited locus in the affirmations of the biblical

texts themselves, not the subsequent and rather recent interpretations of these texts that minimize or eliminate the exclusivistic tendencies found within these texts.

7. Helpful summaries and select bibliography are found in Brown (1992) and Witherington (1995).

8. Clearly, the Klingon empire is not a social subgroup of the Federation, despite the tenuous nature of a peace treaty between the two entities. But it must be remembered that the vision of the *Star Trek* universe is a general view of reality that is epitomized by the Federation. So the fact that the Klingons are not part of the Federation does not significantly diminish this correlation. Besides, Worf is a Klingon who must deal with this component of his faith within the Federation context.

9. In *TNG*'s "Darmok" (1991), the particularity of a community narrative is affirmed despite the great hardships it produces. Picard and the *Enterprise* encounter the Tamarians, a peaceful yet "incomprehensible" race. Their incomprehensibility, as the episode gradually reveals, is due to the Tamarians' verbal communication, which consists entirely of metaphors derived from their own cultural legends. Here, the community narrative is so precisely appropriate to the Tamarians that peaceful interaction, though desired, is immensely difficult. Yet through persistence and tolerance, relations are nevertheless possible.

10. This is not to suggest that there is one single eschatological perspective within Christianity as to how and when the kingdom of God is to come, as a brief perusal of any serious work in systematic theology will reveal.

11. A notable, and recent, exception to this tendency is Fasching (1996).

12. In addition to countless hours viewing TV episodes and movies, several other resources were accessed in refreshing my memories of the original *Star Trek* source materials cited here. Especially helpful were two cyber sources: "Star Trek: Continuum" (1996, 1997), *Microsoft Network*, http://startrek.msn.com; and "Star Trek: the Next Generation" (1987–1995), http://www.ugcs.caltech.edu/st-tng/. Also useful was *Star Trek: 30 Years Special Collector's Edition* (1996). And I must mention the input derived from conversations with friend and Trekker extraordinaire Elisa Bowers.

PART III

Religion and Ritual in Fandom

11

"*Star Trek* to Me Is a Way of Life"

Fan Expressions of Star Trek *Philosophy*

MICHAEL JINDRA

"*S*tar Trek* to me is a way of life" writes a *Star Trek* fan on the Internet. Similar declarations are often made by other fans on the Internet, in letters, or in personal discussions.[1] *Star Trek* has indeed become a way of life for many of its fans. This should not be too surprising, given the serious moral issues that the various *Star Trek* installments frequently address. In fact, it could be said that the most solid evidence of the close relationship between *Star Trek* and religion can be seen in the activities of the fans and the way they have taken a media production and turned it into an unprecedented fan phenomenon. In this chapter, I will journey into fandom and look specifically at some of the ways *Star Trek* philosophy has become a passion for many of its fans.

Previous chapters in this volume have pointed out *Star Trek*'s "religious position," its roots in Gene Roddenberry's optimistic philosophy, and its emphasis on science, progress and technology. Here, I focus on how *Star Trek* philosophy is expressed by fans who have found *Star Trek* to be an admirable presentation of their own beliefs in a "hopeful future." This philosophy has been effectively portrayed by the vivid, optimistic, and consistent universe that has drawn millions of fans across the world

217

into the complex technology, alien worlds, and character histories of the *Star Trek* universe (Zoglin 1994). For many fans, this folk philosophy provides guidance in a pluralistic, often meaningless postmodern world.

Because fandom is so large, it is also diverse, as any look at the myriad of Internet *Star Trek* discussion groups will indicate. Sometimes fans criticize other fans for their "excessive" devotion. Fans have consistently criticized Paramount (the company that produces *Star Trek*) for its inattention to consistency or to "Gene's vision," and its focus on getting as much money as possible from the franchise. Some fans simply sit back and enjoy the episodes, while others extract something deeper from the stories. In this sense, I distinguish the "casual" fan, who occasionally enjoys the show without participating in fan activities, from the "serious" fan, who is drawn in and captivated by the *Star Trek* universe and participates in fan activities. Serious fan activity is commonly signified by fan collections of *Star Trek* episodes on videotapes, or assorted collections of *Trek*-related merchandise or *Star Trek* books or manuals. Convention attendance can also indicate a serious fan, but many serious fans cannot or will not go to conventions. This article applies mostly to serious fans, though I believe the philosophy of *Star Trek* also reflects the views of many casual fans.

STAR TREK AS FOLK PHILOSOPHY

> *Star Trek* presents us with an enlightened, humanistic, peaceful, respectful, hopeful vision of the future. Comparing my own world and moralities to the examples that *Star Trek* makes is the way I find meaning in the *Star Trek* universe.
>
> —Internet message, Strek-L listserv

Instead of overt philosophies or religions marked by doctrines or creeds, many *Star Trek* fans adhere to a *vision* of a universe, portrayed in narrative form in books and film and on television. This substitution of a worldview expressed in narrative form for one expressed in propositions means that *Star Trek* has taken on largely mythological functions (cf. McLaren in this volume). In this sense, *Star Trek* is a "folk philosophy" since it has a large following without being overly institutionalized or codified. Folk philosophy is so named because it describes beliefs found among ordinary people that do not have any central organization or leadership and that are expressions of deep-set cultural convictions. Like folk religions, these beliefs are often not recognized as formal religions, as in Catholic folk religions of South America that mix Catholic beliefs (e.g. saints) with indigenous gods and mythologies (Christian 1987).[2]

The fan use of *Star Trek* has similarities with traditional and folk religions that are expressed largely through myth. Both *Star Trek* and mythological religions (such as those of the Amazonian peoples described by the anthropologist Claude Lévi-Strauss) rise out of the work of story-tellers who weave together compelling narratives out of the characters, values, and context of the contemporary culture (Claus 1976; Jindra 1994: 46). Some of these stories eventually become established as myths that help form (and reflect) the basic cultural values of peoples. Because this connection between popular culture storytelling and the develop-ment of religion is not often recognized, suggestions that *Star Trek* can be used by fans as a "folk philosophy" meet with some skepticism from the public. This skepticism is based partially on prevailing attitudes toward television and film as simply "entertainment" media, not as serious ways to tell stories. In actuality, television functions simply as another commu-nicative medium, much like the oral stories, books, or rituals that have historically been the transmitters of cultural values (Silverstone 1988). Television (and film) fulfills the very serious function of communicating worldviews, moral tales and notions of identity (Martin and Ostwalt 1995). Both the moral/philosophical message of *Trek* and the skepticism with which this kind of message is greeted is evident in the comment of one newspaper writer, who wrote, "One of the messages [of *Star Trek*] is that Picard's mission in life is not just mapping stars but also charting new explanations for human existence. It seems like pretty heady stuff for TV" (Ross 1994).

The ideology of *Star Trek* is rooted in the views of Gene Rodden-berry, who expressed his ideas most explicitly in a thirty-page interview in *The Humanist* magazine just months before his death in 1991 (Alexander 1991). Roddenberry, who was a member of the American Humanist Association (AHA), revealed in the interview that he had a very conscious humanist philosophy that saw humans taking control of their own des-tiny, and thereby controlling the future. His widow, Majel Barret Rod-denberry (who has remained active in *Star Trek* productions), has also car-ried on the humanist torch and recently received the Humanist Award from the AHA. Many humanists regard *Star Trek* as an admirable expres-sion of their faith. The fall 1992 issue of *Free Inquiry* ("an international secular humanist magazine") includes an article titled "*Star Trek:* Human-ism of the Future" (Marsalek 1992), which uses individual episodes to illustrate how much the series illustrates the ideals of secular humanism.

Admittedly, it is ironic to call *Star Trek* "religious," for secular humanism's self-described philosophy (as expressed by the AHA) is in opposition to what they believe to be superstitious religious beliefs. Yet humanism and the scientism (the elevation of science above other values) that draws on it have become "quasi-religious" elements of our culture themselves (Thomas 1990). Also, *Star Trek* fan discourse often takes place on the boundaries between religion and the denial of religion. Many *Star Trek* fans, though denying that their adherence to *Star Trek* is religious, still use religious language to express their fandom. In a manual given to all new members of a fan club, the *Alpha Quadrant*, the leaders wrote the following disclaimer:

> This is not a religious group. While it is true that the ultimate goal of *Alpha Quadrant* is to affect humanity directly, this is not in the least bit religious unless you happen to take *Star Trek* too seriously. Gene Roddenberry's dream would be just as important and vital to the progress of humanity without *Star Trek*; the shows are the medium he used to transmit his feelings to us. We believe in *Star Trek* because we are optimists. You, along with your fellow members, are now taking the first step from being an optimistic observer to being an achiever. (Sanda and Hall 1994)

Ironically, the writers explicitly deny a religious orientation, while at the same time bringing up transcendental notions such as belief and the "progress of humanity," and casting a prophetic Roddenberry "transmitting" messages to the public through the electronic media. This confusion is no doubt generated by the common perception of religion as limited to the worship of deities, and formalized in denominations or other institutions. Religion, however, is much more versatile than this definition implies, and is found in a variety of forms and contexts (Greil and Robbins 1994). In this chapter, religion is given a sociologically broad and "functional" definition as a "symbol system" concerned with "ultimate" questions about the world, human destiny, and "transcendent meaning" (Wuthnow 1992: 102). Based upon this definition, it is not hard to argue that *Star Trek* is religious. *Star Trek* "symbols" such as the *Enterprise* (Selly 1990), along with the narratives of many episodes (e.g. first and last episodes of TNG that "judge" humanity; Spock's, Data's, and the *Voyager* doctor's ruminations on what it means to be human) dwell on transcendent issues of human nature, purpose and destiny.

WHAT IS *STAR TREK* PHILOSOPHY?

In many countries throughout the world (Spelling 1993), fans are taking the messages and morals of *Star Trek* and studying them, discussing them and applying them to their own lives. Many fans point to the Prime Directive and IDIC (Infinite Diversity in Infinite Combinations) as examples of *Star Trek* philosophy. The Prime Directive is the frequently-broken Federation principle allowing no interference in the natural development of other worlds. One college student in Development Studies told me that the Prime Directive illustrated the attitude development experts need to take when working with another culture. Instead of imposing solutions, local peoples themselves need to decide what kind of development they want. In this way, *Star Trek* morals are applied by fans to real-world situations.

The fan desire to find a coherent message in *Star Trek* can also be seen in the extent to which some fans have taken the brief mentions of Vulcan teachings in *Star Trek* and have turned them into an entire philosophy and worldview worthy of emulation. The IDIC philosophy and symbol was only discussed explicitly in one episode of *TOS* ("Is There In Truth No Beauty?" 1968), but fans elaborated on it because it served to summarize key messages of *Star Trek* and gave depth to fan allegiance to the show (even though it may have simply been a marketing ploy by Gene Roddenberry).[3] The "IDIC *Star Trek* fan club," based in Scotland, has over 1,000 members worldwide and, according to the club's leaders, "reflects not only the philosophy of *Star Trek* but our hopes for the club" in having a diverse membership. The father of Vulcan philosophy, Surak, also became a center of attraction for Vulcan fans, and a listserv (Vulcan-L) and Usenet group (alt.fan.surak) devoted to Vulcan philosophy were created. The introduction to the *Free Inquiry* article mentioned earlier summarizes the IDIC philosophy of *Star Trek* and its application:

> The "*Star Trek*" universe is a celebration of pluralism encompassed in the Vulcan philosophy of IDIC—Infinite Diversity in Infinite Combinations. "*Star Trek*" advances a commitment to self-determination, freedom, equality, and individual rights. The *Enterprise* crews are dedicated to using reason, science, and logic . . . in understanding the universe, solving problems, and improving the human condition. (Marsalek 1992: 53)

The culturally relativistic notions of IDIC and the Prime Directive, however, are subsumed within the TV shows themselves under the more powerful motivating philosophy of science, technology, and progress, as others in this volume have pointed out (e.g., Peterson). The narrative of *Star Trek* assumes that, given continual human moral and material progress, society will evolve to near perfection. Fans frequently name the "hopeful future" portrayed by the *Star Trek* universe as the reason the show appeals to them (e.g. Lichtenberg et al. 1975: 106 ff.). For fans, following *Star Trek* precepts such as IDIC and non-interference, along with the pursuit of technological progress, can enable us to attain the kind of world portrayed in the various *Star Trek* installments.

From a cross-cultural perspective, the broadly Euro-American notions of progress, exploration, and independence are clearly visible in *Star Trek* (Kottak 1990: 101–6). This is easily confirmed by comparing the popularity of *Star Trek* in the United States with its popularity in other countries, such as Brazil, where soap operas that focus on family relationships dominate prime-time television.[4] In many places in the world, kinship is the most important cultural value, and the organizing principle is reciprocity or dependence on elders and other relations. *Star Trek*, instead, often negatively portrays situations of dependence, such as *TOS*'s "The Apple" (1967), or the *Star Trek: Voyager* premiere (1995) where the "Caretaker" is the provider for a society. Instead of dependence and unchanging tradition, *Star Trek* promotes independence and self-sufficiency through the use of science and reason. Likewise, it has often been condescending to those cultures and beings it meets that are overtly religious, as Asa and Linford in this volume point out.[5]

Though scientific and rationalist philosophies pointedly exclude mythic modes of knowledge, the emphasis on science, reason, and progress in Western society means that they themselves have become myths of modernity (Robertson 1980; Hegy 1991). These central *Star Trek* themes are drawn from key notions in the history of Western philosophy and social history. Themes of science, reason, and progress began to be expressed most explicitly in the Renaissance and later in the Enlightenment, when humanism and the scientific revolution helped create the "modern" world (Cassirer 1951: 140 ff.; Hopper 1991). The adoption of these expectations by peoples often resulted in utopian beliefs and hopes (Thomas 1990: 100). These utopian hopes are visibly expressed within the narratives of *Star Trek*.

FAN RESPONSES TO *STAR TREK* PHILOSOPHIES

Star Trek draws on themes of humanism and science when it highlights human potential and the power of science to solve problems. These pervasive themes are broad enough to attract fans with otherwise diverse worldviews. *Star Trek* episodes and movies now span four decades and have involved numerous writers, directors, and producers. The end products are episodes so numerous and diverse that fans with many different viewpoints can find something to agree with. *Star Trek* draws together those who love science and technology (Jenkins 1995), along with those who focus on relationships (Bacon-Smith 1992). *Star Trek* does not send a monolithic message, but different episodes give contrasting, sometimes contradictory messages. Science, technology, and progress, for example, must sometimes give way to humanism and the respect for other beings (e.g. *TOS*'s "The Devil in the Dark," 1967). Some episodes and films focus primarily on relationships among the characters (*TNG*'s "Family," 1990), while others rely on science (using technobabble) to resolve situations (*Star Trek VII: Generations*, 1994). As one can see in frequent cyberspace discussions over religion and *Star Trek*, Christians, New Agers, members of Asian religions, and atheists, among others, have all been attracted to *Star Trek*'s discussions of human nature, justice, and being. One fan apparently appreciates *Star Trek*'s ability to address morality in the absence of conventional religion:

> The thing I like about *Star Trek* in general is that they address moral dilemmas without specific references to religion. We see characters torn between what sounds good on paper, e.g., the Prime Directive, and what seems right in a specific situation. I don't want to know where the morality of *Star Trek* characters is grounded. It is enough for me to see that they have a sense of morality, and that this sense is tested on a fairly regular basis. (Usenet post)

How have Christian fans reacted to the humanism of *Star Trek* and its view of myth and religion as mere superstition? Many Christian fans seemingly overlook this aspect of the show, focusing instead on the few times when episodes did show a tolerance for religion, or when Christ-figures were portrayed (Spock, in *Star Trek II* and *III*, gave his life for the crew and was then resurrected).[6] Many Christians with whom I have spoken focused on *TOS*'s "Bread and Circuses" (1968), in which Uhura closed the show with a positive reference to the "Son of God." They also cite its strong focus on justice and ethics and its sense of order. Many Christian fans seem to overlook the side of *Star Trek* that expresses an almost unlimited belief in human potential, which contrasts with Christian notions of human fallenness. This is not surprising, however, given that the optimism of *Star Trek* is such a basic value of middle-class American culture that most people do not see this optimism as something culturally relative and unique (Du Bois 1955; Gellner 1992: 52). Other Christian fans, however, notice and decry the condescension toward religion and the overemphasis on science (e.g. Harris 1988).

The appeal of *Star Trek* among Christians is not surprising when one realizes that both the humanism and the scientism expressed in *Star Trek*, though cut off from Christianity, have their roots in the Christianity of the Early Modern and Renaissance periods. Early Western scientists believed in an orderly, designed universe created by an omnipotent God (Jaki 1978, Whitehead 1925). The humanism of the Renaissance, though in tension with Christianity, was also deeply rooted in it, as in the case of the philosopher Erasmus (Cassirer 1951:134ff). Contemporary humanism, as expressed in *Star Trek* (though not the same as Renaissance humanism) shares concerns with Christianity over justice and human dignity by opposing such notions as racism and promoting human rights. In general, it should not be too surprising to find both secular humanists and Christians among ardent *Star Trek* fans.

Given the diverse makeup of *Star Trek* fandom, it is not surprising to see *Star Trek* interpreted in different ways by fans, particularly with regard to religion. In *Star Trek: Good News in Modern Images*, Caprio (1978) argues that *Star Trek* is essentially Christian in its outlook. She uses passages from the Bible to trace biblical themes of Eden and Paradise throughout *Star Trek* episodes. *Star Trek* fan Skip Borrell understands that Roddenberry's intention was opposed to conventional religion, but still prefers to connect *Star Trek* philosophy with Christianity. In an article entitled "God is a Trekker!" he writes:

> We are told that IDIC is a Vulcan philosophy, but I believe it comes from God. If we look at the opening verses of the book of Genesis we read that God created one person, then two. And God told them to be fruitful and multiply. And so they did. We have gone from two people to billions of people. And through those countless generations we have had infinite diversity through those infinite combinations of people. (Borrell 1993: 4)

Another example of *Trek*/Christian integration is offered by a *Trek* fan who wrote a Ph.D. dissertation based on interviews with Trekker teachers in the southeastern U.S. (Anijar 1994). In the Bible Belt, *Trek* fans (both Christian and non-Christian) use Christian language to articulate their adherence to *Star Trek* beliefs. According to Anijar, teacher fans create a wholly new "syncretized" and "selective tradition" by combining *Star Trek* and traditional "Southern Baptist religious values"(Anijar 1994: 12). Many Bible Belt fans use *Star Trek* to speak of the values of duty, honor, and truth.

Many fans throughout the country do not have to "syncretize" *Star Trek* with another tradition, but simply draw on the underlying humanism, scientism, or optimism of *Star Trek* and make it their folk philosophy of life. Kathe Walker, who with her husband owns several *Star Trek* stores in the Denver area, maintains that "*Star Trek* is more than a show; it's an ideal, a philosophy. It says that the future can be better than the present" (Carrier 1994). Another fan wrote on the Internet:

> I watch the show and try to live my life by Roddenberry's example of hard work, imagination, compassion, curiosity, courage, and keeping an eye on the future while working to make the present better one day at a time. I don't always succeed, and I, we all do, fall prey to our faults, but I keep trying. I'll close by saying that the dream is what is important and it should be protected above all and not turned into a soap opera or the next Scientology.

Some fans view Roddenberry as a "prophet" (e.g. Sanda and Hall 1994; Anijar 1994: 136) much the same way that Elvis fans compare Elvis "the King" with Christ the King (Harrison 1992). Some fans take Gene Roddenberry's word as absolute, and his vision of *Star Trek* and the world as the "correct" one, a view often expressed in debates over the *Star Trek* "canon" (Jindra 1994: 45). Among these fans, the folk philosophy of *Star Trek* begins to show the attributes of an institutionalized religion.[7]

FAN APPLICATIONS OF *STAR TREK* PHILOSOPHY

Star Trek philosophies can be developed and codified both by fans as individuals and through institutions such as fan clubs and classrooms. This process of institutionalization is quite typical for new ideas and beliefs that gain in popularity, some of which eventually become established as religions (Bellah 1970). Jeffrey Mills of the "Central Connecticut *Star Trek* Support Group" teaches classes on the cultural relevance of *Star Trek* at local colleges. "By watching *Star Trek*, studying it and applying its lessons, *Star Trek* almost becomes a sort of Scripture, doesn't it? Like the

Bible, *Star Trek* has excellent stories with heroes and villains; it contains important messages and occasional thou-shalt-nots. What the Bible does in 66 books, *Star Trek* does in 79 episodes" (Mills 1990: 332). Mills has considered turning *Star Trek* into political theory and running for public office, but given the general public's unwillingness to see a TV show such as *Star Trek* as a significant philosophy, it is unlikely he would be taken seriously, so he has not taken that step (Hamilton 1994: C1).

Mills argues that *Star Trek*'s philosophy, expressed in the Prime Directive, assumes a non-aggressive posture that does not interfere in other planets' "social development" (cited in Hamilton 1994: C1). As mentioned above, the evolutionary idea of development, of human and social progress through time, runs throughout the show (Hark 1979: 31 ff.), and is also a strong part of North American culture, as expressed, for example, by the New Age movement (Hexham 1994). Jeffrey Mills describes the evolutionary and teleological theme as such: "*Star Trek* says there's this line of humanoid development, and the best *Trek* stories give us little tips and tools on how we can be moving rightward on getting better" (cited in Hamilton 1994: C1).

Maria Nausch, writing in the *Central Connecticut Star Trek Support Group Newsletter*, describes how fans conceive of their mission in light of the evolution of humanity in *Star Trek*: "They [fans] share a vision of the future and try to make it begin now. I think that in these ways *Star Trek* is more than a religion: it's a way of living and a conception of the world of its own. And it transcends all confession by uniting all of us in the common efforts to make our dream come true" (Nausch 1993: 7).

Fans, of course, express *Star Trek* philosophy in bumper stickers, posters, through Internet discussions and fan club meetings. "Filk" singing is popular at fan-run *Star Trek* conventions, where fans invent their own lyrics, with *Star Trek* themes, to popular tunes. In a song called "Born Again Trek," fandom is spoken of as a "faith," and fans are called upon to "spread the word" (Jenkins 1990: 150). Given the breadth of *Star Trek* fan activities, there is no shortage of places for fans to come together and share their adherence to the vision of *Star Trek*.

Star Trek has had an impact on the lives of many people (Huff 1988). One fan writes: "Having grown up with *Star Trek*, I believe I really have been influenced with Starfleet values" (Internet post). Many have been inspired by *Star Trek* to enter professions such as medicine or engineering. Many others have found a renewed sense of purpose and identity through *Star Trek*. One college student I talked to was not popular in high school and has had problems with self-esteem ever since. She identifies with

Spock as a fellow "outcast." Like Spock, she has had little contact with her parents. *Star Trek* appeals to her because of the diversity it exhibits and encourages, and because of the consideration it gives to those who are different. Fans sense this respect for diversity, and *Star Trek* fandom does seem to draw its share of people who in some ways feel left out by society.

Some fans express their loyalty to *Star Trek* in "ultimate" ways, as befitting a phenomenon that has taken on religious functions. In a cemetery in Carroll, Iowa is a gravestone engraved with the image of the USS *Enterprise* from *TOS*. The top of the stone features a beautiful image of the *Enterprise* so clear that NCC-1701 shows on the facing nacelle. The epitaph read: "His journey ends never, his *Star Trek* will go on forever," and it stands guard over the grave of a young man who died in the 1970s.[8]

Other productions based on *Star Trek* have shown the extent to which *Star Trek* has been able to provide applications, both moral and managerial, to people's lives. The book *All I Really Need to Know I Learned from Watching* Star Trek, by fan Dave Marinaccio (1994) draws lessons of life from the plots and characters of *Star Trek*. For instance, Marinaccio uses the changing role the Klingons have played through various *Star Trek* series to show the wisdom of making your enemies your friends. Likewise, *The Meaning of Star Trek* (Richards 1997), in a more philosophical sense, explains some of the underlying premises of the show. In *Make It So: Leadership for the Next Generation*, Roberts and Ross (1995) draw management lessons from *TNG*, while the U.S. Naval Academy uses *TNG*'s "The First Duty" (1992) featuring Wesley Crusher in an ethical dilemma at Starfleet Academy. Fans have consistently found philosophical and moral depth in their allegiance to *Star Trek*, a trait that distinguishes *Star Trek* and its fans from most other, more superficial, popular culture productions.

FAN CLUBS

Star Trek beliefs have also been institutionalized by the over 500 local *Star Trek* fan clubs found in at least twenty different countries. Many are small, but some, like the USS *Intrepid*, a 500-member club from Detroit, has its own lengthy constitution and bylaws and includes an oath of allegiance and penalties for misconduct (DeSmet 1995).

The serious nature of the fan club phenomenon is indicated by the practices of fans clubs, and by their statements of purpose. The largest fan-organized *Star Trek* club, Starfleet International, is an association of several hundred local fan clubs located around the world. Its 1981 constitution contains the following preamble: "We, the fans of *Star Trek*, in order to organize and promote the concepts of unity, peace and brotherhood in fandom, as espoused by *Star Trek* philosophy and to promote the mutual gain of benefits among members, do ordain and establish this constitution for the organization of Starfleet." Article I (objectives and purposes) of the Constitution states: "The primary purpose of Starfleet shall be the pursuit of unity and brotherhood among members through the promotion of *Star Trek*, its goals and concepts."

These statements reveal that *Star Trek* is more than simple entertainment. *Trek* philosophies stimulate fan activity to the extent that many fans devote major portions of their lives to institutionalizing it in fan clubs. This is no mere escape from real life, but an active and aggressive attempt to give public voice to *Star Trek* and its philosophies in public life.

Charity is one of the chief activities of fan clubs. The USS *Intrepid* has over ten charities to which it regularly contributes time or money. Many clubs raise money for local food banks or contribute to science education programs; others are actively involved in supporting the space program. Club members often dress up for charity events and conventions and role-play in character. Members are given ranks in the club (ensign, lieutenant, etc.) and can gain promotion through participation in club activities. Through these activities, fans express their hopes for a better future, and take action to bring that future into existence, by attempting to make their communities and countries better places to live.

CONCLUSION

> When it comes down to basic questions of life and death and also of life after death, people want to know how to find answers. As someone from India, it is clear to me that many Americans are looking for answers by going to movie theaters or by watching certain TV shows. . . . They may not be aware of what they are doing or what they are looking for, but they are yearning for answers.
>
> —Vishal Mangalwadi, after watching the premiere of *Star Trek: Deep Space Nine* (Mattingly 1993: 1)

Star Trek has succeeded as an ongoing narrative and become one of the largest cultural phenomenons of this century because it has an overarching philosophy that draws on central themes of the Western tradition. It appeals to fans brought up in that tradition, most of whom are found in Europe and North America. For many, *Star Trek* has taken a place alongside the traditional metanarratives and mythologies of Western cultures, largely because it draws on them and portrays humanist, scientific, and Christian themes in the very vivid and attractive media of television and film. The complex and detailed universe portrayed is attractive to fans, and invites fans to think about both that universe and their own.

For some fans, *Star Trek* replaces older religions like Christianity, and for others it supplements them with new ways of expressing the same messages. One feature of contemporary society is the ability people have to pick and choose from among a number of beliefs and create a "personal" religion (Bellah et al. 1985: 220 ff.). *Star Trek* draws together those who love science and technology, along with humanist-oriented fans (both religious and secular), all of whom find aspects of the show (e.g. the political progressiveness and optimism, the morality, or the technology) to appreciate. Through fan clubs and other outlets such as the Internet, and by making it a major part of their lives, serious fans express their adherence to *Star Trek* philosophies.

NOTES

1. In cyberspace, discussion groups of fans can be found almost anywhere; on services such as America-on-Line, in Usenet newsgroups, and on numerous listservs; fan philosophies can also be found on personal or fan club web pages. For letters, issues of *Trek* magazine (or compilations of them in the *Best of Trek* book series) are a good source. See Ruff (1996) for one example of how a fan describes her agreement with the messages of *Star Trek*.

2. "Popular religion," a term similar to "folk religion," could also be applied here (Lippy 1996: 5).

3. According to William Shatner (1993: 287–89), Gene Roddenberry inserted the mention of IDIC, and an IDIC medallion, into this episode mostly as a potential product to exploit through merchandising.

4. There is an active *Star Trek* fan club movement in Brazil, but *Star Trek* has never won the broad popularity it has in North America.

5. Though McLaren and Porter do discuss an increased sensitivity in more recent installments of *Star Trek*.

6. Roddenberry was raised in a Christian fundamentalist environment (Alexander 1991), so it is not surprising to see Christian themes in the show, even though he left Christianity behind in adulthood.

7. Those who view Roddenberry literally as a prophet, however, are in the minority among *Trek* fans, especially since some luster has been taken off Roddenberry by Joel Engel's (1994) unflattering biography.

8. From a post on the rec.arts.startrek.current newsgroup, August 5, 1994.

12

On the Edge of Forever

Understanding the Star Trek *Phenomenon as Myth*

DARCEE L. McLAREN

People do have to have myths . . .—if they don't
believe in the old ones, we must construct new ones
for them

—Wendy Doniger[1]

Star Trek can . . . be defined as a new mythology
because it opens our minds to a new interpretation
of our real universe, past, present, and future.

—Pierre C. Dubreuil, *Star Trek* fan and author

"*Star Trek* is a modern myth" is an often-heard phrase that resonates with, and is used by, scholars and fans alike. Within fandom the phrase justifies loyalty and enthusiasm and legitimizes participation in *Trek* fan activities. Scholars use the phrase as an explanation. The idea that *Star Trek* is a modern myth makes comprehensible the otherwise puzzling behaviour of fans. In either case, fans and scholars treat the concept of myth as a serious dimension of *Star Trek*, accurately naming the powerful sense of "meaning" that fans can find in *Star Trek*. However, very little attention has been given to the referential meaning of the phrase. What do we mean when we say *Star Trek* is a modern myth? At one level, the phrase suggests that the *Star Trek* shows themselves contain meaning of mythic dimension. At another level, to say *Star Trek* is a myth suggests that fans relate to the shows as a myth for modern times. This active participatory aspect of the relationship between myth and community is often overlooked in scholarship concerning *Star Trek* (see Tyrrell 1977; Jewett and Lawrence 1988; Franklin 1994; Harrison et al. 1996). This chapter will argue that *Star Trek* as a myth operates at both levels, that *Star Trek* as a contemporary secular myth provides a set of symbols and meanings, and a concrete direction or model, for an active, creative community of fans.

In his essay, "Myth in Primitive Psychology," anthropologist Bronislaw Malinowski (1992 [1948]: 100) states, "The limitation of the study of myth to the mere examination of texts has been fatal to a proper understanding of its nature." By this, Malinowski means to suggest that myth must be studied in its societal context in order to understand how it is incorporated into the lives of the people who believe it to be true. Furthermore, anthropologist Wendy Doniger (1988: 33) notes that "myths are both events and images, both verbs and nouns. To analyze a myth in terms of either element alone . . . is to reduce and distort it." As stories, myths contain both actions as well as representations, and thus provide models of and for ways of being and behaving. For the purposes of this chapter, Malinowski's and Doniger's observations suggest that the meaning of the *Star Trek* myth and of *Star Trek* in general cannot be separated from the meaning(s) perceived by fans. *Star Trek* as a set of beliefs must be understood in relation to the people who hold those beliefs and participate in the meaning system.

In using a dominantly anthropological approach, this argument begins with the assumption that myth is not significant for what it is, but for what it does. Myth takes many different forms and has many different names in the diverse cultures of the world, but the purpose of myth remains essentially the same: "to reveal the exemplary models for all human rites and all significant human activities—diet or marriage, work or education, art or wisdom" (Eliade 1975: 8; Malinowski 1992 [1948]: 101). Myth "supplies models for human behavior and, by that very fact, gives meaning and value to life" (Eliade 1975: 2). Furthermore, myth can be distinguished from charters, constitutions, and laws by its symbolic content and its story form. A myth is a "true story [and] it is regarded as true not literally, but in its implicit meanings . . . one cannot understand a myth merely by telling it, but only by interpreting it" (Doniger 1988: 31). Myths may be guides, but they are polyvalent guides. They contain many meanings and are thus open to interpretation on many levels, from many angles. Therefore, the "meaning" of a particular myth is not static, but intimately related to the community of "believers." The interpretation of a myth is active and participatory and requires actors and participants. Meaning itself is active and derived within the community of believers, not given from above or outside that community.

THE MEANING OF *STAR TREK*

There is no single meaning of *Star Trek*. If, as we propose, *Star Trek* is a modern myth, then it will have multiple meanings, it will be interpreted differently by the same people at different times and by different people at the same time. However, it is possible to discern a cluster of ideas that have a consistent and powerful set of meanings to a wide cross-section of *Star Trek* fandom. These ideas form the core of what is often referred to as the "vision" of *Star Trek*.

At its most basic level, the vision of *Star Trek* is a positive view of the future of humanity in which there is no poverty or crime and everyone lives together in peace. The authors of *Star Trek Lives!*—a fan-written celebration of *Star Trek*—refer to this vision as "the optimism effect" (Lichtenberg et al. 1975: 106–25), "a vision of what is possible to man" (Lichtenberg et al. 1975: 128). A fan at TorontoTrek XI put it this way: "Original *Star Trek* was a very visionary program and it was an optimistic view of the future. . . . I mean, I think it just inspired a lot of people." This is not to say that *Star Trek* presents a singularly rosy view of the future, rather that it presents plausible options. As Doniger (1988: 28) points out, "myth is persuasive to us because the action itself is persuasive. Even when what happens in the myth is not physically possible in this world (as when, for instance, a man turns into a fish), when the event is described in detail, as something that happened, we can see it happening, and so it enlarges our sense of what might be possible." According to Lichtenberg et al. (1975: 115):

> [*Star Trek*] said: The nature of the universe is such that we can survive, we can cope, we can know, we will prevail. It said: Man is a difficult and dangerous creature; To be human is to be complex. There is a darker side to man; it is a great and terrible thing to be a man, but we can choose the great. It said: We can learn to live together as human beings, as intelligent beings even when we are not "human," and we can learn to cherish our diversity and not destroy each other.

For its fans, *Star Trek* enlarges the sense of what might be possible in the future, and it provides a way to "see" that future happen.

Furthermore, while the possibilities presented in *Star Trek* certainly include aliens and technology, they focus on humanity. In *The Making of Star Trek*, Gene Roddenberry wrote,

> If man survives [to the twenty-third century], he will have learned to take a delight in the essential differences between men and between cultures. He will learn that differences in ideas and attitudes are a delight, part of life's exciting variety, not something to fear. It's a manifestation of the greatness that God, or whatever it is, gave us. This infinite variation and delight, this is part of the optimism we built into *Star Trek*. (Whitfield and Roddenberry 1968: 40)

This "delight in diversity" is symbolized by the ethnic and racial diversity of the original *Star Trek* crew: an African communications officer, a Russian navigator, an Asian helmsman, an American captain and doctor, a Scottish engineer, and a Vulcan science officer. Subsequent *Star Trek* series have continued to represent diversity among the crew members and have extended the concept to include physically challenged individuals, machines, and female commanders. "The greatest challenge—in all four nonanimation incarnations of *Star Trek*—is to determine how the inviolate aloneness of each human person can interface not only with other humans, but machines and other life-forms when—and only when—the human race takes its final leap into maturity" (Fern 1996: 16).

The principle of delight in diversity is recognized by *Star Trek* fans as IDIC (Infinite Diversity in Infinite Combination), a concept introduced in the original *Star Trek* series. Arguably, IDIC is the most central concept in *Trek* fandom (see Ruff 1996; Lichtenberg et al. 1975). However, on its own, IDIC has no referent, no discernible content. It is only the particular interpretation and emphasis placed on the concept within fandom that gives IDIC its meaning. As media scholar Henry Jenkins points out, "many fans trace their commitments to feminism, gay rights, vegetarianism, pacifism and/or multi-culturalism to *Star Trek*'s 'IDIC' philosophy" (Tulloch and Jenkins 1995: 191).[2] In fact, a wide variety of values and causes are attributed by fans to IDIC. For example, in explaining her love of *Star Trek*, one sixteen-year-old wrote, "I love the potential to discuss issues important to those of us who will inherit the Earth— peace, tolerance, hunger, AIDS, integrity, and taking care of this dear old planet" (in Irwin and Love 1994: 72).

These issues, if they are addressed at all, are only addressed in *Star Trek* to a limited extent. There is little direct moralizing in *Star Trek*, particularly in the original series; ideas are expressed through models and relationships more than through rules. As Doniger (1988: 142) suggests, this is typical of myth: "myths are 'lived' not as moral directives ('I will do this because the myth tells me to') nor even as philosophical or theological dogmas ('I now believe this because I learned it from that story') but as patterns within which meaning is discovered or created ('I recognize what sort of a person my new acquaintance is; he is like Pentheus' [or, in this case, Kirk])." Fans draw meaning from the patterns and relationships they perceive within *Star Trek*. For example, as Jenkins (1995: 190) points out, "the close bonds between Kirk and Spock . . . [are] regarded as embodying the series' committment to the acceptance and celebration of cultural difference." Fans consistently interpret IDIC within the framework of the "vision" of *Star Trek* to include those values and causes they find important: justice, tolerance, and equality.[3]

While elements of the idealization of the American way and the frontier spirit do exist in the *Star Trek* text (e.g. Kenas 1986; Jewett and Lawrence 1988; Lalli 1994), fandom emphasizes harmony and equality between all races and gender, the elimination of a class system, and respect for other cultures and beliefs. Innovation, social criticism, and individual responsibility are at the heart of the fan understanding of *Star Trek*. As one fan writes: "The mutual cooperation and the social harmonies among a crew of different races, creeds and planetary origins sets the scene for looking at our own prejudices, social indifferences, and intolerance. 'Through [*Star Trek*, Roddenberry] told the world that the differences among ourselves can be stimulating, exciting, interesting and informative'" (in Sackett 1977: 37). Another fan notes that, for him, "*Star Trek* represents the best in humanity as evidenced in 'principles and life-styles' which can accept, and have accepted, again and again, new and different cultures, and can [learn] the best from them, tolerate the rest, and emerge ever stronger and enriched" (in Irwin and Love 1992: 26).

Joyce Tullock, a well-known and respected fan writer, states, "*Star Trek*'s major theme involves man's greatest adventure—the discovery of himself. In *Star Trek*, nothing is greater than the individual human being—except what the human being can become. Those who need a label would call it the humanistic approach" (in Irwin and Love 1992: 114).

The importance of IDIC is evident in these statements in their emphasis on overcoming and gaining strength from our differences. The IDIC philosophy states that "all people can and will live together in peace, regardless of their differences, and together will become greater than the sum of their parts. It is through IDIC that we will be able to stop wars and decimation of the planet and work as a species toward creating and utilizing resources to benefit us as a whole" (Ruff 1996: 14). Ironically, in textual terms IDIC has a very minor role in *Star Trek*, having been mentioned only once, and very briefly, in the episode "Is There In Truth No Beauty?" (1968). It has even been noted by fans that "IDIC fails at the level of plot (what with Kirk blasting computers, pulverizing perverse cultures, and quoting the U.S. Constitution)" (in Irwin and Love 1992: 3). Yet, fans continue to maintain that IDIC is "Perhaps the most important message in [*Star Trek*;] it can be said that it was [is] the central philosophy of *Star Trek*" (in Irwin and Love 1996: 14).

The optimism of *Star Trek*, while received by fans as a hopeful message, is not interpreted as an inevitable state. The vision must be achieved. In the words of one fan, "I believe that we all must learn and experience the past to move on to the future. *Star Trek* is a reassuring glimpse into a time that proves that we have learned from our mistakes." As media studies scholar Henry Jenkins argues, *Star Trek* fans are not passive consumers of a textual product (see also Parrinder 1980: 29, 45). Jenkins (1991: 196) notes that "it is the fans themselves who are determining what aspects of the original series concept are binding on their play with the program material and to what degree. The fans have embraced *Star Trek* because they found its vision somehow compatible with their own, and they have assimilated only those textual materials that feel comfortable to them" The *Star Trek* text may lean toward American imperialist ideals, as Jewett and Lawrence (1988) suggest, but the fans have determined that *Star Trek* is really about IDIC. The "meaning" of the *Star Trek* myth, therefore, is not something simply received through the media text, meaning is negotiated by the fans in their lives and in their interactions with one another.

FAN PARTICIPATION

This negotiation takes place in many arenas from small discussion groups to internationally organized fan clubs, and conventions that count their attendance figures in the thousands. In all cases, being a fan means more than "being a regular viewer of a particular program," it means "translating that viewing into some kind of cultural activity, by sharing feelings and thoughts about the program content with friends, by joining a 'community' of other fans who share common interests" (Jenkins 1991: 175).

Being a fan requires participation, it requires that the myth be lived. In Malinowski's (1992 [1948]: 101) words, myth "is not an idle tale, but a hard-worked active force; it is not an intellectual explanation or an artistic imagery, but a pragmatic charter of 'faith and moral wisdom.'"

Star Trek fans do live the myth, or at least they profess that the myth should be lived (see Ruff 1996). As in any human endeavour, the reality sometimes fails to live up to the ideal. However, fan committment to IDIC in conjunction with the imperative to act on that committment is consistently revealed in the published statements of fan organizations. For example, the statement of purpose of the International Federation of Trekkers (IFT) (one of the largest fan club organizations) declares that its purpose is:

> To promote the humanistic philosophies and ideals portrayed in the Star Trek mythos in a realistic fashion conducive to the continued existence and responsible advancement of human kind. To provide, promote, and support education and positive legal activism in the areas of human rights, racial and sexual equality, environmental causes, and space exploration. To promote a more positive impression of Star Trek enthusiasts as intelligent, socially conscious, active individuals who are aware and concerned about the real world today.

Likewise, the mission statement of the USS Golden Gate, a chapter of the United Federation of Planets Internationale (UFPI) fan club, states that their mission is "to promote the concept of IDIC—and have fun doing it."

As with the International Federation of Trekkers, many UFPI fan clubs, including the USS Golden Gate, interpret the committment "to promote the concept of IDIC" as an injunction to set an example. In practice, this often takes the form of charity work actually performed by the members of the club as a group activity, or fund-raising done by the club on behalf of recognized charitable organizations. As Jindra (1994: 36) notes, "both Starfleet and KAG [Klingon Assault Group] organizations stress community service projects; this aspect underlies the seriousness with which they take their beliefs about building a better world."

This emphasis on charity can also be found in the smaller fan organizations. One woman at TorontoTrek XI recounted how the Klingon fan organization she belonged to did "a heck of a lot for charity" working for the Red Cross at blood drives, campaigning for the Easter Seal Foundation, and manning the phones for a local public broadcasting station the weekend of their fundraising drive. Another fan noted that

> all of the little starships [local fan club chapters] there's all these little starships—the Yorktown and the Hudson Bay and all they do is work for charity in their areas. . . . And if you wanna join a club and make a difference, you're going to. If you join any club, for any of those clubs upstairs with these people sittin' there tirelessly—I've done it myself—and saying "Would you like to join our club and this is what we do." And without fail it's—we work with the United Way, we work for Ronald McDonald House, whatever the charity is, that's what they do. So, it's not just about makin' ourselves some silly costumes and struttin' around—it is about embracing Gene Roddenberry's vision. I keep saying that, I'm sorry. But no, it's true. It is.

In addition to running a major convention every year for the past eleven years, the fan-run TorontoTrek organization "climbs the stairs of the CN Tower every year without fail and all the money goes to the United Way." As the fans are quick to note, these acts of charity are done in the spirit of Gene Roddenberry's vision, or the spirit of IDIC. Two fans at TorontoTrek XI expressed the idea this way:

> DEB: Why would people care to, why would people bother if they didn't believe in Gene Roddenberry's vision that eventually everybody's gonna come together and love each other? You know, and there's not going to be all of this racism, and criticism and poverty and hunger and . . .
>
> BARB: And you're gonna know what this is about—and this is what it is, people helping people. . . . And havin' a lot of fun doin' it

Charity work is not only ubiquitous in *Star Trek* fandom, it is pro-active. Fandom is consciously oriented toward making the world a better place, toward making the future depicted in *Star Trek* come into being.

Fan clubs dedicated to particular actors also often work to support charity, often the favorite charity of that actor. William Shatner's fan club is involved each year in staging the Hollywood Charity Horse Show, which raises funds for various children's charities. The fan club of Alexander Siddig, of *Star Trek: Deep Space Nine* (*DS9*), does fund-raising for Amnesty International, and the fan clubs of Marc Alaimo and Andrew

Robinson, also of *DS9*, support the Pediatric AIDS Foundation. On paper and in practice, fandom consciously works toward making the world a better place, not through coercion, but through example and participation.

Since the concept of IDIC requires a respect for diversity, it does not lend itself well to coercive missionizing and thus it is common to find an elevation of the concept of role models in *Star Trek* fandom. Fans acknowledge the models provided for them by the show and seek to emulate them thus providing models for others. At conventions, Nichelle Nichols, who played Lieutenant Uhura, will inevitably tell or be asked to tell how Martin Luther King, Jr. asked her to remain with the show because of the positive image she was presenting. Actress Whoopi Goldberg, who played Guinan on *Star Trek: The Next Generation*, tells how she was influenced by Lieutenant Uhura: "Not only was Uhura proof that black folks would actually make it into the future—and that was very important for us to believe back in the '60s—she was beautiful, smart and had power. People listened to her. . . . Watching Nichelle Nichols made me confident that I could make it, too." (in *Farewell to Star Trek: The Next Generation* 1994: 28). Most recently, cast members of *Star Trek: Voyager* are being asked to comment on their involvement with African American and Hispanic teen theatre groups and whether they perceive their characters to be role models.

Fans will also make personal statements about how a particular character in *Star Trek* inspired them. At the Grand Slam convention in Pasadena, California, in 1995, for example, a young woman told Kate Mulgrew, who plays the first female captain of a *Star Trek* ship, that she had been inspired by Mulgrew's character, Captain Janeway, to attend MIT and pursue a career in engineering. Likewise, at the Grand Slam convention in 1996, a young pre-teen girl thanked Nana Visitor and Terry Farrell, both from *DS9*, for being role models for her and inspiring her to "work harder in school and everything." A similar story was recounted by Gene Roddenberry and has become part of *Star Trek* folklore:

> Gene Roddenberry tells of receiving a letter from a young man who had been ready to drop out of high school until he happened to encounter a *Star Trek* episode on television. For him it rekindled an interest in the future, and in machinery. The letter came from the University of Wisconsin, where the young man had become a cum laude student in engineering. (Lichtenberg et al 1975: 109–10; see also Sackett 1977: 89–90)

Within fandom, these stories serve as positive examples of the many small ways in which the values portrayed in *Star Trek* can influence people's lives. *Star Trek*, we are told, is not just to be watched, it is to be lived.

Eliade's phenomenological approach to the study of myth can assist in understanding the need to act and the emphasis on role models apparent in the behaviour of *Star Trek* fans. For Eliade (1975: 18–19), myth

> is always related to a 'creation,' it tells how something came into existence, or how a pattern of behavior, an institution, a manner of working were established; by knowing the myth one knows the 'origin' of things and hence can control and manipulate them at will [and] in one way or another one 'lives' the myth, in the sense that one is seized by the sacred, exalting power of the events recollected or re-enacted.

Since *Star Trek* is set in the future, it is a little unusual to think of it as an origin myth. Yet, *Star Trek* is an origin myth. In seventy-nine episodes, the original series depicted a future of peace and prosperity and told how that future came into existence. Fans are told that the concept of IDIC led to this future Golden Age, and this knowledge empowers them to affect that change. As Eliade (1975: 141) puts it, "myths assure man that what he is about to do has already been done." It takes only a little extra imagination to see that, in *Star Trek*, that which 'has already been done' has been done in the future.[4] *Star Trek* fans, the owners of the myth, are therefore compelled and encouraged to live the myth, to act to bring that future into being, to ensure that it comes into being. In the words of one group of fans, *Star Trek* provides for the fan a "vision of a world [close] to his heart's desire, both as a goal to strive toward and as fuel to power him in striving to reshape the real world closer to that heart's desire" (Lichtenberg et al. 1975: 127). Long-time fan and co-editor of the *Best of Trek* series, G. B. Love (1986: 65) expresses the significance of *Star Trek* quite well when he says:

> *Star Trek* is important. Not for what it gives us, but for what we take from it, and how we use what we take to improve our own lives. Examples of values such as friendship, sacrifice, love, honesty, compassion, etc. abound in *Star Trek*, but the examples are of worth only if we seek out and seize opportunities in the real world to apply those values. *Star Trek* isn't, after all, a place to live . . . it's a way— one way—to live.

For *Star Trek* fans, now and forever, the present and the future, are actively linked by living the myth, and meaning gives rise to and is derived from doing.

Star Trek gives its fans "the experience of what it would be like to live in the world as it should and could be, among human beings as they could and should be" (Lichtenberg et al. 1975: 127). The *Star Trek* myth lives in the sense that it supplies models for human behavior and, by that very fact, gives meaning and value to life (Eliade 1975: 2). Thus, *Star Trek*, as a myth, is transformative as well as conservative. It transforms people's lives and the way they think about the world, and in so doing encourages the attempt to change the world, to remake the world in the image of the myth. Textual analysis of *Star Trek* can help us to understand some of the symbolism and underlying assumptions in the myth, but it cannot tell us how those symbols are interpreted by the people who own the myth or how the myth has affected their lives.

CONCLUSION

Television is not a highly respected forum in North American culture. It frequently comes under attack for everything from moral corruption in its portrayal of sex and violence to the alleged inanity of its sitcoms and soap operas. It is thus not surprising to find that many *Star Trek* fans are ambivalent about expressing what *Star Trek* means to them (e.g. Irwin and Love 1978: 52). Comments about the value *Star Trek* brings to a fan's life are frequently preceded or followed by the phrase "but it's just a TV show." Fans are anxious to establish that they have a very clear sense of what is reality and what is fantasy in their lives. And, in fact, fans live happily and successfully as parents, business people, teachers, colleagues—in any variety of occupations and relationships—in the real world. Yet, at the same time, they will cautiously acknowledge that *Star Trek* is also real.[5] This is the power of myth. It need not be literally true that a man can turn into a fish or that a ship can travel faster than light or that Vulcans are waiting for us to achieve warp speed technology. The details are significant, but do not determine "truth." As Doniger (1988: 31–32) points out:

> Myths are perceived as true when the reality to which they point has "always" been perceived as true or becomes newly perceived as true. And a myth becomes newly perceived as true either by inspiring

people to change the way things are or by enabling people to project their new view of reality over the world, even when that world remains the same.

Similarly, as Eliade (1959: 102) suggests, "it falls to the primordial myth to preserve true history, the history of the human condition; it is in the myth that the principles and paradigms for all conduct must be sought and recovered." As a modern myth, *Star Trek* does inspire its fans, the people who believe the myth, to change the way things are and to see the world differently. For its fans, *Star Trek* provides a philosophy of tolerance, understanding, and appreciation of diversity, and it provides models for conduct that will recover the human capacity to live in peace and prosperity.

To suggest that *Star Trek* is a modern myth is to say it has the power to bring meaning to someone's life, and to transform their life and their world according to the patterns and models inherent in the myth. As even the most brief foray into fandom shows, *Star Trek* has been bringing meaning into the lives of its fans and inspiring them to change the world for over thirty years. In this sense, *Star Trek* is more than just another TV show; it is a modern myth.

NOTES

1. Wendy Doniger (1988: 173 n. 29) a respected anthropologist and professor of religion at the University of Chicago, has also written "to create a myth on purpose for other people to use is an entirely different enterprise [than borrowing a myth from another culture], and one that I distrust." Myths, to the extent that they are "created" should come from within the community and should not be imposed from outside in any way. It should also be noted that Doniger would include science fiction, and very probably *Star Trek*, in a category that she has labeled "kitsch mythology" (1988: 39–41). In her opinion, kitsch mythology "usually lacks the substance that traditional mythology draws from its tradition" (1988: 40). Although space does not permit an exploration of this issue here, I would argue that *Star Trek*, at the very least, is grounded in American traditions and draws fully on its symbol systems. Despite these objections, Doniger's observations about the nature and function of mythology are well suited to a discussion of *Star Trek* and will be used regardless of her aversion to kitsch.

2. Jenkins has written some of the most thorough, sophisticated, and scholarly work yet done on the *Star Trek* phenomenon. Nonetheless, his work has concentrated on those fans involved in the writing and publication of fanzine lit-

erature. As he points out, this field is dominated by women and has its own particular characteristics (see also Bacon-Smith 1992). This chapter is similarly biased, though in a different direction. The fans spoken of here may enjoy the fanzine literature but are rarely involved in the writing and publication of such materials. Thus, their focus, as fans, is quite different and tends to be more involved with local community activities (discussed later).

3. In theory, fans could interpret IDIC in any number of ways and need not be bound by the ideas of cultural relativism, peace, justice, and equality. However, several factors mitigate against a completely arbitrary assignment of value. First, the cultural values of the society in question, in this case North America, will tend to promote certain interpretations over others. Second, the community of *Star Trek* fans exerts its own influence in emphasizing some aspects of the series and not others. Jenkins refers to this latter factor as the "extra-textual discourse" of fandom. For more on the influence of extra-textual discourse, see Jenkins' "Infinite Diversity in Infinite Combinations: Genre and Authorship in *Star Trek*" in Tulloch and Jenkins 1995: 175–195.

4. As Doniger (1988: 29) notes, "It is often asserted that a myth is about an event believed to have taken place in the past, but this is just one side of the situation. Though many myths are indeed set in the past, there are also myths about the future, millenial myths, and eschatological myths, for instance; moreover, as Teilhard de Chardin has pointed out, even the myth of Eden and the myth of the Golden Age are myths not about the past but about the future. Illud tempus, as Mircea Eliade excavated it, exists in the future as much as in the past." This is not to suggest that *Star Trek* is a millenial or eschatological myth, but rather that it is a creation myth of the Eden or Golden Age variety. Rather than depicting a world from which we are descended and to which we hope to return, the *Star Trek* myth represents a world to which we aspire, a world which (we are told) arose out of this most imperfect present.

5. For example, at a convention in 1997, Robert Duncan MacNeil, who plays Lieutenant Paris on *Star Trek: Voyager*, received a thunderous ovation when he commented "This is *Star Trek*, people. This is real." Afterward, a fan who had attended MacNeil's talk repeated this back to me. She followed the comment with "This is real. This is reality." Then, immediately, to clarify she added "This is not our reality. We do have lives." Fans readily acknowledge the reality and truth of *Star Trek* as their myth, yet they have also learned to be skittish about proclaiming this sense of reality to non-fans.

13

To Boldly Go

Star Trek *Convention Attendance as Pilgrimage*

JENNIFER E. PORTER

*S*tar Trek conventions play a major role within the community of *Star Trek* fandom. Conventions provide the primary forum for fans from diverse geographic regions to meet with one another and discuss, negotiate, and explore their mutual love of *Star Trek*. For many fans, traveling to attend a *Star Trek* convention is a deeply meaningful journey, for it is only in this context that fans can step outside their everyday social roles, and fully immerse themselves in a world where love of *Star Trek* unites participants into a community of equals that transcends racial, ethnic, gender, or class lines. The convention setting represents a "place and moment in and out of time," in which fans experience a sense of egalitarian community epitomized, in fan perceptions, by the model of relationships found with the *Star Trek* television series themselves. Through the careful construction and negotiation of this egalitarian ideal by fans within the convention context, the convention provides a time and a space in which the ideals of *Star Trek* are lived and experienced by fans. Drawing upon fieldwork with *Star Trek* fans at the *Trek30* and *GrandSlam IV* conventions in Pasadena, California, in 1995 and 1996, and with fans at the *TorontoTrek 10* and *TorontoTrek 11* conventions in 1996 and 1997, this chapter suggests *Star Trek* convention attendance can be seen as a secular inheritor of religious pilgrimage. In representing a deeply meaningful journey, conducted outside the bounds of everyday social statuses and hierarchies, and made in pursuit of egalitarian communal ideals, *Star Trek* convention attendance represents for some fans a secular pilgrimage.

THEORETICAL PERSPECTIVE

Pilgrimage has been the focus of longstanding and ongoing scholarly research. Victor Turner provides one of the most thorough and intriguing studies of pilgrimage in the anthropological literature. Although recent theoretical critiques of Turner have been proposed (e.g. Eade and Sallnow 1991; Morinis 1992; Coleman and Elsner 1995), Turner's model of pilgrimage remains seminal in the study of both traditional religious and secular pilgrimage journeys. As a result, it is Turner's work that provides the theoretical perspective for the following analysis of *Star Trek* convention attendance as pilgrimage. Turner characterizes pilgrimage as a ritual journey in which participants are temporarily freed from the social constraints of everyday statuses, roles, and expectations. Drawing upon the insights of van Gennep (1909), Turner argues that within complex historical religions, pilgrimage becomes the vehicle through which participants experience a liminal or "liminoid" state of "otherness" similar to that evoked through pre-industrial societies' rites of passage. During this process, the importance of social boundaries diminishes and a state of unmediated egalitarian association between pilgrims becomes possible. This state of "communitas," or communal fellowship, although necessarily impeded to some degree by the organizational and structural imperatives of the pilgrimage itself, is both the goal and the potential outcome of the pilgrimage process (Turner 1969 :131–32). As such, Turner suggests, pilgrimage processes implicitly challenge mainstream social orders and hierarchies.

"Modern" pilgrimage differs somewhat from other pilgrimage contexts for it is situated in the "leisure" domain (Turner and Turner 1978; Turner 1982). Turner suggests (1977: 40; 1982: 35–37) that leisure initially emerged out of the distinction between "ergic" (work) and "ludic" (play) components within complex industrialized societies. Leisure is "anergic-ludic" (1982: 37) and is defined in terms of its relationship to "work." Voluntarism is a key constituent of leisure pursuits, whereas obligatoriness constitutes the frame of tribal ritual. Within the post-industrial context, pilgrimage represents a voluntary journey, and as such falls squarely within the leisure domain (1977: 34–35). Non-religious journeys undertaken in the leisure domain may also be characterized as pilgrimage, for Turner suggests that "many of the symbolic and ludic capacities of tribal religion have [in complex post-industrial societies] migrated into nonreligious genres (1977: 43)." Where formally organized religious contexts are lacking, he suggests (1974b: 260), "the social need for escape from or abandonment of structural commitments seeks cultural expression in ways that are not explicitly religious, though they may become heavily ritualized." Since Turner characterizes pilgrimage as a "liminoid" phenomenon constitutive of a journey during which "communitas" may obtain, secular journeys can be encompassed within the boundaries of pilgrimage in this broader theoretical context. Although *Star Trek* convention attendance is not religious pilgrimage, it may well be an "inheritor" of pilgrimage in the contemporary, secular context.[1]

STAR TREK CONVENTIONS AS LIMINOID

Insofar as *Star Trek* convention attendance constitutes secular, as opposed to religious, pilgrimage, it nonetheless exhibits characteristics identified by Turner as constitutive of religious pilgrimage processes.[2] Analysis of *Star Trek* convention attendance in terms of liminality and communitas reveals marked similarities between this form of secular ritual and Turner's model. *Star Trek* conventions have been bringing *Star Trek* fans together since the first convention was held in 1973. Participants at these conventions often identify the sense of communal belonging, or communitas, and the sense of freedom from everyday statuses and roles, or liminality, that they feel in the convention context as central to their participation. According to Turner (1974a: 197, 1974b: 232), it is in liminality that the potential for communitas emerges, for liminality is by definition a threshold, bridging two sets of status and social role expectations. As such, it constitutes a "place and a moment in and out of time," where social expectations, statuses, and roles are temporarily abandoned, and the potential for unmediated egalitarian relationships with others consequently arise. Turner identifies a wide variety of characteristics inherent in liminoid phenomena, but central to his definition is the abandonment of everyday social statuses and roles, or what Turner calls the "persona" of the individual. According to Turner (1974b: 237), the everyday world of work and family is characterized by "a differentiated, segmented system of structural positions . . . [in which] the individual is segmentalized into roles which he plays." In contrast, liminoid time and space simplify and homogenize social relations, so that individuals relate to one another independent of mundane social categories. In sharing the liminoid experience, participants relate to one another as fully (or merely) human.

It is possible to contextualize *Star Trek* conventions within Turner's conception (1974b) of "outsiderhood" as a defining characteristic of liminoid events. "Outsiderhood" for Turner (1974b: 236–37) refers "to actions and relationships which do not flow from a recognized social status but originate outside it." Often, according to Turner (1977: 47–48), the "social category," defined as "people who are similar in one important characteristic—sex, age, ethnicity, religion, or some [other] aspect"— becomes the basis for categorizing liminoid outsiderhood. Within the context of *Star Trek* convention attendance, fandom becomes the social category that sets participants apart from mainstream statuses and roles. Fandom constitutes a break from everyday status roles and expectations and exists on the margins of central economic, social, and political processes. Furthermore, fandom is stigmatized in mainstream perceptions, which often characterize fans as social misfits unable to distinguish fantasy from reality and who desperately need, to quote actor William Shatner, to "Get a life!"[3] This social stigmatization is evident even among the friends and family of *Star Trek* fans. While many fans categorize the response of their friends and family as "acceptance" or "support" for their fandom, others report responses ranging from "slightly smug and condescending bemusement" to "they think I'm crazy," "they think I'm nuts," and "they think I'm a total psycho." As one fan told me, this kind of reaction on the part of friends and family is at least partly understandable, for it "comes from the label that accompanies *Star Trek* fans."

If *Star Trek* fandom is a stigmatized category, *Star Trek* convention attendance provides a forum for fans to step outside their everyday statuses and roles and meet with others with whom, in the words of Victor Turner (1977: 48), "they share some cultural . . . feature that they take to be their most signal mark of identity." The convention context takes individual fans out of their work and family contexts and places them in a framework within which, for a short period of time, the distinguishing characteristic of their "outsiderness" becomes normative, and their mainstream statuses and roles become irrelevant. As one popular *Star Trek* handbook author notes (Van Hise 1990:11, 90), conventions are like "stepping through an enchanted doorway into another world . . . where every fan is a distant friend [you've] not yet met, [and where] you can easily forget your own troubles as well as those of the world. . . . It's no wonder many people attend as many conventions as they can."

Within the convention framework, fans are free to be fans without apology, and many fans identify meeting other fans as a primary factor in their convention participation. When asked what it was about attending *Star Trek* conventions that appealed to her, one fan's answer epitomized this emphasis: "[it's] the attitudes of the fans. Personal appearance and social standing are *not* important." Another fan responded that "[It's] the fact that I find others who are just like me. They love *Star Trek*, and they like showing it in a weird way." In their provision of a time and a space in which fans are free to be fans, *Star Trek* conventions represent a liminoid frame within which fans are liberated from external social constraint and can form bonds with one another independent of everyday statuses and roles.

LUDIC MASQUERADE

The kind of liminoid frame that *Star Trek* conventions provide is akin to what Turner (1977: 39) calls "public liminality," where temporary release from everyday status roles and expectations occur, temporary forms of mock hierarchies and symbolic status and role-reversals obtain, but where ultimately no change in social status is achieved. Integral to this kind of public liminality are what Turner (1977: 40) has characterized as the "ludic" elements of liminoid phenomena, including the playfulness of ritual role playing and games. According to Turner (1974b: 243), "people have a real need . . . to doff the masks, cloaks, apparel, and insignia of [mainstream social] status from time to time, even if only to don the liberating masks of liminal masquerade."

Within the context of *Star Trek* conventions, it is perhaps within this ludic, role-playing aspect that the liminoid quality or "otherness" of the experience is most clearly expressed. Although only a small percentage of *Star Trek* fans actually literally "don the masks of masquerade," many others don the mark of fandom by wearing *Star Trek*–inspired T-shirts, badges, or jewelry, thereby clearly demarcating themselves as "fans" and distinguishing or separating themselves from their everyday social statuses and roles. A minority of fans *do* "don the masks of masquerade," and here the ludic and liminoid quality of conventions is particularly apparent. Through the donning of *Star Trek*–inspired costumes, fans can abandon their adherence to social structural personas and construct or adopt liminal personas that leave them free to explore aspects of their humanity and personality repressed or ridiculed in mainstream social contexts.

Several of the fans with whom I spoke called the adoption of *Star Trek*–inspired identities "doing" or "building" personas. Unlike the social structural personas of Turner's usage, fan personas are individually constructed alternate personalities that express or exhibit personality traits both consciously and unconsciously chosen for manifestation by the individual. According to two *Star Trek* fans at the *GrandSlam IV* convention in Pasadena, California, in April 1996, "personas" usually take one of two forms. As part of a larger discussion on the nature of fan participation, Liz and John informed me,

> LIZ: Different people have different personas . . . [and] basically, by creating a persona, you either create something totally different from yourself, you know . . . [or you create a persona who reflects your own personality.] My persona, oh, she's quite different from me. I can be quite flighty, quite silly, quite giggly sometimes, [but] she is very much in control, she has a temper, but she keeps it very much under control. . . . But Mark! His persona, our captain's persona . . . he totally created [one who's] really aggressive, straightforward. And so is Mark!
>
> JOHN: He's playing himself but he just gave himself another name!
>
> LIZ: An alien guise! So he's got an excuse for being a mean SOB [laugh].

Whether the persona reflects one's own, perhaps socially stigmatized personality traits, as in the apparent case of Mark, or characteristics not normally expressed by an individual, as in the case of Liz, the liminoid framework of the convention allows fans to express personality traits that might normally go unacknowledged in everyday life.[4]

Fan personas do not require physical costumes for expression, but some fans do use costumes to "get into character," or simply to set themselves apart from their everyday social roles and patterns of behavior. One of the most interesting points observed during fieldwork was the apparent affinity that some female fans felt for the non-human Klingon species. Klingons are characterized within the *Star Trek* universe as a warrior race concerned, as one fan put it, with "honor, family, and a little bloodshed." As Turner argues, liminoid contexts allow individuals to express themselves as fully human in distinction to the segmented and socially regimented roles they are forced to adopt in mainstream settings, and this becomes apparent in the convention context for Klingon fans. The liminoid context of *Star Trek* conventions allows female fans to fully express their humanity through the adoption of Klingon personas, by allowing personality traits suppressed or marginal in everyday contexts to emerge in the convention setting. One woman admiringly characterized a female Klingon persona as "a bitch with an attitude!" and this aggressive, sexual characterization was echoed by several female Klingon-costumed fans to whom I spoke.

According to folklorist Camille Bacon-Smith (1992: 18), women who participate in *Star Trek* fandom, fiction writing, convention attendance, and specifically costuming find in these activities the freedom to break gender stereotypes. According to two women with whom I spoke in depth, it is this challenge to gender roles, and to the limited or constrained social roles that their everyday personas force them to adopt, which underlies their choice of Klingon costuming. Playing a Klingon in the convention context allows them to express, for example, a sexual side of themselves that their work personas require them to repress. Furthermore, this expression of sexuality can be coupled with an aggressive attitude that would normally be culturally inappropriate in a feminine sexual context. The first woman, Anne, a social worker in her early thirties who works with young offenders in a juvenile detention center, explained:

> You know . . . when I go to work I must be [the] staid and stoic pin-stripe suit type. . . . I don't really want to broach [the issue of sexuality] with ten- to sixteen-year-old rapists . . . [so] this is definitely a draw away from what I'm used to. . . . Although, if you think about the Klingon as being the tough and assertive type, I'm required to be that at work. So . . . [as a Klingon] I can be tough and assertive and slightly sexy at the same time.

According to Anne, the constraints of her working life proscribed any expression of sexuality while emphasizing the requirement to be both "tough and assertive." In the liminoid and ludic context of the convention, however, she felt free to express her own sexuality without forsaking aggressive self-assurance or threatening her own well-being. In balancing self-assertiveness and confidence with sexuality in a Klingon persona, she could thereby attain, in Turner's words, the state of being "fully, or merely, human" (Turner 1977: 39–40).

Jane was even more explicit, and reflexive, in her analysis of why she finds her Klingon persona so appealing. According to Jane,

The reason that I think there is an attraction, especially to women to play Klingons, is: we are not encouraged in our society to be aggressive, and to be real sexual . . . we're taught to be sort of meek . . . and in-line and quiet, and subservient, but Klingon women are the total opposite of what we're *supposed* to be. . . . I don't want to get harassed because I'm being outrageous just walking around on the street, but you know here [at the convention], there is a protection, I mean nobody is really going to mess with you. . . . And so, its like you've got an excuse, you know, you go to the convention and you stick your boobs out. . . . And that's another thing . . . you are well protected as a Klingon. I mean... as a woman, sometimes you feel vulnerable if you are walking around alone at night . . . you can't carry a knife like this out on the street! So when you're a Klingon it's like it's encouraged, you are empowered . . . so, it's a real attraction, especially for women.

According to Turner and Turner (1978: 34–35), the liminoid nature of pilgrimage is manifest in numerous ways. Freedom to express yourself fully, as an individual, instead of in conformity to institutional, social, or cultural norms, is one of those ways. So too is the emergence of the full person from the fractured social personas of everyday life. Although not all fans build personas and play at being Klingon or some other *Star Trek*-inspired species, the ludic and liminal nature of the experiences of those who do are evident. For Jane and many other fans, the convention context provides a frame within which to explore their own humanity through a ludic breakdown of normative social structural personas. As such, it constitutes a liminoid time and place that is characteristic of pilgrimage centers.

COMMUNITAS IN THE CONTEXT OF *STAR TREK* CONVENTIONS

Communitas is the second of Turner's two constituent elements of pilgrimage, and like the liminality discussed previously, it is clearly evident in the *Star Trek* convention context. According to Turner, communitas constitutes the goal of pilgrimage processes, for it represents a mode of communal fellowship which the pilgrim cannot attain within the social structural bounds of everyday life. During the fieldwork period, hundreds of people told me that they had journeyed to Pasadena and Toronto—

some from as far away as Australia, Germany, and Brazil, others from all across North America—specifically to attend the *Star Trek* conventions. In making this journey, *Star trek* fans reveal the same pursuit of the communitas ideal that characterizes religious pilgrimages.

According to anthropologist Alan Morinis (1992: 4, 9), "a crucial facet of pilgrimage [is the experience of] an intensified version of some ideal that the pilgrim values but cannot achieve at home." In the liminoid convention context, the primarily meaningful experience for many fans was the sense of communal bond they felt with other fans. "It's so much fun to talk about this love to others . . . who feel like you do," one woman told me. "We are the only ones who understand our obsession." Within this context, many fans felt free to express their love of *Star Trek*, to strike up conversations with strangers with whom they knew they shared an important similarity, to play at being part of the fictional *Star Trek* universe, to buy memorabilia, to hear the actors speak about the show, to be fans together. And as Turner notes (1977: 48), within such secular liminal contexts, "people have a sense of being at times what Buber would call, "an essential We," or what David Schneider would call "symbolically sharing common substance." Even physical illness or hardship is not sufficient to keep fans in search of this communal bond away. One woman's emotional words in particular emphasize the importance of this bond among fans. Speaking both to the visiting guest speakers and to the thousands of listening fans at the *Trek30* convention, she said: "I'm someone who has been through Hell to be here—four back surgeries—and I'd do it all again to be here with you." Within the Turnerian model of pilgrimage, pursuit or attainment of such a communal bond among participants constitutes the communitas he considers integral to pilgrimage journeys.

According to popular culture and media scholar Henry Jenkins (1992: 22–23), "to speak as a [*Star Trek*] fan is to accept . . . an identity constantly belittled or criticized by institutional authorities. Yet it is also to speak from a position of collective identity. . . . Indeed, one of the most often heard comments from new fans is their surprise in discovering how many people share their fascination . . . [and] their pleasure in discovering that they are not 'alone.'" This sense of surprise and of belonging was expressed by one fan at the *GrandSlam IV* convention when he said, "This is my first convention . . . [and] I've met people who are *genuinely* nice and included me into their group. This was a genuine surprise for me, in the total openness they showed [to] me."

According to Turner, the communitas of the pilgrimage experience is epitomized by this sense of openness, inclusiveness, and the homogenization of differences through the realization that all participants share a common bond. Turner and Turner (1974a, 1978) identify three "types" of communitas recognizable in liminoid contexts—which they term "existential, normative, and ideological"—but it is normative communitas that predominates in the pilgrimage context itself. Normative communitas is characterized by Turner (1974b: 232) as a structured framework within which the stressing of equality and comradeship as norms is embedded. Within religious contexts, such a framework is structured, according to Turner (1974a: 169), in attempts to regain the state of existential, or spontaneous, communitas that members of the group believe existed in the mythical or historical past. In the context of *Star Trek* convention attendance, the image of egalitarian fellowship that fans look toward and idealize is the futuristic model of relationships as portrayed in the four *Star Trek* television series. As one fan told me, "I wish we lived in a world that treated every being with [the] respect, honor, and compassion as seen by the crew in [the television series *Star Trek: The*] *Next Generation.*" Another fan expressed a similar wish when she told me, "I hope that people of all races and ethnic backgrounds could someday get along, I hope for a better life for everyone, [and] also for less materialism. [The crews of the starship *Enterprise*] weren't shown to amass riches. . . . Other fans, on the whole, seem to hold the same hopes, are as tolerant, gracious, and friendly." Turner suggests (1974b: 263) that the futuristic visions of science fiction can represent models of communitas as appropriate within complex industrialized societies as the retrospective looking models within religious and tribal contexts. When fans express their hope that the egalitarian relationships portrayed in *Star Trek* might one day be achieved, and their perception that fandom itself presages this egalitarian ideal, normative communitas is revealed.

For several of the fans with whom I spoke, fandom itself was understood to constitute a model of the egalitarian ideal portrayed within the *Star Trek* television series. Turner (1982: 51) suggests that the attempt to conceive of social structural relationships in terms of utopian ideological ideals of "human interconnectedness" and "reverence for life" frequently go hand in hand with the expression of egalitarian ideals in pilgrimage contexts. According to one woman at the *GrandSlam IV* convention in April 1996, the message of *Star Trek* is embodied in the fans who participate in conventions themselves. "*Star Trek,*" she told me, "gives a positive, hopeful outlook for the future. People are treated equally, [and] not judged by race or color. Its even evident at conventions—no one cares who or what you are—you are just another Trek fan!" This homogenization of identity and the embodiment of egalitarian ideals within convention-goers is even more evident in the statement of Karen, a twenty-year-old fan who often worked as a volunteer at conventions in her home town:

> The spirit [of *Star Trek*] is definitely a good motivator for world peace. I mean, look around here [at the convention]. We're all getting along. . . . [We] have a common interest, and so it's easy to identify with someone else. People will just start talking to each other about something, you'll be talking to each other for fifteen minutes before you [finally] introduce yourself. . . . Who you are is less important than what you are [a *Star Trek* fan]. . . . In America, the American dream is to work for yourself, to get ahead by yourself, but here [at the convention] it's more of a community kind of thing, working for others, with others. . . . I think that reaching out to people is a lot harder for some . . . , but [here at conventions] it's a habit [you get into].

The optimistic vision of an egalitarian future presaged by the communitas of fandom itself is almost universally characterized by fans as integral to the popularity of *Star Trek*. This vision of the future, in which prejudice is a thing of the past and relationships are governed by mutual respect among equals regardless of racial, species, or gender difference, transcends the structure of normative communitas and approaches the ideological communitas characterized, according to Turner, by utopian dreams. Ideological communitas is manifest in "a variety of utopian models or blueprints of societies believed by their authors to exemplify or supply the optimal conditions for . . . a homogeneous, unstructured, and free community" (Turner 1974a: 169). Ideological communitas in the context of *Star Trek* conventions is often expressed in terms of Gene Roddenberry's vision, which, as Jindra (1994: 32) notes, is explicitly conceived to be a utopian one by many fans. "I love everything about *Star Trek*," one fan told me. "And I believe in what it stands for. *Star Trek* is a 'utopia,' an ideal universe."

Other fans also characterize their love of *Star Trek* in terms of the idealization of utopia and respect for Roddenberry's vision. According to Dave, a twenty-eight-year-old fan,

> Gene was a visionary and was always trying to get people to put aside their prejudices in a quest for a brighter future. People are

always looking for a better future, [and] *Star Trek* gives a window through which there is always hope for that future. Watching all the grim and violent futuristic films that have been released lately, in conjunction with the everyday newscasts, gives a very negative image of our future, [whereas] *Star Trek* gives people something to look forward to.[5]

Within this understanding of Roddenberry's vision, it is understood that the future will at some point become a better, perhaps even perfect place; by implication, however, the present is seen as sorely lacking. One fan expressed this perception clearly. When asked why she was a fan of *Star Trek*, she responded, "Because I fell in love with the positive view of the future [portrayed in the show.] As a kid who was taught to hide under my desk in case of atomic bombs, *Star Trek* presented a much better outlook altogether." This dual statement of utopian hope and implicit social criticism is also apparent in the almost wistful comment of another female fan: "In this extremely turbulent world, with its terrible problems that seem unsolvable, *Star Trek* gives people hope that the future can be a better place for humanity. Perhaps we *can* overcome all our petty grievances." As Turner suggests (1974b: 238–40), liminality and communitas lend themselves to occasions on which "society takes cognizance of itself," and utopian visions are invariably juxtaposed to the evils of the present age. It is for this reason that Turner suggests (1974b: 268, 1977: 46) ideological or utopian communitas implicitly challenges normative social orders. In looking to the future, ideological communitas criticizes the present. It is in the discrepancy between present and future that fans locate the meaning of *Star Trek* and the content of Roddenberry's vision.

STAR TREK AND THE IDIC ETHIC

There is very little disagreement among *Star Trek* fans about the "true" meaning of *Star Trek*, or the nature of Roddenberry's "vision." When one fan told me that "without Gene Roddenberry's vision there *is* no *Trek*," he was expressing a view on which fans reveal a remarkable degree of consensus (Jenkins 1992: 95). However, this emphasis on Roddenberry's egalitarian vision by no means implies that contention, disagreement, and diversity are lacking in the context of *Star Trek* fandom. As pilgrimage scholars Simon Coleman and John Elsner note (1995: 202), "all social practices are open for contestation," and convention attendance proves no exception. It is the stress on the essential heterogeneity of pilgrimage processes that characterizes recent scholarship on pilgrimage. Anthropologists John Eade and Michael Sallnow (1991: 5), in fact, argue that pilgrimage is characterized by the varied discourses of participants, and is often the site of "mutual *mis*understandings," as people attempt to interpret the actions and motives of others in terms of their own specific discourse.

Fans construct and articulate a system of classifications in which the heterogeneous nature of convention participation is apparent. They base these categorizations on numerous factors, but perhaps the most significant is a fan's own perception of what fandom is or ought to be, and upon his or her self-perceived degree of participation in it.[6] Dominant in fan discourse is a distinction made between those who are *Star Trek* fans because they are either science-fiction fans generally (often negatively characterized by other fans as "techno-babblers" when seen to place an inordinate amount of emphasis on the science and technology and/or special-effect aspects of the show) or fans who love *Star Trek* because of qualities inherent in the *Star Trek* television series alone (including characterization and the philosophy or message of *Star Trek*). According to Jenkins (1992: 95), many fans identify these two camps as the dominant distinction prevalent within *Star Trek* fandom.[7] Although not necessarily representative of the labels attached to these two groups by the majority of fans, one man with whom I spoke characterized the first group (half-jokingly and derogatorily) as "Trekkies," and the other as "Trekkers"; his wife, however, disagreed with these labels.[8] According to Rob and Laura,

> ROB: There are those people that are "out there," though. As an example, today if you were watching, there was that one kid that was always up at the podium, wearing a command duty uniform, long hair, like fourteen, fifteen years old, and . . . it's like he knows all the techno-babble and he lives the techno-babble. . . . That kind of a person really doesn't have a life . . .
>
> LAURA: There are some people, it depends on who you're talking about, that are quite far from reality, who have, I think, no grasp on reality. . . . I mean . . . there are those who have lives, have family, have friends, have responsibilities, and then . . . there is a whole group that has no life outside of *Star Trek*.
>
> ROB: Trekkers and Trekkies.
>
> LAURA: Well no, that's not what I'd separate it out as, I don't separate it that way; I separate it as those who have lives, have careers . . .

ROB: Those are the Trekkers.

LAURA: And then there are those that can't separate it, [for whom *Star Trek*] *is* their life . . .

ROB: Trekkies! There is a big—at least for me—a big difference.

Classifications such as Trekkie versus Trekker, or sci-fi fan versus *Trek* fan, however, are not exclusively representative of fan categories, nor are they necessarily mutually exclusive. Nominal fans might characterize both Trekkies and Trekkers as going too far in their appreciation of *Star Trek*. Further classification of factions in fandom includes those who are considered nominal (often self-identified as such) fans, who enjoy the show for its entertainment value, but do not prioritize their preference for it. Many nominal fans make the disclaimer, "Its just a television show!" to minimize their own participation in fandom.[9] Anthropologist Michael Jindra (1994: 39) cites one dedicated fan who categorized nominal fans at *Star Trek* conventions as "not-a-cluers." At the other extreme from nominal "not-a-cluers" are the hard-core fans, although cultural studies scholars Henry Jenkins (1992: 19–21) and Cassandra Amesley 1989: 338) suggest that this category may, in fact, be entirely fictional.[10] As Amesley (1989: 38) notes, "I have yet to find a self-identified 'hardcore Trekkie.' . . . The idea of a 'hardcore Trekkie' influences [fan] beliefs concerning their own behavior, but does not, except in theory, exist."[11]

The evident factions within *Star Trek* fandom certainly influence fan relationships in the convention context, but they are not the basis for the divisiveness and discord that recent scholarship on pilgrimage might suggest (e.g. Eade and Sallnow 1992.) When asked directly about factionalism in fandom, for example, the majority of fans were quick to minimize such differences. "While I may not agree [with other fans,]" one woman told me, "I believe everyone is entitled to their own opinions." Another insisted that "*Star Trek* is about open minds, and to say [some]one was wrong-headed would be to put yourself in that group."

According to Turner (1974a: 208), the liminoid context of pilgrimage does not abolish social and cultural structures but instead fosters a framework within which "differences are accepted or tolerated rather than aggravated into grounds of aggressive opposition." Within the *Star Trek* convention framework, fans place an overwhelming emphasis on tolerance of difference. Fan discourse is fraught with phrases designed to prevent open discord—qualifiers such as "no offense" and "in my opinion" serve to bracket potentially contentious issues and signal that alternate viewpoints are both acknowledged and validated. Where open disagreements do occur, the ideal of tolerance for diversity will often be explicitly invoked to mediate conflict.

This ideal of tolerance for diversity is symbolized for many fans by the concept of IDIC (Infinite Diversity in Infinite Combination) first introduced in the original *Star Trek* series. As Turner notes (1986: 46), however, there are inevitable tensions between the ideal as conceived within a group and the imperfect real as experienced by members. The failure, at times, to live up to the ideal of tolerance for diversity in the convention and fandom context can become a contentious issue. Some fans, often those most committed to the actualization of *Star Trek*'s ideals, express extreme frustration with other fans for their failure to live up to the IDIC ideal. John, for example, told me that "IDIC is, in one word, tolerance. In two words, celebratory tolerance . . . [but] fans *definitely* do not practice what they preach." The sense of frustration in John's words reveals the tensions between the ideal and the real that Turner (1986: 46) suggests is characteristic among dedicated members of voluntary special interest groups. Such tensions, however, do not negate the communitas experience but rather help to formulate it, for as Turner notes (1974a: 208), the liminoid context of pilgrimage does not abolish social tensions, but instead fosters a framework within which "differences are accepted or tolerated rather than aggravated into grounds of aggressive opposition." No matter how frustrated some fans may be with the failure of other fans to live up to the ideals of *Star Trek*, the liminoid frame of the convention ensures that the ideal of tolerance for diversity is employed to minimize differences and foster a sense of unity even where the ideal and the real are seen to conflict.

For many fans, IDIC has been internalized to the point where the concept has become what Turner and Turner (1978: 10) might characterize as a "root paradigm" of *Star Trek* fandom. IDIC is seen as central to the philosophy of *Star Trek*, and as encapsulating Roddenberry's vision.[12] Significantly, in none of the later *Star Trek* television series produced since the original series has this doctrine been elaborated. Nonetheless, the philosophy of IDIC is of extreme importance to many fans, both to those who were exposed to it while the original series was still in production, and to those who were not yet born at the time.[13] IDIC does not symbolize the goal of homogenizing differences for these fans, however, but symbolizes instead the ideal of celebrating them. As one fan expressed it, "differences should be savored and enjoyed for what they are, because they are so much more interesting than conformity."

According to Turner (1974a: 206), when pilgrimages draw people together from widely dispersed and diverse geographical and social contexts, communitas "becomes, for the groups and individuals . . . a means of binding diversities together and overcoming cleavages." IDIC is the paradigm that actively symbolizes and encapsulates the spirit of communitas in the *Star trek* convention context. IDIC also acts to mute differences when they threaten the communitas of the convention context. Within the frame of *Star Trek* conventions, the "spirit of IDIC"—that is, respect for and acceptance of diversity—is invoked to mediate disputes even in those circumstances where the explicit concept is not articulated. IDIC mediates discrepant perceptions, even when the term itself remains unspoken. As such, it is the philosophy of IDIC that explicitly mediates discrepant views of fans and implicitly fosters the communitas constitutive of the convention experience.

NEGOTIATING THE SACRED

Victor Turner (1986: 44–45) suggests that wherever members of a group based on mutual interest and voluntary affiliation meet, such a group has the potential to become for certain members the focus of intense dedication and energy. It is also in such a group, however, that "social dramas" take place. A social drama, for Turner (1986: 34–35), is "an objectively isolable sequence of social interactions of a conflictive, competitive, or agonistic type." Normative communitas such as that found in pilgrimage contexts does not negate all discrepant perceptions or erase all competing discourses among participants in the liminal process. In fact, Turner suggests (1986: 46) that it is only through such conflictive, competitive, or agonistic instances that the meaning of the group's internalized ideals are negotiated, reformulated, and resolved.

The central foci for conflictive social dramas, according to Turner (1986: 46), are the inevitable tensions between the ideal as conceived within the group and the imperfect real as experienced by members. If one can characterize the ideals of tolerance, freedom, and equality embedded within *Star Trek* as "sacred" (Morinis 1992), social dramas can be understood as those instances in which the sacred is negotiated through conflictive social discourse. The ideal within *Star Trek* fandom and among many convention participants is encapsulated within the egalitarian vision of Gene Roddenberry. The process of negotiation, and the evident points of conflict, arise when individual fans disagree on where and when

this ideal is actualized. One can see this negotiative process in the following conversation between three casual acquaintances who, as members of
an international fan club, journeyed to Pasadena together to attend the
GrandSlam IV convention in April 1996.

Whenever negotiative discourse is analyzed, the ethnographer must
account not only for the explicit meanings embedded within the oral
texts, but also for the implicit messages that members of a shared community pass to one another "telegraphically" (Rosaldo 1986). Anita,
Elaine, and Fran share membership not only in a formally organized *Star
Trek* fan club but within the wider fandom community. As folklorist
Livya Polanyi (1979) notes, it is often necessary to read behind the
explicit text to find the implicit point of narratives. What follows is an
analysis of both the explicit and the implicit point of one instance of fan
negotiation of meaning in the *Star Trek* convention context. The following discussion was initiated as a result of an exchange of narratives
between myself and the three women on the subject of how we came to
be *Star Trek* fans. Anita had earlier expressed the opinion that she would
have preferred to have attended the *Trek30* convention held the previous
November, for it had featured the actors from the original *Star Trek* show,
whereas the *GrandSlam IV* convention featured actors from the more
recent *Star Trek* series of *Next Generation, Deep Space Nine,* and *Voyager.*
Anita's account of how she came to be a *Star Trek* fan clearly highlighted
her sense of affinity for the original television series. This led to a discussion of whether the later *Star Trek* shows accurately reflected the spirit of
Gene Roddenberry's vision. According to Anita,

> In recent years, a lot of characters that were sort of central to *Star
> Trek* have turned their back on Star Fleet. Ro Laren . . . Tom
> Riker. . . . We've [even] had [the character of] *Wesley* turn his back
> on Starfleet, and I mean, he was supposed to be *Gene Roddenberry*
> as a youth, right? . . . [And now] you have the Klingons breaking
> the treaty, starting to become *enemies* of the Federation instead of
> their *allies.* . . . I feel that's just *too far away* from Gene Rodden-
> berry's vision, and I keep saying, "*the noise you hear is Gene spinning
> in his grave.*" I don't think he'd be happy with the way it's going. All
> right, that's just a personal feeling.

According to Turner (1986: 34), social dramas are initiated by what
he calls a "breach of regular norm-governed social relations." In the previous passage, Anita has made a categorical statement regarding her belief

that the creator of *Star Trek* must be "spinning in his grave" in dissatisfaction with the direction the current producers are taking the *Star Trek* series. Although dissatisfaction with the current producers of *Star Trek* is quite prevalent among fans, Anita has gone beyond a mild expression of dissatisfaction to a clear statement of condemnation, and she has marshaled the spirit of Gene Roddenberry in defense of her position. Given Roddenberry's status as the visionary creator of *Star Trek*, appeal to him in this context carries immense weight. Implicit in the examples that Anita chooses to highlight is the theme of disaffection: loved and respected characters of high moral fibre are "turning their backs on Starfleet." By implication, Starfleet—or *Star Trek*—no longer deserves the loyalty and affection of those who have always been true to it in the past. Anita recognizes the potentially divisive nature of her statement, and attempts to offset the vigor of her critique with the phrase, "All right, that's just a personal feeling." However, Anita has opened a door to discord in what amounts to an all-out attack on *Star Trek* in recent years, and the mediating disclaimer is insufficient to smooth over the breach in the normally consensual social relations among fans.

Elaine's response is hesitantly ventured initially, but becomes a clear refutation of Anita's argument. She begins her statement by making a one word acknowledgment of Anita's point ("Yeah,") and then proceeds to argue that Anita is, in fact, missing the point which truly characterizes the spirit of Roddenberry's vision. She says,

> Yeah. But, well, I don't know. They're still thinking about *peace*, and doing things the peaceful way . . . and thinking about *aliens* the same way as what they did in the Classic *Trek* . . . and the *emphasis*, yeah, in *Trek* still hasn't *changed*. . . . I don't think much has changed in that way. I think it's still the same [in current *Star Trek* shows.]. . . . I think that Gene Roddenberry saw that sooner or later in the future, man would realize that . . . *conflict* . . .[is] just not the way to go.

Elaine's response constitutes what Turner calls the "crisis" in social dramas. According to Turner (1986: 35), the crisis is the point in a negotiative process where "people take sides," and where an issue, which might otherwise have gone unremarked, becomes an overt instance of social contention. Elaine's response indicates her understanding that the explicit issue in question is whether "Starfleet" as portrayed within recent *Star Trek* series or episodes can still be said to embody the spirit of *Star Trek* that Gene Roddenberry intended it to convey. Her comments reveal her belief that Roddenberry's vision entails a philosophy of peace and harmony among widely diverse peoples—after all, Starfleet is still "thinking about aliens the same way as they did in Classic *Trek*." This statement communicates to listening *Star Trek* fans that tolerance of diversity remains the governing principle of interspecies contact in current *Star Trek* shows. Current *Star Trek* series, she therefore argues, do indeed still embody the vision of Gene Roddenberry.

In making this point, however, Elaine also reveals an implicit criticism of Anita for contravening the spirit of tolerance integral to *Star Trek*. It is here that the "telegraphic" nature of communication between members of a shared community becomes apparent. According to Elaine, one of the ways in which *Star Trek* continues to embody Roddenberry's vision is in its search for and idealization of a conflict-free world; after all, she notes, the new shows are "still thinking about peace, and doing things the peaceful way." Elaine cites this pacifist emphasis within Roddenberry's vision to *refute* Anita's claim that the spirit of *Star Trek* is no longer present in current *Star Trek* shows. Since Anita explicitly provides an example of warfare and conflict in her initial statement, however, Elaine's comment regarding peace is intended, I suggest, to convey a message other than the simple denial that contemporary *Star Trek* depicts occasional war. Elaine knows that war and conflict are frequently portrayed in *Star Trek* episodes, and so her comments are directed less toward the episodes themselves and more toward Anita personally. This reference to Roddenberry's vision that someday humankind will overcome its propensity for conflict is an implicit criticism of Anita for her critical, and contentious, views. Several fans with whom I spoke explicitly cited IDIC as grounds for not rejecting innovations in current *Star Trek* shows, and Elaine's comments can be contextualized within this framework.[14] In being so overtly negative, Elaine's criticism implies, Anita is guilty of breaching the ethic of tolerance for diversity that is constitutive of the *Star Trek* spirit, and thereby contradicting her own professed idealization of this ethic.

In her subsequent rejoinder, Anita reveals her awareness of this subtextual criticism, for she transforms the implicit accusation of intolerance directed at herself into an explicit condemnation of intolerance in Starfleet as characterized in specific *Star Trek* episodes. Anita claimed,

> But even in [the final episode of *Star Trek: The Next Generation*] there seems to have been this thing, [where] you had to go Star Fleet's way or not at all. Right? If we're talking about *tolerance, har-*

mony, surely, *surely* in a civilization like *that*, everyone is allowed to have their own opinion? [And yet] Starfleet is suddenly saying, well, it's either our way or not at all. And that to me does *not* promote tolerance. Right?

At this point in the negotiative process, the issue in contention has clearly been established as "tolerance for diversity." Explicitly at issue is whether or not this ideal is actualized within the framework of the fictional television shows. Implicitly, however, it is the issue of fan intolerance that is under negotiation. Elaine has implied that Anita is intolerant in her extreme criticisms, and in the previous passage Anita deflects this accusation away from herself, and uses it to contextualize her own criticisms of recent *Star Trek* shows. Further implied in her response is a defense of her own right to make such critical judgements, for all people are "allowed to have their own opinion." To not grant others their right to hold divergent views, she is suggesting, is to contravene the spirit of *Star Trek*. In asking Elaine to confirm this interpretation through her use of the interrogative "right?" Anita contextualizes her criticism of recent *Star Trek* shows within the ideological framework of *Star Trek* itself. Although Anita does not cite the doctrine of IDIC, she is articulating the belief that, within the realm of the *Star Trek* universe, and within the realm of fandom itself, discrepant perceptions should be tolerated if Roddenberry's vision is truly to be actualized.

At this point in the discussion, the third member of the group enters the debate with a position of compromise intended to mediate the discrepant perceptions of Anita and Elaine. Fran comments,

Well, I always thought Gene Roddenberry's vision was about the *human* way, and [how] you kind of *expect* everybody else to follow the human philosophy [of tolerance] but they *don't*. . . . I think you *can* still find the vision there, but maybe it's harder for the *human* part of the Federation to sort of keep going with that vision, when they've got all these other conflicting people coming into it.

Fran's contribution to this negotiative process is effective on two levels. According to Turner (1986: 35), following the initiation of crisis in social dramas, members of a community attempt to institute what he terms "redressive or remedial procedures," whereby participants reflexively sit in judgment and attempt to understand and resolve the issues in contention. Fran's response offers a contribution to the negotiation on the multiple layers of meaning under debate. On the explicit issue of whether the vision of

Gene Roddenberry is still embodied within *Star Trek*, Fran argues that the portrayal of conflict between humans and aliens does not contravene the spirit of Roddenberry's vision, for this vision was of a future in which peacefulness and tolerance governed humanity. It is therefore unproblematic that alien species are being portrayed as conflictive, for no one should expect them to adopt a human-centered vision. If this portrayal of conflict among alien species further makes it difficult for human characters to be true to Roddenberry's vision, this too is in keeping with what *Star Trek* is all about. One need not condemn the current *Star Trek* series, therefore, simply because non-human characters have not yet adopted the IDIC ideal.

On the implicit issue of fan intolerance that is also under negotiation, Fran's comments are of a less compromising nature. At this level of discourse, Fran sides with Elaine in her criticism of Anita's intolerance. Here, Fran's comment that the idealization of tolerance is a "human" philosophy carries a sting. In her condemnation of recent *Star Trek* series, Fran implies, Anita is contributing to the problems that beset *Star Trek* fandom. After all, just as the conflictual natures of non-human species make it that much more difficult for humans within the *Star Trek* universe to live up to their ideals, so too, by implication, do critical and intolerant perspectives on the part of fans make it that much more difficult for other fans to be true to Roddenberry's vision.

Anita responds to this dual compromise/rebuke by backtracking somewhat on her initial forthright condemnation of *Star Trek*. Continuing in the "redressive or remedial" stage of negotiation, Anita articulates a willingness to compromise without recanting completely on her earlier criticisms. She says,

> I guess we've got to learn to be with each other as we are, not as we would like other people to be. I mean, just because I'm saying I'm not liking the way the Federation is going, doesn't mean that I still don't like [the shows]. . . . I still believe that what Gene Roddenberry was trying to say is very much [as] relevant now as it was thirty years ago. You know, I think that's what initially drew me to *Star Trek*, the fact that someone had a positive idea of the future . . . [where] there would be no intolerance, no racism, no prejudice.

In her acknowledgment that "we've got to learn to be with each other as we are, not as we would like other people to be," Anita affirms her commitment to the ideal of tolerance for diversity. She also implicitly acknowledges that she has reevaluated her initial criticisms of recent *Star*

Trek shows in light of the current discussion, and no longer posits the failure of these shows to live up to the vision of Gene Roddenberry. However, Anita also implies in her statement about learning to accept others as they are and not as we would like them to be, that Elaine and Fran must accept that she does not hold a fully appreciative opinion of the more recent *Star Trek* series. She reaffirms her commitment to the philosophy of *Star Trek*, and even admits to a grudging enjoyment in recent *Star Trek* shows, but she continues to disapprove of the direction in which the storylines are being developed.

Elaine then initiates what Turner (1986: 35–36) calls the final stage of social dramas, where consensus is re-established, the group re-integrated, and symbols of unity and continuity re-invigorated. Her comment confirms that the issue under implicit debate has been the issue of fan consensus and the application of Roddenberry's vision to the convention context. She says, "Yeah, and I also think his vision was that everyone could interact together. . . . I think that's a very good vision to have. And, this [the current discussion] is it. This is the sort of thing his vision was." In introducing the idea that the preceding negotiative discourse is constitutive of Roddenberry's vision, Elaine abandons the explicit discussion of whether Roddenberry's vision is portrayed within specific television series in favor of pursuing the implicit (to this point) issue of fandom as constitutive of the IDIC ideal. Her comment in this context reveals her awareness that she and Anita and Fran have been engaging in a negotiative process, and that their differences of opinion have not been allowed to contravene the spirit of tolerance for diversity which characterizes the meaning of *Star Trek*.

In the context of *Star Trek* fandom, negotiative discourse is constitutive of the convention experience. Both negotiation and debate, as Jenkins (1992: 86) notes, are characteristic of fan social interactions. Although this may lead at times to conflict and discord between and among fans, *Star Trek* itself provides a "core" of meaning around which discrepant perceptions of fans cohere. The "meaning" of *Star Trek*, the "vision" of Gene Roddenberry, and the philosophy of IDIC constitute that core. In the example of negotiative discourse above, outright intolerance was rejected as unacceptable in the context of fandom, and fandom itself was posited as a model on which to understand the content of Roddenberry's vision for humanity. Anita maintained her distaste for the conflictual elements in *Star Trek* but, through negotiation, learned to articulate that distaste in ways which did not contravene the ideal of tolerance for diversity. Elaine and Fran maintained their insistence that Roddenberry's vision was in fact actualized within the *Next Generation, Deep Space Nine,* and *Voyager* series, but through negotiation came to grant Anita the right to her opinion. It was through negotiation of these issues that the IDIC ideal came to be constituted, for in asserting the value of tolerance for diversity, mediation of the discrepant perceptions of Anita, Elaine, and Fran became possible. The concept of infinite diversity in infinite combinations was implicitly affirmed in the very negotiative process that mediated and minimized discrepant perceptions of *Star Trek* fandom's sacred ideals. In negotiating the ideal of tolerance for diversity, diversity was minimized through the emergence of consensus on the value of the internalized ideal.

CONCLUSIONS

Star Trek convention attendance can be seen as pilgrimage in a contemporary, secular context. Turner's model of pilgrimage is clearly applicable to the convention experience. In analyzing convention attendance within the framework of Turner's model, it is possible to shed new light on *Star Trek* convention attendance as part of popular culture. *Star Trek* fans experience, in the convention context, the liminality and communitas that Turner suggests is characteristic of pilgrimage journeys. Although recent critics of Turner have suggested that conflict in pilgrimage settings undermines the experience of communitas, within the convention setting conflict or discrepant perceptions are mediated within the bounds of the IDIC principle. Communitas is maintained through the idealization of respect for diversity encapsulated within the IDIC ideal. This mediation of difference, and the idealization of difference in pursuit of common ideals, is characteristic of pilgrimage journeys. Within the increasingly secular and pluralistic framework of North American culture, *Star Trek* conventions provide a sense of meaningful community, an optimistic vision of the future, and a time and space for fans to be free to explore their love of something deeply meaningful in their lives. Although *Star Trek* convention attendance does not represent a religious journey, it does nonetheless constitute a pilgrimage for many fans.

NOTES

1. Anthropologist Simon Coleman and art historian John Elsner (1995: 200) suggest that secular journeys can be seen as the "inheritors" of pilgrimage within industrialized societies.

2. Although this chapter focuses upon the elements of liminality and communitas, other aspects of *Star Trek* convention attendance also resonate with Turner's definition of pilgrimage as a liminoid phenomenon. These include the release of fans from their mundane social and geographical context; the homogenization of status among participants; some degree of hardship, physical or otherwise—including economic; and the reflection on cultural values and the apparent experience of communitas as expressed by fans.

3. Shatner made this comment during a sketch for the irreverent television series *Saturday Night Live*. *Star Trek* fans have since appropriated the phrase and the events surrounding the original comment have become part of *Trek* folklore.

4. The construction of personas is frequently a facet of organized fan clubs. Personas are constructed in the context of fan clubs and enacted in both club and convention contexts.

5. This juxtaposition of "grim and violent" futuristic films with the utopian vision of *Star Trek* is characteristic of what Jindra (1994: 32) calls "two main genres of science fiction, the utopian and the apocalyptic." Drawing upon the insights of Jindra (1994) and Kreuziger (1986), it is possible to see these twin strains in science fiction as symbolizing the tensions between the utopian visions characteristic of ideological communitas, and the social criticism implicit within it.

6. Another basis for making distinctions in fandom is fan loyalty to specific *Star Trek* series or characters. Some fans identify themselves as fans of *Star Trek* the original series; others identify with *Next Generation*, *Deep Space Nine*, or *Voyager* as their primary affiliation. Similar distinctions according to which particular character or actor fans prefer also occur. However, these differences are not considered particularly divisive among fans themselves. As one fan told me, "*Star Trek* is about open minds, and to say one was wrong-headed [about something] would be to put yourself in that group."

7. Jenkins (1992: 95) also cites fans who believe this distinction too simplistic.

8. According to Jenkins (1992: 21), the label "Trekkie" has "increasingly come to refer only to the media constructed stereotype" of the *Star Trek* fan as an immature misfit with "no life." This stereotypical image, however, is "not without a limited factual basis," according to Jenkins (1992: 17). According to Rob, this stereotypical image is definitely based on actual fans. Following the conversation cited here, Rob went on to tell the story of a Trekkie member of his own fan club, who fit the stereotyped image (at least according to Rob's portrayal) perfectly. For a published account of fan characterizations of Trekkies and Trekkers, see Ruff (1996).

9. Dedicated fans also make this disclaimer. This is in part because fans are conscious of the need to communicate to nonfans ("mundanes" or "norms" in fan parlance) their recognition of the leisure/ludic/fantasy basis for their enthusiasm. Jindra (1994) suggests that controversy surrounding *Star Trek* fandom is evoked because of the suspension of *Star Trek* between entertainment and seriousness. Jindra (1994: 48) characterizes this liminal suspension as between the "seriousness" of the fans, and the "entertainment" of nominal fans and non-fans. However, this distinction is only partly correct. It would be more accurate to suggest that the majority of fans themselves find themselves suspended in a liminal frame between seriousness and play. This tension or suspension is epitomized in a comment made by Bob, who told me, "I'm in this for the fun; I'm in this for what, as a whole, we can do as community service . . . that's what it's all about for me. That and fun."

10. Jindra (1994: 48) suggests that at least one fan he spoke to did identify herself as a "hard-core" fan, however. Definitions of "hard-core" vary depending upon a fan's own degree of fandom.

11. According to Eade and Sallnow (1991: 5), a full analysis of pilgrimage must include not only the pilgrims but others who contribute to the pilgrimage process. In addition to fans, further participants include merchandisers, volunteers, organizers, and actors—and possibly local residents as well. Even more broadly, one might want to include the writers, producers, and directors of the television shows and movies and the authors of *Star Trek* novels.

12. Not all fans are familiar with the concept of IDIC. I remember one fan in particular who announced with frustration, "I know its important, but I don't know what it means!" Another fan, attending her first convention, told me she had never heard of the concept until earlier that day. Combined with the absence of the doctrine in later *Star Trek* series (until *Voyager*, no *Star Trek* series except the original series featured a Vulcan character and IDIC is explained as a Vulcan philosophy, hence there has been no easy forum within the television shows for promulgating this concept), this suggests that it may in fact be the convention context itself which is responsible for the maintenance and elaboration of this doctrine in fandom. This possibility requires further research to confirm.

13. The concept of the Prime Directive, explained in the original *Star Trek* series as the "non-interference" directive, has been elaborated extensively in later shows. This directive—understood to impose a hands-off policy on Federation members, so that civilizations without space-travel capability would be left to develop according to their own "natural evolution," has been elaborated by many fans to encompass the doctrine of IDIC, even where they are unaware of the IDIC concept itself. For example, one fan explained the Prime Directive as a philosophy that taught that "acceptance is a virtue. We may not agree with others but we must give credence to [their beliefs]. Don't jump to conclusions because

it just may be that, given the same circumstances, you may do something even more disagreeable than what you see as wrong [in others]." Another defined the Prime Directive as a policy of "live and let live. To each his own. To gain respect, one must respect others." The IDIC principle appears to implicitly underlie fan perceptions of the philosophy of *Star Trek*, therefore, even when it is not consciously articulated.

14. For example, one fan told me, "If we want to go back to the Vulcan IDIC, infinite diversity in infinite combinations, isn't that what it's all about? You can't just stay static. You have to allow all these different elements to enter into it [the *Star Trek* universe], and that just improves the whole thing."

TV Episodes and Movies Cited

TV EPISODES

Star Trek

"The Cage" (1964). Robert Butler, director. Teleplay by Gene Roddenberry.

"Balance of Terror" (1966). Vincent McEveety, director. Teleplay by Paul Schneider.

"Charlie X" (1966). Lawrence Dobkin, director. Teleplay by D. C. Fontana.

"Dagger of the Mind" (1966). Vincent McEveety, director. Teleplay by S. Bar-David.

"Mudd's Women" (1966). Harvey Hart, director. Teleplay by Stephen Kandel.

"The Conscience of the King" (1966). Gerd Oswald, director. Teleplay by Barry Trivers.

"The Enemy Within" (1966). Leo Penn, director. Teleplay by Richard Matheson.

"The Man Trap" (1966). Marc Daniels, director. Teleplay by George Clayton Johnson.

"The Menagerie" (1966). Marc Daniels, director. Teleplay by Gene Roddenberry.

271

"Where No Man Has Gone Before" (1966). James Goldstone, director. Teleplay by Samuel A. Peeples.

"Amok Time" (1967). Joseph Pevney, director. Teleplay by Theodore Sturgeon.

"Errand of Mercy" (1967). John Newland, director. Teleplay by Gene L. Coon.

"I, Mudd" (1967). Robert Lederman, director. Teleplay by Stephen Kandel.

"Metamorphosis" (1967). Ralph Serensky, director. Teleplay by Gene L. Coon.

"Mirror, Mirror" (1967). Marc Daniels, director. Teleplay by Jerome Bixby.

"Operation: Annihilate" (1967). Herschel Daugherty, director. Teleplay by Stephen W, Carabatsos.

"Space Seed" (1967). Marc Daniels, director. Teleplay by Gene L. Coon and Terry Wilbur.

"The Apple" (1967). Joseph Pevney, director. Teleplay by Max Ehrlich and Gene L. Coon.

"The Changeling" (1967). Marc Daniels, director. Teleplay by John Meredyth Lucas.

"The Devil in the Dark" (1967). Joseph Pevney, director. Teleplay by Gene Coon.

"The Doomsday Machine" (1967). Marc Daniels, director. Teleplay by Norman Spinrad.

"The Return of the Archons" (1967). Joseph Pevney, director. Teleplay by Boris Sobelman.

"The Squire of Gothos" (1967). Don McDougall, director. Teleplay by Paul Schneider.

"This Side of Paradise" (1967). Ralph Senensky, director. Teleplay by D. C. Fontana.

"Tomorrow is Yesterday" (1967). Michael O'Herlihy, director. Teleplay by D. C. Fontana

"Who Mourns for Adonais?" (1967). Marc Daniels, director. Teleplay by Gilbert Ralston.

"Wolf in the Fold" (1967). Joseph Pevney, director. Teleplay by Robert Bloch.

"And the Children Shall Lead" (1968). Marvin Chomsky, director. Teleplay by Edward J. Lakso.

"Bread and Circuses" (1968). Ralph Senensky, director. Teleplay by Gene Roddenberry and Gene Coon.

"By Any Other Name" (1968). Marc Daniels, director. Teleplay by D. C. Fontana andJerome Bixby.

"For the World is Hollow and I Have Touched the Sky" (1968). Tony Leader, director. Teleplay by Rik Vollaerts.

"Is There in Truth No Beauty?" (1968). Ralph Senensky, director. Teleplay by Jean Lisette Aroeste.

"Patterns of Force" (1968). Vincent McEveety, director. Teleplay by John Meredyth Lucas.

"Plato's Stepchildren" (1968). David Alexander, director. Teleplay by Meyer Dolinsky.

"Return to Tomorrow," (1968). Ralph Senensky, director. Teleplay by Gene Roddenberry.

"The Day of the Dove" (1968). Marvin Chomsky, director. Teleplay by Jerome Bixby.

"The Empath" (1968). John Erman, director. Teleplay by Joyce Muskat.

"The Gamesters of Triskelion" (1968). Gene Nelson, director. Teleplay by Margaret Armen.

"The Omega Glory" (1968). Vincent McEveety, director. Teleplay by Gene Roddenberry.

"The Paradise Syndrome" (1968). Jud Taylor, director. Teleplay by Margaret Armen.

"The Ultimate Computer" (1968). John Meredyth Lucas, director. Teleplay by D. C. Fontana.

"Let That Be Your Last Battlefield" (1969). Jud Taylor, director. Teleplay by Oliver Crawford.

"Requiem for Methuselah" (1969). Murray Golden, director. Teleplay by Jerome Bixby.

"The Mark of Gideon" (1969). Jud Taylor, director. Teleplay by George F. Slavin and Stanley Adams.

"The Lights of Zetar" (1969). Herb Kenwith, director. Teleplay by Jerome Tarcher and Shari Lewis.

"The Savage Curtain" (1969). Herschel Daugherty, director. Teleplay by Gene Roddenberry and Arthur Heinemann.

"The Way to Eden" (1969). David Alexander, director. Teleplay by Arthur Heinemann.

"Turnabout Intruder" (1969). Herb Wallerstein, director. Teleplay by Gene Roddenberry and Arthur H. Singer.

"Whom Gods Destroy" (1969). Herb Wallerstein, director. Teleplay by Lee Erwin.

Star Trek: The Next Generation

"Code of Honor" (1987). Russ Mayberry, director. Teleplay by Katharyn Powers and Michael Baron.

"Encounter at FarPoint" (1987). Corey Allen, director. Teleplay by D. C. Fontana and Gene Roddenberry.

"Hide and Q" (1987). Cliff Bole, director. Teleplay by C. J. Holland and Gene Roddenberry.

"Justice" (1987). James Conway, director. Teleplay by Worley Thorne.

"Datalore" (1988). Rob Bowman, director. Teleplay by Robert Lewin and Gene Roddenberry.

"Elementary Dear Data" (1988). Rob Bowman, director. Teleplay by Brian Alan Lane.

"Home Soil" (1988). Corey Allen, director. Teleplay by Robert Sabaroff.

"Skin of Evil" (1988). Joseph L. Scanlan, director. Teleplay by Joseph Stephano and Hannah Louise Shearer.

"Symbiosis" (1988). Win Phelps, director. Teleplay by Richard Manning and Hans Beimler.

"The Big Goodbye" (1988). Joseph L. Scanlan, director. Teleplay by Tracy Tormé.

"The Neutral Zone" (1988). James L. Conway, director. Teleplay by Maurice Hurley.

"Where Silence has Lease" (1988). Winrich Kolbe, director. Teleplay by Jack B. Sowards.

"Booby Trap" (1989). Gabrielle Beaumont, director. Teleplay by Ron Roman, Michael Piller and Richard Danus.

"Evolution" (1989). Winrich Kolbe, director. Teleplay by Michael Piller.

"The Bonding" (1989). Winrich Kolbe, director. Teleplay by Ronald Moore.

"The Emissary" (1989). Cliff Bole, director. Teleplay by Richard Manning and Hans Beimler.

"The Measure of a Man" (1989). Robert Scheerer, director. Teleplay by Melinda M. Snodgrass.

"The Schizoid Man" (1989). Les Landau, director. Teleplay by Tracy Tormé.

"Unnatural Selection" (1989). Paul Lynch, director. Teleplay by John Mason and Mike Gray.

"Up the Long Ladder" (1989). Winrich Kolbe, director. Teleplay by Melinda Snodgrass.

"Who Watches the Watchers" (1989). Robert Wiemer, director. Teleplay and story by Richard Manning and Hans Beimler.

"Best of Both Worlds, Part One" (1990). Cliff Bole, Director. Teleplay by Michael Piller.

"Best of Both Worlds, Part Two" (1990) Cliff Bole, Director. Teleplay by Michael Piller.

"Brothers" (1990). Rob Bowman, director. Teleplay by Rick Berman.

"Family" (1990). Les Landau, director. Teleplay by Ronald D. Moore.

"Legacy" (1990). Robert Scheerer, director. Teleplay by Joe Menosky.

"Transfigurations" (1990). Tom Benko, director. Teleplay by Rene Echevarria.

"Yesterday's Enterprise" (1990). David Carson, director. Teleplay by Ira Stephen Behr, Richard Manning, Hans Beimler, and Ronald D. Moore.

"Data's Day" (1991). Robert Weimer, director. Teleplay by Harold Apter and Ronald Moore.

"Devil's Due" (1991). Tom Benko, director. Teleplay by Philip Lazebnik.

"Half a Life" (1991). Les Landau, director. Teleplay by Peter Allan Fields.

"Redemption, Part II" (1991). David Carson, director. Teleplay by Ronald D. Moore.

"The Host" (1991). Marvin V. Rush, director. Teleplay by Michael Horvat.

"Unification" (1991). Les Landau, director. Teleplay by Jeri Taylor.

"Ethics" (1992). Chip Chalmers, director. Teleplay by Ronald Moore.

"The First Duty" (1992). Paul Lynch, director. Teleplay by Ronald D. Moore and Naren Shankar.

"The Next Phase" (1992). David Carson, director. Teleplay by Ronald D. Moore.

"The Outcast" (1992). Robert Scheer, director. Teleplay by Jeri Taylor.

"The Quality of Life" (1992). Jonathan Frakes, director. Teleplay by Naren Shankar.

"Time's Arrow, Part One" (1992). Les Landau, director. Teleplay by Joe Menosky and Michael Pillar.

"Time's Arrow, Part Two" (1992). Les Landau, director. Teleplay by Jeri Taylor.

"True-Q" (1992). Robert Scheerer, director. Teleplay by Rene Echevarria.

"Descent, Part I" (1993). Alexander Singe, director. Teleplay by Ronald D. Moore.

"Inheritance" (1993). Robert Scheerer, director. Teleplay by Dan Koepel and René Echévarria.

"Lessons" (1993). Robert Weimer, director. Teleplay by Ronald Wilkerson and Jean Louise Matthias.

"Rightful Heir" (1993). Winrich Kolbe, director. Teleplay by Ronald Moore.

"Second Chances" (1993). LeVar Burton, director. Teleplay by René Echévarria.

"Ship in a Bottle" (1993). Alexander Singer, director. Teleplay by René Echévarria.

"Tapestry" (1993). Les Landau, director. Teleplay by Ronald D. Moore.

"The Chase" (1993). Jonathan Frakes, director. Teleplay by Joe Menosky.

"Journey's End" (1994). Corey Allen, director. Teleplay by Ronald D. Moore.

"Masks" (1994). Robert Weimer, director. Teleplay by J. Menosky.

Star Trek: Deep Space Nine

"Emissary" (1993). David Carson, director. Teleplay by Michael Pillar.

"In the Hand of the Prophets" (1993). David Livingston, director. Teleplay by Robert Hewitt Wolfe.

"The Circle" (1993). Corey Allen, director. Teleplay by Peter Allen Fields.

"The Homecoming" (1993). Winrich Kolbe, director. Teleplay by Ira Steven Behr.

"Shakaar" (1993). Jonathan West, director. Teleplay by Gordon Dawson.

"Fascination" (1994). Avery Brooks, director. Teleplay by Philip LaZebnik.

"Past Tense, Part One" (1994). Reda Badiyi, director. Teleplay by Robert Hewitt Wolfe.

"The Maquis, Part One" (1994). David Livingston, director. Teleplay by James Crocker.

"The Maquis, Part Two" (1994). Corey Allen, director. Teleplay by Ira Steven Behr.

"Whispers" (1994). Les Landau, director. Teleplay by Paul Robert Coyle.

"Destiny" (1995). Les Landau, director. Teleplay by David S Cohen and Martin A Winer.

"Our Man Bashir" (1995). Winrich Kolbe, director. Teleplay by Ronald D. Moore.

"Past Tense, Part Two" (1995). Jonathan Frakes, director. Teleplay by Ira Steven Behr and Robert Hewitt Wolfe.

"Prophet Motive" (1995). René Auberjonois, director. Teleplay by Ira Steven Behr and Robert Hewitt Wolfe.

"The Visitor" (1995). David Livingston, director. Teleplay by Michael Williams.

"Through the Looking Glass" (1995). Winrich Kolbe, director. Teleplay by Ira Steven Behr, and Robert Hewitt Wolfe.

"Visionary" (1995). Reza Badiyi, director. Teleplay by John Shirley.

"Accession" (1996). Les Landau, director. Teleplay by Jane Espenson.

"Paradise Lost" (1996). Reza Badiyi, director. Teleplay by Ira Steven Behr and Robert Hewitt Wolfe.

"Shattered Mirror" (1996). James L. Conway, director. Teleplay by Steven Behr and Hans Beimler

"Rapture" (1997). Jonathan West, director. Teleplay by Hans Beimler.

"Ties of Blood and Water" (1997). Avery Brooks, director. Teleplay by Robert Hewitt Wolfe.

Star Trek: Voyager

"Cathexis" (1995). Kim Friedman, director. Teleplay by Brannon Braga.

"Initiations" (1995). Rick Kolbe, director. Teleplay by Kenneth Biller.

"State of Flux" (1995). Robert Scheerer, director. Teleplay by Chris Abbott.

"The 37's" (1995). Jim Conway, director. Teleplay by Jeri Taylor and Brannon Braga.

"The Cloud" (1995). David Livingston, director. Telplay by Tom Szollosi and Michael Piller.

"Basics, Part One" (1996). Rick Kolbe, director. Teleplay by Michael Piller.

"Basics, Part Two" (1996). Rick Kolbe, director. Teleplay by Michael Piller.

"Deadlock." (1996). David Livingston, director. Teleplay by Brannon Braga.

"Death Wish" (1996). James L. Conway, director. Teleplay by Michael Piller.

"Resolutions" (1996). Alexander Singer, director. Teleplay by Jeri Taylor.

"Sacred Ground" (1996). Robert Duncan McNeill, director. Teleplay by Lisa Klink.

"Tattoo" (1996). Alexander Singer, director. Teleplay by Michael Piller.

"The Q and the Grey" (1996). Cliff Bole, director. Teleplay by Kenneth Biller.

"Coda" (1997) Les Landau, director. Teleplay by Jeri Taylor.

"Real Life" (1997) Anson Williams, director. Teleplay by Jeri Taylor.

"The Omega Directive" (1998) Victor Lobl, director. Teleplay by Lisa Klink.

MOVIES

Star Trek: The Motion Picture (1979). Robert Wise, director. Paramount Pictures

Star Trek II: The Wrath of Khan (1982). Nicholas Meyer, director. Paramount Pictures

Star Trek III: The Search for Spock (1984). Leonard Nimoy, director. Paramount Pictures

Star Trek IV: The Voyage Home (1986). Leonard Nimoy, director. Paramount Pictures

Star Trek V: The Final Frontier (1989). William Shatner, director. Paramount Pictures

Star Trek VI: The Undiscovered Country (1991). Nicholas Meyer, director. Paramount Pictures

Star Trek: Generations (1994). D. Carson, director. Paramount Pictures

Star Trek: First Contact (1996). Jonathan Frakes, director. Paramount Pictures

Star Trek: Insurrection (1998). Jonathan Frakes, director. Paramount Pictures

Bibliography

Abrahms, M. H. 1981. *A Glossary of Literary Terms*, 4th ed. New York: Holt, Rinehart & Winston.

Albanese, Catherine L. 1996. "Religion and Popular Culture: An Introductory Essay." *Journal of the American Academy of Religion* 59: 733–42

Alexander, Bobby 1994. *Televangelism Reconsidered: Ritual in the Search for Human Community.* American Academy of Religion Studies in Religion 68. Atlanta: Scholars Press.

Alexander, David. 1995 [1994]. *Star Trek Creator: The Authorized Biography of Gene Roddenberry.* New York: Penguin Books.

——. 1991. "Gene Roddenberry. Writer, Producer, Philosopher, Humanist." *The Humanist* 51: 5–38.

Alfred, Mark. 1983. "'He's Dead, Jim.' On Spock's Demise." In Waiter Irwin and G.B. Love, eds. *The Best of Trek #6.* London: Signet Books.

Alter, Robert. 1981. *The Art of Biblical Narrative.* New York: Basic Books.

Altizer, Thomas J. J. 1966. *The Gospel of Christian Atheism.* Philadelphia: Westminster.

Amesley, Cassandra. 1989. "How to Watch *Star Trek.*" *Cultural Studies* 3(3): 323–29.

Amis, Kingsley. 1963. *New Maps of Hell.* London: New English Library.

Anijar, Karen Zapolsky. 1994. *Teaching Towards the Twenty-fourth Century: The Social Curriculum of Star Trek in the Schools.* Ph.D. dissertation, University of North Carolina–Greensboro.

Appleton, G. 1985. *The Oxford Book of Prayer.* Oxford: Oxford University Press.

Asherman, Allen. 1989. *The Star Trek Compendium.* London: Titan Books.

———. 1986. *The Star Trek Compendium.* New York: Pocket Books.

Bacon-Smith, Camille. 1992. *Enterprising Women: Television Fandom and the Creation of Popular Myth.* Philadelphia: University of Pennsylvania Press.

Baker, Carlos. 1961. *Shelley's Major Poetry.* New York: Russell and Russell.

Barbour, Ian G. 1971. *Issues in Science and Religion.* New York: Harper & Row.

Barrett, C. K. 1972. "Mark 10:45—A Ransom for Many." In *New Testament Essays,* pp. 20–26. London: SPCK.

———. 1959. "The Background of Mark 10:45." In A.J.B. Higgins, ed. *New Testament Essays: Studies in Memory of T. W Manson,* pp. 1–18. Manchester: Manchester University Press.

Bascom, William. 1965. "The Forms of Folklore: Prose Narratives." *Journal of American Folklore* 77: 3–20.

Bellah, Robert. 1970. "Religious Evolution." In *Beyond Belief: Essays on Religion in a Post-Traditional World,* pp. 20–50. New York: Harper & Row.

Bellah, Robert, R. Madsen, W. Sullivan, A. Swidler, and S. Tipton. 1985. *Habits of the Heart—Individualism and Commitment in American Life.* New York: Harper & Row.

Berger, Harold L. 1976. *Science Fiction and the New Dark Age.* Bowling Green, Ohio: Popular Press.

Berger, Peter. 1970. *A Rumor of Angels.* New York: Anchor.

Bergman, David, and Daniel Mark Epstein. 1987. *The Heath Guide to Literature,* 2nd ed. Lexington, Mass.: D. C. Heath.

Berkhofer, Robert, Jr. 1978. *The White Man's Indian: Images of the American Indian from Columbus to the Present.* New York: Alfred A. Knopf.

Berlin, Adele. 1983. *Poetics and Interpretation of Biblical Narrative.* Sheffield: Almond.

Best, J. 1937. *The Miracles of Christ in the Light of Our Present-Day Knowledge.* London: SPCK.

Beswick, Norman. 1991. "Glimpses of Ecclesiastical Space." *Foundation* 53: 24–36.

Blair, Karen. 1977. *Meaning in Star Trek.* Chambersburg, Pa.: Anima.

Blake, Douglas. 1987. "Cheaters and Katras: A Short Discussion on Death." In Walter Irwin and G. B. Love, eds. *The Best of Trek #12.* London: Signet Books.

Blish, J. 1959. *A Case of Conscience.* London: Penguin Books.

Blish, James. 1991. *Star Trek—The Classic Episodes,* 3 vols. New York: Bantam Books.

Bonhoeffer, Dietrich. 1974. *Letters and Papers from Prison.* New York: Macmillan.

Borrell, Skip. 1993. "God is a Trekker!" *CCSTSG (Central Connecticut Star Trek Support Group) Newsletter* 32: 4.

Bowman, Marian. 1995. "The Noble Savage and the Global Village: Cultural Evolution in New Age and Neo-Pagan Thought." *Journal of Contemporary Religion* 10(2): 139–49.

Boylan, Richard C. 1996a. "Report on the Star Knowledge Conference." *Spiritweb Org.* http://www.spiritweb.org/Spirit/star-knowledge-conf-06-1996.html (Accessed June 24, 1997).

———. 1996b. "Worlds in Transition: Report on the Star Visions Conference." *Spiritweb Org.* http://www.spiritweb.org/Spirit/star-visions-conf-11-1996.html (Accessed June 24, 1997).

Brown, Colin. 1992. "Historical Jesus, Quest of." In Joel B. Green, Scot McKnight, and I. Howard Marshall, eds. *Dictionary of Jesus and the Gospels,* pp. 326–41. Downers Grove, Ill.: InterVarsity Press.

Bultmann, Rudolph. 1965. "The Idea of God and Modern Man." In Robert W. Funk, ed. *Translating Theology into the Modern Age.* New York: Harper.

———. 1934. *Jesus and the Word.* New York: Scribner's.

Buren, Paul M. van. 1963. *The Secular Meaning of the Gospel.* New York: Macmillan.

Burkert, Walter. 1985. *Greek Religion.* Cambridge: Harvard University Press.

Callahan, Daniel, ed. 1966. *The Secular City Debate.* New York: Macmillan.

Caprio, Betsy. 1978. *Star Trek: Good News in Modern Images*. Kansas City: Sheed Andrews and McNeel

Carrier, Jim. 1994. "Trekkies Among Convention's Star Attractions." *Denver Post*, February 27, PC-2.

Carson, D. A. 1996. *The Gagging of God: Christianity Confronts Pluralism*. Grand Rapids, Mich.: Zondervan.

Cassirer, Ernst. 1951. *The Philosophy of the Enlightenment*. Princeton: Princeton University Press.

Caws, Peter. 1967. "Scientific Method." In *The Encyclopedia of Philosophy*, vol. 7. New York: Macmillan.

Chidester, David. 1996. "The Church of Baseball, the Fetish of Coca-Cola, and the Potlatch of Rock 'n' Roll: Theoretical Models for the Study of Religion in American Popular Culture." *Journal of the American Academy of Religion* 59: 743–65.

Christian Jr., William A. 1987. "Folk Religion." In Mircea Eliade, ed. *The Encyclopedia of Religion*. New York: Macmillan.

Churchill, Ward. 1994. *Indians Are Us? Culture and Genocide in Native North America*. Munroe, Maine: Common Courage Press.

Clark, David Lee. 1966. *Shelley's Prose*. Albuquerque: University of New Mexico Press.

Claus, Peter J. 1976. "A Structuralist Appreciation of Star Trek." In Susan P. Montague and W. Arens, eds. *The American Dimension*,.pp. 15–31. Port Washington, N.Y.: Alfred Publishing.

Clifton, James A., ed. 1990. *The Invented Indian: Cultural Fictions and Government Policies*. New Brunswick, N.J.: Transaction Publishers.

Cohen, Eric. 1992. "Pilgrimage and Tourism: Convergence and Divergence." In Alan Morinis, ed. *Sacred Journeys: The Anthropology of Pilgrimage*, pp. 47–61. New York: Greenwood Press.

Coleman, Simon, and John Elsner, eds. 1995. *Pilgrimage: Past and Present in the World Religions*. Cambridge: Harvard University Press.

Cotterell, P. 1990. *Mission and Meaninglessness*. London: SPCK.

Cox, Harvey. 1967. "The Death of God and the Future of Theology." In Martin E. Marty and Dean G. Peerman, eds. *New Theology No. 4*. New York: Macmillan.

———. 1966. *The Secular City*, rev. ed. New York: Macmillan.

Danker, Frederick W. 1992. "Apollo." In David Noel Freedman, ed. *The Anchor Bible Dictionary*, 1: 297–98. New York: Doubleday.

David, Sister Mary William. 1986. "Star Trek. Odyssey of Salvation." In Walter Irwin and G. B. Love, eds. *The Best of Trek #1*. London: Signet Books.

Davis, S. T. 1993. *Risen Indeed*. London: SPCK.

DeSmet, Kate. 1995. "Trekkers Chase Future with a Religious Zeal." *Detroit News*, March 13, p. A-6.

Devereaux, Barbara. 1990. "New Life, New Creation: Star Trek as Modern Myth." In Walter Irwin and G. B. Love, eds. *The Best of the Best of Trek*, pp. 160–70. New York: Penguin.

Doniger, Wendy. 1988. *Other People's Myths: The Cave of Echoes*. New York: Macmillan.

Du Bois, Cora. 1955. "The Dominant Value Profile of American Culture." *American Anthropologist* 57(6): 1232–39.

Dubreuil, Pierre C. 1994. "A Positive Example of Violation of the Prime Directive: Earth's History of Revealed Religions." In Walter Irwin and G. B. Love eds. *The Best of Trek*, pp. 209–16. New York: Penguin.

Eade, John. 1991. "Order and Power at Lourdes: Lay Helpers and the Organization of a Pilgrimage Shrine," in *Contesting the Sacred: The Anthropology of Christian Pilgrimage*, pp. 51–79. London: Routledge.

Eade, John, and Michael J. Sallnow, eds. 1991. "Introduction." In *Contesting the Sacred: The Anthropology of Christian Pilgrimage*, pp. 1–29. London: Routledge.

Ebeling, Gerhard. 1968. *The Nature of Faith*, trans. Ronald G. Smith. Philadelphia: Fortress.

Edwards, David. L. 1963. *The Honest to God Debate*. Philadelphia: Westminster.

Eliade, Mircea. 1975. *Myth and Reality*. New York: Harper & Row.

———. 1959. *The Sacred and the Profane: The Nature of Religion: The Significance of Religious Myth, Symbolism, and Ritual within Life and Culture*. New York: Harcourt, Brace and World.

———. 1954. *The Myth of Eternal Return*. New York: Pantheon.

Ellington, Jane, and Joseph W. Critelli. 1983. "Analysis of a Modern Myth. The Star Trek Series." *Extrapolation* 24: 241–50.

Engel, Joel. 1995. *Gene Roddenberry: The Man and the Myth*. London: Virgin Books.

————. 1994. *Gene Roddenberry: The Myth and the Man behind Star Trek*. London: Fount.

Englebert, Omer 1979. *St Francis of Assisi*. Ann Arbor, Mich.: Servant Publications.

Erdoes, Richard, and Alfonso Ortiz. 1984. *American Indian Myths and Legends*. New York: Pantheon.

Evans, Christopher. 1973. *Cults of Unreason*. New York: Dell.

Fasching, Darrel J. 1996. *The Coming of the Millenium: Good News for the Whole Human Race*. Valley Forge, Pa : Trinity Press International.

Fedotov, G. P. 1981. *A Treasury of Russian Spirituality*. London: Sheed & Ward.

Ferguson, John. 1970. *The Religions of the Roman Empire*. Ithaca, N.Y.: Cornell University Press.

Ferm, Deane William. 1981. *Contemporary American Theologies*. New York: Seabury.

Fern, Yvonne. 1996. *Gene Roddenberry: The Last Conversation*. New York: Pocket Books.

————. 1995. *Inside the Mind of Gene Roddenberry, the Creator of Star Trek*. London: HarperCollins.

Ferrand, Phil. 1994. *The Nitpicker's Guide for Classic Trekkers*. New York: Dell.

Ferre, Frederick. 1967. *Basic Modern Philosophy of Religion*. New York: Charles Scribners.

Fox, M. 1983. *Original Blessing*. Santa Fe, N.M.: Bear & Company.

Francis, Daniel. 1992. *The Imaginary Indian: The Image of the Indian in Canadian Culture*. Vancouver, B.C.: Arsenal Pulp Press.

Franklin, H. Bruce. 1994. "Star Trek in the Vietnam Era." *Science-Fiction Studies* 21: 24–34.

Frisch, A,. and Martos, J. 1985. "Religious Imagination and Imagined Religion." In Reilly, R. ed. *The Transcendent Adventure: Studies in Science Fiction/Fantasy*. Westport, Conn: Greenwood Press.

Funk, Robert W., Roy W. Hoover, and the Jesus Seminar. 1993. *The Five Gospels: What Did Jesus Really Say?* New York: Macmillan.

Gellner, Ernest. 1992. *Postmodernism, Reason and Religion*. New York: Routledge.

Gennep, Arnold van. 1909. *The Rites of Passage*. London: Routledge & Kegan Paul.

George, David. 1995. "A New Babel? The Television Age and Its Implications for the Communication of Christian Truth." *Vox Evangelica* 25: 33–56.

Gerrold, David. 1984. *The World of Star Trek*. New York: Bluejay Books.

———. 1973. *The World of Star Trek*. New York: Ballantine.

Gilkey, Langdon. 1987. "Religion and Science in an Advanced Scientific Culture." *Zygon* 22(2): 165–78.

———. 1969. *Naming the Whirlwind: The Renewal of God-language*. Indianapolis: Bobbs-Merrill.

———. 1959. *Maker of Heaven and Earth*. New York: Doubleday.

Gitlin, Todd. 1987. *The Sixties: Years of Hope, Days of Rage*. New York: Bantam.

Goethals, Gregor. 1993. "Media Mythologies." In Chris Arthur, ed. *Religion and the Media: An Introductory Reader*. Cardiff: Cardiff University of Wales.

Goswami, Amit. 1983. *The Cosmic Dancers*. New York: Harper & Row.

Goulding, Jay. 1985. *Empire, Aliens and Conquest: Critique of American Ideology in Star Trek and Other Science Fiction Adventures*. Toronto: Sysyphus Press.

Graburn, Nelson H. H. 1989. "Tourism: The Sacred Journey." In Valene L. Smith, ed. *Hosts and Guests: The Anthropology of Tourism*, pp. 17–31. Philadelphia: University of Pennsylvania Press.

Greenberg, Harvey R. 1990. "In Search of Spock: A Psychoanalytic Inquiry." In Walter Irwin and G. B. Love, eds. *The Best of the Best of Trek*, pp. 287–307. New York: Penguin.

Greil, Arthur L. and Thomas Robbins. 1994. *Between Sacred and Secular: Research and Theory on Quasi-Religion, Religion and the Social Order*, vol. 4. Greenwich, Conn.: JAI Press.

Grenz, Stanley. 1995. "The Uniqueness of Christ in a Pluralistic, 'Star Trek' Universe." Paper presented at the 47th Annual Meeting of the Evangelical Theological Society, Philadelphia, Pa.

———. 1994 "Star Trek and the Next Generation: Postmodernism and the Future of Evangelical Theology." *Crux* 30(1): 26.

Gross, Edward, and Mark Altman. 1995. *Captains' Logs: The Unauthorized Complete Trek Voyages*. Boston: Little, Brown & Company.

Gutierrez, G. 1988. *A Theology of Liberation*, 2nd ed. Maryknoll, N.Y.: Orbis Books.

Habgood, J. 1993. *Making Sense*. London: SPCK.

Hamilton, Anne. 1994. "Ellington Man Walks Through Life on Course Plotted by Star Trek." *Hartford Courant,* February 22, p. C-1.

Hamilton, Edith. 1964. *The Greek Way.* New York: Norton.

Hamilton, William. 1961. *The New Essence of Christianity.* New York: Association Press.

Hamilton, William, and Thomas J. J. Altizer. 1966. *Radical Theology and the Death of God.* Indianapolis: Bobbs-Merrill

Hanley, Richard. 1997. *The Metaphysics of Star Trek.* New York: Basic Books.

Hark, Ina Rae. 1979. "Star Trek and Television's Moral Universe." *Extrapolation* 20(1): 20–37.

Harris, Walt. 1988. "Trek Roundtable" (Letter to editor). In W. Irwin and G. B. Love, eds. *The Best of Trek #14,* pp. 215–16. New York: Signet.

Harrison, Paul. 1996. "The Real *Star Trek* theology: Gene Roddenberry's pantheism." http://members.aol.com/Heraklit1/startrek.html.

Harrison, Taylor, Sarah Projansky, and Kent Ono, eds. 1996. *Enterprise Zones: Critical Positions on Star Trek.* Boulder, Colo.: Westview Press.

Harrison, Ted. 1992. *Elvis People: The Cult of the King.* London: Fount.

Heaton, E. W. 1977. *The Old Testament Prophets.* London: Darton, Longman & Todd.

Hegy, Pierre. 1991. *Myth as Foundation for Society and Values: A Sociological Analysis.* Lewiston, N.Y.: Edwin Mellen.

Herbert, A. S. 1975. *The Book of the Prophet Isaiah 40–66.* The Cambridge Bible Commentary, Cambridge: Cambridge University Press.

Hess, David. 1993. *Science in the New Age: The Paranormal, Its Defenders and Debunkers, and American Culture.* Madison: University of Wisconsin Press.

Hexham, Irving. 1994. "Evolution: The Central Mythology of the New Age Movement." *Between Sacred and Secular: Research and Theory on Quasi-Religion. Religion and the Social Order,* vol. 4. Greenwich, Conn.: JAI Press.

Hopper, David H. 1991. *Technology, Theology and the Idea of Progress.* Louisville, Ky.: Knox/Westminster.

Hordern, William E. 1973. *A Layman's Guide to Protestant Theology,* rev. ed. New York: Macmillan.

Huff, Laurie. 1988. "Star Trek and Secularization: A Critical Analysis." In Walter Irwin and G. B. Love, eds. *The Best of Trek #14,* pp. 96–112. New York: Penguin.

Hurley, Neil P. 1983. "Hollywood's New Mythology," *Theology Today* 39: 402–8.

Huxley, Julian. 1967. *The Death of God Debate.* Philadelphia: Westminster.

———. 1957. *Religion without Revelation.* New York: Charles Scribners.

Ice, Jackson Lee, and John Carey, eds. 1967. *The Death of God Debate.* Philadelphia: Westminster.

Irwin, Walter, and G. B. Love, eds. 1996. *The Best of TREK #18.* New York: Penguin.

———. 1994. *The Best of TREK.* New York: Penguin.

———. 1992. *The Best of the Best of TREK II.* New York: Penguin.

———. 1990. *The Best of the Best of TREK.* New York: Penguin.

———. 1988. *The Best of TREK #14.* New York: Penguin.

———. 1986. *The Best of TREK #10.* New York: Penguin.

Jaki, Stanley L. 1978. *The Origins of Science and the Science of Its Origins.* South Bend, Ind.: Regnery/Gateway.

James, Edward. 1994. *Science Fiction in the 20th Century.* New York: Oxford University Press.

Jenkins, Henry. 1995. "How Many StarFleet Officers Does It Take to Change a Lightbulb?: Star Trek at MIT." In J. Tullock and H. Jenkins, eds. *Science Fiction Audiences.* New York: Routledge.

———. 1992. *Textual Poachers: Television Fans and Participatory Culture.* New York and London: Routledge

———. 1991. "Star Trek Rerun, Reread, Rewritten: Fan Writing as Textual Poaching." In Constance Penley, Elisabeth Lyon, Lynn Spigel, and Janet Bergstrom, eds. *Close Encounters: Film, Feminism, and Science Fiction.* Minneapolis: University of Minnesota Press.

———. 1990. "If I Could Speak with Your Sound." *Camera Obscura* 23: 149–76.

Jewett, Robert, and John S. Lawrence. 1988 [1977]. *The American Monomyth,* 2nd ed. Lanham, Md.: University Press of America.

Jindra, Michael. 1994. "*Star Trek* Fandom as a Religious Phenomenon." *Sociology of Religion* 55: 27–51.

Johnson, Luke Timothy. 1996. *The Real Jesus.* San Francisco: HarperSanFrancisco.

Johnson, Paul C. 1995. "Shamanism from Ecuador to Chicago: A Case Study in New Age Ritual Appropriation." *Religion* 25: 163–78.

Johnston, Linda M. 1986. "The Classic Star Trek." In Walter Irwin and G. B. Love, eds. *The Best of Trek #1*. New York: Signet.

Kenas, Lisa. 1986. "The American Ideal in Star Trek." In Walter Irwin and G. B. Love, eds. *The Best of Trek #10*, pp. 110–14. New York: Penguin.

King-Hele, Desmond. 1963. *Shelley: The Man and the Poet*. New York: Thomas Yoseloff.

Kottak, Conrad. 1990. *Prime Time Society*. Belmont, Calif.: Wadsworth.

Krauss, Lawrence M. 1995. *The Physics of Star Trek*. New York: Basic Books.

Kreitzer, Larry J. 1996. "The Cultural Veneer of Star Trek," *The Journal of Popular Culture* 30: 1–28.

——— . 1990. *The Gospel According to John*. Oxford. Regent's Park College.

Kreuziger, Frederick. 1986. *The Religion of Science Fiction*. Bowling Green, Ohio: Popular Press.

——— . 1982. *Apocalypse and Science Fiction: A Dialectic of Religious and Secular Soteriologies*. AAR Academy Series #40. Chico, California: Scholars Press.

Kung, Hans. 1980. *Does God Exist?* New York: Doubleday.

Kusik, Michelle A. 1988. "Intrarelationships." In Walter Irwin and G. B. Love, eds. *The Best of Trek #14*. New York: Penguin.

Kyle, Richard. 1995. *The New Age Movement in American Culture*. Lanham, Md.: University Press of America.

Lalli, Tom. 1994. "Starship America: Politics and the Star Trek Films." In Walter Irwin and G. B. Loves, eds. *The Best of Trek*, pp. 197–208. New York: Penguin.

Leach, Edmund. 1967. "Genesis as Myth," In John Middleton, ed. *Myth and Cosmos: Readings in Mythology and Symbolism*, pp. 1–13. Austin: University of Texas Press.

Lévi-Strauss, Claude. 1955. "The Structural Study of Myth," In Thomas A. Sebeok, ed. *Myth: A Symposium*. Bloomington: Indiana University Press.

Lewis, James R. 1992. "Approaches to the Study of the New Age Movement." In James R. Lewis and J. Gordon Melton, eds. *Perspectives on the New Age*, pp. 1–12. Albany: State University of New York Press.

Lichtenberg, Jaqueline, Sondra Marshak, and Joan Winston. 1975. *Star Trek Lives!: Personal Notes and Anecdotes*. New York: Bantam.

Lippy, Charles H. 1996. *Modern American Popular Religion*. Westport, Conn.: Greenwood.

Lossky, V. 1991. *The Mystical Theology of the Eastern Church*. Worcester, U.K.: Clark & Company.

Love, G. B. 1986. "Star Trek and Me." In Walter Irwin and G. B. Love, eds. *The Best of Trek #14*, pp. 62–65. New York: Penguin.

MacDonald, Alan. 1991. *Films in Close-Up*. Leicester: Frameworks/IVP Press.

Macquarrie, John. 1967. *New Directions in Theology Today*, vol. 3, *God and Secularity*. Philadelphia: Westminster.

Malinowski, Bronislaw. 1992 [1948]. "Myth in Primitive Psychology." In *Magic, Science and Religion and Other Essays*. Prospect Heights, Ill.: Waveland Press.

Marinaccio, Dave. 1994. *All I Really Need to Know I Learned from Watching Star Trek*. New York: Crown Books.

Marsalek, Kenneth. 1992. "*Star Trek*: Humanism of the Future." *Free Inquiry* 12(4): 53–56.

Martin, Joel W., and Conrad E. Ostwalt Jr., eds. 1995. *Screening the Sacred: Religion, Myth and Ideology in Popular American Film*. Boulder, Colo.: Westview Press.

Marty, Martin E. 1966. *Varieties of Unbelief*. New York: Anchor.

Mattingly, Terry. 1993. "To Boldly Go Where Gurus Have Gone Before." *Houston Chronicle*, March 23.

May, John R. 1982. "The Demonic in American Cinema." In John R. May and Michael Bird, eds. *Religion in Film*. Knoxville: University of Tennessee Press.

McClellan, J. 1996. "Warp Factor." *The Guardian Review*, December 13, pp. 2, 19.

McGaa, Ed. 1990. *Mother Earth Spirituality: Native American Paths to Healing Ourselves and Our World*. San Francisco: HarperSanFrancisco.

McGrath, A. E. 1987. *Understanding the Trinity*. Eastbourne: Kingsway.

Melton, J. Gordon. 1992. *Encyclopedic Handbook of Cults in America*, rev. ed. New York: Garland.

Mills, Jeffrey H. 1990. "Star Trek in the Classroom," In W. Irwin and G. B. Love, eds. *The Best of the Best of Trek*, pp. 324–35. New York: ROC Press.

Moltmann, J. 1974. *The Crucified God*. London: SCM.

More, Thomas. 1965. *Utopia*. London: Penguin.

Morinis, Alan, ed. 1992. *Sacred Journeys: The Anthropology of Pilgrimage.* New York: Greenwood.

Morris, Colin. 1984. *God-In-A-Box: Christian Strategy in the Television Age.* London: Hodder & Stoughton.

Moulder, W. J. 1977–78. "The Old Testament Background and the Interpretation of Mark X.45." *New Testament Studies* 24: 120–27.

Murchland, Bernard Murchland, ed. 1967. *The Meaning of the Death of God.* New York: Random House.

Myers, David G. 1993. *A Postmodern Reader.* Albany: State University of New York Press.

———. 1980. *The Inflated Self.* New York: Seabury.

Natoli, Joseph, and Linda Hutcheon, eds. 1993. *A Post-Modern Reader.* Albany: State University of New York Press

Nausch, Maria. 1993. Letter to the editor. *CCSTSG (Central Connecticut Star Trek Support Group) Newsletter* 32: 7.

Nichols, Nichelle. 1994. *Beyond Uhura.* New York: Putnam.

Nimoy, Leonard. 1995. *I Am Spock.* Hyperion.

North, Christopher R. 1948. *The Suffering Servant in Deutero-Isaiah: An Historical and Critical Study.* Oxford: Oxford University Press.

Okuda, Michael, and Denise Okuda. 1996. *The Star Trek Chronology: The History of the Future.* New York: Pocket Books.

Okuda, Michael, Denise Okuda, and Debbie Mirek. 1994. *The Star Trek Encyclopedia: A Reference Guide to the Future.* New York: Pocket Books.

Ostwalt, C., and Joel Martin. 1995. *Screening the Sacred: Religion, Myth and Ideology in Popular American Film.* Boulder: Westview Press.

Page, S. 1992. "Ransom Saying." In Joel B. Green, Scott McKnight, and I. H. Marshall, eds. *Dictionary of Jesus and the Gospels.* Leicester, U.K.: InterVarsity Press.

Parrinder, Patrick. 1980. *Science Fiction: Its Criticism and Teaching.* New York: Methuen.

Peck, Janice. 1993. *The Gods of Televangelism: The Crisis of Meaning and the Appeal of Religious Television.* Cresskill, N.Y.: Hampton Press.

Peters, Ted. 1997. "Theology and Natural Science." In David F. Ford, ed. *The Modern Theologians*, 2nd ed. Oxford: Blackwell.

———. 1991. *The Cosmic Self.* San Francisco: HarperSanFrancisco.

Pinnock, C. et al. 1994. *The Openness of God.* Chicago, Ill.: Inter Varsity Press.

Pinnock, C., and R. Brow. 1994. *Unbounded Love.* Chicago, Ill.: Inter Varsity Press.

Polanyi, Livia. 1979. "So What's the Point?" *Semiotica* 25: 207–41.

Porter, Jennifer. 1996. "Spiritualists, Aliens and UFOs: Extraterrestrials as Spirit Guides." *Journal of Contemporary Religion* 11(3): 337–53.

———. 1995. Science and Spiritual Vibrations: Contemporary Spiritualism and the Discourse of Science. Unpublished Ph.D. dissertation. McMaster University.

Pringle, David, ed. 1996. *The Ultimate Encyclopedia of Science Fiction.* North Dighton, Mass.: JG Press.

Reeves-Stevens, Judith, and Garfield Reeves-Stevens. 1997. *Star Trek: The Next Generation: The Continuing Mission A Tenth Anniversary Tribute.* New York: Pocket Books.

Richards, Thomas. 1997. *The Meaning of Star Trek.* New York: Doubleday.

Richardson, Alan. 1961. *The Bible in the Age of Science.* Philadelphia: Westminster.

———. 1950. *The Gospel and Modern Thought.* London: Oxford.

Ridpath, Ian. 1978. *Messages from the Stars.* New York: Harper & Row.

Roberts, Wess, and Bill Ross. 1995. *Make It So: Leadership for the Next Generation.* New York: Pocket Books.

Robertson, James Oliver. 1980. *American Myth, American Reality.* New York: Hill & Wang.

Robinson, John A. T. 1963. *Honest to God.* Philadelphia: Westminster.

Robinson, Marilynne. 1993. "Hearing Silence: Western Myth Reconsidered." In Kurt Browne, ed. *The True Subject: Writers on Life and Craft.* St. Paul: Grey Wolf Press.

Roof, Wade Clark. 1993. *A Generation of Seekers.* San Francisco: HarperSanFrancisco.

Rosaldo, Renato. 1986. "Ilongot Hunting as Story and Experience." In Victor Turner and E. Bruner, eds. *The Anthropology of Experience.* Urbana: University of Illinois Press.

Rose, Pamela Rose. 1990. "Women in the Federation." In Walter Irwin and G. B. Love, eds. *The Best of the Best of Trek*, pp. 21–26. New York: Penguin.

Ross, Deborah. 1994. "Final Voyage: Fans Beam in Next Generation's Last Episode." *Phoenix Gazette*, May 24, p. D1.

Roth, Lane. 1987. "Death and Rebirth in '*Star Trek* II: The Wrath of Khan,'" *Extrapolation* 28(2): 159–66.

Rourke, Mary. 1994. "Cross Examination." *Los Angeles Times*. February 24, pp. E1, E5.

Rubenstein, Richard L. 1966. "Cox's Vision of the Secular City." In Daniel Callahan, ed. *The Secular City Debate*. New York: Macmillan.

Ruff, Miriam. 1996. Fandom, What A Concept." In Walter Irwin and G. B. Love eds. *The Best of Trek #18: From the Magazine for Star Trek Fans*, pp. 11–19. New York: Penguin.

Ruppersberg, Hugh. 1990. "The Alien Messiah." In Annette Kuhn, ed. *Alien Zone: Cultural Theory and Contemporary Science Fiction*. London: Verso Books.

Rust, Eric. 1967. *Science and Faith*. New York: Oxford University Press.

Sackett, Susan, ed. 1977. *Letters To Star Trek*. New York: Ballantine.

Sackett, Susan and Gene Roddenberry. 1980. *The Making of Star Trek: The Motion Picture*. New York: Pocket.

Saliba, John A. 1995. "Religious Dimensions of UFO Phenomena." In James R. Lewis, ed. *The Gods Have Landed: New Religions from Other Worlds*. Albany: State University of New York Press.

Sallnow, Michael J. 1981. "Communitas Reconsidered: The Sociology of Andean Pilgrimage." *Man* 16: 163–82.

Sanda, Jeffrey, and Max Hall Jr. 1994. *Alpha Quadrant Membership Manual*. Madison, Wisc. Self-published.

Sartre, Jean-Paul. 1964. *The Words*. New York: George Braziller.

Sawyer, John F. A. 1996. *The Fifth Gospel: Isaiah in the History of Christianity*. Cambridge: Cambridge University Press.

Schilling, S. Paul. 1969. *God in an Age of Atheism*. Nashville: Abingdon.

Schultze, Quentin J. 1991. *Televangelism and American Culture: The Business of Popular Religion*. Grand Rapids: Baker Book House.

Selly, April. 1990. "Transcendentalism in Star Trek: The Next Generation." *Journal of American Culture* 13(1): 31–34.

Shatner, Lisabeth. 1989. *Captain's Log: William Shatner's Personal Account of the Making of Star Trek V: The Final Frontier*. New York: Pocket.

Shatner, William. 1994. *Star Trek Movie Memories.* New York: HarperCollins.

Shatner, William, with Chris Kreski. 1993. *Star Trek Memories.* New York: HarperCollins.

Sheppard, D. 1983. *Bias to the Poor.* London: Hodder & Stoughton.

Short, Robert. 1983. *The Gospel from Outer Space.* New York: Harper & Row.

Silverstone, Roger. 1988. "Television Myth and Culture." In James W. Carey, ed. *Media Myths and Narratives*, pp. 20–47. Newbury Park, Calif.: Sage.

Skill, Thomas. 1994. "The Portrayal of Religion and Spirituality in Fictional Network Television." *Review of Religious Research* 35(3): 251–67.

Solow, Herbert, and Robert Justman. 1996. *Inside Star Trek.* New York: Pocket.

Spelling, Ian. 1993. "Grandma Trek Runs Network of Volunteers" *Houston Chronicle*, October 30, p. 2.

Spinrad, Norman. 1990. *Science Fiction in the Real World.* Carbondale: Southern Illinois University Press.

Sternberg, Meir. 1985. *The Poetics of Biblical Narrative.* Bloomington: Indiana University Press.

Stuhlmacher, Peter. 1986. *Reconciliation, Law and Righteousness: Essays in Biblical Theology.* Philadelphia: Fortress.

Suvin, Darko. 1988. *Positions and Presuppositions in Science Fiction.* Kent, Ohio: Kent State University Press.

Swain, Joseph Ward, and William H. Armstrong. 1959. *The Peoples of the Ancient World.* New York: Harper & Row.

Sweeney, Terrance A. 1985. *God &.* Minneapolis: Winston Press.

Taylor, J. V. 1992. *The Christlike God.* London: SCM.

Thomas, J. Mark. 1990. "Are Science and Technology Quasi-Religions?" *Research in Philosophy and Technology* 10: 93–102. Greenwich, Conn.: JAI Press.

Tillich, Paul. 1968. *A History of Christian Thought.* New York: Simon & Schuster.

Tippler, Frank J. 1994. *The Physics of Immortality.* New York: Anchor.

Trimble, Bjo. 1995. *Star Trek Concordance.* New York: Citadel.

Tulloch, John, and Henry Jenkins. 1995. *Science Fiction Audiences: Watching Dr. Who and Star Trek.* London and New York: Routledge.

Tullock, Joyce. 1980. "'Just' a Simple Country Doctor?" In Walter Irwin and G. B. Love, eds. *The Best of Trek #2.* New York: Penguin.

Turner, Victor. 1986. "Social Dramas in Brazilian Umbanda: The Dialectics of Meaning." In *The Anthropology of Performance*, pp. 33–71. New York: PAJ Publications.

———. 1982. "Liminal to Liminoid, in Play, Flow, Ritual: An Essay in Comparative Symbology," in *From Ritual to Theatre: The Human Seriousness of Play*, pp. 20–60. New York: Performing Arts Journal Publications.

———. 1977. "Variations on a theme of liminality." In Sally F. Moore and Barbara G. Meyerhoff, eds. *Secular Ritual*, pp. 36–52. Amsterdam: Van Gorcum.

———. 1974a. "Pilgrimages as Social Processes." In Victor Turner, ed. *Dramas, Fields and Metaphors: Symbolic Action in Human Society*, pp. 166–230. Ithaca, N.Y.: Cornell University Press.

———. 1974b. "Passages, Margins, and Poverty: Religious Symbols of Communitas," in *Dramas, Fields and Metaphors: Symbolic Action in Human Society*, pp. 231–271. Ithaca, N.Y.: Cornell University Press.

———. 1969. *The Ritual Process: Structure and Anti-Structure*. Ithaca, N.Y.: Cornell University Press.

Turner, Victor, and Edith Turner. 1978. *Image and Pilgrimage in Christian Culture*. New York: Columbia University Press.

TV Guide. 1994. *Farewell to Star Trek: The Next Generation.* Toronto: Telemedia Communications.

Tyrrell, William B. 1977. "Star Trek as Myth and Television as Myth Maker." *Journal of Popular Culture* 10: 711–19.

Vahanian, Gabriel. 1961. *The Death of God: The Culture of Our Post-Christian Era.* New York: George Braziller.

Van de Weyer R. 1990. *Celtic Fire.* London: DLT.

Van Hise, James. 1992. "Trek—The Making of the Movies." Las Vegas, Nev.: Pioneer Books.

———. 1991. *History of Trek.* New York: Harper Prism.

———. 1990. *The Trek Fan's Handbook.* Las Vegas: Pioneer Books.

Wagner, Jon, and Jan Lundeen. 1998. *Deep Space and Sacred Time: Star Trek in the American Mythos.* Westpor, Conn. and London: Praeger.

Wallis, Roy. 1975. "Reflections on When Prophecy Fails." *Zetetic Scholar* 4: 9–14.

Watts, John D. W. 1987. *Isaiah 34–66.* Waco, Tex.: Word Books.

Weber, Max. 1952. "Science as a Vocation." In H. H. Gerth and C. W. Mills, eds. *Max Weber: Essays in Sociology*. London: Routledge & Kegan Paul.

Wendland, Albert. 1985. *Science, Myth, and the Fictional Creation of Alien Worlds*. Ann Arbor, Mich.: UMI Research Press.

Whitehead, Alfred N. 1925. *Science and the Modern World*. New York: Macmillan.

Whitfield, Stephen E., and Gene Roddenberry. 1968. *The Making of Star Trek*. New York: Ballantine.

Whybray, R. N. 1987. *Isaiah 40–66*. Grand Rapids, Mich.: Eerdmans.

Wilkens, Michael J., and J. P. Moreland, eds. 1995. *Jesus Under Fire*. Grand Rapids, Mich.: Zondervan.

Williams, H. A. 1972. *True Resurrection*. London: Mitchell Beazley.

Witherington III, Ben. 1995. *The Jesus Quest*. Downers Grove, Ill.: InterVarsity Press.

Wolf, Eric. 1958. "The Virgin of Guadalupe: A Mexican National Symbol." *Journal of American Folklore* 71: 34–39.

Wood, B. 1986. *Our World, God's World*. Oxford: BRF.

Woodman, Ross. 1963. *The Apocalyptic Vision in the Poetry of Shelley*. Toronto: University of Toronto Press.

Wuthnow, Robert. 1992. *Rediscovering the Sacred: Perspectives on Religion in Contemporary Society*. Grand Rapids, Mich.: Eerdmans.

Wybrew, H. 1989. *The Orthodox Liturgy*. London: SPCK.

Yeats, William Butler. 1956. "Sailing to Byzantium," in *The Collected Poems of W. B. Yeats*, pp. 191–92. New York: Macmillan.

York, Michael. 1995. *The Emerging Network: A Sociology of the New Age and Neo-Pagan Movements*. Lanham, Md.: Rowman & Littlefield.

Zimmerli, Walther, and Joachim Jeremias. 1965. *The Servant of God*. 2nd ed. London: SCM.

Zoglin, Richard. 1994. "Trekking Onward." *Time*. November 28, pp. 72–79.

List of Contributors

Robert Asa is a Professor of Religion at the Chapman School of Religious Studies, Oakland City University, Oakland City, IN.

Michael Jindra is an Assistant Professor of Social Science at Bethany Lutheran College, Greenville, PA. He is the author of the first published academic article on *Star Trek* fandom and religion.

Larry Kreitzer is a Tutor in New Testament Studies and Tutor for Graduates at Regent's Park College, Oxford, U.K. He is the author of *The New Testament in Fiction and Film* (Biblical Seminar Series, Sheffield Academic Press, 1993) and *The Old Testament in Fiction and Film* (Biblical Seminar Series, Sheffield Academic Press, 1994). He is also an ordained Baptist minister.

Jeffrey Scott Lamp is an Adjunct Professor of Religion at Oral Roberts University. He is also an ordained Deacon in the United Methodist Church.

Peter Linford is a Ph.D. candidate at the University College of St. Martin, Lancaster, U.K. and News Editor for Church Net U.K.

Ian Maher is a Tutor and Lecturer in Ethics and World Religions, Wilson Carlile College of Evangelism, Sheffield, U.K. He holds a diploma in Evangelism Studies.

Darcee L. McLaren has been an Adjunct Professor at McMaster University, Hamilton, Ontario and holds a Ph.D. in Religious Studies with a specialization in myth and Native American religions.

Anne Mackenzie Pearson is a postdoctoral fellow and Adjunct Professor at McMaster University, Hamilton, Ontario. She is the author of *Because it gives me Peace of Mind: Ritual Fasts in the Religious Lives of Hindu Women* (State University of New York Press, 1996).

Gregory Peterson is an Assistant Professor at Thiel College, Greenville, Pa.

Jennifer E. Porter is an Assistant Professor of Religion and Modern Culture at Memorial University, St. John's, Newfoundland.

Jon Wagner is a Professor of Anthropology at Knox College, Galesburg, Ill. He is a co-author of *Deep Space and Sacred Time: Star Trek in the American Mythos* (Praeger Publishers, 1998).

Index